THE BEST POEMS IN THE ENGLISH LANGUAGE

The Golden Treasury is a comprehensive and definitive collection of the great lyrical poems of the English language. Published by Francis Turner Palgrave in 1861, it has achieved a permanent place in the affections of poetry lovers as well as a wide acceptance by schools and colleges.

This centennial edition contains in Books One through Four the exact original *Golden Treasury*. Books Five to Seven, chosen by Oscar Williams, contain poems unknown to or omitted by Mr. Palgrave. Among these is a generous representation of the work of the twentieth-century poets, including those who have achieved recognition since 1950.

Mr. Williams has arranged the poems within each book by theme. In this latest edition he has added thirty-two pages of poetry, as well as eight pages of photographs of ninety-six poets.

In quality and variety this new *Golden Treasury* is truly a treasure more golden than gold, a summation of man's highest lyrical achievements.

Εἰς τὸν λειμῶνα καθίσας,
ἔδοεπεν ἕτερον ἐρ ἑτέρῳ
αἱρόμενος ἄγρευμ' ἀνθέων
ἁδομένᾳ ψυχᾷ.

[Eurip. *frag.* 754.]

['He sat in the meadow and plucked
with glad heart the spoil of the
flowers, gathering them one by one.']

F. T. _Palgrave's_

The GOLDEN
TREASURY

Of The BEST SONGS And LYRICAL POEMS

CENTENNIAL EDITION

Revised, Greatly Enlarged and Brought Up to Date
by

OSCAR WILLIAMS

MENTOR

A MENTOR BOOK

PUBLISHED BY THE NEW AMERICAN LIBRARY

PR 1175 .P34 1961

Palgrave, Francis Turner,
1824-1897.

The golden treasury of the
best songs and lyrical

MENTOR BOOKS are published by
The New American Library of World Literature, Inc.
501 Madison Avenue, New York 22, New York

CONTENTS

See pages 555 to 564 for the Alphabetical Index of Authors and Titles.

PREFACE

to the First Edition of *The Golden Treasury*

THIS little Collection differs, it is believed, from others in the attempt made to include in it all the best original Lyrical pieces and Songs in our language, by writers not living,—and none beside the best. Many familiar verses will hence be met with; many also which should be familiar:—the Editor will regard as his fittest readers those who love Poetry so well, that he can offer them nothing not already known and valued.

The Editor is acquainted with no strict and exhaustive definition of Lyrical Poetry; but he has found the task of practical decision increase in clearness and in facility as he advanced with the work, whilst keeping in view a few simple principles. Lyrical has been here held essentially to imply that each Poem shall turn on some single thought, feeling, or situation. In accordance with this, narrative, descriptive, and didactic poems,—unless accompanied by rapidity of movement, brevity, and the colouring of human passion,—have been excluded. Humorous poetry, except in the very unfrequent instances where a truly poetical tone pervades the whole, with what is strictly personal, occasional, and religious, has been considered foreign to the idea of the book. Blank verse and the ten-syllable couplet, with all pieces markedly dramatic, have been rejected as alien from what is commonly understood by Song, and rarely conforming to Lyrical conditions in treatment. But it is not anticipated, nor is it possible, that all readers shall think the line accurately drawn. Some poems, as Gray's "Elegy," the "Allegro" and "Penseroso," Wordsworth's "Ruth" or Campbell's "Lord Ullin," might be claimed with perhaps equal justice for a narrative or descriptive selection: whilst with reference especially to Ballads and Sonnets, the Editor can only state that he has taken his utmost pains to decide without caprice or partiality.

This also is all he can plead in regard to a point even more liable to question;—what degree of merit should give rank among the Best. That a Poem shall be worthy of the writer's genius,—that it shall reach a perfection commensurate with its aim,—that we should require finish in proportion to brevity, —that passion, colour, and originality cannot atone for serious imperfections in clearness, unity, or truth,—that a few good lines do not make a good poem,—that popular estimate is serviceable as a guidepost more than as a compass,—above all, that Excellence should be looked for rather in the Whole than in the Parts,—such and other such canons have been always steadily regarded. He may however add that the pieces

en, and a far larger number rejected, have been carefully
ad repeatedly considered; and that he has been aided throughout by two friends of independent and exercised judgment,
besides the distinguished person addressed in the Dedication.*
It is hoped that by this procedure the volume has been freed
from that onesidedness which must beset individual decisions:
—but for the final choice the Editor is alone responsible.

It would obviously have been invidious to apply the standard
aimed at in this Collection to the Living. Nor, even in the cases
where this might be done without offence, does it appear wise
to attempt to anticipate the verdict of the Future on our con-
temporaries. Should the book last, poems by Tennyson, Bryant,
Clare, Lowell, and others, will no doubt claim and obtain their
place among the best. But the Editor trusts that this will be
effected by other hands, and in days far distant.

Chalmer's vast collection, with the whole works of all acces-
sible poets not contained in it, and the best Anthologies of different periods, have been twice systematically read through:
and it is hence improbable that any omissions which may be
regretted are due to oversight. The poems are printed entire,
except in a very few instances where a stanza has been omitted.
The omissions have been risked only when the piece could be
thus brought to a closer lyrical unity: and, as essentially opposed to this unity, extracts, obviously such, are excluded. In
regard to the text, the purpose of the book has appeared to
justify the choice of the most poetical version, wherever more
than one exists: and much labour has been given to present
each poem, in disposition, spelling, and punctuation, to the
greatest advantage.

For the permission under which the copyright pieces are
inserted, thanks are due to the respective Proprietors, without
whose liberal concurrence the scheme of the collection would
have been defeated.

In the arrangement, the most poetically-effective order has
been attempted. The English mind has passed through phases
of thought and cultivation so various and so opposed during
these three centuries of Poetry, that a rapid passage between
Old and New, like rapid alteration of the eye's focus in looking
at the landscape, will always be wearisome and hurtful to the
sense of Beauty. The poems have been therefore distributed
into Books corresponding, I to the ninety years closing about
1616, II thence to 1700, III to 1800, IV to the half century just
ended. Or, looking at the Poets who more or less give each
portion its distinctive character, they might be called the Books
of Shakespeare, Milton, Gray, and Wordsworth. The volume,
in this respect, so far as the limitations of its range allow, accu-

* *Alfred, Lord Tennyson.*

rately reflects the natural growth and evolution of our Po
A rigidly chronological sequence, however, rather fits a cc
lection aiming at instruction than at pleasure, and the Wisdon
which comes through Pleasure:—within each book the pieces
have therefore been arranged in gradations of feeling or subject. The development of the symphonies of Mozart and Beethoven has been here thought of as a model, and nothing
placed without careful consideration. And it is hoped that the
contents of this Anthology will thus be found to present a
certain unit; "as episodes," in the noble language of Shelley,
"to that great Poem which all poets, like the co-operating
thoughts of one great mind, have built up since the beginning
of the world."

As he closes his long survey, the Editor trusts he may add
without egotism, that he has found the vague general verdict
of popular Fame more just than those have thought, who, with
too severe a criticism, would confine judgements on Poetry to
"the selected few of many generations." Not many appear to
have gained reputation without some gift or performance that,
in due degree, deserved it: and if no verses by certain writers
who show less strength than sweetness, or more thought than
mastery in expression, are printed in this volume, it should not
be imagined that they have been excluded without much hesitation and regret,—far less that they have been slighted.
Throughout this vast and pathetic array of Singers now silent,
few have been honoured with the name Poet, and have not
possessed a skill in words, a sympathy with beauty, a tenderness of feeling, or seriousness in reflection, which render their
works, although never perhaps attaining that loftier and finer
excellence here required,—better worth reading than much
of what fills the scanty hours that most men spare for self-
improvement, or for pleasure in any of its more elevated and
permanent forms.—And if this be true of even mediocre
poetry, for how much more are we indebted to the best! Like
the fabled fountain of the Azores, but with a more various
power, the magic of this Art can confer on each period of life
its appropriate blessing: on early years Experience, on ma
turity Calm, on age Youthfulness. Poetry gives treasures "more
golden than gold," leading us in higher and healthier ways than
those of the world, and interpreting to us the lessons of
Nature. But she speaks best for herself. Her true accents, i
the plan has been executed with success, may be heard through
out the following pages:—wherever the Poets of England are
honoured, wherever the dominant language of the world i
spoken, it is hoped that they will find fit audience.

F. T. PALGRAVE

May, 1861

PREFACE

to the Centennial Edition of *The Golden Treasury*

A full century has passed since F. T. Palgrave issued his *The Golden Treasury of the Best Songs and Lyrical Poems*. In that time changes of custom and attitude have been as decided as changes brought about by invention and the upheavals of history. Modern readers still take pleasure in *The Golden Treasury* and find its only serious flaw that of the incompleteness made apparent by the passage of time. The present edition was compiled to remedy this fault.

Palgrave, publishing in 1861, did not include any poets alive after 1855. He did not venture into prophecy as to what contemporary verse would stand the test of time. Modern critics and readers are not so conservative but are willing to allow greatness to the living poet, and are eager to accord him fame as soon as he has earned it by giving them poems that excite them, whether or not posterity is to have the last word. The present extension of *The Golden Treasury* departs somewhat from Palgrave's minor principles by including the verse of living poets and certain poems unknown to or unused by him. But throughout the work of amplification, Palgrave's main intention of presenting the finest lyrical expression of the English language has been carefully kept in view. His own definition of the lyrical as unity of feeling or thought, as stated in his own preface, has been a determinant of choice. Each book falls into a time period, and in that way the arrangement is chronological, but within the books the grouping is according to theme, "in gradations of feeling or subject," as planned by Palgrave. This half thematic, half chronological sequence of the poems has always given a special charm to *The Golden Treasury* and has been retained for the supplementary matter.

A glance at the table of contents will reveal the plan I have followed. The entire first edition of *The Golden Treasury*, consisting of four Books, has been retained exactly as edited by Palgrave. Book Five, which contains poems drawn from the same periods covered by Palgrave, but which were either omitted by or unknown to him, is not meant as an adverse criticism of his taste, but rather as a guess as to what that taste might have become if he had lived on into our own time. Thus, except for one poem latterly ascribed to Donne (but to Anonymous in the original *Treasury*), Palgrave omitted Donne, Blake, Traherne and others who are here included, as are further selections from Shakespeare, Milton, Marvell, Coleridge, Keats, etc., thus amplifying their representations in accordance

with the verdicts of time. Book Six contains lyrics of the la
half of the Nineteenth Century and the important Victoria
poets. Tennyson, Browning, Poe, Whitman, Arnold and the
rest are fully presented, thus rounding out Palgrave's own century. Book Seven adds to *The Golden Treasury* the work of the
Twentieth Century poets, including those now writing. As I
compiled it, I often thought of Palgrave's astonishment if he
had been able to travel forward in time and read the works of
Gerard Manley Hopkins, William Butler Yeats, Thomas
Stearns Eliot, E. A. Robinson, George Barker, Robert Frost,
W. H. Auden, Dylan Thomas, Gene Derwood, Richard
Eberhart, etc.—massively shocking to a Victorian sensibility,
yet incontestably great with their new techniques, richness
of vocabulary and depth of understanding in areas once considered outside the scope of poetry. The poems of Hopkins,
Bridges, Housman, Dickinson and some others will be found
in both Books Six and Seven, since in time they belong to the
Nineteenth, in influence and publication to the Twentieth centuries. Taken together, Books Six and Seven constitute an
anthology of the lyrics of the full century after Palgrave.

All of the selections are true and complete lyrical poems,
and short. No added poem is longer than the longest selected
by Palgrave for the original edition. I have deviated slightly
from the rule of the first edition that all poems have rhyme and
meter by including selections of both blank and free verse,
when they were, to the modern taste, lyrical. Thus, a few pieces
by such diverse poets as Shakespeare and Whitman will be
found, though Palgrave might have excluded them for lack
of rhyme. I hope however that he would be, on the whole,
pleased with the magnification of his collection and feel that
the hands that effected it in "days far distant" were not too
incompetent.

OSCAR WILLIAMS

January, 1961, NEW YORK, N. Y.

Publisher's Note to The Centennial Edition

This present edition is an enlargement of previously published editions. It was considered feasible and necessary, not
only to honor Palgrave's centennial, but also to reflect the
advances of the last decade in American and English poetry.
Book Seven alone contains a complete anthology of 200 modern poems, almost as many as in Palgrave's original edition of
288 poems. We hope the reader will also find attractive the
portfolio of 96 poets' portraits.

The Golden Treasury

of the Best Songs and Lyrical Poems

❦

Books One to Four

selected by

F. T. PALGRAVE

❦

Books Five to Seven

selected by

OSCAR WILLIAMS

THE GOLDEN TREASURY

BOOK ONE

1

Spring

Spring, the sweet Spring, is the year's pleasant king;
Then blooms each thing, then maids dance in a ring,
Cold doth not sting, the pretty birds do sing,
   Cuckoo, jug-jug, pu-we, to-witta-woo!

The palm and may make country houses gay,
Lambs frisk and play, the shepherds pipe all day,
And we hear ay birds tune this merry lay,
   Cuckoo, jug-jug, pu-we, to-witta-woo!

The fields breathe sweet, the daisies kiss our feet,
Young lovers meet, old wives a-sunning sit,
In every street these tunes our ears do greet,
   Cuckoo, jug-jug, pu-we, to-witta-woo!
    Spring! the sweet Spring!

Thomas Nash

2

Summons to Love

    Phoebus, arise!
   And paint the sable skies
   With azure, white, and red:
Rouse Memnon's mother from her Tithon's bed
That she thy career may with roses spread:
The nightingales thy coming each-where sing:
   Make an eternal spring,
Give life to this dark world which lieth dead;
   Spread forth thy golden hair
In larger locks than thou wast wont before,
   And emperor-like decore
With diadem of pearl thy temples fair:
   Chase hence the ugly night
Which serves but to make dear thy glorious light.

   —This is that happy morn,
   That day, long-wishéd day
   Of all my life so dark,

3

(If cruel stars have not my ruin sworn
        And fates my hopes betray),
        Which, purely white, deserves
An everlasting diamond should it mark.
This is the morn should bring unto this grove
My Love, to hear and recompense my love.
        Fair King, who all preserves,
        But show thy blushing beams,
        And thou two sweeter eyes
Shalt see than those which by Peneüs' streams
        Did once thy heart surprise.
Now, Flora, deck thyself in fairest guise:
        If that ye, winds, would hear
A voice surpassing far Amphion's lyre,
        Your furious chiding stay;
        Let Zephyr only breathe,
        And with her tresses play.
        —The winds all silent are,
        And Phoebus in his chair
        Ensaffroning sea and air
        Makes vanish every star:
        Night like a drunkard reels
Beyond the hills, to shun his flaming wheels:
The fields with flowers are deck'd in every hue,
The clouds with orient gold spangle their blue;
        Here is the pleasant place—
And nothing wanting is, save She, alas!
                        William Drummond of Hawthornden

3   **Time and Love**

I] When I have seen by Time's fell hand defaced
    The rich proud cost of out-worn buried age;
    When sometime lofty towers I see down-razed,
    And brass eternal slave to mortal rage;
    When I have seen the hungry ocean gain
    Advantage on the kingdom of the shore,
    And the firm soil win of the watery main,
    Increasing store with loss, and loss with store;
    When I have seen such interchange of state,
    Or state itself confounded to decay,
    Ruin hath taught me thus to ruminate—
    That Time will come and take my Love away:
    —This thought is as a death, which cannot choose
    But weep to have that which it fears to lose.
                        William Shakespeare

II] Since brass, nor stone, nor earth, nor boundless sea,
But sad mortality o'ersways their power,
How with this rage shall beauty hold a plea,
Whose action is no stronger than a flower?
O how shall summer's honey breath hold out
Against the wreckful siege of battering days,
When rocks impregnable are not so stout
Nor gates of steel so strong, but time decays?
O fearful meditation! where, alack!
Shall Time's best jewel from Time's chest lie hid?
Or what strong hand can hold his swift foot back,
Or who his spoil of beauty can forbid?
O! none, unless this miracle have might,
That in black ink my love may still shine bright.

William Shakespeare

5   The Passionate Shepherd to His Love*

Come live with me and be my Love,
And we will all the pleasures prove
That hills and valleys, dale and field,
And all the craggy mountains yield.

There will we sit upon the rocks
And see the shepherds feed their flocks,
By shallow rivers, to whose falls
Melodious birds sing madrigals.

There will I make thee beds of roses
And a thousand fragrant posies,
A cap of flowers, and a kirtle
Embroider'd all with leaves of myrtle.

A gown made of the finest wool,
Which from our pretty lambs we pull,
Fair linéd slippers for the cold,
With buckles of the purest gold.

A belt of straw and ivy buds
With coral clasps and amber studs:
And if these pleasures may thee move,
Come live with me and be my Love.

Thy silver dishes for thy meat
As precious as the gods do eat,
Shall on an ivory table be
Prepared each day for thee and me.

* See Poem No. 376.

The shepherd swains shall dance and sing
For thy delight each May-morning:
If these delights thy mind may move,
Then live with me and be my Love.

Christopher Marlowe

6

A Madrigal

Crabbed Age and Youth
Cannot live together:
  Youth is full of pleasance,
Age is full of care;
  Youth like summer morn,
Age like winter weather,
  Youth like summer brave,
Age like winter bare:
  Youth is full of sport,
  Age's breath is short,
Youth is nimble, Age is lame:
  Youth is hot and bold,
  Age is weak and cold,
Youth is wild, and Age is tame:—
  Age, I do abhor thee,
  Youth, I do adore thee;
O! my Love, my Love is young!
  Age, I do defy thee—
  O sweet shepherd, hie thee,
For methinks thou stay'st too long.

William Shakespeare

7

Under the greenwood tree
Who loves to lie with me,
And turn his merry note
Unto the sweet bird's throat—
Come hither, come hither, come hither!
    Here shall he see
    No enemy
But winter and rough weather.

Who doth ambition shun
And loves to live i' the sun,
Seeking the food he eats
And pleased with what he gets—
Come hither, come hither, come hither!
    Here shall he see
    No enemy
But winter and rough weather.   *William Shakespeare*

It was a lover and his lass
  With a hey and a ho, and a hey-nonino!
That o'er the green cornfield did pass
In the spring time, the only pretty ring time,
When birds do sing hey ding a ding ding:
  Sweet lovers love the Spring.

Between the acres of the rye
These pretty country folks would lie:
This carol they began that hour,
How that a life was but a flower:

And therefore take the present time
  With a hey and a ho, and a hey-nonino!
For love is crownéd with the prime
In spring time, the only pretty ring time,
When birds do sing hey ding a ding ding:
  Sweet lovers love the Spring.

William Shakespeare

9   **Present in Absence**

Absence, hear thou my protestation
      Against thy strength,
      Distance, and length;
Do what thou canst for alteration:
    For hearts of truest mettle
    Absence doth join, and Time doth settle.

Who loves a mistress of such quality,
      He soon hath found
      Affection's ground
Beyond time, place, and all mortality.
    To hearts that cannot vary
    Absence is Present, Time doth tarry.

By absence this good means I gain,
      That I can catch her,
      Where none can watch her,
In some close corner of my brain:
    There I embrace and kiss her;
    And so I both enjoy and miss her.

Anon.*

* *John Donne.*

10   Absence

Being your slave, what should I do but tend
Upon the hours and times of your desire?
I have no precious time at all to spend
Nor services to do, till you require:
Nor dare I chide the world-without-end hour
Whilst I, my sovereign, watch the clock for you,
Nor think the bitterness of absence sour
When you have bid your servant once adieu:
Nor dare I question with my jealous thought
Where you may be, or your affairs suppose,
But like a sad slave, stay and thing of nought
Save, where you are, how happy you make those;—
So true a fool is love, that in your will,
Though you do anything, he thinks no ill.

William Shakespear

11   How like a winter hath my absence been
From Thee, the pleasure of the fleeting year!
What freezings have I felt, what dark days seen,
What old December's bareness everywhere!
And yet this time removed was summer's time;
The teeming autumn, big with rich increase,
Bearing the wanton burden of the prime
Like widow'd wombs after their lords' decease:
Yet this abundant issue seem'd to me
But hope of orphans, and unfather'd fruit;
For summer and his pleasures wait on thee,
And, thou away, the very birds are mute;
Or if they sing, 'tis with so dull a cheer,
That leaves look pale, dreading the winter's near.

William Shakespear

12   A Consolation

When in disgrace with fortune and men's eyes
I all alone beweep my outcast state,
And trouble deaf heaven with my bootless cries,
And look upon myself, and curse my fate;
Wishing me like to one more rich in hope,
Featured like him, like him with friends possest,
Desiring this man's art, and that man's scope,
With what I most enjoy contented least:

Yet in these thoughts myself almost despising,
Haply I think on Thee—and then my state,
Like to the lark at break of day arising
From sullen earth, sings hymns at heaven's gate;
For thy sweet love remember'd such wealth brings,
That then I scorn to change my state with kings.

                              William Shakespeare

13   **The Unchangeable**

O never say that I was false of heart,
Though absence seem'd my flame to qualify:
As easy might I from myself depart
As from my soul, which in thy breast doth lie;
That is my home of love; if I have ranged,
Like him that travels, I return again;
Just to the time, not with the time exchanged,
So that myself bring water for my stain.
Never believe, though in my nature reign'd
All frailties that besiege all kinds of blood,
That it could so preposterously be stain'd
To leave for nothing all thy sum of good:
For nothing this wide universe I call,
Save thou, my rose: in it thou art my all.

                              William Shakespeare

14   To me, fair Friend, you never can be old,
For as you were when first your eye I eyed
Such seems your beauty still. Three winters cold
Have from the forests shook three summers' pride;
Three beauteous springs to yellow autumn turn'd
In process of the seasons have I seen,
Three April perfumes in three hot Junes burn'd,
Since first I saw you fresh, which yet are green.
Ah! yet doth beauty, like a dial-hand,
Steal from his figure, and no pace perceived;
So your sweet hue, which methinks still doth stand,
Hath motion, and mine eye may be deceived:
For fear of which, hear this, thou age unbred,—
Ere you were born, was beauty's summer dead.

                              William Shakespeare

15   Diaphenia

Diaphenia like the daffadowndilly,
  White as the sun, fair as the lily,
Heigh ho, how I do love thee!
  I do love thee as my lambs
  Are belovéd of their dams;
How blest were I if thou would'st prove me.

Diaphenia like the spreading roses,
  That in thy sweets all sweets encloses,
Fair sweet, how I do love thee!
  I do love thee as each flower
  Loves the sun's life-giving power;
For dead, thy breath to life might move me.

Diaphenia like to all things blesséd
  When all thy praises are expresséd,
Dear joy, how I do love thee!
  As the birds do love the spring,
  Or the bees their careful king:
Then in requite, sweet virgin, love me!
                            Henry Constable

16   Rosalynde

Like to the clear in highest sphere
  Where all imperial glory shines,
Of selfsame colour is her hair
  Whether unfolded, or in twines:
      Heigh ho, fair Rosalynde!
Her eyes are sapphires set in snow,
  Refining heaven by every wink;
The Gods do fear whenas they glow,
  And I do tremble when I think
      Heigh ho, would she were mine!

Her cheeks are like the blushing cloud
  That beautifies Aurora's face,
Or like the silver crimson shroud
  That Phoebus' smiling looks doth grace;
      Heigh ho, fair Rosalynde!
Her lips are like two budded roses
  Whom ranks of lilies neighbour nigh,
Within which bounds she balm encloses
  Apt to entice a deity:
      Heigh ho, would she were mine!

Her neck is like a stately tower
 Where Love himself imprison'd lies,
To watch for glances every hour
 From her divine and sacred eyes:
  Heigh ho, for Rosalynde!
Her paps are centres of delight,
 Her breasts are orbs of heavenly frame,
Where Nature moulds the dew of light
 To feed perfection with the same:
  Heigh ho, would she were mine!

With orient pearl, with ruby red,
 With marble white, with sapphire blue
Her body every way is fed,
 Yet soft in touch and sweet in view:
  Heigh ho, fair Rosalynde!
Nature herself her shape admires;
 The Gods are wounded in her sight;
And Love forsakes his heavenly fires
 And at her eyes his brand doth light:
  Heigh ho, would she were mine!

Then muse not, Nymphs, though I bemoan
 The absence of fair Rosalynde,
Since for a fair there's fairer none,
 Nor for her virtues so divine:
  Heigh ho, fair Rosalynde;
Heigh ho, my heart! would God that she were mine!
        Thomas Lodge

17   Colin

Beauty sat bathing by a spring
 Where fairest shades did hide her;
The winds blew calm, the birds did sing,
 The cool streams ran beside her.
My wanton thoughts enticed mine eye
 To see what was forbidden:
But better memory said, fie!
 So vain desire was chidden:—
  Hey nonny nonny O!
  Hey nonny nonny!

Into a slumber then I fell,
 When fond imagination
Seemed to see, but could not tell

Her feature or her fashion.
But ev'n as babes in dreams do smile,
 And sometimes fall a-weeping,
So I awaked, as wise this while
 As when I fell a-sleeping:—
  Hey nonny nonny O!
  Hey nonny nonny!
   The Shepherd Tony (Anthony Munday)

18   **To His Love**

Shall I compare thee to a summer's day?
Thou art more lovely and more temperate:
Rough winds do shake the darling buds of May,
And summer's lease hath all too short a date:
Sometime too hot the eye of heaven shines,
And often is his gold complexion dimm'd:
And every fair from fair sometime declines,
By chance, or nature's changing course, untrimm'd:
But thy eternal summer shall not fade
Nor lose possession of that fair thou owest;
Nor shall death brag thou wanderest in his shade,
When in eternal lines to time thou growest:
So long as men can breathe, or eyes can see,
So long lives this, and this gives life to thee.
                    William Shakespeare

19   **To His Love**

When in the chronicle of wasted time
I see descriptions of the fairest wights,
And beauty making beautiful old rhyme
In praise of ladies dead, and lovely knights;
Then in the blazon of sweet beauty's best
Of hand, of foot, of lip, of eye, of brow,
I see their antique pen would have exprest
Ev'n such a beauty as you master now.
So all their praises are but prophecies
Of this our time, all you prefiguring;
And, for they look'd but with divining eyes,
They had not skill enough your worth to sing:
For we, which now behold these present days,
Have eyes to wonder but lack tongues to praise.
                    William Shakespeare

Love's Perjuries

On a day, alack the day!
Love, whose month is ever May,
Spied a blossom passing fair
Playing in the wanton air:
Through the velvet leaves the wind,
All unseen, 'gan passage find;
That the lover, sick to death,
Wish'd himself the heaven's breath.
Air, quoth he, thy cheeks may blow;
Air, would I might triumph so!
But, alack, my hand is sworn
Ne'er to pluck thee from thy thorn:
Vow, alack, for youth unmeet;
Youth so apt to pluck a sweet.
Do not call it sin in me
That I am forsworn for thee:
Thou for whom Jove would swear
Juno but an Ethiope were,
And deny himself for Jove,
Turning mortal for thy love.

William Shakespeare

A Supplication

Forget not yet the tried intent
Of such a truth as I have meant;
My great travail so gladly spent,
               Forget not yet!
Forget not yet when first began
The weary life ye know, since whan
The suit, the service none tell can;
               Forget not yet!
Forget not yet, the great assays,
The cruel wrong, the scornful ways,
The painful patience in delays,
               Forget not yet!
Forget not! O, forget not this,
How long ago hath been, and is
The mind that never meant amiss—
               Forget not yet!
Forget not then thine own approved
The which so long hath thee so loved,
Whose steadfast faith yet never moved—
               Forget not this!

Sir Thomas Wyatt

22   **To Aurora**

O if thou knew'st how thou thyself dost harm,
And dost prejudge thy bliss, and spoil my rest;
Then thou would'st melt the ice out of thy breast
And thy relenting heart would kindly warm.
O if thy pride did not our joys controul,
What world of loving wonders should'st thou see!
For if I saw thee once transform'd in me,
Then in thy bosom I would pour my soul;
Then all my thoughts should in thy visage shine,
And if that aught mischanced thou should'st not moan
Nor bear the burthen of thy griefs alone;
No, I would have my share in what were thine:
And whilst we thus should make our sorrows one,
This happy harmony would make them none.

                        William Alexander, Earl of Sterl

23   **True Love**

Let me not to the marriage of true minds
Admit impediments. Love is not love
Which alters when it alteration finds,
Or bends with the remover to remove:—
O no! it is an ever-fixéd mark
That looks on tempests, and is never shake.
It is the star to every wandering bark,
Whose worth's unknown, although his height be taken.
Love's not Time's fool, though rosy lips and cheeks
Within his bending sickle's compass come;
Love alters not with his brief hours and weeks,
But bears it out ev'n to the edge of doom:—
If this be error, and upon me proved,
I never writ, nor no man ever loved.

                        William Shakespea

24   **A Ditty**

My true-love hath my heart, and I have his,
    By just exchange one for another given:
I hold his dear, and mine he cannot miss,
    There never was a better bargain driven:
        My true-love hath my heart, and I have his.

His heart in me keeps him and me in one,
    My heart in him his thoughts and senses guides:
He loves my heart, for once it was his own.

I cherish his because in me it bides:
> My true-love hath my heart, and I have his.

> > *Sir Philip Sidney*

Love's Omnipresence

Were I as base as is the lowly plain,
And you, my Love, as high as heaven above,
Yet should the thoughts of me your humble swain
Ascend to heaven, in honour of my Love.
Were I as high as heaven above the plain,
And you, my Love, as humble and as low
As are the deepest bottoms of the main,
Wheresoe'er you were, with you my love should go.
Were you the earth, dear Love, and I the skies,
My love should shine on you like to the sun,
And look upon you with ten thousand eyes
Till heaven wax'd blind, and till the world were done.
Wheresoe'er I am, below, or else above you,
Wheresoe'er you are, my heart shall truly love you.

> > *Joshua Sylvester*

Carpe Diem

O Mistress mine, where are you roaming?
O stay and hear! your true-love's coming
> > That can sing both high and low;
Trip no further, pretty sweeting,
Journeys end in lovers' meeting—
> > Every wise man's son doth know.

What is love? 'tis not hereafter;
Present mirth hath present laughter;
> > What's to come is still unsure:
In delay there lies no plenty,—
Then come kiss me, Sweet-and-twenty,
> > Youth's a stuff will not endure.

> > *William Shakespeare*

Winter

When icicles hang by the wall
> And Dick the shepherd blows his nail,
And Tom bears logs into the hall,
> And milk comes frozen home in pail;

When blood is nipt, and ways be foul,
Then nightly sings the staring owl
       Tuwhoo!
Tuwhit! tuwhoo! A merry note!
While greasy Joan doth keel the pot.

When all aloud the wind doth blow,
   And coughing drowns the parson's saw,
And birds sit brooding in the snow,
   And Marian's nose looks red and raw;
When roasted crabs hiss in the bowl—
Then nightly sings the staring owl
       Tuwhoo!
Tuwhit! tuwhoo! A merry note!
While greasy Joan doth keel the pot.

William Shakespea

28   That time of year thou may'st in me behold
When yellow leaves, or none, or few, do hang
Upon those boughs which shake against the cold,
Bare ruin'd choirs, where late the sweet birds sang.
In me thou see'st the twilight of such day
As after sunset fadeth in the west,
Which by and by black night doth take away,
Death's second self, that seals up all in rest.
In me thou see'st the glowing of such fire,
That on the ashes of his youth doth lie
As the death-bed whereon it must expire,
Consumed with that which it was nourish'd by:
—This thou perceiv'st, which makes thy love more
    strong,
To love that well which thou must leave ere long.

William Shakespea

29   When to the sessions of sweet silent thought
I summon up remembrance of things past,
I sigh the lack of many a thing I sought,
And with old woes new wail my dear time's waste;
Then can I drown an eye, unused to flow,
For precious friends hid in death's dateless night,
And weep afresh love's long-since-cancell'd woe,
And moan the expense of many a vanish'd sight.

Then can I grieve at grievances foregone,
And heavily from woe to woe tell o'er
The sad account of fore-bemoanéd moan,
Which I new pay as if not paid before:
—But if the while I think on thee, dear friend,
All losses are restored, and sorrows end.

William Shakespeare

Revolutions

Like as the waves make towards the pebbled shore,
So do our minutes hasten to their end;
Each changing place with that which goes before,
In sequent toil all forwards do contend.
Nativity, once in the main of light,
Crawls to maturity, wherewith being crown'd,
Crooked eclipses 'gainst his glory fight,
And Time that gave doth now his gift confound.
Time doth transfix the flourish set on youth,
And delves the parallels in beauty's brow;
Feeds on the rarities of nature's truth,
And nothing stands but for his scythe to mow:
And yet, to times in hope, my verse shall stand
Praising thy worth, despite his cruel hand.

William Shakespeare

Farewell! thou art too dear for my possessing,
And like enough thou know'st thy estimate:
The charter of thy worth gives thee releasing;
My bonds in thee are all determinate.
For how do I hold thee but by thy granting?
And for that riches where is my deserving?
The cause of this fair gift in me is wanting,
And so my patent back again is swerving.
Thyself thou gav'st, thy own worth then not knowing,
Or me, to whom thou gav'st it, else mistaking;
So thy great gift, upon misprision growing,
Comes home again, on better judgement making.
Thus have I had thee as a dream doth flatter;
In sleep, a king; but waking, no such matter.

William Shakespeare

32   **The Life Without Passion**

They that have power to hurt, and will do none,
That do not do the thing they most do show,
Who, moving others, are themselves as stone,
Unmovéd, cold, and to temptation slow,—
They rightly do inherit Heaven's graces,
And husband nature's riches from expense;
They are the lords and owners of their faces,
Others, but stewards of their excellence.
The summer's flower is to the summer sweet,
Though to itself it only live and die;
But if that flower with base infection meet,
The basest weed outbraves his dignity:
For sweetest things turn sourest by their deeds;
Lilies that fester smell far worse than weeds.

William Shakespea

33   **The Lover's Appeal**

And wilt thou leave me thus?
  Say nay! say nay! for shame!
  To save thee from the blame
  Of all my grief and grame.
And wilt thou leave me thus?
  Say nay! say nay!

And wilt thou leave me thus,
  That hath loved thee so long
  In wealth and woe among?
  And is thy heart so strong
As for to leave me thus?
  Say nay! say nay!

And wilt thou leave me thus,
  That hath given thee my heart
  Never for to depart
  Neither for pain nor smart?
And wilt thou leave me thus?
  Say nay! say nay!

And wilt thou leave me thus,
And have no more pity
  Of him that loveth thee?
  Alas! thy cruelty!
And wilt thou leave me thus?
  Say nay! say nay!   *Sir Thomas Wy*

The Nightingale

As it fell upon a day
In the merry month of May,
Sitting in a pleasant shade
Which a grove of myrtles made,
Beasts did leap and birds did sing,
Trees did grow and plants did spring,
Every thing did banish moan
Save the Nightingale alone.
She, poor bird, as all forlorn,
Lean'd her breast up-till a thorn,
And there sung the dolefull'st ditty
That to hear it was great pity.
Fie, fie, fie, now would she cry;
Tereu, tereu, by and by:
That to hear her so complain
Scarce I could from tears refrain;
For her griefs so lively shown
Made me think upon mine own.
—Ah, thought I, thou mourn'st in vain,
None takes pity on thy pain:
Senseless trees, they cannot hear thee,
Ruthless beasts, they will not cheer thee;
King Pandion, he is dead,
All thy friends are lapp'd in lead:
All thy fellow birds do sing
Careless of thy sorrowing:
Even so, poor bird, like thee
None alive will pity me.   *Richard Barnfield*

5   Care-charmer Sleep, son of the sable Night,
Brother to Death, in silent darkness born,
Relieve my languish, and restore the light;
With dark forgetting of my care return.
And let the day be time enough to mourn
The shipwreck of my ill-adventured youth:
Let waking eyes suffice to wail their scorn,
Without the torment of the night's untruth.
Cease, dreams, the images of day-desires,
To model forth the passions of the morrow;
Never let rising Sun approve you liars
To add more grief to aggravate my sorrow:
Still let me sleep, embracing clouds in vain,
And never wake to feel the day's disdain.
                        Samuel Daniel

36   **Madrigal**

Take, O take those lips away
    That so sweetly were forsworn,
And those eyes, the break of day,
    Lights that do mislead the morn:
But my kisses bring again,
            Bring again—
Seals of love, but seal'd in vain,
            Seal'd in vain!

                                William Shakespear

37   **Love's Farewell**

Since there's no help, come let us kiss and part,—
Nay I have done, you get no more of me;
And I am glad, yea, glad with all my heart,
That thus so cleanly I myself can free;
Shake hands for ever, cancel all our vows,
And when we meet at any time again,
Be it not seen in either of our brows
That we one jot of former love retain.
Now at the last gasp of love's latest breath,
When, his pulse failing, passion speechless lies,
When faith is kneeling by his bed of death,
And innocence is closing up his eyes,
—Now if thou would'st, when all have given him over,
From death to life thou might'st him yet recover!

                                Michael Drayte

38   **To His Lute**

My lute, be as thou wert when thou didst grow
With thy green mother in some shady grove,
When immelodious winds but made thee move,
And birds their ramage did on thee bestow.
Since that dear Voice which did thy sounds approve,
Which wont in such harmonious strains to flow,
Is reft from Earth to tune those spheres above,
What art thou but a harbinger of woe?
Thy pleasing notes be pleasing notes no more,
But orphans' wailings to the fainting ear;
Each stroke a sigh, each sound draws forth a tear;
For which be silent as in woods before:
Or if that any hand to touch thee deign,
Like widow'd turtle still her loss complain.

                        William Drummond of Hawthorrde

39

Blind Love

O me! what eyes hath love put in my head
Which have no correspondence with true sight:
Or if they have, where is my judgement fled
That censures falsely what they see aright?
If that be fair whereon my false eyes dote,
What means the world to say it is not so?
If it be not, then love doth well denote
Love's eye is not so true as all men's: No,
How can it? O how can love's eye be true,
That is so vex'd with watching and with tears?
No marvel then though I mistake my view:
The sun itself sees not till heaven clears.
O cunning Love! with tears thou keep'st me blind,
Lest eyes well-seeing thy foul faults should find!

William Shakespeare

40   **The Unfaithful Shepherdess**

While that the sun with his beams hot
    Scorchéd the fruits in vale and mountain,
Philon the shepherd, late forgot,
    Sitting beside a crystal fountain,
    In shadow of a green oak tree
    Upon his pipe this song play'd he:
Adieu Love, adieu Love, untrue Love,
Untrue Love, untrue Love, adieu Love;
Your mind is light, soon lost for new love.

So long as I was in your sight
    I was your heart, your soul, and treasure;
And evermore you sobb'd and sigh'd
    Burning in flames beyond all measure:
    —Three days endured your love to me,
    And it was lost in other three!
Adieu Love, adieu Love, untrue Love,
Untrue Love, untrue Love, adieu Love;
Your mind is light, soon lost for new love.

Another Shepherd you did see
    To whom your heart was soon enchainéd;
Full soon your love was leapt from me,
    Full soon my place he had obtainéd.
        Soon came a third, your love to win,
        And we were out and he was in.

Adieu Love, adieu Love, untrue Love,
Untrue Love, untrue Love, adieu Love;
Your mind is light, soon lost for new love.

Sure you have made me passing glad
   That you your mind so soon removéd,
Before that I the leisure had
   To choose you for my best belovéd:
      For all your love was past and done
      Two days before it was begun:—
Adieu Love, adieu Love, untrue Love,
Untrue Love, untrue Love, adieu Love;
Your mind is light, soon lost for new love.

Anon.

41   **A Renunciation**

If women could be fair, and yet not fond,
   Or that their love were firm, not fickle still,
I would not marvel that they make men bond
   By service long to purchase their good will;
But when I see how frail those creatures are,
I muse that men forget themselves so far.

To mark the choice they make, and how they change,
   How oft from Phoebus they do flee to Pan;
Unsettled still, like haggards wild they range,
   These gentle birds that fly from man to man;
Who would not scorn and shake them from the fist,
And let them fly, fair fools, which way they list?

Yet for disport we fawn and flatter both,
   To pass the time when nothing else can please,
And train them to our lure with subtle oath,
   Till, weary of their wiles, ourselves we ease;
And then we say when we their fancy try,
To play with fools, O what a fool was I!

Edward Vere, Earl of Oxford

42   Blow, blow, thou winter wind,
                     Thou art not so unkind
                        As man's ingratitude;
                     Thy tooth is not so keen

Because thou art not seen,
  Although thy breath be rude.
Heigh ho! sing heigh ho! unto the green holly:
Most friendship is feigning, most loving mere folly:
  Then, heigh ho! the holly!
  This life is most jolly.

Freeze, freeze, thou bitter sky,
That dost not bite so nigh
  As benefits forgot:
Though thou the waters warp,
Thy sting is not so sharp
  As friend remember'd not.
Heigh ho! sing heigh ho! unto the green holly:
Most friendship is feigning, most loving mere folly:
  Then, heigh ho! the holly!
  This life is most jolly.

William Shakespeare

43   Madrigal

My thoughts hold mortal strife
I do detest my life,
And with lamenting cries,
Peace to my soul to bring,
Oft call that prince which here doth monarchize:
—But he, grim grinning King,
Who caitiffs scorns, and doth the blest surprise,
Late having deck'd with beauty's rose his tomb,
Disdains to crop a weed, and will not come.
William Drummond of Hawthornden

44   Dirge of Love

Come away, come away, Death,
And in sad cypress let me be laid;
  Fly away, fly away, breath;
I am slain by a fair cruel maid.
My shroud of white, stuck all with yew,
  O prepare it!
My part of death, no one so true
  Did share it.

Not a flower, not a flower sweet
On my black coffin let there be strown;

Not a friend, not a friend greet
My poor corpse, where my bones shall be thrown:
A thousand thousand sighs to save,
    Lay me, O where
Sad true lover never find my grave,
    To weep there.

William Shakespeare

45   **Fidele**

Fear no more the heat o' the sun
    Nor the furious winter's rages;
Thou thy worldly task hast done,
    Home art gone and ta'en thy wages;
Golden lads and girls all must,
As chimney-sweepers, come to dust.

Fear no more the frown o' the great,
    Thou art past the tyrant's stroke;
Care no more to clothe and eat;
    To thee the reed is as the oak:
The sceptre, learning, physic, must
All follow this, and come to dust.

Fear no more the lightning-flash
    Nor the all-dreaded thunder-stone;
Fear not slander, censure rash;
    Thou hast finish'd joy and moan;
All lovers young, all lovers must
Consign to thee, and come to dust.

William Shakespeare

46   **A Sea Dirge**

Full fathom five thy father lies:
    Of his bones are coral made;
Those are pearls that were his eyes:
    Nothing of him that doth fade
But doth suffer a sea-change
Into something rich and strange.
Sea-nymphs hourly ring his knell:
Hark! now I hear them,—
    Ding, dong, bell.

William Shakespeare

47
A Land Dirge

Call for the robin-redbreast and the wren,
    Since o'er shady groves they hover
    And with leaves and flowers do cover
The friendless bodies of unburied men.
    Call unto his funeral dole
    The ant, the field-mouse, and the mole,
To rear him hillocks that shall keep him warm
And (when gay tombs are robb'd) sustain no harm;
But keep the wolf far thence, that's foe to men,
For with his nails he'll dig them up again.

John Webster

48
Post Mortem

If thou survive my well-contented day
When that churl Death my bones with dust shall cover,
And shalt by fortune once more re-survey
These poor rude lines of thy deceasèd lover;
Compare them with the bettering of the time,
And though they be outstripp'd by every pen,
Reserve them for my love, not for their rhyme
Exceeded by the height of happier men.
O then vouchsafe me but this loving thought—
'Had my friend's muse grown with this growing age,
A dearer birth than this his love had brought,
To march in ranks of better equipage:
But since he died, and poets better prove,
Theirs for their style I'll read, his for his love.'

William Shakespeare

49
The Triumph of Death

No longer mourn for me when I am dead
Than you shall hear the surly sullen bell
Give warning to the world, that I am fled
From this vile world, with vilest worms to dwell;
Nay, if you read this line, remember not
The hand that writ it; for I love you so,
That I in your sweet thoughts would be forgot
If thinking on me then should make you woe.
O if, I say, you look upon this verse
When I perhaps compounded am with clay,

Do not so much as my poor name rehearse,
But let your love even with my life decay;
Lest the wise world should look into your moan,
And mock you with me after I am gone.

William Shakespeare

50   **Madrigal**

Tell me where is Fancy bred,
Or in the heart, or in the head?
How begot, how nourishéd?
        Reply, reply.

It is engender'd in the eyes,
With gazing fed; and Fancy dies
In the cradle where it lies:
        Let us all ring Fancy's knell;
        I'll begin it,—Ding, dong, bell.
            —Ding, dong, bell.

William Shakespeare

51   **Cupid and Campaspe**

Cupid and my Campaspe play'd
At cards for kisses; Cupid paid:
He stakes his quiver, bow, and arrows,
His mother's doves, and team of sparrows;
Loses them too; then down he throws
The coral of his lip, the rose
Growing on 's cheek (but none knows how);
With these, the crystal of his brow,
And then the dimple of his chin;
All these did my Campaspe win:
At last he set her both his eyes—
She won, and Cupid blind did rise.
        O Love! has she done this to thee?
        What shall, alas! become of me?

John Lyly

52   Pack, clouds, away, and welcome day,
            With night we banish sorrow;
        Sweet air blow soft, mount lark aloft
            To give my Love good-morrow!
        Wings from the wind to please her mind
            Notes from the lark I'll borrow;

Bird prune thy wing, nightingale sing,
　　To give my Love good-morrow;
　　　　To give my Love good-morrow
　　　　Notes from them all I'll borrow.

Wake from thy nest, Robin-red-breast,
　　Sing birds in every furrow;
And from each bill, let music shrill
　　Give my fair Love good-morrow!
Blackbird and thrush in every bush,
　　Stare, linnet, and cock-sparrow,
You pretty elves, amongst yourselves
　　Sing my fair Love good-morrow!
　　　　To give my Love good-morrow
　　　　Sing birds in every furrow!

Thomas Heywood

53 **Prothalamion**

Calm was the day, and through the trembling air
　　Sweet-breathing Zephyrus did softly play—
　　A gentle spirit, that lightly did delay
Hot Titan's beams, which then did glister fair;
　　　　When I (whom sullen care,
Through discontent of my long fruitless stay
　　In princes' court, and expectation vain
Of idle hopes, which still do fly away
　　Like empty shadows, did afflict my brain)
　　　　Walk'd forth to ease my pain
Along the shore of silver-streaming Thames;
Whose rutty bank, the which his river hems,
　　Was painted all with variable flowers,
And all the meads adorn'd with dainty gems
　　　　Fit to deck maidens' bowers,
　　　　And crown their paramours
Against the bridal day, which is not long:
Sweet Thames! run softly, till I end my song.

There in a meadow by the river's side
　　A flock of nymphs I chancéd to espy,
　　All lovely daughters of the flood thereby,
With goodly greenish locks all loose untied
　　　　As each had been a bride;
And each one had a little wicker basket
　　Made of fine twigs, entailéd curiously,
In which they gather'd flowers to fill their flasket,
　　And with fine fingers cropt full feateously

The tender stalks on high.
Of every sort which in that meadow grew
They gather'd some; the violet, pallid blue,
    The little daisy that at evening closes,
The virgin lily and the primrose true,
      With store of vermeil roses,
      To deck their bridegrooms' posies
Against the bridal day, which was not long:
Sweet Thames! run softly, till I end my song.

With that I saw two swans of goodly hue
    Come softly swimming down along the lee;
    Two fairer birds I yet did never see;
The snow which doth the top of Pindus strow
     Did never whiter show,
Nor Jove himself, when he a swan would be
    For love of Leda, whiter did appear;
Yet Leda was (they say) as white as he,
    Yet not so white as these, nor nothing near;
     So purely white they were,
That even the gentle stream, the which them bare,
Seem'd foul to them, and bade his billows spare
    To wet their silken feathers, lest they might
Soil their fair plumes with water not so fair,
     And mar their beauties bright,
     That shone as Heaven's light
Against their bridal day, which was not long:
Sweet Thames! run softly, till I end my song.

Eftsoons the nymphs, which now had flowers their fill,
    Ran all in haste to see that silver brood
    As they came floating on the crystal flood;
Whom when they saw, they stood amazéd still
     Their wondering eyes to fill;
Them seem'd they never saw a sight so fair
    Of fowls, so lovely, that they sure did deem
Them heavenly born, or to be that same pair
    Which through the sky draw Venus' silver team;
    For sure they did not seem
To be begot of any earthly seed,
But rather angels, or of angels' breed;
    Yet were they bred of summer's heat, they say,
In sweetest season, when each flower and weed
     The earth did fresh array;
     So fresh they seem'd as day,
Even as their bridal day, which was not long:
Sweet Thames! run softly, till I end my song.

Then forth they all out of their baskets drew
  Great store of flowers, the honour of the field,
  That to the sense did fragrant odours yield,
All which upon those goodly birds they threw
  And all the waves did strew,
That like old Peneus' waters they did seem
  When down along by pleasant Tempe's shore
Scatter'd with flowers, through Thessaly they stream,
  That they appear, through lilies' plenteous store,
    Like a bride's chamber-floor.
Two of those nymphs meanwhile two garlands bound
Of freshest flowers which in that mead they found,
  The which presenting all in trim array,
Their snowy foreheads therewithal they crown'd;
    Whilst one did sing this lay
    Prepared against that day,
Against their bridal day, which was not long:
Sweet Thames! run softly, till I end my song.

'Ye gentle birds! the world's fair ornament,
  And Heaven's glory, whom this happy hour
  Doth lead unto your lovers' blissful bower,
Joy may you have, and gentle heart's content
    Of your love's couplement:
And let fair Venus, that is queen of love,
  With her heart-quelling son upon you smile,
Whose smile, they say, hath virtue to remove
  All love's dislike, and friendship's faulty guile
    For ever to assoil.
Let endless peace your steadfast hearts accord,
And blessed plenty wait upon your board;
  And let your bed with pleasures chaste abound,
That fruitful issue may to you afford
    Which may your foes confound,
    And make your joys redound
Upon your bridal day, which is not long:
Sweet Thames! run softly, till I end my song.'

So ended she; and all the rest around
  To her redoubled that her undersong,
  Which said their bridal day should not be long:
And gentle Echo from the neighbour ground
    Their accents did resound.
So forth those joyous birds did pass along
  Adown the lee that to them murmur'd low,
As he would speak but that he lack'd a tongue,
  Yet did by signs his glad affection show,

Making his stream run slow.
And all the fowl which in his flood did dwell
'Gan flock about these twain, that did excel
   The rest, so far as Cynthia doth shend
The lesser stars. So they, enrangéd well,
     Did on those two attend,
   And their best service lend
Against their wedding day, which was not long:
Sweet Thames! run softly, till I end my song.

At length they all to merry London came,
  To merry London, my most kindly nurse,
  That to me gave this life's first native source,
Though from another place I take my name,
    An house of ancient fame:
There when they came whereas those bricky towers
  The which on Thames' broad aged back do ride,
Where now the studious lawyers have their bowers,
  There whilome wont the Templar-knights to bide,
    Till they decay'd through pride;
Next whereunto there stands a stately place,
Where oft I gainéd gifts and goodly grace
  Of that great lord, which therein wont to dwell,
Whose want too well now feels my friendless case;
    But ah! here fits not well
    Old woes, but joys, to tell
Against the bridal day, which is not long:
Sweet Thames! run softly, till I end my song.

Yet therein now doth lodge a noble peer,
  Great England's glory and the world's wide wonder,
  Whose dreadful name late through all Spain did thunder,
And Hercules' two pillars standing near
    Did make to quake and fear:
Fair branch of honour, flower of chivalry!
  That fillest England with thy triumphs' fame,
Joy have thou of thy noble victory,
  And endless happiness of thine own name
    That promiseth the same;
That through thy prowess and victorious arms
Thy country may be freed from foreign harms,
  And great Eliza's glorious name may ring
Through all the world, fill'd with thy wide alarms,
    Which some brave Muse may sing
    To ages following,
Upon the bridal day, which is not long:
Sweet Thames! run softly, till I end my song.

From those high towers this noble lord issúing
   Like radiant Hesper, when his golden hair
   In th' ocean billows he hath bathéd fair,
Descended to the river's open viewing
    With a great train ensuing.
Above the rest were goodly to be seen
   Two gentle knights of lovely face and feature,
Beseeming well the bower of any queen,
   With gifts of wit and ornaments of nature,
    Fit for so goodly stature,
That like the twins of Jove they seem'd in sight
Which deck the baldric of the Heavens bright;
   They two, forth pacing to the river's side,
Received those two fair brides, their love's delight;
    Which, at th' appointed tide,
    Each one did make his bride
Against their bridal day, which is not long:
Sweet Thames! run softly, till I end my song.

Edmund Spenser

54   The Happy Heart

Art thou poor, yet hast thou golden slumbers?
       O sweet content!
Art thou rich, yet is thy mind perplexed?
       O punishment!
Dost thou laugh to see how fools are vexed
To add to golden numbers, golden numbers?
O sweet content! O sweet, O sweet content!
  Work apace, apace, apace, apace;
  Honest labour bears a lovely face;
Then hey nonny nonny, hey nonny nonny!

Canst drink the waters of the crispéd spring?
       O sweet content!
Swimm'st thou in wealth, yet sink'st in thine own tears?
       O punishment!
Then he that patiently want's burden bears
No burden bears, but is a king, a king!
O sweet content! O sweet, O sweet content!
  Work apace, apace, apace, apace;
  Honest labour bears a lovely face;
Then hey nonny nonny, hey nonny nonny!

Thomas Dekker

55
   This Life, which seems so fair,
  Is like a bubble blown up in the air
    By sporting children's breath,
    Who chase it everywhere
 And strive who can most motion it bequeath.
 And though it sometime seem of its own might,
  Like to an eye of gold, to be fix'd there,
 And firm to hover in that empty height,
 That only is because it is so light.
  —But in that pomp it doth not long appear;
 For, when 'tis most admired, in a thought,
 Because it erst was nought, it turns to nought.
      William Drummond of Hawthornden

56
Soul and Body

Poor Soul, the centre of my sinful earth,
[Fool'd by] those rebel powers that thee array,
Why dost thou pine within, and suffer dearth,
Painting thy outward walls so costly gay?
Why so large cost, having so short a lease,
Dost thou upon thy fading mansion spend?
Shall worms, inheritors of this excess,
Eat up thy charge? is this thy body's end?
Then, Soul, live thou upon thy servant's loss,
And let that pine to aggravate thy store;
Buy terms divine in selling hours of dross;
Within be fed, without be rich no more:—
So shalt thou feed on death, that feeds on men,
And death once dead, there's no more dying then.
      William Shakespeare

57
Life

The World's a bubble, and the Life of Man
   Less than a span:
In his conception wretched, from the womb
   So to the tomb;
Curst from the cradle, and brought up to years
   With cares and fears.
Who then to frail mortality shall trust,
But limns the water, or but writes in dust.

Yet since with sorrow here we live opprest,
   What life is best?
Courts are but only superficial schools
   To dandle fools:

The rural parts are turn'd into a den
      Of savage men:
And where's a city from all vice so free,
But may be term'd the worst of all the three?

Domestic cares afflict the husband's bed,
      Or pains his head:
Those that live single, take it for a curse,
      Or do things worse:
Some would have children: those that have them moan
      Or wish them gone:
What is it, then, to have, or have no wife,
But single thraldom, or a double strife?

Our own affections still at home to please
      Is a disease:
To cross the sea to any foreign soil,
      Perils and toil:
Wars with their noise affright us; when they cease,
      We are worse in peace;—
What then remains, but that we still should cry
Not to be born, or, being born, to die?   *Francis Bacon*

58   The Lessons of Nature

Of this fair volume which we World do name
If we the sheets and leaves could turn with care,
Of Him who it corrects, and did it frame,
We clear might read the art and wisdom rare:
Find out His power which wildest powers doth tame,
His providence extending everywhere,
His justice which proud rebels doth not spare,
In every page, no period of the same.
But silly we, like foolish children, rest
Well pleased with colour'd vellum, leaves of gold,
Fair dangling ribbands, leaving what is best,
On the great Writer's sense ne'er taking hold;
Or if by chance we stay our minds on aught,
It is some picture on the margin wrought.
          William Drummond of Hawthornden

59   Doth then the world go thus, doth all thus move?
    Is this the justice when on Earth we find?
    Is this that firm decree which all both bind?
    Are these your influences, Powers above?

Those souls which vice's moody mists most blind,
Blind Fortune, blindly, most their friend doth prove;
And they who thee, poor idol, Virtue! love,
Ply like a feather toss'd by storm and wind,
Oh! if a Providence doth sway this all,
Why should best minds groan under most distress?
Or why should pride humility make thrall,
And injuries the innocent oppress?
Heavens! hinder, stop this fate; or grant a time
When good may have, as well as bad, their prime.

William Drummond of Hawthornden

60   **The World's Way**

Tired with all these, for restful death I cry—
As, to behold desert a beggar born,
And needy nothing trimm'd in jollity,
And purest faith unhappily forsworn,
And gilded honour shamefully misplaced,
And maiden virtue rudely strumpeted,
And right perfection wrongfully disgraced,
And strength by limping sway disabled,
And art made tongue-tied by authority,
And folly, doctor-like, controlling skill,
And simple truth miscall'd simplicity,
And captive Good attending captain Ill:—
—Tired with all these, from these would I be gone,
Save that, to die, I leave my Love alone.

William Shakespeare

61   **Saint John Baptist**

The last and greatest Herald of Heaven's King
Girt with rough skins, hies to the deserts wild,
Among that savage brood the woods forth bring,
Which he more harmless found than man, and mild.
His food was locusts, and what there doth spring,
With honey that from virgin hives distill'd;
Parch'd body, hollow eyes, some uncouth thing
Made him appear, long since from earth exiled.
There burst he forth: 'All ye whose hopes rely
On God, with me amidst these deserts mourn,
Repent, repent, and from old errors turn!'
—Who listen'd to his voice, obey'd his cry?
Only the echoes, which he made relent,
Rung from their flinty caves, Repent! Repent!

William Drummond of Hawthornden

THE GOLDEN TREASURY

BOOK TWO

62   ### Ode on the Morning of Christ's Nativity

This is the month, and this the happy morn
      Wherein the Son of Heaven's Eternal King
Of wedded maid and virgin mother born,
      Our great redemption from above did bring;
      For so the holy sages once did sing
That He our deadly forfeit should release,
And with His Father work us a perpetual peace.

That glorious Form, that Light unsufferable,
      And that far-beaming blaze of Majesty
Wherewith He wont at Heaven's high council-table
      To sit in the midst of Trinal Unity.
      He laid aside; and, here with us to be,
Forsook the courts of everlasting day,
And chose with us a darksome house of mortal clay.

Say, heavenly Muse, shall not thy sacred vein
      Afford a present to the Infant God?
Hast thou no verse, no hymn, or solemn strain
      To welcome Him to this His new abode,
      Now while the heaven, by the sun's team untrod,
Hath took no print of the approaching light,
And all the spangled host keep watch in squadrons bright?

See how from far, upon the eastern road,
      The star-led wizards haste with odours sweet:
O run, prevent them with they humble ode
      And lay it lowly at His blessed feet;
      Have thou the honour first thy Lord to greet,
And join they voice unto the angel quire
From out His secret altar touch'd with hallow'd fire.

The Hymn

It was the winter wild
While the heaven-born Child
All meanly wrapt in the rude manger lies;
Nature in awe to Him

Had doff'd her gaudy trim,
With her great Master so to sympathize:
　　It was no season then for her
To wanton with the sun, her lusty paramour.

　　　Only with speeches fair
　　　She woos the gentle air
To hide her guilty front with innocent snow;
　　　And on her naked shame,
　　　Pollute with sinful blame,
The saintly veil of maiden white to throw;
　　Confounded, that her Maker's eyes
Should look so near upon her foul deformities.

　　　But He, her fears to cease,
　　　Sent down the meek-eyed Peace;
She, crown'd with olive green, came softly sliding
　　　Down through the turning sphere,
　　　His ready harbinger,
With turtle wing the amorous clouds dividing;
　　And waving wide her myrtle wand,
She strikes a universal peace through sea and land.

　　　No war, or battle's sound
　　　Was heard the world around:
The idle spear and shield were high uphung;
　　　The hookéd chariot stood
　　　Unstain'd with hostile blood;
The trumpet spake not to the arméd throng;
　　And kings sat still with awful eye,
As if they surely knew their sovran Lord was by.

　　　But peaceful was the night
　　　Wherein the Prince of Light
His reign of peace upon the earth began:
　　　The winds, with wonder whist,
　　　Smoothly the waters kist,
Whispering new joys to the mild oceân—
　　Who now hath quite forgot to rave,
While birds of calm sit brooding on the charméd wave.

　　　The stars, with deep amaze,
　　　Stand fix'd in steadfast gaze,
Bending one way their precious influence;
　　　And will not take their flight
　　　For all the morning light,
Or Lucifer that often warn'd them thence;

But in their glimmering orbs did glow
Until their Lord Himself bespake, and bid them go.

And though the shady gloom
Had given day her room,
The sun himself withheld his wonted speed,
And hid his head for shame,
As his inferior flame
The new-enlighten'd world no more should need:
He saw a greater Sun appear
Than his bright throne or burning axletree could bear.

The shepherds on the lawn
Or ere the point of dawn
Sate simply chatting in a rustic row;
Full little thought they than
That the mighty Pan
Was kindly come to live with them below;
Perhaps their loves, or else their sheep
Was all that did their silly thoughts so busy keep.

When such music sweet
Their hearts and ears did greet
As never was by mortal finger strook—
Divinely-warbled voice
Answering the stringéd noise,
As all their souls in blissful rapture took:
The air, such pleasure loth to lose,
With thousand echoes still prolongs each heavenly close.

Nature that heard such sound
Beneath the hollow round
Of Cynthia's seat the airy region thrilling,
Now was almost won
To think her part was done,
And that her reign had here its last fulfilling;
She knew such harmony alone
Could hold all heaven and earth in happier union.

At last surrounds their sight
A globe of circular light,
That with long beams the shamefaced night array'd;
The helméd Cherubim
And sworded Seraphim
Are seen in glittering ranks with wings display'd,
Harping in loud and solemn quire
With unexpected notes, to Heaven's new-born Heir.

Such music (as 'tis said)
Before was never made
But when of old the sons of morning sung,
While the Creator great
His constellations set
And the well-balanced world on hinges hung;
And cast the dark foundations deep,
And bid the weltering waves their oozy channel keep.

Ring out, ye crystal spheres!
Once bless our human ears,
If ye have power to touch our senses so;
And let your silver chime
Move in melodious time;
And let the bass of heaven's deep organ blow,
And with your ninefold harmony
Make up full consort to the angelic symphony.

For if such holy song,
Enwrap our fancy long,
Time will run back, and fetch the age of gold;
And speckled vanity
Will sicken soon and die,
And leprous sin will melt from earthly mould;
And Hell itself will pass away,
And leave her dolorous mansions to the peering day.

Yea, Truth and Justice then
Will down return to men,
Orb'd in a rainbow; and, like glories wearing,
Mercy will sit between
Throned in celestial sheen,
With radiant feet the tissued clouds down steering;
And Heaven, as at some festival,
Will open wide the gates of her high palace hall.

But wisest Fate says No;
This must not yet be so;
The Babe yet lies in smiling infancy
That on the bitter cross
Must redeem our loss;
So both Himself and us to glorify;
Yet first, to those ychain'd in sleep
The wakeful trump of doom must thunder through the deep,

With such a horrid clang
As on mount Sinai rang
With unexpressive notes, to Heaven's new-born Heir.

The aged Earth aghast
With terror of that blast
Shall from the surface to the centre shake,
When, at the world's last sessión,
The dreadful Judge in middle air shall spread His throne.

And then at last our bliss
Full and perfect is,
But now begins; for from this happy day
The old Dragon under ground,
In straiter limits bound,
Not half so far casts his usurpéd sway;
And, wroth to see his kingdom fail,
Swinges the scaly horror of his folded tail.

The oracles are dumb;
No voice or hideous hum
Runs through the archéd roof in words deceiving:
Apollo from his shrine
Can no more divine,
With hollow shriek the steep of Delphos leaving:
No nightly trance or breathéd spell
Inspires the pale-eyed priest from the prophetic cell.

The lonely mountains o'er
And the resounding shore
A voice of weeping heard, and loud lament;
From haunted spring and dale
Edged with poplar pale
The parting Genius is with sighing sent;
With flower-woven tresses torn
The nymphs in twilight shade of tangled thickets mourn.

In consecrated earth
And on the holy hearth
The Lars and Lemures moan with midnight plaint;
In urns, and altars round
A drear and dying sound
Affrights the Flamens at their service quaint;
And the chill marble seems to sweat,
While each peculiar Power forgoes his wonted seat.

Peor and Baalim
Forsake their temples dim,
With that twice-batter'd god of Palestine;
And moonéd Ashtaroth
Heaven's queen and mother both,

Now sits not girt with tapers' holy shine;
   The Lybic Hammon shrinks his horn,
In vain the Tyrian maids their wounded Thammuz mourn.

     And sullen Moloch, fled.
      Hath left in shadows dread
His burning idol all of blackest hue;
     In vain with cymbals' ring
     They call the grisly king,
In dismal dance about the furnace blue;
   The brutish gods of Nile as fast,
Isis, and Orus, and the dog Anubis, haste.

     Nor is Osiris seen
     In Memphian grove, or green,
Trampling the unshower'd grass with lowings loud:
     Nor can he be at rest
     Within his sacred chest;
Nought but profoundest hell can be his shroud;
   In vain with timbrell'd anthems dark
The sable-stoléd sorcerers bear his worshipt ark.

     He feels from Juda's land
     The dreaded infant's hand;
The rays of Bethlehem blind his dusky eyn;
     Nor all the gods beside
     Longer dare abide,
Not Typhon huge ending in snaky twine:
   Our Babe, to show his Godhead true,
Can in His swaddling bands control the damnéd crew.

     So, when the sun in bed
     Curtain'd with cloudy red
Pillows his chin upon an orient wave,
     The flocking shadows pale
     Troop to the infernal jail,
Each fetter'd ghost slips to his several grave;
   And the yellow-skirted fays
Fly after the night-steeds, leaving their moon-loved maze.

     But see, the Virgin blest
     Hath laid her Babe to rest;
Time is, our tedious song should here have ending:
     Heaven's youngest-teeméd star
     Hath fix'd her polish'd car,
Her sleeping Lord with hand-maid lamp attending:
   And all about the courtly stable
Bright-harness'd angels sit in order serviceable.

                 John Milton

Song for Saint Cecilia's Day, 1687

From Harmony, from heavenly Harmony
 This universal frame began:
 When Nature underneath a heap
  Of jarring atoms lay
 And could not heave her head,
The tuneful voice was heard from high
  Arise, ye more than dead!
Then cold, and hot, and moist, and dry
In order to their stations leap,
  And Music's power obey.
From harmony, from heavenly harmony
  This universal frame began:
  From harmony to harmony
Through all the compass of the notes it ran,
The diapason closing full in Man.

What passion cannot Music raise and quell?
  When Jubal struck the chorded shell
 His listening brethren stood around,
  And, wondering, on their faces fell
 To worship that celestial sound.
Less than a god they thought there could not dwell
  Within the hollow of that shell
  That spoke so sweetly and so well.
What passion cannot Music raise and quell?

 The trumpet's loud clangor
  Excites us to arms,
 With shrill notes of anger
  And mortal alarms.
 The double double double beat
  Of the thundering drum
  Cries 'Hark! the foes come;
Charge, charge, 'tis too late to retreat!'

The soft complaining flute
 In dying notes discovers
 The woes of hopeless lovers,
Whose dirge is whisper'd by the warbling lute.

 Sharp violins proclaim
Their jealous pangs and desperation,
Fury, frantic indignation,
Depth of pains, and height of passion
 For the fair disdainful dame.

But oh! what art can teach,
What human voice can reach
    The sacred organ's praise?
Notes inspiring holy love,
    Notes that wing their heavenly ways
To mend the choirs above.

Orpheus could lead the savage race,
And trees unrooted left their place
    Sequacious of the lyre:
But bright Cecilia raised the wonder higher:
When to her Organ vocal breath was given,
An Angel heard, and straight appear'd—
    Mistaking Earth for Heaven!

Grand Chorus

As from the power of sacred lays
    The spheres began to move.
And sung the great Creator's praise
    To all the blest above;
So when the last and dreadful hour
This crumbling pageant shall devour
The trumpet shall be heard on high,
The dead shall live, the living die,
And Music shall untune the sky.

John Dryden

64   On the Late Massacre in Piedmont

Avenge, O Lord! Thy slaughter'd Saints, whose bones
Lie scatter'd on the Alpine mountains cold;
Even them who kept Thy truth so pure of old,
When all our fathers worshipt stocks and stones,
Forget not: in Thy book record their groans
Who were Thy sheep, and in their ancient fold
Slain by the bloody Piemontese, that roll'd
Mother with infant down the rocks. Their moans
The vales redoubled to the hills, and they
To Heaven. Their martyr'd blood and ashes sow
O'er all the Italian fields, where still doth sway
The triple tyrant: that from these may grow
A hundred-fold, who, having learnt Thy way,
Early may fly the Babylonian woe.

John Milton

65 Horatian Ode upon Cromwell's Return from Ireland

The forward youth that would appear,
Must now forsake his Muses dear,
    Nor in the shadows sing
    His numbers languishing.

'Tis time to leave the books in dust,
And oil th' unuséd armour's rust,
    Removing from the wall
    The corslet of the hall.

So restless Cromwell could not cease
In the inglorious arts of peace,
    But through adventurous war
    Urgéd his active star:

And like the three-fork'd lightning, first
Breaking the clouds where it was nurst,
    Did thorough his own side
    His fiery way divide:

(For 'tis all one to courage high
The emulous, or enemy;
    And with such, to enclose
    Is more than to oppose;)

Then burning through the air he went
And palaces and temples rent;
    And Caesar's head at last
    Did through his laurels blast.

'Tis madness to resist or blame
The face of angry heaven's flame;
    And if we would speak true,
    Much to the man is due

Who, from his private gardens, where
He lived reservéd and austere
    (As if his highest plot
    To plant the bergamot),

Could by industrious valour climb
To ruin the great work of Time,
    And cast the Kingdoms old
    Into another mould;

Though Justice against Fate complain,
And plead the ancient Rights in vain—
    But those do hold or break
    As men are strong or weak.

Nature, that hateth emptiness,
Allows of penetration less,
    And therefore must make room
    Where greater spirits come.

What field of all the Civil War
Where his were not the deepest scar?
    And Hampton shows what part
    He had of wiser art;

Where, twining subtle fears with hope,
He wove a net of such a scope
    To Charles himself might chase
    To Carisbrook's narrow case;

That thence the Royal actor borne
The tragic scaffold might adorn:
    While round the arméd bands
    Did clap their bloody hands;

He nothing common did or mean
Upon that memorable scene,
    But with his keener eye
    The axe's edge did try;

Nor call'd the Gods, with vulgar spite,
To vindicate his helpless right;
    But bow'd his comely head
    Down, as upon a bed.

—This was that memorable hour
Which first assured the forcéd power
    So when they did design
    The Capitol's first line,

A Bleeding Head, where they begun,
Did fright the architects to run;
    And yet in that the State
    Foresaw its happy fate!

And now the Irish are ashamed
To see themselves in one year tamed:
    So much one man can do
    That does both act and know.

They can affirm his praises best,
And have, though overcome, confest
    How good he is, how just
    And fit for highest trust;

Nor yet grown stiffer with command,
But still in the Republic's hand—
How fit he is to sway
That can so well obey!—

He to the Commons' feet presents
A Kingdom for his first year's rents,
And (what he may) forbears
His fame, to make it theirs:

And has his sword and spoils ungirt
To lay them at the Public's skirt.
So when the falcon high
Falls heavy from the sky,

She, having kill'd, no more does search
But on the next green bough to perch,
Where, when he first does lure,
The falconer has her sure.

—What may not then our Isle presume
While victory his crest does plume?
What may not others fear
If thus he crowns each year?

As Caesar he, ere long, to Gaul,
To Italy an Hannibal,
And to all states not free
Shall climacteric be.

The Pict no shelter now shall find
Within his parti-colour'd mind,
But from this valour sad,
Shrink underneath the plaid—

Happy, if in the tufted brake
The English hunter him mistake,
Nor lay his hounds in near
The Caledonian deer.

But thou, the War's and Fortune's son,
March indefatigably on;
And for the last effect
Still keep the sword erect:

Besides the force it has to fright
The spirits of the shady night,
The same arts that did gain
A power, must it maintain.

Andrew Marvell

Lycidas

Elegy on a Friend drowned in the Irish Channel

Yet once more, O ye laurels, and once more
Ye myrtles brown, with ivy never sere,
I come to pluck your berries harsh and crude,
And with forced fingers rude
Shatter your leaves before the mellowing year.
Bitter constraint, and sad occasion dear
Compels me to disturb your season due:
For Lycidas is dead, dead ere his prime,
Young Lycidas, and hath not left his peer:
Who would not sing for Lycidas? he knew
Himself to sing, and build the lofty rhyme.
He must not float upon his watery bier
Unwept, and welter to the parching wind,
Without the meed of some melodious tear.

Begin then, Sisters of the sacred well
That from beneath the seat of Jove doth spring,
Begin, and somewhat loudly sweep the string.
Hence with denial vain and coy excuse:
So may some gentle Muse
With lucky words favour my destined urn;
And as he passes, turn
And bid fair peace be to my sable shroud.

For we were nursed upon the self-same hill,
Fed the same flock by fountain, shade, and rill.
Together both, ere the high lawns appear'd
Under the opening eye-lids of the morn,
We drove a-field, and both together heard
What time the gray-fly winds her sultry horn,
Battening our flocks with the fresh dews of night,
Oft till the star, that rose at evening bright,
Toward heaven's descent had sloped his westering wheel.
Meanwhile the rural ditties were not mute,
Temper'd to the oaten flute;
Rough Satyrs danced, and Fauns with cloven heel
From the glad sound would not be absent long;
And old Damaetas loved to hear our song.

But O the heavy change, now thou art gone,
Now thou art gone, and never must return!
Thee, Shepherd, thee the woods, and desert caves,
With wild thyme and the gadding vine o'ergrown,
And all their echoes, mourn:

The willows and the hazel copses green
Shall now no more be seen
Fanning their joyous leaves to thy soft lays.
As killing as the canker to the rose,
Or taint-worm to the weanling herds that graze,
Or frost to flowers, that their gay wardrobe wear
When first the white-thorn blows;
Such, Lycidas, thy loss to shepherd's ear.

Where were ye, Nymphs, when the remorseless deep
Closed o'er the head of your loved Lycidas?
For neither were ye playing on the steep
Where your old bards, the famous Druids, lie,
Nor on the shaggy top of Mona high,
Nor yet where Deva spreads her wizard stream:
Ay me! I fondly dream—
Had ye been there—for what could that have done?
What could the Muse herself that Orpheus bore,
The Muse herself, for her enchanting son,
Whom universal nature did lament,
When by the rout that made the hideous roar
His gory visage down the stream was sent,
Down the swift Hebrus to the Lesbian shore?

Alas! what boots it with uncessant care
To tend the homely, slighted, shepherd's trade
And strictly meditate the thankless Muse?
Were it not better done, as others use,
To sport with Amaryllis in the shade,
Or with the tangles of Neaera's hair?
Fame is the spur that the clear spirit doth raise
(That last infirmity of noble mind)
To scorn delights, and live laborious days;
But the fair guerdon when we hope to find,
And think to burst out into sudden blaze,
Comes the blind Fury with the abhorréd shears
And slits the thin-spun life. 'But not the praise',
Phoebus replied, and touch'd my trembling ears;
'Fame is no plant that grows on mortal soil,
Nor in the glistering foil
Set off to the world, nor in broad rumour lies:
But lives and spreads aloft by those pure eyes
And perfect witness of all-judging Jove;
As he pronounces lastly on each deed,
Of so much fame in heaven expect thy meed.'

O fountain Arethuse, and thou honour'd flood
Smooth-sliding Mincius, crown'd with vocal reeds,

That strain I heard was of a higher mood:
But now my oat proceeds,
And listens to the herald of the sea
That came in Neptune's plea;
He ask'd the waves, and ask'd the felon winds,
What hard mishap hath doom'd this gentle swain?
And question'd every gust of rugged wings
That blows from off each beakéd promontory:
They knew not of his story;
And sage Hippotades their answer brings,
That not a blast was from his dungeon stray'd;
The air was calm, and on the level brine
Sleek Panope with all her sisters play'd.
It was that fatal and perfidious bark
Built in the eclipse, and rigg'd with curses dark,
That sunk so low that sacred head of thine.

Next Camus, reverend sire, went footing slow,
His mantle hairy, and his bonnet sedge,
Inwrought with figures dim, and on the edge
Like to that sanguine flower inscribed with woe:
'Ah! who hath reft,' quoth he, 'my dearest pledge?'
Last came, and last did go
The pilot of the Galilean lake;
Two massy keys he bore of metals twain
(The golden opes, the iron shuts amain);
He shook his mitred locks, and stern bespake:
How well could I have spared for thee, young swain,
Enow of such as for their bellies' sake
Creep and intrude and climb into the fold!
Of other care they little reckoning make
Than how to scramble at the shearers' feast,
And shove away the worthy bidden guest.
Blind mouths! that scarce themselves know how to hold
A sheep-hook, or have learn'd aught else the least
That to the faithful herdman's art belongs!
What recks it them? What need be? They are sped;
And when they list, their lean and flashy songs
Grate on their scrannel pipes of wretched straw;
The hungry sheep look up, and are not fed,
But swoln with wind and the rank mist they draw
Rot inwardly, and foul contagion spread:
Besides what the grim wolf with privy paw
Daily devours apace, and nothing said:
—But that two-handed engine at the door
Stands ready to smite once, and smite no more.'

Return, Alpheus, the dread voice is past
That shrunk thy streams; return, Sicilian Muse,
And call the vales, and bid them hither cast
Their bells and flowerets of a thousand hues.
Ye valleys low, where the mild whispers use
Of shades, and wanton winds, and gushing brooks,
On whose fresh lap the swart star sparely looks,
Throw hither all your quaint enamell'd eyes
That on the green turf suck the honey'd showers
And purple all the ground with vernal flowers.
Bring the rathe primrose that forsaken dies;
The tufted crow-toe, and pale jessamine,
The white pink, and the pansy freak'd with jet,
The glowing violet,
The musk-rose, and the well-attired woodbine,
With cowslips wan that hang the pensive head,
And every flower that sad embroidery wears:
Bid amarantus all his beauty shed,
And daffadillies fill their cups with tears
To strew the laureat hearse where Lycid lies.
For, so to interpose a little ease,
Let our frail thoughts dally with false surmise;
Ay me! whilst thee the shores and sounding seas
Wash far away,—where'er thy bones are hurl'd,
Whether beyond the stormy Hebrides
Where thou perhaps, under the whelming tide,
Visitest the bottom of the monstrous world;
Or whether thou, to our moist vows denied,
Sleep'st by the fable of Bellerus old,
Where the great Vision of the guarded mount
Looks toward Namancos and Bayona's hold,
—Look homeward, Angel, now, and melt with ruth:
—And, O ye dolphins, waft the hapless youth!

Weep no more, woeful shepherds, weep no more,
For Lycidas, your sorrow, is not dead,
Sunk though he be beneath the watery floor;
So sinks the day-star in the ocean-bed,
And yet anon repairs his drooping head
And tricks his beams, and with new-spangled ore
Flames in the forehead of the morning sky:
So Lycidas sunk low, but mounted high
Through the dear might of Him that walk'd the waves;
Where, other groves and other streams along,
With nectar pure his oozy locks he laves,
And hears the unexpressive nuptial song
In the blest kingdoms meek of joy and love.

There entertain him all the saints above
In solemn troops, and sweet societies,
That sing, and singing in their glory move,
And wipe the tears for ever from his eyes.
Now, Lycidas, the shepherds weep no more;
Henceforth thou art the Genius of the shore
In thy large recompense, and shalt be good
To all that wander in that perilous flood.

Thus sang the uncouth swain to the oaks and rills,
While the still morn went out with sandals grey;
He touch'd the tender stops of various quills,
With eager thought warbling his Doric lay:
And now the sun had stretch'd out all the hills,
And now was dropt into the western bay:
At last he rose, and twitch'd his mantle blue:
To-morrow to fresh woods, and pastures new.

                                        John Milton

67   On the Tombs in Westminster Abbey

Mortality, behold and fear,
What a change of flesh is here!
Think how many royal bones
Sleep within these heaps of stones;
Here they lie, had realms and lands,
Who now want strength to stir their hands,
Where from their pulpits seal'd with dust
They preach, 'In greatness is no trust.'
Here's an acre sown indeed
With the richest royallest seed
That the earth did e'er suck in
Since the first man died for sin:
Here the bones of birth have cried
'Though gods they were, as men they died!'
Here are sands, ignoble things,
Dropt from the ruin'd sides of kings:
Here's a world of pomp and state
Buried in dust, once dead by fate.

                                        Francis Beaumont

68   The Last Conqueror

Victorious men of earth, no more
    Proclaim how wide your empires are;
Though you bind-in every shore,
    And your triumphs reach as far

As night or day,
Yet you, proud monarchs, must obey
And mingle with forgotten ashes, when
Death calls ye to the crowd of common men.

Devouring Famine, Plague, and War,
　Each able to undo mankind,
Death's servile emissaries are;
　Nor to these alone confined,
　　He hath at will
　More quaint and subtle ways to kill;
A smile or kiss, as he will use the art,
Shall have the cunning skill to break a heart.

James Shirley

69　　**Death the Leveller**

The glories of our blood and state
　Are shadows, not substantial things;
There is no armour against fate;
　Death lays his icy hand on kings:
　　Sceptre and Crown
　　Must tumble down,
And in the dust be equal made
With the poor crooked scythe and spade.

Some men with swords may reap the field,
　And plant fresh laurels where they kill:
But their strong nerves at last must yield;
　They tame but one another still:
　　Early or late
　　They stoop to fate,
And must give up their murmuring breath
When they, pale captives, creep to death.

The garlands wither on your brow;
　Then boast no more your mighty deeds;
Upon Death's purple altar now
　See where the victor-victim bleeds:
　　Your heads must come
　　To the cold tomb;
Only the actions of the just
Smell sweet, and blossom in their dust.

James Shirley

70   **When the Assault Was Intended to the City**

Captain, or Colonel, or Knight in arms,
  Whose chance on these defenceless doors may seize,
  If deed of honour did thee ever please,
Guard them, and him within protect from harms.
He can requite thee; for he knows the charms
  That call fame on such gentle acts as these,
  And he can spread thy name o'er lands and seas,
Whatever clime the sun's bright circle warms.
Lift not thy spear against the Muses' bower:
  The great Emathian conqueror bid spare
  The house of Pindarus, when temple and tower
Went to the ground: and the repeated air
  Of sad Electra's poet had the power
  To save the Athenian walls from ruin bare.

                                        John Milton

71   **On His Blindness**

When I consider how my light is spent
  Ere half my days, in this dark world and wide,
  And that one talent which is death to hide
Lodged with me useless, though my soul more bent
To serve therewith my Maker, and present
  My true account, lest He returning chide,—
Doth God exact day-labour, light denied?
  I fondly ask:—But Patience, to prevent
That murmur, soon replies; God doth not need
  Either man's work, or His own gifts: who best
Bear His mild yoke, they serve Him best: His state
Is kingly; thousands at His bidding speed
  And post o'er land and ocean without rest:—
  They also serve who only stand and wait.

                                        John Milton

72   **Character of a Happy Life**

How happy is he born or taught
    That serveth not another's will;
Whose armour is his honest thought,
    And silly truth his highest skill!

Whose passions not his masters are,
    Whose soul is still prepared for death;
Untied unto the world with care
    Of princely love or vulgar breath;

Who hath his life from rumours freed,
 Whose conscience is his strong retreat
Whose state can neither flatterers feed,
 Nor ruin make accusers great;

Who envieth none whom chance doth raise
 Or vice; who never understood
How deepest wounds are given with praise;
 Nor rules of state, but rules of good:

Who God doth late and early pray
 More of his grace than gifts to lend;
Who entertains the harmless day
 With a well-chosen book or friend;

—This man is free from servile bands
 Of hope to rise, or fear to fall;
Lord of himself, though not of lands;
 And having nothing, he hath all.

Sir Henry Wotton

73 The Noble Nature

It is not growing like a tree
 In bulk, doth make Man better be;
Or standing long an oak, three hundred year,
To fall a log at last, dry, bald, and sere:
  A lily of a day
  Is fairer far in May,
 Although it fall and die that night;
 It was the plant and flower of Light.
In small proportions we just beauties see;
And in short measures life may perfect be.

Ben Jonson

74 The Gifts of God

When God at first made Man,
Having a glass of blessings standing by;
Let us (said He) pour on him all we can:
Let the world's riches, which dispersèd lie,
 Contract into a span.

So strength first made a way;
Then beauty flow'd, then wisdom, honour, pleasure:
When almost all was out, God made a stay,

Perceiving that alone, of all His treasure,
    Rest in the bottom lay.

For if I should (said He)
Bestow this jewel also on my creature,
He would adore my gifts instead of me,
And rest in Nature, not the God of Nature:
    So both should losers be.

Yet let him keep the rest;
But keep them with repining restlessness:
Let him be rich and weary, that at least,
If goodness lead him not, yet weariness
    May toss him to my breast.

George Herbert

75   **The Retreat**

Happy those early days, when I
Shined in my Angel-infancy!
Before I understood this place
Appointed for my second race,
Or taught my soul to fancy aught
But a white, celestial thought;
When yet I had not walk'd above
A mile or two from my first Love,
And looking back, at that short space
Could see a glimpse of His bright face;
When on some gilded cloud or flower
My gazing soul would dwell an hour,
And in those weaker glories spy
Some shadows of eternity;
Before I taught my tongue to wound
My conscience with a sinful sound,
Or had the black art to dispense
A several sin to every sense,
But felt through all this fleshly dress
Bright shoots of everlastingness.

O how I long to travel back,
And tread again that ancient track!
That I might once more reach that plain,
Where first I left my glorious train;
From whence th' enlighten'd spirit sees
That shady City of Palm trees!
But ah, my soul with too much stay

Is drunk, and staggers in the way:—
Some men a forward motion love,
But I by backward steps would move;
And when this dust falls to the urn,
In that state I came, return.

Henry Vaughan

76   **To Mr. Lawrence**

Lawrence, of virtuous father virtuous son,
Now that the fields are dank and ways are mire,
Where shall we sometimes meet, and by the fire
Help waste a sullen day, what may be won
From the hard season gaining? Time will run
On smoother, till Favonius re-inspire
The frozen earth, and clothe in fresh attire
The lily and rose, that neither sow'd nor spun.

What neat repast shall feast us, light and choice,
Of Attic taste, with wine, whence we may rise
To hear the lute well touch'd, or artful voice
Warble immortal notes and Tuscan air?
He who of those delights can judge, and spare
To interpose them oft, is not unwise.

John Milton

77   **To Cyriack Skinner**

Cyriack, whose grandsire, on the royal bench
Of British Themis, with no mean applause
Pronounced, and in his volumes taught, our laws,
Which others at their bar so often wrench;
To-day deep thoughts resolve with me to drench
In mirth, that after no repenting draws;
Let Euclid rest, and Archimedes pause,
And what the Swede intend, and what the French.

To measure life learn thou betimes, and know
Toward solid good what leads the nearest way;
For other things mild Heaven a time ordains,
And disapproves that care, though wise in show,
That with superfluous burden loads the day,
And, when God sends a cheerful hour, refrains.

John Milton

78

Hymn to Diana

Queen and Huntress, chaste and fair,
  Now the sun is laid to sleep,
Seated in thy silver chair
  State in wonted manner keep:
    Hesperus entreats thy light,
    Goddess excellently bright.

Earth, let not thy envious shade
  Dare itself to interpose;
Cynthia's shining orb was made
  Heaven to clear when day did close:
    Bless us then with wishéd sight,
    Goddess excellently bright.

Lay thy bow of pearl apart
  And thy crystal-shining quiver;
Give unto the flying hart
  Space to breathe, how short soever:
    Thou that mak'st a day of night,
    Goddess excellently bright!

Ben Jonson

79

Wishes for the (Supposed) Mistress

    Whoe'er she be,
  That not impossible She
That shall command my heart and me;

    Where'er she lie,
  Lock'd up from mortal eye
In shady leaves of destiny:

    Till that ripe birth
  Of studied Fate stand forth,
And teach her fair steps tread our earth;

    Till that divine
  Idea take a shrine
Of crystal flesh, through which to shine:

    —Meet you her, my Wishes,
  Bespeak her to my blisses,
And be ye call'd, my absent kisses.

    I wish her beauty
  That owes not all its duty
To gaudy tire, or glist'ring shoe-tie:

Something more than
Taffata or tissue can,
Or rampant feather, or rich fan.

A face that's best
By its own beauty drest,
And can alone commend the rest:

A face made up
Out of no other shop
Than what Nature's white hand sets ope.

Sidneian showers
Of sweet discourse, whose powers
Can crown old Winter's head with flowers.

Whate'er delight
Can make day's forehead bright
Or give down to the wings of night.

Soft silken hours,
Open suns, shady bowers;
'Bove all, nothing within that lowers.

Days, that need borrow
No part of their good morrow
From a fore-spent night of sorrow:

Days, that in spite
Of darkness, by the light
Of a clear mind are day and night.

Life, that dares send
A challenge to his end,
And when it comes, say, 'Welcome, friend.'

I wish her store
Of worth may leave her poor
Of wishes; and I wish——no more.

—Now, if Time knows
That Her, whose radiant brows
Weave them a garland of my vows;

Her that dares be
What these lines wish to see:
I seek no further, it is She.

'Tis She, and here
Lo! I unclothe and clear.
My wishes' cloudy character.

Such worth as this is
Shall fix my flying wishes,
And determine them to kisses.

Let her full glory,
My fancies, fly before ye;
Be ye my fictions:—but her story.

Richard Crashaw

80   **The Great Adventurer**

Over the mountains
    And over the waves,
Under the fountains
    And under the graves,
Under floods that are deepest,
    Which Neptune obey;
Over rocks that are steepest
    Love will find out the way.

Where there is no place
    For the glow-worm to lie;
Where there is no space
    For receipt of a fly;
Where the midge dares not venture
    Lest herself fast she lay;
If love come, he will enter
    And soon find out his way.

You may esteem him
    A child for his might;
Or you may deem him
    A coward from his flight;
But if she whom love doth honour
    Be conceal'd from the day,
Set a thousand guards upon her,
    Love will find out the way.

Some think to lose him
    By having him confined;
And some do suppose him,
    Poor thing, to be blind;
But if ne'er so close ye wall him,
    Do the best that you may,
Blind love, if so ye call him,
    Will find out his way.

You may train the eagle
  To stoop to your fist;
Or you may inveigle
  The phoenix of the east;
The lioness, ye may move her
  To give o'er her prey;
But you'll ne'er stop a lover:
  He will find out his way.

Anon.

81   **Child and Maiden**

Ah, Chloris! that I now could sit
  As unconcern'd as when
Your infant beauty could beget
  No pleasure, nor no pain!
When I the dawn used to admire,
  And praised the coming day,
I little thought the growing fire
  Must take my rest away.

Your charms in harmless childhood lay
  Like metals in the mine;
Age from no face took more away
  Then youth conceal'd in thine.
But as your charms insensibly
  To their perfection prest,
Fond love as unperceived did fly,
  And in my bosom rest.

My passion with your beauty grew,
  And Cupid at my heart,
Still as his mother favour'd you,
  Threw a new flaming dart:
Each gloried in their wanton part;
  To make a lover, he
Employ'd the utmost of his art—
  To make a beauty, she.

Sir Charles Sedley

82   **Counsel to Girls**

Gather ye rose-buds while ye may,
  Old Time is still a-flying:
And this same flower that smiles to-day,
  To-morrow will be dying.

The glorious Lamp of Heaven, the Sun,
  The higher he's a-getting
The sooner will his race be run,
  And nearer he's to setting.

That age is best which is the first,
  When youth and blood are warmer;
But being spent, the worse, and worst
  Times, still succeed the former.

Then be not coy, but use your time;
  And while ye may, go marry:
For having lost but once your prime,
  You may for ever tarry.

Robert Herrick

83   **To Lucasta, on Going to the Wars**

Tell me not, Sweet, I am unkind
  That from the nunnery
Of thy chaste breast and quiet mind
  To war and arms I fly.

True, a new mistress now I chase,
  The first foe in the field;
And with a stronger faith embrace
  A sword, a horse, a shield.

Yet this inconstancy is such
  As you too shall adore;
I could not love thee, Dear, so much,
  Loved I not Honour more.

Richard Lovelace

84   **Elizabeth of Bohemia**

You meaner beauties of the night,
  That poorly satisfy our eyes
More by your number than your light,
  You common people of the skies,
What are you, when the Moon shall rise?

You curious chanters of the wood
  That warble forth dame Nature's lays,
Thinking your passions understood
  By your weak accents; what's your praise
When Philomel her voice shall raise?

You violets that first appear,
  By your pure purple mantles known
Like the proud virgins of the year,
  As if the spring were all your own,—
What are you, when the Rose is blown?

So when my Mistress shall be seen
  In form and beauty of her mind,
By virtue first, then choice, a Queen,
  Tell me, if she were not design'd
Th' eclipse and glory of her kind?

Sir Henry Wotton

85 **To the Lady Margaret Ley**

Daughter to that good Earl, once President
Of England's Council and her Treasury,
Who lived in both, unstain'd with gold or fee,
And left them both, more in himself content,
Till the sad breaking of that Parliament
Broke him, as that dishonest victory
At Chaeronea, fatal to liberty,
Kill'd with report that old man eloquent;—
Though later born than to have known the days
Wherein your father flourish'd, yet by you,
Madam, methinks I see him living yet;
So well your words his noble virtues praise,
That all both judge you to relate them true,
And to possess them, honour'd Margaret.

John Milton

86 **The Loveliness of Love**

It is not Beauty I demand,
  A crystal brow, the moon's despair,
Nor the snow's daughter, a white hand,
  Nor mermaid's yellow pride of hair:

Tell me not of your starry eyes,
  Your lips that seem on roses fed,
Your breasts, where Cupid trembling lies
  Nor sleeps for kissing of his bed:—

A bloomy pair of vermeil cheeks
  Like Hebe's in her ruddiest hours,
A breath that softer music speaks
  Than summer winds a-wooing flowers,

These are but gauds: nay, what are lips?
    Coral beneath the ocean-stream,
Whose brink when your adventurer sips
    Full oft he perisheth on them.

And what are cheeks, but ensigns oft
    That wave hot youth to fields of blood?
Did Helen's breast, though ne'er so soft,
    Do Greece or Ilium any good?

Eyes can with baleful ardour burn;
    Poison can breathe, that erst perfumed;
There's many a white hand holds an urn
    With lovers' hearts to dust consumed.

For crystal brows—there's nought within;
    They are but empty cells for pride;
He who the Syren's hair would win
    Is mostly strangled in the tide.

Give me, instead of Beauty's bust,
    A tender heart, a loyal mind
Which with temptation I could trust,
    Yet never link'd with error find,—

One in whose gentle bosom I
    Could pour my secret heart of woes,
Like the care-burthen'd honey-fly
    That hides his murmurs in the rose,—

My earthly Comforter! whose love
    So indefeasible might be
That, when my spirit won above,
    Hers could not stay, for sympathy.

*Anon.**

87   **The True Beauty**

He that loves a rosy cheek
    Or a coral lip admires,
Or from star-like eyes doth seek
    Fuel to maintain his fires;
As old Time makes these decay,
So his flames must waste away.

* *George Darley*

But a smooth and steadfast mind,
    Gentle thoughts, and calm desires,
Hearts with equal love combined,
    Kindle never-dying fires:—
Where these are not, I despise
Lovely cheeks or lips or eyes.

Thomas Carew

88

To Dianeme

Sweet, be not proud of those two eyes
Which starlike sparkle in their skies;
Nor be you proud, that you can see
All hearts your captives; yours yet free:
Be you not proud of that rich hair
Which wantons with the lovesick air;
Whenas that ruby which you wear,
Sunk from the tip of your soft ear,
Will last to be a precious stone
When all your world of beauty's gone.

Robert Herrick

89

    Go, lovely Rose!
Tell her, that wastes her time and me,
    That now she knows,
When I resemble her to thee,
How sweet and fair she seems to be.

    Tell her that's young
And shuns to have her graces spied,
    That hadst thou sprung
In deserts, where no men abide,
Thou must have uncommended died.

    Small is the worth
Of beauty from the light retired:
    Bid her come forth,
Suffer herself to be desired,
And not blush so to be admired.

    Then die! that she
The common fate of all things rare
    May read in thee:
How small a part of time they share
That are so wondrous sweet and fair!

Edmund Waller

90   **To Celia**

Drink to me only with thine eyes,
   And I will pledge with mine;
Or leave a kiss but in the cup
   And I'll not look for wine.
The thirst that from the soul doth rise
   Doth ask a drink divine;
But might I of Jove's nectar sup,
   I would not change for thine.

I sent thee late a rosy wreath,
   Not so much honouring thee
As giving it a hope that there
   It could not wither'd be;
But thou thereon didst only breathe
   And sent'st it back to me;
Since when it grows, and smells, I swear,
   Not of itself but thee!

Ben Jonson

91   **Cherry-Ripe**

There is a garden in her face
   Where roses and white lilies grow;
A heavenly paradise is that place,
   Wherein all pleasant fruits do flow;
There cherries grow which none may buy,
Till 'Cherry-Ripe' themselves do cry.

Those cherries fairly do enclose
   Of orient pearl a double row,
Which when her lovely laughter shows,
   They look like rose-buds fill'd with snow:
Yet them nor peer nor prince can buy,
Till 'Cherry-Ripe' themselves do cry.

Her eyes like angels watch them still;
   Her brows like bended bows do stand,
Threat'ning with piercing frowns to kill
   All that attempt with eye or hand
Those sacred cherries to come nigh,
—Till 'Cherry-Ripe' themselves do cry!

Thomas Campion

92   **The Poetry of Dress**
                       I

A sweet disorder in the dress
Kindles in clothes a wantonness:—
A lawn about the shoulders thrown
Into a fine distractión,—
An erring lace, which here and there
Enthrals the crimson stomacher—
A cuff neglectful, and thereby
Ribbands to flow confusedly,—
A winning wave, deserving note,
In the tempestuous petticoat,—
A careless shoe-string, in whose tie
I see a wild civility,—
Do more bewitch me, than when art
Is too precise in every part.

Robert Herrick

93   II

Whenas in silks by Julia goes
Then, then (methinks) how sweetly flows
That liquefaction of her clothes.

Next, when I cast mine eyes and see
That brave vibration each way free;
O how that glittering taketh me!

Robert Herrick

94   III

My Love in her attire doth shew her wit,
      It doth so well become her:
For every season she hath dressings fit,
      For Winter, Spring, and Summer.
      No beauty she doth miss
          When all her robes are on:
      But Beauty's self she is
          When all her robes are gone.

Anon.

95   **On a Girdle**

That which her slender waist confined
Shall now my joyful temples bind:
No monarch but would give his crown
His arms might do what this has done.

It was my Heaven's extremest sphere,
  The pale which held that lovely deer:
My joy, my grief, my hope, my love
  Did all within this circle move.

A narrow compass! and yet there
  Dwelt all that's good, and all that's fair:
Give me but what this ribband bound,
  Take all the rest the Sun goes round.

Edmund Waller

96   **To Anthea Who May Command Him Any Thing**

Bid me to live, and I will live
    Thy Protestant to be:
Or bid me love, and I will give
    A loving heart to thee.

A heart as soft, a heart as kind,
    A heart as sound and free
As in the whole world thou canst find,
    That heart I'll give to thee.

Bid that heart stay, and it will stay,
    To honour thy decree:
Or bid it languish quite away,
    And 't shall do so for thee.

Bid me to weep, and I will weep
    While I have eyes to see:
And, having none, yet I will keep
    A heart to weep for thee.

Bid me despair, and I'll despair
    Under that cypress tree:
Or bid me die, and I will dare
    E'en Death, to die for thee.

Thou art my life, my love, my heart,
    The very eyes of me,
And hast command of every part,
    To live and die for thee.

Robert Herrick

97

Love not me for comely grace,
    For my pleasing eye or face,
Nor for any outward part,
No, nor for my constant heart,—
        For those may fail, or turn to ill,
            So thou and I shall sever:
    Keep therefore a true woman's eye,
    And love me still, but know not why—
        So hast thou the same reason still
            To dote upon me ever!

Anon.

98

Not, Celia, that I juster am
    Or better than the rest;
For I would change each hour, like them,
    Were not my heart at rest.

But I am tied to very thee
    By every thought I have;
Thy face I only care to see,
    Thy heart I only crave.

All that in woman is adored
    In thy dear self I find—
For the whole sex can but afford
    The handsome and the kind.

Why then should I seek further store,
    And still make love anew?
When change itself can give no more,
    'Tis easy to be true.

Sir Charles Sedley

99

To Althea from Prison

When Love with unconfinéd wings
    Hovers within my gates,
And my divine Althea brings
    To whisper at the grates;
When I lie tangled in her hair
    And fetter'd to her eye,
The Gods that wanton in the air
    Know no such liberty.

When flowing cups run swiftly round
　　With no allaying Thames,
Our careless heads with roses crown'd,
　　Our hearts with loyal flames;
When thirsty grief in wine we steep,
　　When healths and draughts go free—
Fishes that tipple in the deep
　　Know no such liberty.

When, like committed linnets, I
　　With shriller throat shall sing
The sweetness, mercy, majesty
　　And glories of my King;
When I shall voice aloud how good
　　He is, how great should be,
Enlargèd winds, that curl the flood,
　　Know no such liberty.

Stone walls do not a prison make,
　　Nor iron bars a cage;
Minds innocent and quiet take
　　That for an hermitage:
If I have freedom in my love
　　And in my soul am free,
Angels alone, that soar above,
　　Enjoy such liberty.

Richard Lovelace

100　　**To Lucasta, on Going Beyond the Seas**

If to be absent were to be
　　Away from thee;
Or that when I am gone
　　You or I were alone;
Then, my Lucasta, might I crave
Pity from blustering wind, or swallowing wave.

Though seas and land betwixt us both,
　　Our faith and troth,
Like separated souls,
　　All time and space controls:
Above the highest sphere we meet
Unseen, unknown, and greet as Angels greet.

So then we do anticipate
　　Our after-fate,

And are alive i' the skies,
If thus our lips and eyes
Can speak like spirits unconfined
In Heaven, their earthly bodies left behind.

Richard Lovelace

101 **Encouragements to a Lover**

Why so pale and wan, fond lover?
Prythee, why so pale?
Will, when looking well can't move her,
Looking ill prevail?
Prythee, why so pale?

Why so dull and mute, young sinner?
Prythee, why so mute?
Will, when speaking well can't win her,
Saying nothing do't?
Prythee, why so mute?

Quit, quit, for shame! this will not move,
This cannot take her;
If of herself she will not love,
Nothing can make her:
The devil take her!

Sir John Suckling

102 **A Supplication**

Awake, awake, my Lyre!
And tell thy silent master's humble tale
In sounds that may prevail;
Sounds that gentle thoughts inspire:
Though so exalted she
And I so lowly be,
Tell her, such different notes make all thy harmony.

Hark, how the strings awake:
And, though the moving hand approach not near,
Themselves with awful fear
A kind of numerous trembling make.
Now all thy forces try;
Now all thy charms apply;
Revenge upon her ear the conquests of her eye.

Weak Lyre! thy virtue sure
Is useless here, since thou art only found

To cure, but not to wound,
And she to wound, but not to cure.
Too weak, too, wilt thou prove
My passion to remove;
Physic to other ills, thou'rt nourishment to love.

Sleep, sleep again, my Lyre!
For thou canst never tell my humble tale
In sounds that will prevail,
Nor gentle thoughts in her inspire;
All thy vain mirth lay by,
Bid thy strings silent lie,
Sleep, sleep again, my Lyre, and let thy master die.

Abraham Cowley

103   **The Manly Heart**

Shall I, wasting in despair,
Die because a woman's fair?
Or make pale my cheeks with care
'Cause another's rosy are?
Be she fairer than the day
Or the flowery meads in May—
    If she think not well of me,
    What care I how fair she be?

Shall my silly heart be pined
'Cause I see a woman kind;
Or a well disposéd nature
Joinéd with a lovely feature?
Be she meeker, kinder, than
Turtle-dove or pelican,
    If she be not so to me,
    What care I how kind she be?

Shall a woman's virtues move
Me to perish for her love?
Or her well-deservings known
Make me quite forget mine own?
Be she with that goodness blest
Which may merit name of Best;
    If she be not such to me,
    What care I how good she be?

'Cause her fortune seems too high,
Shall I play the fool and die?

She that bears a noble mind
If not outward helps she find,
Thinks what with them he would do
That without them dares her woo;
    And unless that mind I see,
    What care I how great she be?

Great or good, or kind or fair,
I will ne'er the more despair;
If she love me, this believe,
I will die ere she shall grieve;
If she slight me when I woo,
I can scorn and let her go;
    For if she be not for me,
    What care I for whom she be?

George Wither

104   **Melancholy**

Hence, all you vain delights,
  As short as are the nights
    Wherein you spend your folly:
There's nought in this life sweet,
  If man were wise to see't,
    But only melancholy,
    O sweetest melancholy!
Welcome, folded arms, and fixéd eyes,
A sigh that piercing mortifies,
A look that's fasten'd to the ground,
A tongue chain'd up without a sound!
Fountain heads and pathless groves,
Places which pale passion loves!
Moonlight walks, when all the fowls
Are warmly housed, save bats and owls!
A midnight bell, a parting groan—
These are the sounds we feed upon;
Then stretch our bones in a still gloomy valley;
Nothing's so dainty sweet as lovely melancholy.

John Fletcher

105   **To a Lock of Hair**

Thy hue, dear pledge, is pure and bright
As in that well-remember'd night
When first thy mystic braid was wove,
And first my Agnes whisper'd love.

Since then how often hast thou prest
The torrid zone of this wild breast,
Whose wrath and hate have sworn to dwell
With the first sin that peopled hell;
A breast whose blood's a troubled ocean,
Each throb the earthquake's wild commotion!
O if such clime thou canst endure
Yet keep thy hue unstain'd and pure,
What conquest o'er each erring thought
Of that fierce realm had Agnes wrought!
I had not wander'd far and wide
With such an angel for my guide;
Nor heaven nor earth could then reprove me
If she had lived, and lived to love me.
Not then this world's wild joys had been
To me one savage hunting scene,
My sole delight the headlong race
And frantic hurry of the chase;
To start, pursue, and bring to bay,
Rush in, drag down, and rend my prey,
Then—from the carcass turn away!
Mine ireful mood had sweetness tamed,
And soothed each wound which pride inflamed:—
Yes, God and man might now approve me
If thou hadst lived, and lived to love me!

Sir Walter Scott

106   **The Forsaken Bride**

O waly waly up the bank,
    And waly waly down the brae,
And waly waly you burn-side
    Where I and my Love wont to gae!
I leant my back unto an aik,
    I thought it was a trusty tree;
But first it bow'd, and syne it brak,
    Sae my true Love did lichtly me.

O waly waly, but love be bonny
    A little time while it is new;
But when 'tis auld, it waxeth cauld
    And fades awa' like morning dew.
O wherefore should I busk my head?
    Or wherefore should I kame my hair?
For my true Love has me forsook,
    And says he'll never loe me mair.

Now Arthur-seat sall be my bed;
  The sheets shall ne'er be 'fil'd by me:
Saint Anton's well sall be my drink,
  Since my true Love has forsaken me.
Marti'mas wind, when wilt thou blaw
  And shake the green leaves aff the tree?
O gentle Death, when wilt thou come?
  For of my life I am wearíe.

'Tis not the frost, that freezes fell,
  Nor blawing snaw's inclemencie;
'Tis not sic cauld that makes me cry,
  But my Love's heart grown cauld to me.
When we came in by Glasgow town
  We were a comely sight to see;
My Love was clad in the black velvét,
  And I myself in cramasie.

But had I wist, before I kist,
  That love had been sae ill to win;
I had lockt my heart in a case of gowd
  And pinn'd it with a siller pin.
And, O! if my young babe were born,
  And set upon the nurse's knee,
And I mysell were dead and gane,
  For a maid again I'll never be.   *Anon.*

107   Fair Helen

I wish I were where Helen lies;
Night and day on me she cries;
O that I were where Helen lies
  On fair Kirconnell lea!

Curst be the heart that thought the thought,
And curst the hand that fired the shot,
When in my arms burd Helen dropt,
  And died to succour me!

O think na but my heart was sair
When my Love dropt down and spak nae mair!
I laid her down wi' meikle care
  On fair Kirconnell lea.

As I went down the water-side,
None but my foe to be my guide,

None but my foe to be my guide,
    On fair Kirconnell lea;

I lighted down my sword to draw,
I hackéd him in pieces sma',
I hackéd him in pieces sma',
    For her sake that died for me.

O Helen fair, beyond compare!
I'll make a garland of thy hair
Shall bind my heart for evermair
    Until the day I die.

O that I were where Helen lies!
Night and day on me she cries;
Out of my bed she bids me rise,
    Says, 'Haste and come to me!'

O Helen fair! O Helen chaste!
If I were with thee, I were blest,
Where thou lies low and takes thy rest
    On fair Kirconnell lea.

I wish my grave were growing green,
A winding-sheet drawn ower my een,
And I in Helen's arms lying,
    On fair Kirconnell lea.

I wish I were where Helen lies;
Night and day on me she cries;
And I am weary of the skies,
    Since my Love died for me.

Anon.

108   **The Twa Corbies**

As I was walking all alane
I heard twa corbies making a mane;
The tane unto the t'other say,
'Where sall we gang and dine to-day?'

'—In behint yon auld fail dyke,
I wot there lies a new-slain Knight;
And naebody kens that he lies there,
But his hawk, his hound, and lady fair.

'His hound is to the hunting gane,
His hawk to fetch the wild-fowl hame,

His lady's ta'en another mate,
So we may make our dinner sweet.

'Ye'll sit on his white hause-bane,
And I'll pick out his bonny blue een:
Wi' ae lock o' his gowden hair
We'll theek our nest when it grows bare.

'Mony a one for him makes mane,
But nane sall ken where he is gane;
O'er his white banes, when they are bare,
The wind sall blaw for evermair.'

Anon.

109 ### To Blossoms

Fair pledges of a fruitful tree,
    Why do ye fall so fast?
    Your date is not so past,
But you may stay yet here awhile
    To blush and gently smile,
      And go at last.

What, were ye born to be
    An hour or half's delight,
    And so to bid good-night?
'Twas pity Nature brought ye forth
    Merely to show your worth,
      And lose you quite.

But you are lovely leaves, where we
    May read how soon things have
    Their end, though ne'er so brave:
And after they have shown their pride
    Like you awhile, they glide
      Into the grave.

Robert Herrick

110 ### To Daffodils

Fair Daffodils, we weep to see
    You haste away so soon:
As yet the early-rising Sun
    Has not attain'd his noon.
      Stay, stay,
    Until the hasting day

        Has run
        But to the even-song;
And, having pray'd together, we
        Will go with you along.

We have short time to stay, as you,
        We have as short a Spring;
As quick a growth to meet decay
        As you, or any thing.
        We die,
As your hours do, and dry
        Away
Like to the Summer's rain;
Or as the pearls of morning's dew,
        Ne'er to be found again.

Robert Herrick

111   **Thoughts in a Garden**

How vainly men themselves amaze
To win the palm, the oak, or bays,
And their uncessant labours see
Crown'd from some single herb or tree,
Whose short and narrow-vergéd shade
Does prudently their toils upbraid;
While all the flowers and trees do close
To weave the garlands of repose.

Fair Quiet, have I found thee here,
And Innocence thy sister dear!
Mistaken long, I sought you then
In busy companies of men:
Your sacred plants, if here below,
Only among the plants will grow:
Society is all but rude
To this delicious solitude.

No white nor red was ever seen
So amorous as this lovely green.
Fond lovers, cruel as their flame,
Cut in these trees their mistress' name:
Little, alas, they know or heed
How far these beauties hers exceed!
Fair trees! wheres'e'er your barks I wound,
No name shall but your own be found.

When we have run our passions' heat
Love hither makes his best retreat:
The gods, that mortal beauty chase,
Still in a tree did end their race:
Apollo hunted Daphne so,
Only that she might laurel grow:
And Pan did after Syrinx speed
Not as a nymph, but for a reed.

What wondrous life in this I lead!
Ripe apples drop about my head;
The luscious clusters of the vine
Upon my mouth do crush their wine;
The nectarine and curious peach
Into my hands themselves do reach;
Stumbling on melons, as I pass,
Ensnared with flowers, I fall on grass.

Meanwhile the mind, from pleasure less,
Withdraws into its happiness;
The mind, that ocean where each kind
Does straight its own resemblance find;
Yet it creates, transcending these,
Far other worlds, and other seas;
Annihilating all that's made
To a green thought in a green shade.

Here at the fountain's sliding foot
Or at some fruit-tree's mossy root,
Casting the body's vest aside,
My soul into the boughs does glide;
There, like a bird, it sits and sings,
Then whets and combs its silver wings,
And, till prepared for longer flight,
Waves in its plumes the various light.

Such was that happy Garden-state
While man there walk'd without a mate:
After a place so pure and sweet,
What other help could yet be meet!
But 'twas beyond a mortal's share
To wander solitary there:
Two paradises 'twere in one,
To live in Paradise alone.

How well the skilful gardener drew
Of flowers and herbs this dial new!

Where, from above, the milder sun
Does through a fragrant zodiac run:
And, as it works, th' industrious bee
Computes its time as well as we.
How could such sweet and wholesome hours
Be reckon'd, but with herbs and flowers!

Andrew Marvell

112   **L'Allegro**

Hence, loathéd Melancholy,
Of Cerberus and blackest Midnight born
    In Stygian cave forlorn
'Mongst horrid shapes, and shrieks, and sights unholy!
    Find out some uncouth cell,
Where brooding Darkness spreads his jealous wings
    And the night-raven sings;
There, under ebon shades and low-brow'd rocks
    As ragged as thy locks,
In dark Cimmerian desert ever dwell.

    But come, thou Goddess fair and free,
    In heaven yclep'd Euphrosyne,
    And by men, heart-easing Mirth,
    Whom lovely Venus at a birth
    With two sister Graces more
    To ivy-crownéd Bacchus bore:
    Or whether (as some sager sing)
    The frolic wind that breathes the spring,
    Zephyr, with Aurora playing,
    As he met her once a-Maying—
    There on beds of violets blue
    And fresh-blown roses wash'd in dew
    Fill'd her with thee, a daughter fair,
    So buxom, blithe, and debonair.
    Haste thee, Nymph, and bring with thee
    Jest, and youthful jollity,
    Quips, and cranks, and wanton wiles,
    Nods, and becks, and wreathéd smiles,
    Such as hang on Hebe's cheek,
    And love to live in dimple sleek;
    Sport that wrinkled Care derides,
    And Laughter holding both his sides.
    Come, and trip it as you go
    On the light fantastic toe;
    And in thy right hand lead with thee

The mountain nymph, sweet Liberty;
And if I give thee honour due,
Mirth, admit me of thy crew,
To live with her, and live with thee
In unreprovéd pleasures free;
To hear the lark begin his flight
And singing startle the dull night
From his watch-tower in the skies,
Till the dappled dawn doth rise;
Then to come, in spite of sorrow,
And at my window bid good-morrow
Through the sweetbriar, or the vine,
Or the twisted eglantine:
While the cock with lively din
Scatters the rear of darkness thin,
And to the stack, or the barn-door,
Stoutly struts his dames before:
Oft listening how the hounds and horn
Cheerly rouse the slumbering morn,
From the side of some hoar hill,
Through the high wood echoing shrill.
Sometime walking, not unseen,
By hedge-row elms, on hillocks green,
Right against the eastern gate
Where the great Sun begins his state
Robed in flames and amber light,
The clouds in thousand liveries dight;
While the ploughman, near at hand,
Whistles o'er the furrow'd land,
And the milkmaid singeth blithe,
And the mower whets his scythe,
And every shepherd tells his tale
Under the hawthorn in the dale.
　　Straight mine eye hath caught new pleasures
Whilst the landscape round it measures;
Russet lawns, and fallows grey,
Where the nibbling flocks do stray;
Mountains, on whose barren breast
The labouring clouds do often rest;
Meadows trim with daisies pied,
Shallow brooks, and rivers wide;
Towers and battlements it sees
Bosom'd high in tufted trees,
Where perhaps some Beauty lies,
The Cynosure of neighbouring eyes.
　　Hard by, a cottage chimney smokes
From betwixt two aged oaks,

Where Corydon and Thyrsis, met,
Are at their savoury dinner set
Of herbs, and other country messes
Which the neat-handed Phillis dresses;
And then in haste her bower she leaves
With Thestylis to bind the sheaves;
Or, if the earlier season lead,
To the tann'd haycock in the mead.

Sometimes with secure delight
The upland hamlets will invite,
When the merry bells ring round,
And the jocund rebecks sound
To many a youth and many a maid,
Dancing in the chequer'd shade;
And young and old come forth to play
On a sunshine holy-day,
Till the live-long daylight fail;
Then to the spicy nut-brown ale,
With stories told of many a feat,
How Faery Mab the junkets eat;
She was pinch'd, and pull'd, she said;
And he, by Friar's lantern led;
Tells how the drudging Goblin sweat
To earn his cream-bowl duly set,
When in one night, ere glimpse of morn,
His shadowy flail hath thresh'd the corn
That ten day-labourers could not end;
Then lies him down the lubber fiend,
And, stretch'd out all the chimney's length,
Basks at the fire his hairy strength;
And crop-full out of doors he flings,
Ere the first cock his matin rings.
Thus done the tales, to bed they creep,
By whispering winds soon lull'd asleep.

Tower'd cities please us then
And the busy hum of men,
Where throngs of knights and barons hold,
In weeds of peace high triumphs hold,
With store of ladies, whose bright eyes
Rain influence, and judge the prize
Of wit or arms, while both contend
To win her grace, whom all commend.
There let Hymen oft appear
In saffron robe, with taper clear,
And pomp, and feast, and revelry,
With mask, and antique pageantry;
Such sights as youthful poets dream

On summer eves by haunted stream.
Then to the well-trod stage anon,
If Jonson's learned sock be on,
Or sweetest Shakespeare, Fancy's child,
Warble his native wood-notes wild.
    And ever against eating cares
Lap me in soft Lydian airs
Married to immortal verse,
Such as the meeting soul may pierce
In notes, with many a winding bout
Of linkéd sweetness long drawn out,
With wanton heed and giddy cunning,
The melting voice through mazes running,
Untwisting all the chains that tie
The hidden soul of harmony;
That Orpheus' self may heave his head
From golden slumber, on a bed
Of heap'd Elysian flowers, and hear
Such strains as would have won the ear
Of Pluto, to have quite set free
His half-regain'd Eurydice.

    These delights if thou canst give,
Mirth, with thee I mean to live.

John Milton

113   Il Penseroso

Hence, vain deluding Joys,
The brood of Folly without father bred!
    How litle you bestead
Or fill the fixéd mind with all your toys!
    Dwell in some idle brain,
And fancies fond with gaudy shapes possess
    As thick and numberless
As the gay motes that people the sunbeams,
    Or likest hovering dreams
The fickle pensioners of Morpheus' train.

      But hail, thou goddess sage and holy,
    Hail, divinest Melancholy!
Whose saintly visage is too bright
To hit the sense of human sight,
And therefore to our weaker view
O'erlaid with black, staid Wisdom's hue;
Black, but such as in esteem
Prince Memnon's sister might beseem,

Or that starr'd Ethiop queen that strove
To set her beauty's praise above
The sea-nymphs, and their powers offended:
Yet thou art higher far descended:
Thee bright-hair'd Vesta, long of yore,
To solitary Saturn bore;
His daughter she; in Saturn's reign
Such mixture was not held a stain:
Oft in glimmering bowers and glades
He met her, and in secret shades
Of woody Ida's inmost grove,
Whilst yet there was no fear of Jove.
   Come, pensive nun, devout and pure,
Sober, steadfast, and demure,
All in a robe of darkest grain
Flowing with majestic train,
And sable stole of cypres lawn
Over thy decent shoulders drawn
Come, but keep thy wonted state,
With even step, and musing gait,
And looks commercing with the skies,
Thy rapt soul sitting in thine eyes:
There, held in holy passion still,
Forget thyself to marble, till
With a sad leaden downward cast
Thou fix them on the earth as fast:
And join with thee calm Peace, and Quiet,
Spare Fast, that oft with gods doth diet,
And hears the Muses in a ring
Ay round about Jove's altar sing:
And add to these retired Leisure
That in trim gardens takes his pleasure:—
But first, and chiefest, with thee bring
Him that yon soars on golden wing
Guiding the fiery-wheeléd throne,
The cherub Contemplatión;
And the mute Silence hist along,
'Less Philomel will deign a song
In her sweetest saddest plight,
Smoothing the rugged brow of Night,
While Cynthia checks her dragon yoke
Gently o'er the accustom'd oak.
—Sweet bird, that shunn'st the noise of folly,
Most musical, most melancholy!
Thee, chauntress, oft, the woods among
I woo, to hear thy even-song;
And missing thee, I walk unseen

On the dry smooth-shaven green,
To behold the wandering Moon
Riding near her highest noon,
Like one that had been led astray
Through the heaven's wide pathless way,
And oft, as if her head she bow'd,
Stooping through a fleecy cloud.

Oft, on a plat of rising ground
I hear the far-off curfeu sound
Over some wide-water'd shore,
Swinging slow with sullen roar:
Or, if the air will not permit,
Some still removéd place will fit,
Where glowing embers through the room
Teach light to counterfeit a gloom;
Far from all resort of mirth,
Save the cricket on the hearth,
Or the bellman's drowsy charm
To bless the doors from nightly harm.

Or let my lamp at midnight hour
Be seen in some high lonely tower,
Where I may oft out-watch the Bear
With thrice-great Hermes, or unsphere
The spirit of Plato, to unfold
What worlds or what vast regions hold
The immortal mind, that hath forsook
Her mansion in this fleshly nook:
And of those demons that are found
In fire, air, flood, or under ground,
Whose power hath a true consent
With planet, or with element.
Sometime let gorgeous Tragedy
In scepter'd pall come sweeping by,
Presenting Thebes, or Pelops' line,
Or the tale of Troy divine;
Or what (though rare) of later age
Ennobled hath the buskin'd stage.

But, O sad Virgin, that thy power
Might raise Musaeus from his bower,
Or bid the soul of Orpheus sing
Such notes as, warbled to the string,
Drew iron tears down Pluto's cheek
And made Hell grant what Love did seek!
Or call up him that left half-told
The story of Cambuscan bold,
Of Camball, and of Algarsife,
And who had Canacé to wife,

That own'd the virtuous ring and glass;
And of the wondrous horse of brass
On which the Tartar king did ride:
And if aught else great bards beside
In sage and solemn tunes have sung
Of turneys, and of trophies hung,
Of forests, and enchantments drear,
Where more is meant than meets the ear.

   Thus, Night, oft see me in thy pale career,
Till civil-suited Morn appear,
Not trick'd and frounced as she was wont
With the Attic Boy to hunt,
But kercheft in a comely cloud
While rocking winds are piping loud,
Or usher'd with a shower still,
When the gust hath blown his fill,
Ending on the rustling leaves
With minute drops from off the eaves.
And when the sun begins to fling
His flaring beams, me, goddess, bring
To archéd walks of twilight groves,
And shadows brown, that Sylvan loves,
Of pine, or monumental oak,
Where the rude axe, with heavéd stroke,
Was never heard the nymphs to daunt
Or fright them from their hallow'd haunt.
There in close covert by some brook
Where no profaner eye may look,
Hide me from day's garish eye,
While the bee with honey'd thigh,
That at her flowery work doth sing,
And the waters murmuring,
With such consort as they keep
Entice the dewy-feather'd Sleep;
And let some strange mysterious dream
Wave at his wings in airy stream
Of lively portraiture display'd,
Softly on my eyelids laid:
And, as I wake, sweet music breathe
Above, about, or underneath,
Sent by some Spirit to mortals good,
Or the unseen Genius of the wood.

   But let my due feet never fail
To walk the studious cloister's pale,
And love the high-embowéd roof,
With antique pillars massy-proof,
And storied windows richly dight

Casting a dim religious light:
There let the pealing organ blow
To the full-voiced quire below
In service high and anthems clear,
As may with sweetness, through mine ear,
Dissolve me into ecstasies,
And bring all Heaven before mine eyes.
  And may at last my weary age
Find out the peaceful hermitage,
The hairy gown and mossy cell
Where I may sit and rightly spell
Of every star that heaven doth show,
And of every herb that sips the dew;
Till old experience do attain
To something like prophetic strain.

  These pleasures, Melancholy, give,
And I with thee will choose to live.

John Milton

114   Song of the Emigrants in Bermuda

Where the remote Bermudas ride
In the ocean's bosom unespied,
From a small boat that row'd along
The listening winds received this song:
  'What should we do but sing His praise
That led us through the watery maze
Unto an isle so long unknown,
And yet far kinder than our own?
Where He the huge sea-monsters wracks,
That lift the deep upon their backs,
He lands us on a grassy stage,
Safe from the storms and prelate's rage:
He gave us this eternal spring
Which here enamels everything,
And sends the fowls to us in care
On daily visits through the air;
He hangs in shades the orange bright
Like golden lamps in a green night,
And does in the pomegranates close
Jewels more rich than Ormus shows:
He makes the figs our mouths to meet,
And throws the melons at our feet;
But apples plants of such a price,
No tree could ever bear them twice.
With cedars chosen by His hand

From Lebanon He stores the land;
And makes the hollow seas that roar
Proclaim the ambergris on shore.
He cast (of which we rather boast)
The Gospel's pearl upon our coast;
And in these rocks for us did frame
A temple where to sound His name.
Oh! let our voice His praise exalt
Till it arrive at Heaven's vault,
Which thence (perhaps) rebounding may
Echo beyond the Mexique bay!'
Thus sung they in the English boat
An holy and a cheerful note:
And all the way, to guide their chime,
With falling oars they kept the time.

Andrew Marvell

115   **At a Solemn Music**

Blest pair of Sirens, pledges of Heaven's joy,
    Sphere-born harmonious Sisters, Voice and Verse!
Wed your divine sounds, and mixt power employ
    Dead things with inbreathed sense able to pierce;
And to our high-raised phantasy present
That undisturbéd Song of pure consent
Ay sung before the sapphire-colour'd throne
            To Him that sits thereon,
With saintly shout and solemn jubilee;
Where the bright Seraphim in burning row
Their loud uplifted angel-trumpets blow;
And the Cherubic host in thousand quires
Touch their immortal harps of golden wires,
With those just Spirits that wear victorious palms,
            Hymns devout and holy psalms
            Singing everlastingly:
That we on earth, with undiscording voice
May rightly answer that melodious noise;
As once we did, till disproportion'd sin
Jarr'd against nature's chime, and with harsh din
Broke the fair music that all creatures made
To their great Lord, whose love their motion sway'd
In perfect diapason, whilst they stood
In first obedience, and their state of good.
O may we soon again renew that Song,

And keep in tune with Heaven, till God ere long
  To His celestial consort us unite,
To live with Him, and sing in endless morn of light.
                            John Milton

116   Alexander's Feast, or, The Power of Music

'Twas at the royal feast for Persia won
    By Philip's warlike son—
    Aloft in awful state
    The godlike hero sate
    On his imperial throne;
His valiant peers were placed around,
Their brows with roses and with myrtles bound
    (So should desert in arms be crown'd);
    The lovely Thais by his side
    Sate like a blooming eastern bride
    In flower of youth and beauty's pride:—
      Happy, happy, happy pair!
        None but the brave
        None but the brave
    None but the brave deserves the fair!

    Timotheus placed on high
    Amid the tuneful quire
With flying fingers touch'd the lyre:
The trembling notes ascend the sky
    And heavenly joys inspire.
    The song began from Jove
Who left his blissful seats above—
Such is the power of mighty love!
A dragon's fiery form belied the god;
Sublime on radiant spires he rode
When he to fair Olympia prest,
And while he sought her snowy breast,
    Then round her slender waist he curl'd,
And stamp'd an image of himself, a sovereign of the world
  —The listening crowd admire the lofty sound;
  A present deity! they shout around:
A present deity! the vaulted roofs rebound:
      With ravish'd ears
      The monarch hears,
      Assumes the god,
      Affects to nod
    And seems to shake the spheres.

The praise of Bacchus then the sweet musician sung,
  Of Bacchus ever fair and ever young:
    The jolly god in triumph comes!
    Sound the trumpets, beat the drums!
      Flush'd with a purple grace
      He shows his honest face:
Now give the hautboys breath; he comes, he comes!
    Bacchus, ever fair and young,
    Drinking joys did first ordain;
    Bacchus' blessings are a treasure,
    Drinking is the soldier's pleasure:
      Rich the treasure,
      Sweet the pleasure,
    Sweet is pleasure after pain.

Soothed with the sound, the king grew vain;
  Fought all his battles o'er again,
And thrice he routed all his foes, and thrice he slew the slain.
    The master saw the madness rise,
    His glowing cheeks, his ardent eyes;
    And while he Heaven and Earth defied
    Changed his hand and check'd his pride.
      He chose a mournful Muse
      Soft pity to infuse:
    He sung Darius great and good,
      By too severe a fate
    Fallen, fallen, fallen, fallen,
      Fallen from his high estate,
    And weltering in his blood;
Deserted, at his utmost need,
By those his former bounty fed;
On the bare earth exposed he lies
With not a friend to close his eyes.
  —With downcast looks the joyless victor sate,
Revolving in his alter'd soul
  The various turns of Chance below;
And now and then a sigh he stole,
  And tears began to flow.

    The mighty master smiled to see
That love was in the next degree;
'Twas but a kindred-sound to move,
For pity melts the mind to love.
Softly sweet, in Lydian measures
Soon he soothed his soul to pleasures.
War, he sung, is toil and trouble,

Honour but an empty bubble;
Never ending, still beginning,
   Fighting still, and still destroying;
If the world by worth thy winning,
   Think, O think, it worth enjoying:
Lovely Thais sits beside thee,
Take the good the gods provide thee!
—The many rend the skies with loud applause;
So Love was crown'd, but Music won the cause.
The prince, unable to conceal his pain,
    Gazed on the fair
    Who caused his care,
And sigh'd and look'd, sigh'd and look'd,
Sigh'd and look'd, and sigh'd again:
At length with love and wine at once opprest
The vanquish'd victor sunk upon her breast.

   Now strike the golden lyre again:
A louder yet, and yet a louder strain!
Break his bands of sleep asunder
And rouse him like a rattling peal of thunder.
Hark, hark! the horrid sound
   Has raised up his head:
   As awaked from the dead
And amazed he stares around.
Revenge, revenge, Timotheus cries,
See the Furies arise!
   See the snakes that they rear
   How they hiss in their hair,
And the sparkles that flash from their eyes!
    Behold a ghastly band,
    Each a torch in his hand!
Those are Grecian ghosts, that in battle were slain
    And unburied remain
    Inglorious on the plain:
    Give the vengeance due
    To the valiant crew!
Behold how they toss their torches on high,
How they point to the Persian abodes
And glittering temples of their hostile gods.
—The princes applaud with a furious joy:
And the King seized a flambeau with zeal to destroy;
    Thais led the way
    To light him to his prey,
And like another Helen, fired another Troy!

    —Thus, long ago,
Ere heaving bellows learn'd to blow,
    While organs yet were mute,
    Timotheus, to his breathing flute
      And sounding lyre,
Could swell the soul to rage, or kindle soft desire.
    At last divine Cecilia came,
    Inventress of the vocal frame;
The sweet enthusiast from her sacred store
    Enlarged the former narrow bounds,
    And added length to solemn sounds,
With Nature's mother-wit, and arts unknown before.
—Let old Timotheus yield the prize
    Or both divide the crown;
He raised a mortal to the skies;
    She drew an angel down!

John Dryden

THE GOLDEN TREASURY

BOOK THREE

117   **Ode on the Pleasure Arising from Vicissitude**

Now the golden Morn aloft
   Waves her dew-bespangled wing,
With vermeil cheek and whisper soft
   She woos the tardy Spring:
Till April starts, and calls around
The sleeping fragrance from the ground,
And lightly o'er the living scene
Scatters his freshest, tenderest green.

New-born flocks, in rustic dance,
   Frisking ply their feeble feet;
Forgetful of their wintry trance
   The birds his presence greet:
But chief, the sky-lark warbles high
His trembling thrilling ecstasy;
And lessening from the dazzled sight,
Melts into air and liquid light.

Yesterday the sullen year
   Saw the snowy whirlwind fly;
Mute was the music of the air,
   The herd stood drooping by:
Their raptures now that wildly flow
No yesterday nor morrow know;
'Tis Man alone that joy descries
With forward and reverted eyes.

Smiles on past Misfortune's brow
   Soft Reflection's hand can trace,
And o'er the cheek of Sorrow throw
   A melancholy grace;
While Hope prolongs our happier hour,
Or deepest shades, that dimly lour
And blacken round our weary way,
Gilds with a gleam of distant day.

Still, where rosy Pleasure leads,
   See a kindred Grief pursue;

Behind the steps that Misery treads
   Approaching Comfort view:
The hues of bliss more brightly glow
Chastised by sabler tints of woe,
And blended form, with artful strife,
The strength and harmony of life.

See the wretch that long has tost
   On the thorny bed of pain,
At length repair his vigour lost
   And breathe and walk again:
The meanest floweret of the vale,
The simplest note that swells the gale,
The common sun, the air, the skies,
To him are opening Paradise.

                    Thomas Gray

118   The Quiet Life

Happy the man, whose wish and care
   A few paternal acres bound,
Content to breathe his native air
        In his own ground.

Whose herds with milk, whose fields with bread,
   Whose flocks supply him with attire;
Whose trees in summer yield him shade,
        In winter fire.

Blest, who can unconcern'dly find
   Hours, days, and years slide soft away
In health of body, peace of mind,
        Quiet by day,

Sound sleep by night; study and ease
   Together mix'd; sweet recreation,
And innocence, which most does please
        With meditation.

Thus let me live, unseen, unknown;
   Thus unlamented let me die;
Steal from the world, and not a stone
        Tell where I lie.

                  Alexander Pope

The Blind Boy

O say what is that thing call'd Light,
　Which I must ne'er enjoy;
What are the blessings of the sight,
　O tell your poor blind boy!

You talk of wondrous things you see,
　You say the sun shines bright;
I feel him warm, but how can he
　Or make it day or night?

My day or night myself I make
　Whene'er I sleep or play;
And could I ever keep awake
　With me 'twere always day.

With heavy sighs I often hear
　You mourn my hapless woe;
But sure with patience I can bear
　A loss I ne'er can know.

Then let not what I cannot have
　My cheer of mind destroy:
Whilst thus I sing, I am a king,
　Although a poor blind boy.

Colley Cibber

120 On a Favourite Cat, Drowned in a Tub of Goldfishes

'Twas on a lofty vase's side,
Where China's gayest art had dyed
　The azure flowers that blow,
Demurest of the tabby kind,
The pensive Selima, reclined,
　Gazed on the lake below.

Her conscious tail her joy declared:
The fair round face, the snowy beard,
　The velvet of her paws,
Her coat that with the tortoise vies,
Her ears of jet, and emerald eyes,
　She saw; and purr'd applause.

Still had she gazed, but 'midst the tide
Two angel forms were seen to glide,
　The Genii of the stream:

Their scaly armour's Tyrian hue
Through richest purple to the view
    Betray'd a golden gleam.

The hapless Nymph with wonder saw:
A whisker first, and then a claw
    With many an ardent wish
She stretch'd, in vain, to reach the prize—
What female heart can gold despise?
    What Cat's averse to Fish?

Presumptuous maid! with looks intent
Again she stretch'd, again she bent,
    Nor knew the gulf between—
Malignant Fate sat by and smiled—
The slippery verge her feet beguiled;
    She tumbled headlong in!

Eight times emerging from the flood
She mew'd to every watery God
    Some speedy aid to send:—
No Dolphin came, no Nereid stirr'd,
Nor cruel Tom nor Susan heard—
    A favourite has no friend!

From hence, ye Beauties, undeceived,
Know one false step is ne'er retrieved,
    And be with caution bold:
Not all that tempts your wandering eyes
And heedless hearts, is lawful prize,
    Nor all that glisters, gold!

Thomas Gray

121   **To Charlotte Pulteney**

Timely blossom, Infant fair,
Fondling of a happy pair,
Every morn and every night
Their solicitous delight,
Sleeping, waking, still at ease,
Pleasing, without skill to please,
Little gossip, blithe and hale,
Tattling many a broken tale,
Singing many a tuneless song,
Lavish of a heedless tongue;
Simple maiden, void of art,
Babbling out the very heart,

Yet abandon'd to thy will,
Yet imagining no ill,
Yet too innocent to blush;
Like the linnet in the bush
To the mother-linnet's note
Moduling her slender throat;
Chirping forth thy petty joys,
Wanton in the change of toys,
Like the linnet green, in May
Flitting to each gloomy spray;
Wearied then and glad of rest,
Like the linnet in the nest:—
This thy present happy lot,
This, in time will be forgot:
Other pleasures, other cares,
Ever-busy Time prepares;
And thou shalt in thy daughter see,
This picture, once, resembled thee.

Ambrose Philips

122   **Rule, Britannia**

When Britain first at Heaven's command
    Arose from out the azure main,
This was the charter of the land,
    And guardian angels sung this strain:
Rule, Britannia! rule the waves!
Britons never will be slaves.

The nations not so blest as thee
    Must in their turns to tyrants fall,
While thou shalt flourish great and free,
    The dread and envy of them all.

Still more majestic shalt thou rise,
    More dreadful from each foreign stroke;
As the loud blast that tears the skies
    Serves but to root thy native oak.

Thee haughty tyrants ne'er shall tame;
    All their attempts to bend thee down
Will but arouse thy generous flame,
    But work their woe and thy renown.

To thee belongs the rural reign;
    Thy cities shall with commerce shine;

All thine shall be the subject main,
  And every shore it circles thine!

The Muses, still with Freedom found,
  Shall to thy happy coast repair;
Blest Isle, with matchless beauty crown'd,
  And manly hearts to guard the fair:—
Rule, Britannia! rule the waves!
  Britons never will be slaves!

James Thomson

123 **The Bard**

A Pindaric Ode

'Ruin seize thee, ruthless King!
  Confusion on thy banners wait!
Tho' fann'd by Conquest's crimson wing
  They mock the air with idle state.
Helm, nor hauberk's twisted mail,
Nor e'en thy virtues, tyrant, shall avail
To save thy secret soul from nightly fears,
From Cambria's curse, from Cambria's tears!'
—Such were the sounds that o'er the crested pride
  Of the first Edward scatter'd wild dismay,
As down the steep of Snowdon's shaggy side
  He wound with toilsome march his long array:—
Stout Glo'ster stood aghast in speechless trance;
'To arms!' cried Mortimer, and couch'd his quivering lance.

On a rock, whose haughty brow
  Frowns o'er old Conway's foaming flood,
  Robed in the sable garb of woe,
With haggard eyes the Poet stood;
(Loose his beard and hoary hair
Stream'd like a meteor to the troubled air;)
And with a master's hand and prophet's fire
Struck the deep sorrows of his lyre:
'Hark, how each giant oak and desert cave
  Sighs to the torrent's awful voice beneath!
O'er thee, O King! their hundred arms they wave,
  Revenge on thee in hoarser murmurs breathe;
Vocal no more, since Cambria's fatal day,
To high-born Hoel's harp, or soft Llewellyn's lay.

'Cold is Cadwallo's tongue,
  That hush'd the stormy main:
Brave Urien sleeps upon his craggy bed:

Mountains, ye mourn in vain
   Modred, whose magic song
Made huge Plinlimmon bow his cloud-topt head.
   On dreary Arvon's shore they lie
Smear'd with gore and ghastly pale:
Far, far aloof the affrighted ravens sail;
   The famish'd eagle screams, and passes by.
Dear lost companions of my tuneful art,
   Dear as the light that visits these sad eyes,
Dear as the ruddy drops that warm my heart,
   Ye died amidst your dying country's cries—
No more I weep. They do not sleep;
   On yonder cliffs, a griesly band,
I see them sit; they linger yet,
   Avengers of their native land:
With me in dreadful harmony they join,
And weave with bloody hands the tissue of thy line.'

'Weave the warp and weave the woof,
   The winding-sheet of Edward's race:
Give ample room and verge enough
   The characters of hell to trace.
Mark the year and mark the night
When Severn shall re-echo with affright
The shrieks of death thro' Berkley's roofs that ring,
Shrieks of an agonizing king!
   She-wolf of France, with unrelenting fangs
That tear'st the bowels of thy mangled mate,
   From thee be born, who o'er thy country hangs
The scourge of Heaven! What terrors round him wait!
Amazement in his van, with Flight combined,
And Sorrow's faded form, and Solitude behind.

'Mighty victor, mighty lord,
   Low on his funeral couch he lies!
No pitying heart, no eye, afford
   A tear to grace his obsequies.
Is the sable warrior fled?
Thy son is gone. He rests among the dead.
The swarm that in thy noon-tide beam were born?
—Gone to salute the rising morn.
Fair laughs the Morn, and soft the zephyr blows,
   While proudly riding o'er the azure realm
In gallant trim the gilded Vessel goes:
   Youth on the prow, and Pleasure at the helm:
Regardless of the sweeping Whirlwind's sway,
That, hush'd in grim repose, expects his evening prey.

'Fill high the sparkling bowl,
The rich repast prepare;
   Reft of a crown, he yet may share the feast:
Close by the regal chair
   Fell Thirst and Famine scowl
   A baleful smile upon their baffled guest.
Heard ye the din of battle bray,
   Lance to lance, and horse to horse?
Long years of havoc urge their destined course,
And thro' the kindred squadrons mow their way.
Ye towers of Julius, London's lasting shame,
With many a foul and midnight murder fed,
   Revere his Consort's faith, his Father's fame,
And spare the meek usurper's holy head!
Above, below, the rose of snow,
   Twined with her blushing foe, we spread:
The bristled boar in infant-gore
   Wallows beneath the thorny shade.
Now, brothers, bending o'er the acccurséd loom,
Stamp we our vengeance deep, and ratify his doom.

'Edward, lo! to sudden fate
   (Weave we the woof; The thread is spun;)
Half of thy heart we consecrate.
   (The web is wove; The work is done.)'
'Stay, O stay! nor thus forlorn
Leave me unbless'd, unpitied, here to mourn:
In yon bright track that fires the western skies
They melt, they vanish from my eyes.
But O! what solemn scenes on Snowdon's height
   Descending slow their glittering skirts unroll?
Visions of glory, spare my aching sight,
   Ye unborn ages, crowd not on my soul!
No more our long-lost Arthur we bewail:—
All hail, ye genuine kings! Britannia's issue, hail!

   'Girt with many a baron bold
Sublime their starry fronts they rear;
   And gorgeous dames, and statesmen old
In bearded majesty, appear.
In the midst a form divine!
Her eye proclaims her of the Briton-Line:
Her lion-port, her awe-commanding face
Attemper'd sweet to virgin-grace.
What strings symphonious tremble in the air,
   What strains of vocal transport round her play?
Hear from the grave, great Taliessin, hear;

They breathe a soul to animate thy clay.
Bright Rapture calls, and soaring as she sings,
Waves in the eye of Heaven her many-colour'd wings.

'The verse adorn again
  Fierce War, and faithful Love,
And Truth severe, by fairy Fiction drest.
  In buskin'd measures move
Pale Grief, and pleasing Pain,
With Horror, tyrant of the throbbing breast.
A voice as of the cherub-choir
  Gales from blooming Eden bear,
  And distant warblings lessen on my ear,
That lost in long futurity expire.
Fond impious man, think'st thou yon sanguine cloud
  Raised by thy breath, has quench'd the orb of day?
To-morrow he repairs the golden flood
  And warms the nations with redoubled ray.
  Enough for me: with joy I see
  The different doom our fates assign:
Be thine Despair and sceptred Care;
  To triumph and to die are mine.'
—He spoke, and headlong from the mountain's height
Deep in the roaring tide he plunged to endless night.

Thomas Gray

124   **Ode Written in 1746**

How sleep the Brave who sink to rest
By all their Country's wishes blest!
When Spring, with dewy fingers cold,
Returns to deck their hallow'd mould,
She there shall dress a sweeter sod
Than Fancy's feet have ever trod.

By fairy hands their knell is rung,
By forms unseen their dirge is sung:
There Honour comes, a pilgrim grey,
To bless the turf that wraps their clay;
And Freedom shall awhile repair
To dwell, a weeping hermit, there!

William Collins

125   **Lament for Culloden**

The lovely lass o' Inverness,
  Nae joy nor pleasure can she see;

For e'en and morn she cries, Alas!
　　And ay the saut tear blin's her ee:
Drumossie moor—Drumossie day—
　　A waefu' day it was to me!
For there I lost my father dear,
　　My father dear, and brethren three.

Their winding-sheet the bluidy clay,
　　Their graves are growing green to see:
And by them lies the dearest lad
　　That ever blest a woman's ee!
Now wae to thee, thou cruel lord,
　　A bluidy man I trow thou be;
For mony a heart thou hast made sair
　　That ne'er did wrang to thine or thee.

Robert Burns

126   Lament for Flodden

I've heard them lilting at the ewe-milking,
　　Lasses a' lilting before dawn of day;
But now they are moaning on ilka green loaning—
　　The Flowers of the Forest are a' wede away.

At bughts, in the morning, nae blythe lads are scorning,
　　Lasses are lonely and dowie and wae;
Nae daffing, nae gabbing, but sighing and sabbing,
　　Ilk ane lifts her leglin and hies her away.

In har'st, at the shearing, nae youths now are jeering,
　　Bandsters are runkled, and lyart, or grey;
At fair or at preaching, nae wooing, nae fleeching—
　　The Flowers of the Forest are a' wede away.

At e'en, in the gloaming, nae younkers are roaming
　　'Bout stacks with the lasses at bogle to play;
But ilk maid sits dreary, lamenting her dearie—
　　The Flowers of the Forest are weded away.

Dool and wae for the order, sent our lads to the Border!
　　The English, for ance, by guile wan the day;
The Flowers of the Forest, that fought aye the foremost,
　　The prime of our land, are cauld in the clay.

We'll hear nae mair lilting at the ewe-milking;
　　Women and bairns are heartless and wae;
Sighing and moaning on ilka green loaning—
　　The Flowers of the Forest are a' wede away.

Jane Elliot

127   The Braes of Yarrow

'Thy braes were bonny, Yarrow stream,
    When first on them I met my lover;
Thy braes how dreary, Yarrow stream,
    When now thy waves his body cover!
For ever now, O Yarrow stream,
    Thou art to me a stream of sorrow;
For never on thy banks shall I
    Behold my love, the flower of Yarrow.

'He promised me a milk-white steed
    To bear me to his father's bowers;
He promised me a little page
    To squire me to his father's towers;
He promised me a wedding-ring,—
    The wedding-day was fix'd to-morrow;—
Now he is wedded to his grave,
    Alas, his watery grave, in Yarrow!

'Sweet were his words when last we met;
    My passion I as freely told him;
Clasp'd in his arms, I little thought
    That I should never more behold him!
Scarce was he gone, I saw his ghost;
    It vanish'd with a shriek of sorrow;
Thrice did the water-wraith ascend,
    And gave a doleful groan thro' Yarrow.

'His mother from the window look'd
    With all the longing of a mother;
His little sister weeping walk'd
    The green-wood path to meet her brother;
They sought him east, they sought him west,
    They sought him all the forest thorough;
They only saw the cloud of night,
    They only heard the roar of Yarrow.

'No longer from thy window look—
    Thou hast no son, thou tender mother!
No longer walk, thou lovely maid;
    Alas, thou hast no more a brother!
No longer seek him east or west
    And search no more the forest thorough;
For, wandering in the night so dark,
    He fell a lifeless corpse in Yarrow.

'The tear shall never leave my cheek,
　No other youth shall be my marrow—
I'll seek thy body in the stream,
　And then with thee I'll sleep in Yarrow.'
—The tear did never leave her cheek,
　No other youth became her marrow;
She found his body in the stream,
　And now with him she sleeps in Yarrow.

John Logan

128　　　　　**Willy Drowned in Yarrow**

Down in yon garden sweet and gay
　Where bonnie grows the lily,
I heard a fair maid sighing say,
　'My wish be wi' sweet Willie!

'Willie's rare, and Willie's fair,
　And Willie's wondrous bonny;
And Willie hecht to marry me
　Gin e'er he married ony.

'Oh gentle wind, that bloweth south
　From where my Love repaireth,
Convey a kiss frae his dear mouth
　And tell me how he fareth!

'O tell sweet Willie to come doun
　And hear the mavis singing,
And see the birds on ilka bush
　And leaves around them hinging

'The lav'rock there, wi' her white breast
　And gentle throat sae narrow;
There's sport eneuch for gentlemen
　On Leader haughs and Yarrow.

'O Leader haughs are wide and braid
　And Yarrow haughs are bonny;
There Willie hecht to marry me
　If e'er he married ony.

'But Willie's gone, whom I thought on,
　And does not hear me weeping;
Draws many a tear frae 's true love's e'e
　When other maids are sleeping.

'Yestreen I made my bed fu' braid,
   The night I'll mak' it narrow,
For a' the live-lang winter night
   I lie twined o' my marrow.

'O came ye by yon water-side?
   Pou'd you the rose or lily?
Or came you by yon meadow green,
   Or saw you my sweet Willie?'

She sought him up, she sought him down,
   She sought him braid and narrow;
Syne, in the cleaving of a craig,
   She found him drown'd in Yarrow!

Anon.

129   Loss of the Royal George

   Toll for the brave!
The brave that are no more!
   All sunk beneath the wave
Fast by their native shore!

   Eight hundred of the brave,
Whose courage well was tried,
   Had made the vessel heel
And laid her on her side.

   A land-breeze shook the shrouds
And she was overset;
   Down went the Royal George,
With all her crew complete.

   Toll for the brave!
Brave Kempenfelt is gone;
   His last sea-fight is fought,
His work of glory done.

   It was not in the battle;
No tempest gave the shock;
   She sprang no fatal leak,
She ran upon no rock.

   His sword was in the sheath,
His fingers held the pen,
   When Kempenfelt went down
With twice four hundred men.

Weigh the vessel up
 Once dreaded by our foes,
  And mingle with your cup
The tears that England owes.

 Her timbers yet are sound,
And she may float again
  Full charged with England's thunder,
And plough the distant main:

 But Kempenfelt is gone,
His victories are o'er;
  And he and his eight hundred
Must plough the wave no more.

William Cowper

130 Black-Eyed Susan

All in the Downs the fleet was moor'd,
 The streamers waving in the wind,
When black-eyed Susan came aboard;
 'O! where shall I my true-love find?
Tell me, ye jovial sailors, tell me true
If my sweet William sails among the crew.'

William, who high upon the yard
 Rock'd with the billow to and fro,
Soon as her well-known voice he heard,
 He sigh'd, and cast his eyes below:
The cord slides swiftly through his glowing hands,
And quick as lightning on the deck he stands.

So the sweet lark, high poised in air,
 Shuts close his pinions to his breast
If chance his mate's shrill call he hear,
 And drops at once into her nest:—
The noblest captain in the British fleet
Might envy William's lips those kisses sweet.

'O Susan, Susan, lovely dear,
 My vows shall ever true remain;
Let me kiss off that falling tear;
 We only part to meet again.
Change as ye list, ye winds; my heart shall be
The faithful compass that still points to thee.

'Believe not what the landmen say
  Who tempt with doubts thy constant mind:
They'll tell thee, sailors, when away,
  In every port a mistress find:
Yes, yes, believe them when they tell thee so,
For Thou art present wheresoe'er I go.

'If to far India's coast we sail,
  Thy eyes are seen in diamonds bright,
Thy breath is Afric's spicy gale,
  Thy skin is ivory so white.
Thus every beauteous object that I view
Wakes in my soul some charm of lovely Sue.

'Though battle call me from thy arms
  Let not my pretty Susan mourn;
Though cannons roar, yet safe from harms
  William shall to his Dear return.
Love turns aside the balls that round me fly,
Lest precious tears should drop from Susan's eye.'

The boatswain gave the dreadful word,
  The sails their swelling bosom spread;
No longer must she stay aboard;
  They kiss'd, she sigh'd, he hung his head.
Her lessening boat unwilling rows to land;
'Adieu!' she cries; and waved her lily hand.

John Gay

131   **Sally in Our Alley**

Of all the girls that are so smart
  There's none like pretty Sally;
She is the darling of my heart,
  And she lives in our alley.
There is no lady in the land
  Is half so sweet as Sally;
She is the darling of my heart,
  And she lives in our alley.

Her father he makes cabbage-nets
  And through the streets does cry 'em;
Her mother she sells laces long
  To such as please to buy 'em:
But sure such folks could ne'er beget
  So sweet a girl as Sally!

She is the darling of my heart,
 And she lives in our alley.

When she is by, I leave my work,
 I love her so sincerely;
My master comes like any Turk,
 And bangs me most severely—
But let him bang his bellyful,
 I'll bear it all for Sally;
She is the darling of my heart,
 And she lives in our alley.

Of all the days that's in the week
 I dearly love but one day—
And that's the day that comes betwixt
 A Saturday and Monday;
For then I'm drest all in my best
 To walk abroad with Sally;
She is the darling of my heart,
 And she lives in our alley.

My master carries me to church,
 And often am I blamed
Because I leave him in the lurch
 As soon as text is named;
I leave the church in sermon-time
 And slink away to Sally;
She is the darling of my heart,
 And she lives in our alley.

When Christmas comes about again
 O then I shall have money;
I'll hoard it up, and box and all,
 I'll give it to my honey:
I would it were ten thousand pound,
 I'd give it all to Sally;
She is the darling of my heart,
 And she lives in our alley.

My master and the neighbours all
 Make game of me and Sally,
And, but for her, I'd better be
 A slave and row a galley;
But when my seven long years are out
 O then I'll marry Sally,—
O then we'll wed, and then we'll bed,
 But not in our alley!

Henry Carey

132
A Farewell

Go fetch to me a pint o' wine,
    An' fill it in a silver tassie;
That I may drink before I go
    A service to my bonnie lassie:
The boat rocks at the pier o' Leith,
    Fu' loud the wind blaws frae the Ferry,
The ship rides by the Berwick-law,
    And I maun leave my bonnie Mary.

The trumpets sound, the banners fly,
    The glittering spears are rankéd ready;
The shouts o' war are heard afar,
    The battle closes thick and bloody;
But it's not the roar o' sea or shore
    Wad make me langer wish to tarry;
Nor shout o' war that's heard afar—
    It's leaving thee, my bonnie Mary.

Robert Burns

133
If doughty deeds my lady please
    Right soon I'll mount my steed;
And strong his arm, and fast his seat,
    That bears frae me the meed.
I'll wear thy colours in my cap,
    Thy picture in my heart;
And he that bends not to thine eye
    Shall rue it to his smart.
        Then tell me how to woo thee, love;
           O tell me how to woo thee!
        For thy dear sake, nae care I'll take,
           Tho' ne'er another trow me.

If gay attire delight thine eye
    I'll dight me in array;
I'll tend thy chamber door all night,
    And squire thee all the day.
If sweetest sounds can win thine ear,
    These sounds I'll strive to catch;
Thy voice I'll steal to woo thysell,
    That voice that nane can match.

But if fond love thy heart can gain,
    I never broke a vow;
Nae maiden lays her skaith to me,
    I never loved but you.

For you alone I ride the ring,
    For you I wear the blue;
For you alone I strive to sing,
    O tell me how to woo!
      Then tell me how to woo thee, love;
        O tell me how to woo thee!
      For thy dear sake, nae care I'll take,
        Tho' ne'er another trow me.

Robert Graham of Gartmore

134   To a Young Lady

Sweet stream, that winds through yonder glade,
Apt emblem of a virtuous maid—
Silent and chaste she steals along,
Far from the world's gay busy throng:
With gentle yet prevailing force,
Intent upon her destined course;
Graceful and useful all she does,
Blessing and blest where'er she goes;
Pure-bosom'd as that watery glass,
And Heaven reflected in her face.

William Cowper

135   The Sleeping Beauty

Sleep on, and dream of Heaven awhile—
    Tho' shut so close thy laughing eyes,
Thy rosy lips still wear a smile
    And move, and breathe delicious sighs!

Ah, now soft blushes tinge her cheeks
    And mantle o'er her neck of snow:
Ah, now she murmurs, now she speaks
    What most I wish—and fear to know!

She starts, she trembles, and she weeps!
    Her fair hands folded on her breast:
—And now, how like a saint she sleeps!
    A seraph in the realms of rest!

Sleep on secure! Above control
    Thy thoughts belong to Heaven and thee:
And may the secret of thy soul
    Remain within its sanctuary!

Samuel Rogers

136

For ever, Fortune, wilt thou prove
An unrelenting foe to Love,
And when we meet a mutual heart
Come in between, and bid us part?

Bid us sigh on from day to day,
And wish and wish the soul away;
Till youth and genial years are flown,
And all the life of life is gone?

But busy, busy, still art thou,
To bind the loveless joyless vow,
The heart from pleasure to delude,
And join the gentle to the rude.

For once, O Fortune, hear my prayer,
And I absolve thy future care;
All other blessings I resign,
Make but the dear Amanda mine.

James Thomson

137

The merchant, to secure his treasure,
    Conveys it in a borrow'd name:
Euphelia serves to grace my measure,
    But Cloe is my real flame.

My softest verse, my darling lyre
    Upon Euphelia's toilet lay—
When Cloe noted her desire
    That I should sing, that I should play.

My lyre I tune, my voice I raise,
    But with my numbers mix my sighs;
And whilst I sing Euphelia's praise,
    I fix my soul on Cloe's eyes.

Fair Cloe blush'd: Euphelia frown'd:
    I sung, and gazed; I play'd, and trembled:
And Venus to the Loves around
    Remark'd how ill we all dissembled.

Matthew Prior

138   When lovely woman stoops to folly
    And finds too late that men betray,—
What charm can soothe her melancholy,
    What art can wash her guilt away?

The only art her guilt to cover,
    To hide her shame from every eye,
To give repentance to her lover
    And wring his bosom, is—to die.

                          Oliver Goldsmi

139   Ye flowery banks o' bonnie Doon,
    How can ye bloom sae fair!
How can ye chant, ye little birds,
    And I sae fu' o' care!

Thou'll break my heart, thou bonnie bird
    That sings upon the bough;
Thou minds me o' the happy days
    When my fause Luve was true.

Thou'll break my heart, thou bonnie bird
    That sings beside thy mate;
For sae I sat, and sae I sang,
    And wist na o' my fate.

Aft hae I roved by bonnie Doon
    To see the woodbine twine;
And ilka bird sang o' its love,
    And sae did I o' mine.

Wi' lightsome heart I pu'd a rose,
    Frae aff its thorny tree;
And my fause luver staw the rose,
    But left the thorn wi' me.

                          Robert Burr

140   **The Progress of Poesy**

A Pindaric Ode

Awake, Aeolian lyre, awake,
And give to rapture all thy trembling strings.
From Helicon's harmonious springs
    A thousand rills their mazy progress take:
The laughing flowers that round them blow

Drink life and fragrance as they flow.
Now the rich stream of Music winds along
Deep, majestic, smooth, and strong,
Through verdant vales and Ceres' golden reign;
Now rolling down the steep amain,
Headlong, impetuous, see it pour:
The rocks and nodding groves rebellow to the roar.

    O Sovereign of the willing soul,
Parent of sweet and solemn-breathing airs,
Enchanting shell! the sullen Cares
    And frantic Passions hear thy soft control.
On Thracia's hills the Lord of War
Has curb'd the fury of his car
And dropt his thirsty lance at thy command.
Perching on the sceptred hand
Of Jove, thy magic lulls the feather'd king
With ruffled plumes, and flagging wing:
Quench'd in dark clouds of slumber lie
The terror of his beak, and lightnings of his eye.

Thee the voice, the dance, obey
Temper'd to thy warbled lay.
    O'er Idalia's velvet green
    The rosy-crownéd Loves are seen
On Cytherea's day,
    With antic Sports, and blue-eyed Pleasures,
    Frisking light in frolic measures;
Now pursuing, now retreating,
    Now in circling troops they meet:
To brisk notes in cadence beating
    Glance their many-twinkling feet.
Slow melting strains their Queen's approach declare:
    Where'er she turns the Graces homage pay:
With arms sublime that float upon the air
    In gliding state she wins her easy way:
O'er her warm cheek and rising bosom move
The bloom of young Desire and purple light of Love.

    Man's feeble race what ills await!
Labour, and Penury, the racks of Pain,
Disease, and Sorrow's weeping train,
    And Death, sad refuge from the storms of Fate!
The fond complaint, my song, disprove,
And justify the laws of Jove.
Say, has he given in vain the heavenly Muse?
Night, and all her sickly dews,

Her spectres wan, and birds of boding cry
He gives to range the dreary sky:
Till down the eastern cliffs afar
Hyperion's march they spy, and glittering shafts of war.

In climes beyond the solar road,
Where shaggy forms o'er ice-built mountains roam,
The Muse has broke the twilight gloom
　　To cheer the shivering native's dull abode.
And oft, beneath the odorous shade
Of Chili's boundless forests laid,
She deigns to hear the savage youth repeat
In loose numbers wildly sweet
Their feather-cinctured chiefs, and dusky loves.
Her track, where'er the Goddess roves,
Glory pursue, and generous Shame,
Th' unconquerable Mind, and Freedom's holy flame.

Woods, that wave o'er Delphi's steep,
Isles, that crown th' Aegean deep,
　　Fields that cool Ilissus laves,
　　Or where Maeander's amber waves
In lingering lab'rinths creep,
　　How do your tuneful echoes languish,
　　Mute, but to the voice of anguish!
Where each old poetic mountain
　　Inspiration breath'd around;
Every shade and hallow'd fountain
　　Murmur'd deep a solemn sound:
Till the sad Nine, in Greece's evil hour,
　　Left their Parnassus for the Latian plains.
Alike they scorn the pomp of tyrant Power,
　　And coward Vice, that revels in her chains.
When Latium had her lofty spirit lost,
They sought, O Albion, next thy sea-encircled coast.

Far from the sun and summer-gale
In thy green lap was Nature's Darling laid,
What time, where lucid Avon stray'd,
　　To him the mighty Mother did unveil
Her awful face: the dauntless Child
Stretch'd forth his little arms, and smiled.
This pencil take (she said), whose colours clear
Richly paint the vernal year:
Thine, too, these golden keys, immortal Boy!
This can unlock the gates of Joy;
Of Horror that, and thrilling Fears,
Or ope the sacred source of sympathetic Tears.

Nor second He, that rode sublime
Upon the seraph-wings of Ecstasy,
The secrets of the Abyss to spy:
  He pass'd the flaming bounds of Place and Time:
The living Throne, the sapphire-blaze,
Where Angels tremble while they gaze,
He saw; but blasted with excess of light,
Closed his eyes in endless night.
Behold where Dryden's less presumptuous car
Wide o'er the fields of Glory bear
Two coursers of ethereal race
With necks in thunder clothed, and long-resounding pace.

Hark, his hands the lyre explore!
Bright-eyed Fancy, hovering o'er,
  Scatters from her pictur'd urn
  Thoughts that breathe, and words that burn.
But ah! 'tis heard no more————
  O! Lyre divine, what daring Spirit
  Wakes thee now? Tho' he inherit
Nor the pride, nor ample pinion,
  That the Theban Eagle bear,
Sailing with supreme dominion
  Thro' the azure deep of air:
Yet oft before his infant eyes would run
  Such forms as glitter in the Muse's ray
With orient hues, unborrow'd of the sun:
  Yet shall he mount, and keep his distant way
Beyond the limits of a vulgar fate:
Beneath the Good how far—but far above the Great.

Thomas Gray

141   **The Passions**

An Ode for Music

When Music, heavenly maid, was young,
While yet in early Greece she sung,
The Passions oft, to hear her shell,
Throng'd around her magic cell
Exulting, trembling, raging, fainting,
Possest beyond the Muse's painting;
By turns they felt the glowing mind
Disturb'd, delighted, rais'd, refin'd:
Till once, 'tis said, when all were fir'd,
Fill'd with fury, rapt, inspir'd,
From the supporting myrtles round

They snatch'd her instruments of sound,
And, as they oft had heard apart
Sweet lessons of her forceful art,
Each, for Madness ruled the hour,
Would prove his own expressive power.

First Fear his hand, its skill to try,
    Amid the chords bewilder'd laid,
And back recoil'd, he knew not why,
    E'en at the sound himself had made.

Next Anger rush'd, his eyes on fire,
    In lightnings own'd his secret stings;
In one rude clash he struck the lyre
    And swept with hurried hand the strings.

With woeful measures wan Despair,
    Low sullen sounds, his grief beguiled,
A solemn, strange, and mingled air,
    'Twas sad by fits, by starts 'twas wild.

But thou, O Hope, with eyes so fair,
    What was thy delightful measure?
Still it whisper'd promised pleasure
    And bade the lovely scenes at distance hail!

Still would her touch the strain prolong;
    And from the rocks, the woods, the vale,
She call'd on Echo still through all the song;
    And, where her sweetest theme she chose,
    A soft responsive voice was heard at every close;
And Hope enchanted smiled, and waved her golden hair.

And longer had she sung,—but with a frown
    Revenge impatient rose:
He threw his blood-stain'd sword in thunder down;
    And with a withering look
The war-denouncing trumpet took,
And blew a blast so loud and dread,
Were ne'er prophetic sounds so full of woe.
    And ever and anon he beat
    The doubling drum with furious heat;
And, though sometimes, each dreary pause between,
    Dejected Pity at his side
    Her soul-subduing voice applied,
Yet still he kept his wild unalter'd mien,
While each strain'd ball of sight seem'd bursting from his head

Thy numbers, Jealousy, to nought were fix'd:
  Sad proof of thy distressful state!
Of differing themes the veering song was mix'd;
  And now it courted Love, now raving call'd on Hate.

With eyes up-rais'd, as one inspir'd,
Pale Melancholy sat retir'd;
And from her wild sequester'd seat,
In notes by distance made more sweet,
Pour'd through the mellow horn her pensive soul:
    And dashing soft from rocks around
    Bubbling runnels join'd the sound;
Through glades and glooms the mingled measure stole,
  Or, o'er some haunted stream, with fond delay,
    Round an holy calm diffusing,
    Love of peace and lonely musing,
  In hollow murmurs died away.

But O! how alter'd was its sprightlier tone,
When Cheerfulness, a nymph of healthiest hue,
  Her bow across her shoulder flung,
  Her buskins gemm'd with morning dew,
Blew an inspiring air, that dale and thicket rung,
  The hunter's call to Faun and Dryad known!
The oak-crown'd Sisters and their chaste-eyed Queen,
  Satyrs and Sylvan Boys, were seen
  Peeping from forth their alleys green:
Brown Exercise rejoic'd to hear;
  And Sport leap'd up, and seiz'd his beechen spear.

Last came Joy's ecstatic trial:
He, with viny crown advancing,
  First to the lively pipe his hand addrest:
But soon he saw the brisk awak'ning viol,
  Whose sweet entrancing voice he lov'd the best:
They would have thought who heard the strain
    They saw, in Tempe's vale, her native maids
    Amidst the festal-sounding shades
To some unwearied minstrel dancing;
While, as his flying fingers kiss'd the strings,
  Love fram'd with Mirth a gay fantastic round:
  Loose were her tresses seen, her zone unbound;
  And he, amidst his frolic play,
  As if he would the charming air repay,
Shook thousand odours from his dewy wings.
O Music! sphere-descended maid,
Friend of Pleasure, Wisdom's aid!
Why, goddess, why, to us denied,

Lay'st thou thy ancient lyre aside?
As in that lov'd Athenian bower
You learn'd an all-commanding power,
Thy mimic soul, O nymph endear'd,
Can well recall what then it heard.
Where is thy native simple heart
Devote to Virtue, Fancy, Art?
Arise, as in that elder time,
Warm, energic, chaste, sublime!
Thy wonders in that god-like age
Fill thy recording Sister's page;—
'Tis said, and I believe the tale,
Thy humblest reed could more prevail,
Had more of strength, diviner rage,
Than all which charms this laggard age,
E'en all at once together found,
Cecilia's mingled world of sound:—
O bid our vain endeavours cease:
Revive the just designs of Greece:
Return in all thy simple state!
Confirm the tales her sons relate!

William Collins

142   Ode on the Spring

Lo! where the rosy-bosom'd Hours,
   Fair Venus' train, appear,
Disclose the long-expecting flowers
   And wake the purple year!
The Attic warbler pours her throat
Responsive to the cuckoo's note,
The untaught harmony of Spring:
   While, whispering pleasure as they fly,
   Cool Zephyrs through the clear blue sky
Their gather'd fragrance fling.

Where'er the oak's thick branches stretch
   A broader, browner shade,
Where'er the rude and moss-grown beech
   O'er-canopies the glade,
Beside some water's rushy brink
With me the Muse shall sit, and think
(At ease reclined in rustic state)
   How vain the ardour of the Crowd,
   How low, how little are the Proud,
How indigent the Great!

Still is the toiling hand of Care;
  The panting herds repose;
Yet hark, how through the peopled air
  The busy murmur grows!
The insect youth are on the wing,
Eager to taste the honied spring
And float amid the liquid noon:
  Some lightly o'er the current skim,
  Some show their gaily-gilded trim
Quick-glancing to the sun.

To Contemplation's sober eye
  Such is the race of Man:
And they that creep, and they that fly,
  Shall end where they began.
Alike the busy and the gay
But flutter through life's little day,
In Fortune's varying colours drest;
  Brush'd by the hand of rough Mischance,
  Or chill'd by Age, their airy dance
They leave, in dust to rest.

Methinks I hear in accents low
  The sportive kind reply:
Poor moralist; and what art thou?
  A solitary fly!
Thy joys no glittering female meets,
No hive hast thou of hoarded sweets,
No painted plumage to display:
  On hasty wings thy youth is flown;
  Thy sun is set, thy spring is gone—
We frolic while 'tis May.

Thomas Gray

143 **The Poplar Field**

The poplars are fell'd; farewell to the shade
And the whispering sound of the cool colonnade;
The winds play no longer and sing in the leaves,
Nor Ouse on his bosom their image receives.

Twelve years have elapsed since I first took a view
Of my favourite field, and the bank where they grew:
And now in the grass behold they are laid,
And the tree is my seat that once lent me a shade.

The blackbird has fled to another retreat,
Where the hazels afford him a screen from the heat;
And the scene where his melody charm'd me before
Resounds with his sweet-flowing ditty no more.

My fugitive years are all hasting away,
And I must ere long lie as lowly as they,
With a turf on my breast and a stone at my head,
Ere another such grove shall arise in its stead.

'Tis a sight to engage me, if anything can,
To muse on the perishing pleasures of man;
Though his life be a dream, his enjoyments, I see,
Have a being less durable even than he.

William Cowper

144   **To a Mouse**

On turning her up in her nest with the plough

Wee, sleekit, cow'rin', tim'rous beastie,
O what a panic's in thy breastie!
Thou need na start awa sae hasty,
    Wi' bickering brattle!
I wad be laith to rin an' chase thee
    Wi' murd'ring pattle!

I'm truly sorry man's dominion
Has broken nature's social union,
An' justifies that ill opinion
    Which makes thee startle
At me, thy poor earth-born companion,
    An' fellow-mortal!

I doubt na, whiles, but thou may thieve;
What then? poor beastie, thou maun live?
A daimen-icker in a thrave
    'S a sma' request:
I'll get a blessin' wi' the lave,
    And never miss't!

Thy wee bit housie, too, in ruin!
Its silly wa's the win's are strewin':
And naething, now, to big a new ane,
    O' foggage green!
An' bleak December's winds ensuin'
    Baith snell an' keen!

Thou saw the fields laid bare and waste
An' weary winter comin' fast,
An' cozie here, beneath the blast,
   Thou thought to dwell,
Till, crash! the cruel coulter past
   Out thro' thy cell.

That wee bit heap o' leaves an' stibble
Has cost thee mony a weary nibble!
Now thou's turn'd out, for a' thy trouble,
   But house or hald,
To thole the winter's sleety dribble
   An' cranreuch cauld!

But, Mousie, thou art no thy lane
In proving foresight may be vain:
The best laid schemes o' mice an' men
   Gang aft a-gley,
An' lea'e us nought but grief an' pain,
   For promised joy.

Still thou art blest, compared wi' me!
The present only toucheth thee:
But, och! I backward cast my e'e
   On prospects drear!
An' forward, tho' I canna see,
   I guess an' fear!

Robert Burns

145   A Wish

Mine be a cot beside the hill;
   A bee-hive's hum shall soothe my ear;
A willowy brook that turns a mill,
   With many a fall shall linger near.

The swallow, oft, beneath my thatch
   Shall twitter from her clay-built nest;
Oft shall the pilgrim lift the latch,
   And share my meal, a welcome guest.

Around my ivied porch shall spring
   Each fragrant flower that drinks the dew;
And Lucy, at her wheel, shall sing
   In russet gown and apron blue.

The village-church among the trees
   Where first our marriage-vows were given,
With merry peals shall swell the breeze
   And point with taper spire to Heaven.

                 Samuel Rogers

146   **To Evening**

If aught of oaten stop or pastoral song
May hope, O pensive Eve, to soothe thine ear,
   Like thy own brawling springs,
   Thy springs, and dying gales;

O Nymph reserved,—while now the bright-hair'd sun
Sits in yon western tent, whose cloudy skirts
   With brede ethereal wove
   O'erhang his wavy bed;

Now air is hush'd, save where the weak-ey'd bat
With short shrill shriek flits by on leathern wing,
   Or where the beetle winds
   His small but sullen horn,

As oft he rises 'midst the twilight path,
Against the pilgrim borne in heedless hum,—
   Now teach me, maid composed,
   To breathe some soften'd strain,

Whose numbers, stealing through thy dark'ning vale,
May not unseemly with its stillness suit;
   As musing slow I hail
   Thy genial loved return.

For when thy folding-star arising shows
His paly circlet, at his warning lamp
   The fragrant Hours, and Elves
   Who slept in buds the day,

And many a Nymph who wreathes her brows with sedge
And sheds the freshening dew, and lovelier still
   The pensive Pleasures sweet,
   Prepare thy shadowy car.

Then let me rove some wild and heathy scene;
Or find some ruin midst its dreary dells,
   Whose walls more awful nod
   By thy religious gleams.

Or if chill blustering winds or driving rain
Prevent my willing feet, be mine the hut
    That, from the mountain's side,
    Views wilds and swelling floods,

And hamlets brown, and dim-discover'd spires;
And hears their simple bell; and marks o'er all
    Thy dewy fingers draw
    The gradual dusky veil.

While Spring shall pour his showers, as oft he wont,
And bathe thy breathing tresses, meekest Eve!
    While Summer loves to sport
    Beneath thy lingering light;

While sallow Autumn fills thy lap with leaves;
Or Winter, yelling through the troublous air,
    Affrights thy shrinking train
    And rudely rends thy robes;

So long, regardful of thy quiet rule,
Shall Fancy, Friendship, Science, smiling Peace,
    Thy gentlest influence own,
    And love thy favourite name!

William Collins

147   Elegy Written in a Country Church-Yard

The curfew tolls the knell of parting day,
  The lowing herd wind slowly o'er the lea,
The ploughman homeward plods his weary way,
  And leaves the world to darkness, and to me.

Now fades the glimmering landscape on the sight,
  And all the air a solemn stillness holds,
Save where the beetle wheels his droning flight,
  And drowsy tinklings lull the distant folds:

Save that from yonder ivy-mantled tower
  The moping owl does to the moon complain
Of such as, wandering near her secret bower,
  Molest her ancient solitary reign.

Beneath those rugged elms, that yew-tree's shade,
  Where heaves the turf in many a mouldering heap,
Each in his narrow cell for ever laid,
  The rude Forefathers of the hamlet sleep.

The breezy call of incense-breathing morn,
  The swallow twittering from the straw-built shed,
The cock's shrill clarion, or the echoing horn,
  No more shall rouse them from their lowly bed.

For them no more the blazing hearth shall burn,
  Or busy housewife ply her evening care:
No children run to lisp their sire's return,
  Or climb his knees the envied kiss to share.

Oft did the harvest to their sickle yield,
  Their furrow oft the stubborn glebe has broke;
How jocund did they drive their team afield!
  How bow'd the woods beneath their sturdy stroke!

Let not Ambition mock their useful toil,
  Their homely joys, and destiny obscure;
Nor Grandeur hear with a disdainful smile
  The short and simple annals of the Poor.

The boast of heraldry, the pomp of power,
  And all that beauty, all that wealth e'er gave,
Awaits alike th' inevitable hour:—
  The paths of glory lead but to the grave.

Nor you, ye Proud, impute to these the fault
  If Memory o'er their tomb no trophies raise,
Where through the long-drawn aisle and fretted vault
  The pealing anthem swells the note of praise.

Can storied urn or animated bust
  Back to its mansion call the fleeting breath?
Can Honour's voice provoke the silent dust,
  Or Flattery soothe the dull cold ear of Death?

Perhaps in this neglected spot is laid
  Some heart once pregnant with celestial fire;
Hands, that the rod of empire might have sway'd,
  Or waked to ecstasy the living lyre:

But Knowledge to their eyes her ample page,
  Rich with the spoils of time, did ne'er unroll;
Chill Penury repress'd their noble rage,
  And froze the genial current of the soul.

Full many a gem of purest ray serene
  The dark unfathom'd caves of ocean bear:

Full many a flower is born to blush unseen,
    And waste its sweetness on the desert air.

Some village-Hampden, that with dauntless breast
    The little tyrant of his fields withstood,
Some mute inglorious Milton here may rest,
    Some Cromwell, guiltless of his country's blood.

Th' applause of list'ning senates to command,
    The threats of pain and ruin to despise,
To scatter plenty o'er a smiling land,
    And read their history in a nation's eyes,

Their lot forbad: nor circumscribed alone
    Their growing virtues, but their crimes confined;
Forbad to wade through slaughter to a throne,
    And shut the gates of mercy on mankind,

The struggling pangs of conscious truth to hide,
    To quench the blushes of ingenuous shame,
Or heap the shrine of Luxury and Pride
    With incense kindled at the Muse's flame.

Far from the madding crowd's ignoble strife,
    Their sober wishes never learn'd to stray;
Along the cool sequester'd vale of life
    They kept the noiseless tenour of their way.

Yet e'en these bones from insult to protect
    Some frail memorial still erected nigh,
With uncouth rhymes and shapeless sculpture deck'd,
    Implores the passing tribute of a sigh.

Their name, their years, spelt by th' unletter'd Muse,
    The place of fame and elegy supply:
And many a holy text around she strews,
    That teach the rustic moralist to die.

For who, to dumb forgetfulness a prey,
    This pleasing anxious being e'er resign'd,
Left the warm precincts of the cheerful day,
    Nor cast one longing lingering look behind?

On some fond breast the parting soul relies,
    Some pious drops the closing eye requires;
E'en from the tomb the voice of Nature cries,
    E'en in our ashes live their wonted fires.

For thee, who, mindful of th' unhonour'd dead,
    Dost in these lines their artless tale relate;
If chance, by lonely contemplation led,
    Some kindred spirit shall inquire thy fate,

Haply some hoary-headed swain may say,
    'Oft have we seen him at the peep of dawn
Brushing with hasty steps the dews away,
    To meet the sun upon the upland lawn;

'There at the foot of yonder nodding beech
    That wreathes its old fantastic roots so high.
His listless length at noontide would he stretch,
    And pore upon the brook that babbles by.

'Hard by yon wood, now smiling as in scorn,
    Muttering his wayward fancies he would rove;
Now drooping, woeful wan, like one forlorn,
    Or crazed with care, or cross'd in hopeless love.

'One morn I miss'd him on the custom'd hill,
    Along the heath, and near his favourite tree;
Another came; nor yet beside the rill,
    Nor up the lawn, nor at the wood was he;

'The next with dirges due in sad array
    Slow through the church-way path we saw him borne,—
Approach and read (for thou canst read) the lay
    Graved on the stone beneath yon aged thorn.'

THE EPITAPH

Here rests his head upon the lap of Earth
    A Youth, to Fortune and to Fame unknown;
Fair Science frown'd not on his humble birth,
    And Melancholy mark'd him for her own.

Large was his bounty, and his soul sincere;
    Heaven did a recompense as largely send:
He gave to Misery all he had, a tear,
    He gain'd from Heaven, 'twas all he wish'd, a friend.

No farther seek his merits to disclose,
    Or draw his frailties from their dread abode,
(There they alike in trembling hope repose,)
    The bosom of his Father and his God.

Thomas Gray

148

148   Mary Morison

O Mary, at thy window be,
  It is the wish'd, the trysted hour!
Those smiles and glances let me see
  That make the miser's treasure poor:
  How blythely wad I bide the stoure,
A weary slave frae sun to sun,
  Could I the rich reward secure,
The lovely Mary Morison.

Yestreen, when to the trembling string
  The dance gaed thro' the lighted ha',
To thee my fancy took its wing,—
  I sat, but neither heard nor saw:
  Tho' this was fair, and that was braw,
And yon the toast of a' the town,
  I sigh'd, and said amang them a',
'Ye are na Mary Morison.'

O Mary, canst thou wreck his peace
  Wha for thy sake wad gladly dee?
Or canst thou break that heart of his,
  Whase only faut is loving thee?
  If love for love thou wiltna gie,
At least be pity to me shown;
  A thought ungentle canna be
The thought o' Mary Morison.

                    Robert Burns

149   Bonnie Lesley

O saw ye bonnie Lesley
  As she gaed o'er the border?
She's gane, like Alexander,
  To spread her conquests farther.

To see her is to love her,
  And love but her for ever;
For nature made her what she is,
  And never made anither!

Thou art a queen, fair Lesley,
  Thy subjects we, before thee;
Thou art divine, fair Lesley,
  The hearts o' men adore thee.

The deil he couldna scaith thee,
   Or aught that wad belang thee;
He'd look into thy bonnie face,
   And say 'I canna wrang thee!"

The Powers aboon will tent thee;
   Misfortune sha'na steer thee;
Thou'rt like themselves sae lovely,
   That ill they'll ne'er let near thee.

Return again, fair Lesley,
   Return to Caledonie!
That we may brag we hae a lass
   There's nane again sae bonnie.

                  Robert Burns

150

O my Luve's like a red, red rose
   That's newly sprung in June:
O my Luve's like the melodie
   That's sweetly play'd in tune.

As fair art thou, my bonnie lass,
   So deep in luve am I:
And I will luve thee still, my dear,
   Till a' the seas gang dry:

Till a' the seas gang dry, my dear,
   And the rocks melt wi' the sun;
I will luve thee still, my dear,
   While the sands o' life shall run.

And fare thee weel, my only Luve!
   And fare thee weel a while!
And I will come again, my Luve,
   Tho' it were ten thousand mile.

                  Robert Burns

151   **Highland Mary**

Ye banks and braes and streams around
   The castle o' Montgomery,
Green be your woods, and fair your flowers,
   Your waters never drumlie!

There simmer first unfauld her robes,
 And there the langest tarry;
For there I took the last fareweel
 O' my sweet Highland Mary.

How sweetly bloom'd the gay green birk,
 How rich the hawthorn's blossom,
As underneath their fragrant shade
 I clasp'd her to my bosom!
The golden hours on angel wings
 Few o'er me and my dearie;
For dear to me as light and life
 Was my sweet Highland Mary.

Wi' mony a vow and lock'd embrace
 Our parting was fu' tender;
And pledging aft to meet again,
 We tore oursels asunder;
But, oh! fell Death's untimely frost,
 That nipt my flower sae early!
Now green's the sod, and cauld's the clay,
 That wraps my Highland Mary!

O pale, pale now, those rosy lips,
 I aft hae kiss'd sae fondly!
And closed for ay the sparkling glance
 That dwelt on me sae kindly;
And mouldering now in silent dust
 That heart that lo'ed me dearly!
But still within my bosom's core
 Shall live my Highland Mary.

Robert Burns

152   Auld Robin Gray

When the sheep are in the fauld, and the kye at hame,
And a' the warld to rest are gane,
The waes o' my heart fa' in showers frae my e'e,
While my gudeman lies sound by me.

Young Jamie lo'ed me weel, and sought me for his bride;
But saving a croun he had naething else beside:
To make the croun a pund, young Jamie gaed to sea;
And the croun and the pund were baith for me.

He hadna been awa' a week but only twa,
When my father brak his arm, and the cow was stown awa;
My mother she fell sick, and my Jamie at the sea—
And auld Robin Gray came a-courtin' me.

My father couldna work, and my mother couldna spin;
I toil'd day and night, but their bread I couldna win;
Auld Rob maintain'd them baith, and wi' tears in his e'e
Said, Jennie, for their sakes, O, marry me!

My heart it said nay; I look'd for Jamie back;
But the wind it blew high, and the ship it was a wrack;
His ship it was a wrack—why didna Jamie dee?
Or why do I live to cry, Wae's me?

My father urgit sair: my mother didna speak;
But she look'd in my face till my heart was like to break:
They gi'ed him my hand, but my heart was at the sea;
Sae auld Robin Gray he was gudeman to me.

I hadna been a wife a week but only four,
When mournfu' as I sat on the stane at the door,
I saw my Jamie's wraith, for I couldna think it he—
Till he said, I'm come hame to marry thee.

O sair, sair did we greet, and muckle did we say;
We took but ae kiss, and I bad him gang away:
I wish that I were dead, but I'm no like to dee;
And why was I born to say, Wae's me!

I gang like a ghaist, and I carena to spin;
I daurna think on Jamie, for that wad be a sin;
But I'll do my best a gude wife ay to be,
For auld Robin Gray he is kind unto me.

Lady Anne Lindsay

153   Duncan Gray

Duncan Gray cam here to woo,
    Ha, ha, the wooing o't,
On blythe Yule night when we were fou,
    Ha, ha, the wooing o't:
Maggie coost her head fu' high,
Look'd asklent and unco skeigh,
Gart poor Duncan stand abeigh;
    Ha, ha, the wooing o't!

Duncan fleech'd, and Duncan pray'd;
Meg was deaf as Ailsa Craig;
Duncan sigh'd baith out and in,
Grat his een baith bleer't and blin',
Spak o' lowpin ower a linn!

Time and chance are but a tide,
Slighted love is sair to bide;
Shall I, like a fool, quoth he,
For a haughty hizzie dee?
She may gae to—France for me!

How it comes let doctors tell,
Meg grew sick—as he grew heal;
Something in her bosom wrings,
For relief a sigh she brings;
And O, her een, they spak sic things!

Duncan was a lad o' grace;
    Ha, ha, the wooing o't!
Maggie's was a piteous case;
    Ha, ha, the wooing o't!
Duncan couldna be her death,
Swelling pity smoor'd his wrath;
Now they're crouse and canty baith:
    Ha, ha, the wooing o't!

Robert Burns

154   The Sailor's Wife

And are ye sure the news is true?
    And are ye sure he's weel?
Is this a time to think o' wark?
    Ye jades, lay by your wheel;
Is this the time to spin a thread,
    When Colin's at the door?
Reach down my cloak, I'll to the quay,
    And see him come ashore.
For there's nae luck about the house,
    There's nae luck at a';
There's little pleasure in the house
    When our gudeman's awa'.

And gie to me my bigonet,
    My bishop's satin gown;
For I maun tell the baillie's wife
    That Colin's in the town.

My Turkey slippers maun gae on,
   My stockins pearly blue;
It's a' to pleasure our gudeman,
   For he's baith leal and true.

Rise, lass, and mak a clean fireside,
   Put on the muckle pot;
Gie little Kate her button gown
   And Jock his Sunday coat;
And mak their shoon as black as slaes,
   Their hose as white as snaw;
It's a' to please my ain gudeman,
   For he's been long awa'.

There's twa fat hens upo' the coop
   Been fed this month and mair;
Mak haste and thraw their necks about,
   That Colin weel may fare;
And spread the table neat and clean,
   Gar ilka thing look braw,
For wha can tell how Colin fared
   When he was far awa'?

Sae true his heart, sae smooth his speech,
   His breath like caller air;
His very foot has music in't
   As he comes up the stair—
And will I see his face again?
   And will I hear him speak?
I'm downright dizzy wi' the thought,
   In troth I'm like to greet!

If Colin's weel, and weel content,
   I hae nae mair to crave:
And gin I live to keep him sae,
   I'm blest aboon the lave:
And will I see his face again,
   And will I hear him speak?
I'm downright dizzy wi' the thought,
   In troth I'm like to greet.
For there's nae luck about the house,
   There's nae luck at a';
There's little pleasure in the house
   When our gudeman's awa'.

W. J. Mickle

Jean

Of a' the airts the wind can blaw
   I dearly like the West,
For there the bonnie lassie lives,
   The lassie I lo'e best:
There wild woods grow, and rivers row,
   And mony a hill between;
But day and night my fancy's flight
   Is ever wi' my Jean.

I see her in the dewy flowers,
   I see her sweet and fair:
I hear her in the tunefu' birds,
   I hear her charm the air:
There's not a bonnie flower that springs
   By fountain, shaw, or green,
There's not a bonnie bird that sings
   But minds me o' my Jean.

O blaw ye westlin winds, blaw saft
   Amang the leafy trees;
Wi' balmy gale, frae hill and dale
   Bring hame the laden bees;
And bring the lassie back to me
   That's ay sae neat and clean;
Ae smile o' her wad banish care,
   Sae charming is my Jean.

What sighs and vows amang the knowes
   Hae pass'd atween us twa!
How fond to meet, how wae to part
   That night she gaed awa!
The Powers aboon can only ken
   To whom the heart is seen,
That nane can be sae dear to me
As my sweet lovely Jean!

Robert Burns

John Anderson

John Anderson my jo, John,
   When we were first acquent
Your locks were like the raven,
   Your bonnie brow was brent;
But now your brow is beld, John,
   Your locks are like the snow;
But blessings on your frosty pow,
   John Anderson my jo.

John Anderson my jo, John,
  We clamb the hill thegither,
And mony a canty day, John,
  We've had wi' ane anither:
Now we maun totter down, John,
  But hand in hand we'll go,
And sleep thegither at the foot,
  John Anderson my jo.

Robert Burns

157   **The Land 'o the Leal**

I'm wearing awa', Jean,
Like snaw when it's thaw, Jean,
I'm wearing awa'
  To the land o' the leal.
There's nae sorrow there, Jean,
There's neither cauld nor care, Jean,
The day is ay fair
  In the land o' the leal.

Ye were ay leal and true, Jean,
Your task's ended noo, Jean,
And I'll welcome you
  To the land o' the leal.
Our bonnie bairn's there, Jean,
She was baith guid and fair, Jean:
O we grudged her right sair
  To the land o' the leal!

Then dry that tearfu' e'e, Jean,
My soul langs to be free, Jean,
And angels wait on me
  To the land o' the leal.
Now fare ye weel, my ain Jean,
This warld's care is vain, Jean;
We'll meet and ay be fain
  In the land o' the leal.

Lady Carolina Nairne

158   **Ode on a Distant Prospect of Eton College**

Ye distant spires, ye antique towers
  That crown the watery glade,
Where grateful Science still adores
  Her Henry's holy shade;

And ye, that from the stately brow
Of Windsor's heights th' expanse below
    Of grove, of lawn, of mead survey,
Whose turf, whose shade, whose flowers among
Wanders the hoary Thames along
    His silver-winding way:

Ah happy hills! ah pleasing shade!
    Ah fields beloved in vain!
Where once my careless childhood stray'd,
    A stranger yet to pain!
I feel the gales that from ye blow
A momentary bliss bestow,
    As waving fresh their gladsome wing
My weary soul they seem to soothe,
And, redolent of joy and youth,
    To breathe a second spring.

Say, Father Thames, for thou hast seen
    Full many a sprightly race
Disporting on thy margent green
    The paths of pleasure trace;
Who foremost now delight to cleave
With pliant arm, thy glassy wave?
    The captive linnet which enthral?
What idle progeny succeed
To chase the rolling circle's speed
    Or urge the flying ball?

While some on earnest business bent
    Their murmuring labours ply
'Gainst graver hours, that bring constraint
    To sweeten liberty:
Some bold adventurers disdain
The limits of their little reign
    And unknown regions dare descry:
Still as they run they look behind,
They hear a voice in every wind,
    And snatch a fearful joy.

Gay hope is theirs by fancy fed,
    Less pleasing when possest;
The tear forgot as soon as shed,
    The sunshine of the breast:
Theirs buxom health, of rosy hue,
Wild wit, invention ever new,
    And lively cheer, of vigour born;

The thoughtless day, the easy night,
The spirits pure, the slumbers light
    That fly th' approach of morn.

Alas! regardless of their doom
    The little victims play!
No sense have they of ills to come
    Nor care beyond to-day:
Yet see how all around them wait
The Ministers of human fate
    And black Misfortune's baleful train!
Ah show them where in ambush stand
To seize their prey, the murderous band!
    Ah, tell them they are men!

These shall the fury Passions tear,
    The vultures of the mind,
Disdainful Anger, pallid Fear,
    And Shame that skulks behind;
Or pining Love shall waste their youth,
Or Jealousy with rankling tooth
    That inly gnaws the secret heart,
And Envy wan, and faded Care,
Grim-visaged comfortless Despair,
    And Sorrow's piercing dart.

Ambition this shall tempt to rise,
    Then whirl the wretch from high,
To bitter Scorn a sacrifice
    And grinning Infamy.
The stings of Falsehood those shall try,
And hard Unkindness' alter'd eye,
    That mocks the tear it forced to flow;
And keen Remorse with blood defiled,
And moody Madness laughing wild
    Amid severest woe.

Lo, in the vale of years beneath
    A griesly troop are seen,
The painful family of Death,
    More hideous than their Queen:
This racks the joints, this fires the veins,
That every labouring sinew strains,
    Those in the deeper vitals rage:
Lo, Poverty, to fill the band,
That numbs the soul with icy hand,
    And slow-consuming Age.

To each his sufferings: all are men,
   Condemn'd alike to groan;
The tender for another's pain,
   Th' unfeeling for his own.
Yet, ah! why should they know their fate,
Since sorrow never comes too late,
   And happiness too swiftly flies?
Thought would destroy their paradise.
No more;—where ignorance is bliss,
   'Tis folly to be wise.   *Thomas Gray*

159   Hymn to Adversity

Daughter of Jove, relentless power,
   Thou tamer of the human breast,
Whose iron scourge and torturing hour
   The bad affright, afflict the best!
Bound in thy adamantine chain
The proud are taught to taste of pain,
And purple tyrants vainly groan
With pangs unfelt before, unpitied and alone.

When first thy Sire to send on earth
   Virtue, his darling child, design'd,
To thee he gave the heavenly birth
   And bade to form her infant mind.
Stern, rugged Nurse! thy rigid lore
With patience many a year she bore:
What sorrow was, thou bad'st her know,
And from her own she learn'd to melt at others' woe.

Scared at thy frown terrific, fly
   Self-pleasing Folly's idle brood,
Wild Laughter, Noise, and thoughtless Joy,
   And leave us leisure to be good.
Light they disperse, and with them go
The summer Friend, the flattering Foe;
By vain Prosperity received,
To her they vow their truth, and are again believed.

Wisdom in sable garb array'd
   Immersed in rapturous thought profound,
And Melancholy, silent maid,
   With leaden eye, that loves the ground,
Still on thy solemn steps attend:
Warm Charity, the general friend,
With Justice, to herself severe,
And Pity dropping soft the sadly-pleasing tear.

O, gently on thy suppliant's head
　　Dread Goddess, lay thy chastening hand!
Not in thy Gorgon terrors clad,
　　Nor circled with the vengeful band
(As by the impious thou art seen)
With thundering voice, and threatening mien,
With screaming Horror's funeral cry,
Despair, and fell Disease, and ghastly Poverty:

Thy form benign, O Goddess, wear,
　　Thy milder influence impart,
Thy philosophic train be there
　　To soften, not to wound my heart.
The generous spark extinct revive,
Teach me to love and to forgive,
Exact my own defects to scan,
What others are to feel, and know myself a Man.

Thomas Gray

160　　　**The Solitude of Alexander Se'kirk**

I am monarch of all I survey,
　　My right there is none to dispute;
From the centre all round to the sea
　　I am lord of the fowl and the brute.
O solitude! where are the charms
　　That sages have seen in thy face?
Better dwell in the midst of alarms
　　Than reign in this horrible place.

I am out of humanity's reach.
　　I must finish my journey alone,
Never hear the sweet music of speech;
　　I start at the sound of my own.
The beasts that roam over the plain
　　My form with indifference see;
They are so unacquainted with man,
　　Their tameness is shocking to me.

Society, friendship, and love
　　Divinely bestow'd upon man,
O had I the wings of of a dove
　　How soon would I taste you again!
My sorrows I then might assuage
　　In the ways of religion and truth,
Might learn from the wisdom of age,
　　And be cheer'd by the sallies of youth.

Ye winds that have made me your sport,
　Convey to this desolate shore
Some cordial endearing report
　Of a land I shall visit no more:
My friends, do they now and then send
　A wish or a thought after me?
O tell me I yet have a friend,
　Though a friend I am never to see.

How fleet is a glance of the mind!
　Compared with the speed of its flight,
The tempest itself lags behind,
　And the swift-wingéd arrows of light.
When I think of my own native land
　In a moment I seem to be there;
But, alas! recollection at hand
　Soon hurries me back to despair.

But the seafowl is gone to her nest,
　The beast is laid down in his lair;
Even here is a season of rest,
　And I to my cabin repair.
There is mercy in every place,
　And mercy, encouraging thought!
Gives even affliction a grace
　And reconciles man to his lot.

William Cowper

161　To Mary Unwin

Mary! I want a lyre with other strings,
Such aid from heaven as some have feign'd they drew,
An eloquence scarce given to mortals, new
And undebased by praise of meaner things,
That ere through age or woe I shed my wings
I may record thy worth with honour due,
In verse as musical as thou art true,
Verse that immortalizes whom it sings:—
But thou hast little need. There is a Book
By seraphs writ with beams of heavenly light,
On which the eyes of God not rarely look,
A chronicle of actions just and bright—
There all thy deeds, my faithful Mary, shine;
And since thou own'st that praise, I spare thee mine.

William Cowper

To the Same

The twentieth year is well-nigh past
Since first our sky was overcast;
Ah, would that this might be the last!
    My Mary!

Thy spirits have a fainter flow,
I see thee daily weaker grow—
'Twas my distress that brought thee low,
    My Mary!

Thy needles, once a shining store,
For my sake restless heretofore,
Now rust disused, and shine no more;
    My Mary!

For though thou gladly wouldst fulfil
The same kind office for me still,
Thy sight now seconds not thy will,
    My Mary!

But well thou play'dst the housewife's part,
And all thy threads with magic art
Have wound themselves about this heart,
    My Mary!

Thy indistinct expressions seem
Like language utter'd in a dream;
Yet me they charm, whate'er the theme,
    My Mary!

Thy silver locks, once auburn bright,
Are still more lovely in my sight
Than golden beams of orient light,
    My Mary!

For could I view nor them nor thee,
What sight worth seeing could I see?
The sun would rise in vain for me,
    My Mary!

Partakers of thy sad decline
Thy hands their little force resign;
Yet, gently press'd, press gently mine,
    My Mary!

Such feebleness of limbs thou prov'st
That now at every step thou mov'st
Upheld by two; yet still thou lov'st,
    My Mary!

And still to love, though press'd with ill,
In wintry age to feel no chill,
With me is to be lovely still,
    My Mary!

But ah! by constant heed I know
How oft the sadness that I show
Transforms thy smiles to looks of woe,
        My Mary!
And should my future lot be cast
With much resemblance of the past,
Thy worn-out heart will break at last—
        My Mary!

                                William Cowper

163   **The Dying Man in His Garden**

Why, Damon, with the forward day
Dost thou thy little spot survey
From tree to tree, with doubtful cheer,
Observe the progress of the year,
What winds arise, with rains descend,
When thou before that year shalt end?

What do thy noonday walks avail,
To clear the leaf, and pick the snail
Then wantonly to death decree
An insect usefuller than thee?
Thou and the worm are brother-kind,
As low, as earthy, and as blind.

Vain wretch! canst thou expect to see
The downy peach make court to thee?
Or that thy sense shall ever meet
The bean-flower's deep-embosom'd sweet
Exhaling with an evening's blast?
Thy evenings then will all be past!

Thy narrow pride, thy fancied green
(For vanity's in little seen),
All must be left when Death appears,
In spite of wishes, groans, and tears;
Nor one of all thy plants that grow
    But Rosemary will with thee go.

                                George Sewell

164   **To-Morrow**

In the downhill of life, when I find I'm declining,
    May my lot no less fortunate be
Than a snug elbow-chair can afford for reclining,
    And a cot that o'erlooks the wide sea;

With an ambling pad-pony to pace o'er the lawn,
　　While I carol away idle sorrow,
And blithe as the lark that each day hails the dawn
　　Look forward with hope for to-morrow.

With a porch at my door, both for shelter and shade too,
　　As the sunshine or rain may prevail;
And a small spot of ground for the use of the spade too,
　　With a barn for the use of the flail:
A cow for my dairy, a dog for my game,
　　And a purse when a friend wants to borrow;
I'll envy no nabob his riches or fame,
　　Nor what honours await him to-morrow.

From the bleak northern blast may my cot be completely
　　Secured by a neighbouring hill;
And at night may repose steal upon me more sweetly
　　By the sound of a murmuring rill:
And while peace and plenty I find at my board,
　　With a heart free from sickness and sorrow,
With my friends may I share what to-day may afford,
　　And let them spread the table to-morrow.

And when I at last must throw off this frail covering
　　Which I've worn for three-score years and ten,
On the brink of the grave I'll not seek to keep hovering,
　　Nor my thread wish to spin o'er again:
But my face in the glass I'll serenely survey,
　　And with smiles count each wrinkle and furrow;
As this old worn-out stuff, which is threadbare to-day,
　　May become everlasting to-morrow.

John Collins

165　　Life! I know not what thou art,
　　　　But know that thou and I must part;
　　　　And when, or how, or where we met
　　　　I own to me's a secret yet.
　　　　　　Life! we've been long together
　　　　Through pleasant and through cloudy weather;
　　　　'Tis hard to part when friends are dear—
　　　　Perhaps 'twill cost a sigh, a tear;
　　　　—Then steal away, give little warning,
　　　　　　Choose thine own time;
　　　　Say not Good Night,—but in some brighter clime
　　　　　　Bid me Good Morning.

Anna Letitia Barbauld

THE GOLDEN TREASURY

BOOK FOUR

166

On First Looking into Chapman's Homer

Much have I travell'd in the realms of gold
And many goodly states and kingdoms seen;
Round many western islands have I been
Which bards in fealty to Apollo hold.
Oft of one wide expanse had I been told
That deep-brow'd Homer ruled as his demesne;
Yet did I never breathe its pure serene
Till I heard Chapman speak out loud and bold:
Then felt I like some watcher of the skies
When a new planet swims into his ken;
Or like stout Cortez, when with eagle eyes
He stared at the Pacific—and all his men
Look'd at each other with a wild surmise—
Silent, upon a peak in Darien.

John Keats

167

Ode on the Poets

Bards of Passion and of Mirth
Ye have left your souls on earth!
Have ye souls in heaven too,
Double-lived in regions new?

Yes, and those of heaven commune
With the spheres of sun and moon;
With the noise of fountains wond'rous
And the parle of voices thund'rous;
With the whisper of heaven's trees
And one another, in soft ease
Seated on Elysian lawns
Brows'd by none but Dian's fawns;
Underneath large blue-bells tented,
Where the daisies are rose-scented,
And the rose herself has got
Perfume which on earth is not;
Where the nightingale doth sing
Not a senseless, trancéd thing,

But divine melodious truth;
Philosophic numbers smooth;
Tales and golden histories
Of heaven and its mysteries.

Thus ye live on high, and then
On the earth ye live again;
And the souls ye left behind you
Teach us, here, the way to find you,
Where your other souls are joying,
Never slumber'd, never cloying.
Here, your earth-born souls still speak
To mortals, of their little week;
Of their sorrows and delights;
Of their passions and their spites;
Of their glory and their shame;
What doth strengthen and what maim:—
Thus ye teach us, every day,
Wisdom, though fled far away.

Bards of Passion and of Mirth
Ye have left your souls on earth!
Ye have souls in heaven too,
Double-lived in regions new!

John Keats

168   Love

All thoughts, all passions, all delights,
    Whatever stirs this mortal frame,
All are but ministers of Love,
        And feed his sacred flame.

Oft in my waking dreams do I
    Live o'er again that happy hour,
When midway on the mount I lay
        Beside the ruin'd tower.

The moonshine stealing o'er the scene
    Had blended with the lights of eve;
And she was there, my hope, my joy,
        My own dear Genevieve!

She lean'd against the arméd man,
    The statue of the arméd knight;
She stood and listen'd to my lay,
        Amid the lingering light.

Few sorrows hath she of her own,
  My hope! my joy! my Genevieve!
She loves me best whene'er I sing
    The songs that make her grieve.

I play'd a soft and doleful air,
  I sang an old and moving story—
An old rude song, that suited well
    That ruin wild and hoary.

She listen'd with a flitting blush,
  With downcast eyes and modest grace;
For well she knew I could not choose
    But gaze upon her face.

I told her of the Knight that wore
  Upon his shield a burning brand;
And that for ten long years he woo'd
    The Lady of the Land.

I told her how he pined; and ah!
  The deep, the low, the pleading tone
With which I sang another's love
    Interpreted my own.

She listen'd with a flitting blush,
  With downcast eyes and modest grace;
And she forgave me, that I gazed
    Too fondly on her face.

But when I told the cruel scorn
  That crazed that bold and lovely Knight,
And that he cross'd the mountain-woods,
    Nor rested day nor night;

That sometimes from the savage den,
  And sometimes from the darksome shade,
And sometimes starting up at once
    In green and sunny glade

There came and look'd him in the face
  An angel beautiful and bright;
And that he knew it was a Fiend,
    This miserable Knight!

And that, unknowing what he did,
  He leap'd amid a murderous band,
And saved from outrage worse than death
    The Lady of the Land;

And how she wept, and clasp'd his knees
   And how she tended him in vain;
And ever strove to expiate
      The scorn that crazed his brain;

And that she nursed him in a cave,
   And how his madness went away,
When on the yellow forest leaves
      A dying man he lay;

—His dying words—but when I reach'd
   That tenderest strain of all the ditty,
My faltering voice and pausing harp
      Disturb'd her soul with pity!

All impulses of soul and sense
   Had thrill'd guileless Genevieve;
The music and the doleful tale,
      The rich and balmy eve;

And hopes, and fears that kindle hope,
   An undistinguishable throng,
And gentle wishes long subdued,
      Subdued and cherish'd long!

She wept with pity and delight,
   She blush'd with love and virgin shame;
And like the murmur of a dream,
      I heard her breathe my name.

Her bosom heaved—she stepp'd aside,
   As conscious of my look she stept—
Then suddenly, with timorous eye
      She fled to me and wept.

She half enclosed me with her arms,
   She press'd me with a meek embrace;
And bending back her head, look'd up,
      And gazed upon my face.

'Twas partly love, and partly fear,
   And partly 'twas a bashful art,
That I might rather feel, than see,
      The swelling of her heart.

I calm'd her fears, and she was calm,
   And told her love with virgin pride;
And so I won my Genevieve,
      My bright and beauteous Bride.

                Samuel Taylor Coleridge

169   **All for Love**

O talk not to me of a name great in story;
The days of our youth are the days of our glory;
And the myrtle and ivy of sweet two-and-twenty
Are worth all your laurels, though ever so plenty.

What are garlands and crowns to the brow that is wrinkled?
'Tis but as a dead flower with May-dew besprinkled:
Then away with all such from the head that is hoary—
What care I for the wreaths that can only give glory?

O Fame!—If I e'er took delight in thy praises,
'Twas less for the sake of thy high-sounding phrases,
Than to see the bright eyes of the dear one discover
She thought that I was not unworthy to love her.

There chiefly I sought thee, there only I found thee;
Her glance was the best of the rays that surround thee;
When it sparkled o'er aught that was bright in my story,
I knew it was love, and I felt it was glory.

                                    George Gordon, Lord Byron

170   **The Outlaw**

    O Brignall banks are wild and fair,
        And Greta woods are green,
    And you may gather garlands there
        Would grace a summer queen.
    And as I rode by Dalton Hall
        Beneath the turrets high,
    A Maiden on the castle-wall
        Was singing merrily:
    'O Brignall banks are fresh and fair,
        And Greta woods are green;
    I'd rather rove with Edmund there
        Than reign our English queen.'

    'If, Maiden, thou wouldst wend with me,
        To leave both tower and town,
    Thou first must guess what life lead we
        That dwell by dale and down.
    And if thou canst that riddle read,
        As read full well you may,
    Then to the greenwood shalt thou speed
        As blithe as Queen of May!

Yet sung she, 'Brignall banks are fair,
  And Greta woods are green;
I'd rather rove with Edmund there
  Than reign our English queen.

'I read you by your bugle-horn
  And by your palfrey good,
I read you for a ranger sworn
  To keep the king's greenwood.'
'A ranger, lady, winds his horn,
  And 'tis at peep of light;
His blast is heard at merry morn,
  And mine at dead of night.'
Yet sung she, Brignall banks are fair,
  And Greta woods are gay;
I would I were with Edmund there
  To reign his Queen of May!

'With burnish'd brand and musketoon
  So gallantly you come,
I read you for a bold Dragoon
  That lists the tuck of drum.'
'I list no more the tuck of drum
  No more the trumpet hear;
But when the beetle sounds his hum
  My comrades take the spear.
And O! though Brignall banks be fair
  And Greta woods be gay,
Yet mickle must the maiden dare
  Would reign my Queen of May!

'Maiden! a nameless life I lead,
  A nameless death I'll die;
The fiend whose lantern lights the mead
  Were better mate than I!
And when I'm with my comrades met
  Beneath the greenwood bough,—
What once we were we all forget,
  Nor think what we are now.'

Chorus

Yet Brignall banks are fresh and fair,
  And Greta woods are green,
And you may gather garlands there
  Would grace a summer queen.

Sir Walter Scott

171

There be none of Beauty's daughters
    With a magic like thee;
And like music on the waters
    Is thy sweet voice to me:
When, as if its sound were causing
The charméd ocean's pausing,
The waves lie still and gleaming,
And the lull'd winds seem dreaming:

And the midnight moon is weaving
    Her bright chain o'er the deep,
Whose breast is gently heaving
    As an infant's asleep:
So the spirit bows before thee
To listen and adore thee;
With a full but soft emotion,
Like the swell of Summer's ocean.

                    George Gordon, Lord Byron

172

Lines to an Indian Air

I arise from dreams of thee
    In the first sweet sleep of night,
When the winds are breathing low
    And the stars are shining bright:
I arise from dreams of thee,
    And a spirit in my feet
Has led me—who knows how?
    To thy chamber-window, sweet!

The wandering airs they faint
    On the dark, the silent stream—
The champak odours fail
    Like sweet thoughts in a dream;
The nightingale's complaint
    It dies upon her heart,
As I must die on thine,
    O belovéd as thou art!

O lift me from the grass!
    I die, I faint, I fail!
Let thy love in kisses rain
    On my lips and eyelids pale.

My cheek is cold and white, alas!
   My heart beats loud and fast;
O! press it close to thine again
   Where it will break at last.

Percy Bysshe Shelley

173   She walks in beauty, like the night
       Of cloudless climes and starry skies,
     And all that's best of dark and bright
       Meet in her aspect and her eyes,
     Thus mellow'd to that tender light
       Which heaven to gaudy day denies.

     One shade the more, one ray the less,
       Had half impair'd the nameless grace
     Which waves in every raven tress,
       Or softly lightens o'er her face,
     Where thoughts serenely sweet express
       How pure, how dear their dwelling-place.

     And on that cheek and o'er that brow
       So soft, so calm, yet eloquent,
     The smiles that win, the tints that glow,
       But tell of days in goodness spent,
     A mind at peace with all below,
       A heart whose love is innocent.

George Gordon, Lord Byron

174   She was a phantom of delight
     When first she gleam'd upon my sight;
     A lovely apparition, sent
     To be a moment's ornament;
     Her eyes as stars of Twilight fair;
     Like Twilight's, too, her dusky hair;
     But all things else about her drawn
     From May-time and the cheerful dawn;
     A dancing shape, an image gay,
     To haunt, to startle, and waylay.

     I saw her upon nearer view,
     A spirit, yet a woman too!
     Her household motions light and free,
     And steps of virgin-liberty;

A countenance in which did meet
Sweet records, promises as sweet;
A creature not too bright or good
For human nature's daily food,
For transient sorrows, simple wiles,
Praise, blame, love, kisses, tears, and smiles.

And now I see with eye serene
The very pulse of the machine;
A being breathing thoughtful breath,
A traveller between life and death:
The reason firm, the temperate will,
Endurance, foresight, strength, and skill;
A perfect woman, nobly plann'd
To warn, to comfort, and command;
And yet a Spirit still, and bright
With something of angelic light.

William Wordsworth

175

She is not fair to outward view
    As many maidens be;
Her loveliness I never knew
    Until she smiled on me.
O then I saw her eye was bright,
A well of love, a spring of light.

But now her looks are coy and cold,
    To mine they ne'er reply,
And yet I cease not to behold
    The love-light in her eye:
Her very frowns are fairer far
Than smiles of other maidens are.

Hartley Coleridge

176

I fear thy kisses, gentle maiden;
    Thou needest not fear mine;
My spirit is too deeply laden
    Ever to burthen thine.

I fear thy mien, thy tones, thy motion;
    Thou needest not fear mine;
Innocent is the heart's devotion
    With which I worship thine.

Percy Bysshe Shelley

177   **The Lost Love**

She dwelt among the untrodden ways
    Beside the springs of Dove;
A maid whom there were none to praise,
    And very few to love:

A violet by a mossy stone
    Half hidden from the eye!
—Fair as a star, when only one
    Is shining in the sky.

She lived unknown, and few could know
    When Lucy ceased to be;
But she is in her grave, and oh,
    The difference to me!

                              William Wordsworth

178   I travell'd among unknown men
            In lands beyond the sea;
        Nor, England! did I know till then
            What love I bore to thee.

        'Tis past, that melancholy dream!
            Nor will I quit thy shore
        A second time; for still I seem
            To love thee more and more.

        Among thy mountains did I feel
            The joy of my desire;
        And she I cherish'd turn'd her wheel
            Beside an English fire.

        Thy mornings show'd, thy nights conceal'd
            The bowers where Lucy play'd;
        And thine too is the last green field
            That Lucy's eyes surveyed.

                              William Wordsworth

179   **The Education of Nature**

Three years she grew in sun and shower;
Then Nature said, 'A lovelier flower
    On earth was never sown:

This child I to myself will take;
She shall be mine, and I will make
 A lady of my own.

'Myself will to my darling be
Both law and impulse: and with me
 The girl, in rock and plain,
In earth and heaven, in glade and bower,
Shall feel an overseeing power
 To kindle or restrain.

'She shall be sportive as the fawn
That wild with glee across the lawn
 Or up the mountain springs;
And hers shall be the breathing balm,
And hers the silence and the calm
 Of mute insensate things.

'The floating clouds their state shall lend
To her; for her the willow bend;
 Nor shall she fail to see
E'en in the motions of the storm
Grace that shall mould the maiden's form
 By silent sympathy.

'The stars of midnight shall be dear
To her; and she shall lean her ear
 In many a secret place
Where rivulets dance their wayward round,
And beauty born of murmuring sound
 Shall pass into her face.

'And vital feelings of delight
Shall rear her form to stately height,
 Her virgin bosom swell;
Such thoughts to Lucy I will give
While she and I together live
 Here in this happy dell.'

Thus Nature spake—The work was done—
How soon my Lucy's race was run!
 She died, and left to me
This heath, this calm and quiet scene;
The memory of what has been,
 And never more will be.

       William Wordsworth

180

A slumber did my spirit seal;
    I had no human fears:
She seemed a thing that could not feel
    The touch of earthly years.

No motion has she now, no force;
    She neither hears nor sees;
Roll'd round in earth's diurnal course
    With rocks, and stones, and trees.

                    William Wordsworth

181   Lord Ullin's Daughter

A Chieftain to the Highlands bound
    Cries 'Boatman, do not tarry!
And I'll give thee a silver pound
    To row us o'er the ferry!'

'Now who be ye, would cross Lochgyle
    This dark and stormy water?'
'O I'm the chief of Ulva's isle,
    And this, Lord Ullin's daughter.

'And fast before her father's men
    Three days we've fled together,
For should he find us in the glen,
    My blood would stain the heather.

'His horsemen hard behind us ride—
    Should they our steps discover,
Then who will cheer my bonny bride
    When they have slain her lover?'

Out spoke the hardy Highland wight,
    'I'll go, my chief, I'm ready:
It is not for your silver bright,
    But for your winsome lady:—

'And by my word! the bonny bird
    In danger shall not tarry;
So though the waves are raging white
    I'll row you o'er the ferry.'

By this the storm grew loud apace,
    The water-wraith was shrieking;

And in the scowl of heaven each face
  Grew dark as they were speaking.

But still as wilder blew the wind
  And as the night grew drearer,
Adown the glen rode arméd men,
  Their trampling sounded nearer.

'O haste thee, haste!' the lady cries,
  'Though tempests round us gather;
I'll meet the raging of the skies,
  But not an angry father.'

The boat has left a stormy land,
  A stormy sea before her,—
When, oh! too strong for human hand
  The tempest gather'd o'er her.

And still they row'd amidst the roar
  Of waters fast prevailing:
Lord Ullin reach'd that fatal shore,—
  His wrath was changed to wailing.

For, sore dismay'd, through storm and shade
  His child he did discover:—
One lovely hand she stretch'd for aid,
  And one was round her lover.

'Come back! come back! he cried in grief
  'Across this stormy water:
And I'll forgive your Highland chief,
  My daughter!—O, my daughter!'

'Twas vain: the loud waves lash'd the shore,
  Return or aid preventing:
The water wild went o'er his child,
  And he was left lamenting.

                              Thomas Campbell

182   **Jock o' Hazeldean**

'Why weep ye by the tide, ladie?
  Why weep ye by the tide?
I'll wed ye to my youngest son,
  And ye sall be his bride:
And ye sall be his bride, ladie,
  Sae comely to be seen'—

But aye she loot the tears down fa'
   For Jock o' Hazeldean.

'Now let this wilfu' grief be done,
   And dry that cheek so pale;
Young Frank is chief of Errington
   And lord of Langley-dale;
His step is first in peaceful ha',
   His sword in battle keen'—
But aye she loot the tears down fa'
   For Jock o' Hazeldean.

'A chain of gold ye sall not lack,
   Nor braid to bind your hair;
Nor mettled hound, nor managed hawk,
   Nor palfrey fresh and fair;
And you, the foremost o' them a',
   Shall ride our forest queen'—
But aye she loot the tears down fa'
   For Jock o' Hazeldean.

The kirk was deck'd at morning-tide,
   The tapers glimmer'd fair;
The priest and bridegroom wait the bride,
   And dame and knight are there.
They sought her baith by bower and ha';
   The ladie was not seen!
She's o'er the Border, and awa'
   Wi' Jock o' Hazeldean.

Sir Walter Scott

183   **Freedom and Love**

How delicious is the winning
Of a kiss at love's beginning,
When two mutual hearts are sighing
For the knot there's no untying!

Yet remember, 'midst your wooing,
Love has bliss, but Love has ruing;
Other smiles may make you fickle,
Tears for other charms may trickle.

Love he comes, and Love he tarries,
Just as fate or fancy carries;
Longest stays, when sorest chidden;
Laughs and flies, when press'd and bidden.

Bind the sea to slumber stilly,
Bind its odour to the lily,
Bind the aspen ne'er to quiver,
Then bind Love to last for ever.

Love's a fire that needs renewal
Of fresh beauty for its fuel:
Love's wing moults when caged and captured,
Only free, he soars enraptured.

Can you keep the bee from ranging
Or the ringdove's neck from changing?
No! nor fetter'd Love from dying
In the knot there's no untying.

Thomas Campbell

184　　　　　**Love's Philosophy**

The fountains mingle with the river
　And the rivers with the ocean,
The winds of heaven mix for ever
　With a sweet emotion;
Nothing in the world is single,
　All things by a law divine
In one another's being mingle—
　Why not I with thine?

See the mountains kiss high heaven
　And the waves clasp one another;
No sister-flower would be forgiven
　If it disdain'd its brother:
And the sunlight clasps the earth,
　And the moonbeams kiss the sea—
What are all these kissings worth,
　If thou kiss not me?

Percy Bysshe Shelley

185　　　　　**Echoes**

How sweet the answer Echo makes
　To Music at night,
When, roused by lute or horn, she wakes,
And far away o'er lawns and lakes
　Goes answering light!

Yet Love hath echoes truer far
　And far more sweet

Than e'er, beneath the moonlight's star,
Of horn or lute or soft guitar
   The songs repeat.

'Tis when the sigh,—in youth sincere
   And only then—
The sigh that's breathed for one to hear,
Is by that one, that only Dear
   Breathed back again.

           Thomas Moore

186   A Serenade

Ah! County Guy, the hour is nigh,
   The sun has left the lea,
The orange flower perfumes the bower,
   The breeze is on the sea.
The lark, his lay who trill'd all day,
   Sits hush'd his partner nigh;
Breeze, bird, and flower confess the hour,
   But where is County Guy?

The village maid steals through the shade
   Her shepherd's suit to hear;
To beauty shy, by lattice high,
   Sings high-born Cavalier.
The star of Love, all stars above,
   Now reigns o'er earth and sky,
And high and low the influence know—
   But where is County Guy?

           Sir Walter Scott

187   To the Evening Star

Gem of the crimson-colour'd Even,
   Companion of retiring day,
Why at the closing gates of heaven,
   Belovéd Star, dost thou delay?

So fair thy pensile beauty burns
   When soft the tear of twilight flows;
So due thy plighted love returns
   To chambers brighter than the rose;

To Peace, to Pleasure, and to Love
   So kind a star thou seem'st to be,
Sure some enamour'd orb above
   Descends and burns to meet with thee.

Thine is the breathing, blushing hour,
  When all unheavenly passions fly,
Chased by the soul-subduing power
  Of Love's delicious witchery.

O! sacred to the fall of day,
  Queen of propitious stars, appear,
And early rise, and long delay,
  When Caroline herself is here!

Shine on her chosen green resort,
  Whose trees the sunward summit crown,
And wanton flowers, that well may court
  An angel's feet to tread them down.

Shine on her sweetly-scented road,
  Thou star of evening's purple dome,
That lead'st the nightingale abroad,
  And guid'st the pilgrim to his home.

Shine where my charmer's sweeter breath
  Embalms the soft exhaling dew,
Where dying winds a sigh bequeath
  To kiss the cheek of rosy hue.

Where, winnow'd by the gentle air,
  Her silken tresses darkly flow,
And fall upon her brow so fair,
  Like shadows on the mountain snow.

Thus, ever thus, at day's decline
  In converse sweet to wander far—
O bring with thee my Caroline,
  And thou shalt be my Ruling Star!

Thomas Campbell

To the Night

188

Swiftly walk over the western wave
      Spirit of Night!
Out of the misty eastern cave,
  Where, all the long and lone daylight,
Thou wovest dreams of joy and fear
Which make thee terrible and dear,—
      Swift be thy flight!

Wrap thy form in a mantle grey
      Star-inwrought!

Blind with thine hair the eyes of Day,
　　Kiss her until she be wearied out,
Then wander o'er city, and sea, and land,
Touching all with thine opiate wand—
　　　　Come, long-sought!

When I arose and saw the dawn,
　　　　I sigh'd for thee;
When light rode high, and the dew was gone,
　　And noon lay heavy on flower and tree,
And the weary Day turn'd to his rest,
Lingering like an unloved guest,
　　　　I sigh'd for thee.

Thy brother Death came, and cried,
　　　　'Wouldst thou me?'
Thy sweet child Sleep, the filmy-eyed,
　　Murmur'd like a noontide bee,
'Shall I nestle near thy side?
Wouldst thou me?'—And I replied,
　　　　'No, not thee!'

Death will come when thou art dead,
　　　　Soon, too soon—
Sleep will come when thou art fled;
　　Of neither would I ask the boon
I ask of thee, belovéd Night—
Swift be thine approaching flight,
　　　　Come soon, soon!
　　　　　　　　　　Percy Bysshe Shelley

189　　　　　**To a Distant Friend**

Why art thou silent? Is thy love a plant
　　Of such weak fibre that the treacherous air
　　Of absence withers what was once so fair?
Is there no debt to pay, no boon to grant?
Yet have my thoughts for thee been vigilant,
　　Bound to thy service with unceasing care—
The mind's least generous wish a mendicant
　　For nought but what thy happiness could spare.
Speak!—though this soft warm heart, once free to hold
　　A thousand tender pleasures, thine and mine,
Be left more desolate, more dreary cold
Than a forsaken bird's-nest fill'd with snow
　　'Mid its own bush of leafless eglantine—
Speak, that my torturing doubts their end may know!
　　　　　　　　　　William Wordsworth

190

When we two parted
  In silence and tears,
Half broken-hearted,
  To sever for years,
Pale grew thy cheek and cold,
  Colder thy kiss;
Truly that hour foretold
  Sorrow to this!

The dew of the morning
  Sunk chill on my brow;
It felt like the warning
  Of what I feel now.
Thy vows are all broken,
  And light is thy fame:
I hear thy name spoken
  And share in its shame.

They name thee before me,
  A knell to mine ear;
A shudder comes o'er me—
  Why wert thou so dear?
They know not I knew thee
  Who knew thee too well:
Long, long shall I rue thee
  Too deeply to tell.

In secret we met:
  In silence I grieve
That thy heart could forget,
  Thy spirit deceive.
If I should meet thee
  After long years,
How should I greet thee?
  With silence and tears.
    George Gordon, Lord Byron

191   ## Happy Insensibility

In a drear-nighted December,
  Too happy, happy tree,
Thy branches ne'er remember
  Their green felicity:
The north cannot undo them
With a sleety whistle through them,
Nor frozen thawings glue them
  From budding at the prime.

In a drear-nighted December,
  Too happy, happy brook,
Thy bubblings ne'er remember
  Apollo's summer look;
But with a sweet forgetting
They stay their crystal fretting,
Never, never petting
  About the frozen time.

Ah, would 'twere so with many
  A gentle girl and boy!
But were there ever any
  Writhed not at passéd joy?

To know the change and feel it,
When there is none to heal it
Nor numbéd sense to steel it—
    Was never said in rhyme.

John Keats

192   Where shall the lover rest
                Whom the fates sever
        From his true maiden's breast,
                Parted for ever?
        Where, through groves deep and high,
                Sounds the far billow,
        Where early violets die
                Under the willow. Eleu loro!
                Soft shall be his pillow.

        There, through the summer day,
                Cool streams are laving:
        There, while the tempests sway,
                Scarce are boughs waving;
        There thy rest shalt thou take,
                Parted for ever,
        Never again to wake,
                Never, O never! Eleu loro!
                Never, O never!

        Where shall the traitor rest,
                He, the deceiver,
        Who could win maiden's breast,
                Ruin, and leave her?
        In the lost battle,
                Borne down by the flying,
        Where mingles war's rattle
                With groans of the dying; Eleu loro!
                There shall he be lying.

        Her wing shall the eagle flap
                O'er the falsehearted;
        His warm blood the wolf shall lap
                Ere life be parted:
        Shame and dishonour sit
                By his grave ever;
        Blessing shall hallow it
                Never, O never! Eleu loro!
                Never, O never!

Sir Walter Scott

La Belle Dame Sans Merci

'O what can ail thee, knight-at-arms,
　　Alone and palely loitering?
The sedge has wither'd from the Lake,
　　And no birds sing.

'O what can ail thee, knight-at-arms!
　　So haggard and so woebegone?
The squirrel's granary is full,
　　And the harvest's done.

'I see a lily on thy brow
　　With anguish moist and fever dew,
And on thy cheeks a fading rose
　　Fast withereth too.'

'I met a Lady in the Meads,
　　Full beautiful—a fairy's child,
Her hair was long, her foot was light,
　　And her eyes were wild.

'I made a garland for her head,
　　And bracelets too, and fragrant zone;
She look'd at me as she did love,
　　And made sweet moan.

'I set her on my pacing steed
　　And nothing else saw all day long,
For sidelong would she bend, and sing
　　A fairy's song.

'She found me roots of relish sweet,
　　And honey wild and manna dew,
And sure in language strange she said
　　"I love thee true."

'She took me to her elfin grot,
　　And there she wept, and sigh'd full sore,
And there I shut her wild wild eyes
　　With kisses four.

'And there she lulléd me asleep,
　　And there I dream'd—Ah! woe betide!
The latest dream I ever dream'd
　　On the cold hill side.

'I saw pale Kings and Princes too,
　　Pale warriors, death-pale were they all;
They cried—"La belle Dame sans Merci
　　Thee hath in thrall!"

'I saw their starved lips in the gloam
　　With horrid warning gapéd wide,
And I awoke and found me here
　　On the cold hill's side.

'And this is why I sojourn here
　　Alone and palely loitering,
Though the sedge is wither'd from the Lake
　　And no birds sing.'

John Keats

194　The Rover

'A weary lot is thine, fair maid,
　　A weary lot is thine!
To pull the thorn thy brow to braid,
　　And press the rue for wine.
A lightsome eye, a soldier's mien,
　　A feather of the blue,
A doublet of the Lincoln green—
　　No more of me you knew, my love!
No more of me you knew.

'This morn is merry June, I trow,
　　The rose is budding fain;
But she shall bloom in winter snow
　　Ere we two meet again.'
He turn'd his charger as he spake
　　Upon the river shore,
He gave his bridle-reins a shake,
　　Said 'Adieu for evermore, my love!
And adieu for evermore.'

Sir Walter Scott

195　The Flight of Love

When the lamp is shattered,
　　The light in the dust lies dead—
When the cloud is scattered,
　　The rainbow's glory is shed.
When the lute is broken,

Sweet tones are remembered not;
When the lips have spoken,
　　Love accents are soon forgot.

As music and splendour
　　Survive not the lamp and the lute,
The heart's echoes render
　　No song when the spirit is mute—
No song but sad dirges,
　　Like the wind through a ruined cell,
Or the mournful surges
　　That ring the dead seaman's knell.

When hearts have once mingled,
　　Love first leaves the well-built nest;
The weak one is singled
　　To endure what it once possest.
O Love! who bewailest
　　The frailty of all things here,
Why choose you the frailest
　　For your cradle, your home, and your bier?

Its passions will rock thee
　　As the storms rock the raven on high;
Bright reason will mock thee
　　Like the sun from a wintry sky.
From thy nest every rafter
　　Will rot, and thine eagle home
Leave thee naked to laughter,
　　When leaves fall and cold winds come.
　　　　　　　　　　　Percy Bysshe Shelley

196　　　　　　　　**The Maid of Neidpath**

O lovers' eyes are sharp to see,
　　And lovers' ears in hearing;
And love, in life's extremity,
　　Can lend an hour of cheering.
Disease had been in Mary's bower
　　And slow decay from mourning,
Though now she sits on Neidpath's tower
　　To watch her love's returning.

All sunk and dim her eyes so bright,
　　Her form decay'd by pining,
Till through her wasted hand, at night,
　　You saw the taper shining.

By fits a sultry hectic hue
  Across her cheek was flying;
By fits so ashy pale she grew
  Her maidens thought her dying.

Yet keenest powers to see and hear
  Seem'd in her frame residing;
Before the watch-dog prick'd his ear
  She heard her lover's riding;
Ere scarce a distant form was kenn'd
  She knew and waved to greet him,
And o'er the battlement did bend
  As on the wing to meet him.

He came—he pass'd—an heedless gaze,
  As o'er some stranger glancing;
Her welcome, spoke in faltering phrase,
  Lost in his courser's prancing—
The castle-arch, whose hollow tone
  Returns each whisper spoken,
Could scarcely catch the feeble moan
  Which told her heart was broken.

Sir Walter Scott

197   The Maid of Neidpath

Earl March look'd on his dying child,
  And, smit with grief to view her—
'The youth,' he cried, 'whom I exiled
  Shall be restored to woo her.'

She's at the window many an hour
  His coming to discover:
And he look'd up to Ellen's bower
  And she look'd on her lover—

But ah! so pale, he knew her not,
  Though her smile on him was dwelling—
'And am I then forgot—forgot?'
  It broke the heart of Ellen.

In vain he weeps, in vain he sighs,
  Her cheek is cold as ashes;
Nor love's own kiss shall wake those eyes
  To lift their silken lashes.

Thomas Campbell

198 Bright Star, would I were steadfast as thou art—
Not in lone splendour hung aloft the night,
And watching, with eternal lids apart,
Like nature's patient sleepless Eremite,
The moving waters at their priestlike task
Of pure ablution round earth's human shores,
Or gazing on the new soft-fallen mask
Of snow upon the mountains and the moors—
No—yet still steadfast, still unchangeable,
Pillow'd upon my fair love's ripening breast,
To feel for ever its soft fall and swell,
Awake for ever in a sweet unrest;
Still, still to hear her tender-taken breath,
And so live ever,—or else swoon to death.

John Keats

199

The Terror of Death

When I have fears that I may cease to be
Before my pen has glean'd my teeming brain,
Before high-pilèd books, in charact'ry
Hold like rich garners the full-ripen'd grain;
When I behold, upon the night's starr'd face,
Huge cloudy symbols of a high romance,
And think that I may never live to trace
Their shadows, with the magic hand of chance;
And when I feel, fair creature of an hour!
That I shall never look upon thee more,
Never have relish in the fairy power
Of unreflecting love—then on the shore
Of the wide world I stand alone, and think
Till love and fame to nothingness do sink.

John Keats

200

Desideria

Surprised by joy—impatient as the wind—
I turn'd to share the transport—O with whom
But Thee—deep buried in the silent tomb,
That spot which no vicissitude can find?
Love, faithful love recall'd thee to my mind—
But how could I forget thee? Through what power
Even for the least division of an hour
Have I been so beguiled as to be blind
To my most grievous loss?—That thought's return

Was the worst pang that sorrow ever bore,
   Save one, one only, when I stood forlorn,
     Knowing my heart's best treasure was no more;
   That neither present time, nor years unborn
     Could to my sight that heavenly face restore.

                            William Wordsworth

201

At the mid hour of night, when stars are weeping, I fly
To the lone vale we loved, when life shone warm in thine eye;
And I think oft, if spirits can steal from the regions of air
To revisit past scenes of delight, thou wilt come to me there
And tell me our love is remember'd, even in the sky!

Then I sing the wild song it once was rapture to hear,
When our voices, commingling, breathed like one on the ear;
And as Echo far off through the vale my sad orison rolls,
I think, O my Love! 'tis thy voice, from the Kingdom of Souls
Faintly answering still the notes that once were so dear.

                              Thomas Moore

202   **Elegy on Thyrza**

  And thou art dead, as young and fair
    As aught of mortal birth;
  And form so soft and charms so rare
    Too soon return'd to Earth!
  Though Earth received them in her bed,
  And o'er the spot the crowd may tread
    In carelessness or mirth,
  There is an eye which could not brook
  A moment on that grave to look.

  I will not ask where thou liest low,
    Nor gaze upon the spot;
  There flowers or weeds at will may grow,
    So I behold them not:
  It is enough for me to prove
  That what I loved and long must love
    Like common earth can rot;
  To me there needs no stone to tell
  'Tis Nothing that I loved so well.

  Yet did I love thee to the last,
    As fervently as thou,

Who didst not change through all the past
　And canst not alter now.
The love where Death has set his seal
Nor age can chill, nor rival steal,
　Nor falsehood disavow:
And, what were worse, thou canst not see
Or wrong, or change, or fault in me.

The better days of life were ours;
　The worst can be but mine:
The sun that cheers, the storm that lours,
　Shall never more be thine.
The silence of that dreamless sleep
I envy now too much to weep;
　Nor need I to repine
That all those charms have pass'd away
I might have watch'd through long decay.

The flower in ripen'd bloom unmatch'd
　Must fall the earliest prey;
Though by no hand untimely snatch'd,
　The leaves must drop away.
And yet it were a greater grief
To watch it withering, leaf by leaf,
　Than see it pluck'd to-day;
Since earthly eye but ill can bear
To trace the change to foul from fair.

I know not if I could have borne
　To see thy beauties fade;
The night that follow'd such a morn
　Had worn a deeper shade:
Thy day without a cloud hath past,
And thou wert lovely to the last,
　Extinguish'd, not decay'd;
As stars that shoot along the sky
Shine brightest as they fall from high.

As once I wept, if I could weep,
　My tears might well be shed,
To think I was not near, to keep
　One vigil o'er thy bed:
To gaze, how fondly! on thy face,
To fold thee in a faint embrace,
　Uphold thy drooping head;
And show that love, however vain,
Nor thou nor I can feel again.

Yet how much less it were to gain,
　　Though thou hast left me free,
The loveliest things that still remain
　　Than thus remember thee!
The all of thine that cannot die
Through dark and dread Eternity
　　Returns again to me,
And more thy buried love endears
Than aught except its living years.

George Gordon, Lord Byron

203

One word is too often profaned
　　For me to profane it,
One feeling too falsely disdain'd
　　For thee to disdain it;
One hope is too like despair
　　For prudence to smother,
And Pity from thee more dear
　　Than that from another.

I can give not what men call love;
　　But wilt thou accept not
The worship the heart lifts above
　　And the Heavens reject not,—
The desire of the moth for the star,
　　Of the night for the morrow,
The devotion to something afar
　　From the sphere of our sorrow?

Percy Bysshe Shelley

204　　　**Gathering Song of Donald the Black**

Pibroch of Donuil Dhu,
　　Pibroch of Dunuil,
Wake thy wild voice anew,
　　Summon Clan Conuil.
Come away, come away,
　　Hark to the summons!
Come in your war-array,
　　Gentles and commons.

Come from deep glen, and
　　From mountain so rocky;

The war-pipe and pennon
    Are at Inverlocky.
Come every hill-plaid, and
    True heart that wears one,
Come every steel blade, and
    Strong hand that bears one.

Leave untended the herd,
    The flock without shelter;
Leave the corpse uninterr'd,
    The bride at the altar;
Leave the deer, leave the steer,
    Leave nets and barges:
Come with your fighting gear,
    Broadswords and targes.

Come as the winds come, when
    Forests are rended;
Come as the waves come, when
    Navies are stranded:
Faster come, faster come,
    Faster and faster,
Chief, vassal, page and groom,
    Tenant and master.

Fast they come, fast they come;
    See how they gather!
Wide waves the eagle plume,
    Blended with heather.
Cast your plaids, draw your blades,
    Forward each man set!
Pibroch of Donuil Dhu
    Knell for the onset!

                                Sir Walter Scott

205   A wet sheet and a flowing sea,
            A wind that follows fast
        And fills the white and rustling sail
            And bends the gallant mast;
        And bends the gallant mast, my boys,
            While like the eagle free
        Away the good ship flies, and leaves
            Old England on the lee.

O for a soft and gentle wind!
   I heard a fair one cry;
But give to me the snoring breeze
   And white waves heaving high;
And white waves heaving high, my lads,
   The good ship tight and free—
The world of waters is our home,
   And merry men are we.

There's tempest in yon hornéd moon,
   And lightning in yon cloud;
But hark the music, mariners!
   The wind is piping loud;
The wind is piping loud, my boys,
   The lightning flashes free—
While the hollow oak our palace is,
   Our heritage the sea.

           Allan Cunningham

206   Ye Mariners of England
   That guard our native seas,
Whose flag has braved, a thousand years,
   The battle and the breeze,
Your glorious standard launch again
   To match another foe:
And sweep through the deep,
   While the stormy winds do blow;
While the battle rages loud and long
   And the stormy winds do blow.

The spirits of your fathers
   Shall start from every wave—
For the deck it was their field of fame,
   And Ocean was their grave.
Where Blake and mighty Nelson fell
   Your manly hearts shall glow,
As ye sweep through the deep,
   While the stormy winds do blow;
While the battle rages loud and long
   And the stormy winds do blow.

Britannia needs no bulwarks,
   No towers along the steep;
Her march is o'er the mountain waves,
   Her home is on the deep.

With thunders from her native oak
   She quells the floods below—
As they roar on the shore,
   When the stormy winds do blow;
When the battle rages loud and long,
   And the stormy winds do blow.

The meteor flag of England
   Shall yet terrific burn;
Till danger's troubled night depart
   And the star of peace return.
Then, then, ye ocean warriors!
   Our song and feast shall flow
To the fame of your name,
   When the storm has ceased to blow;
When the fiery fight is heard no more,
   And the storm has ceased to blow.

Thomas Campbell

207   Battle of the Baltic

Of Nelson and the North
Sing the glorious day's renown,
   When to battle fierce came forth
All the might of Denmark's crown,
And her arms along the deep proudly shone;
   By each gun the lighted brand
   In a bold, determined hand,
   And the Prince of all the land
      Led them on.
      Like leviathans afloat
Lay their bulwarks on the brine;
   While the sign of battle flew
On the lofty British line:
It was ten of April morn by the chime:
   As they drifted on their path
   There was silence deep as death;
   And the boldest held his breath
      For a time.
      But the might of England flush'd
To anticipate the scene;
   And her van the fleeter rush'd
O'er the deadly space between.
'Hearts of oak!' our captains cried, when each gun
   From its adamantine lips
   Spread a death-shade round the ships,
   Like the hurricane eclipse

Of the sun.
Again! again! again!
And the havoc did not slack,
Till a feeble cheer the Dane
To our cheering sent us back;
Their shots along the deep slowly boom:
Then ceased—and all is wail,
As they strike the shatter'd sail;
Or in conflagration pale
Light the gloom.
Out spoke the victor then
As he hail'd them o'er the wave,
'Ye are brothers! ye are men!
And we conquer but to save:
So peace instead of death let us bring:
But yield, proud foe, thy fleet
With the crews, at England's feet,
And make submission meet
To our King.'
Then Denmark blest our chief
That he gave her wounds repose;
And the sounds of joy and grief
From her people wildly rose,
As death withdrew his shades from the day:
While the sun look'd smiling bright
O'er a wide and woeful sight,
Where the fires of funeral light
Died away.
Now joy, old England, raise
For the tidings of thy might,
By the festal cities' blaze,
Whilst the wine cup shines in light;
And yet amidst that joy and uproar,
Let us think of them that sleep
Full many a fathom deep
By thy wild and stormy deep,
Elsinore!
Brave hearts! to Britain's pride
Once so faithful and so true,
On the deck of fame that died
With the gallant good Riou:
Soft sigh the winds of heaven o'er their grave!
While the billow mournful rolls
And the mermaid's song condoles,
Singing glory to the souls
Of the brave!

Thomas Campbell

Ode to Duty

Stern Daughter of the Voice of God!
O Duty! if that name thou love
Who art a light to guide, a rod
To check the erring, and reprove;
Thou, who art victory and law
When empty terrors overawe,
From vain temptations dost set free,
And calm'st the weary strife of frail humanity!

There are who ask not if thine eye
Be on them; who, in love and truth
Where no misgiving is, rely
Upon the genial sense of youth:
Glad hearts! without reproach or blot,
Who do thy work, and know it not:
O! if through confidence misplaced
They fail, thy saving arms, dread Power! around
them cast.

Serene will be our days and bright,
And happy will our nature be,
When love is an unerring light,
And joy its own security.
And they a blissful course may hold
Ev'n now, who, not unwisely bold,
Live in the spirit of this creed,
Yet seek thy firm support, according to their need.

I, loving freedom, and untried,
No sport of every random gust,
Yet being to myself a guide,
Too blindly have reposed my trust:
And oft, when in my heart was heard
Thy timely mandate, I deferr'd
The task, in smoother walks to stray;
But thee I now would serve more strictly, if I may.

Through no disturbance of my soul
Or strong compunction in me wrought,
I supplicate for thy control,
But in the quietness of thought:
Me this uncharter'd freedom tires;
I feel the weight of chance desires:
My hopes no more must change their name;
I long for a repose that ever is the same.

Stern Lawgiver! yet thou dost wear
   The Godhead's most benignant grace;
Nor know we anything so fair
   As is the smile upon thy face:
Flowers laugh before thee on their beds,
And fragrance in thy footing treads;
Thou dost preserve the stars from wrong;
And the most ancient heavens, through thee, are
     fresh and strong.

To humbler functions, awful Power!
   I call thee: I myself commend
Unto thy guidance from this hour;
   O let my weakness have an end!
Give unto me, made lowly wise,
The spirit of self-sacrifice;
The confidence of reason give;
And in the light of Truth thy bondman let me live.

                     William Wordsworth

209   On the Castle of Chi'lon

Eternal Spirit of the chainless Mind!
Brightest in dungeons, Liberty, thou art—
For there thy habitation is the heart—
The heart which love of Thee alone can bind;
And when thy sons to fetters are consign'd,
To fetters, and the damp vault's dayless gloom,
Their country conquers with their martyrdom,
And Freedom's fame finds wings on every wind.
Chillon! thy prison is a holy place
And thy sad floor an altar, for 'twas trod,
Until his very steps have left a trace
Worn, as if thy cold pavement were a sod,
By Bonnivard! May none those marks efface!
For they appeal from tyranny to God.

              George Gordon, Lord Byron

210   England and Switzerland, 1802

Two Voices are there, one is of the Sea,
One of the Mountains, each a mighty voice:
In both from age to age thou didst rejoice,
They were thy chosen music, Liberty!
There came a tyrant, and with holy glee
Thou fought'st against him,—but hast vainly striven:

Thou from thy Alpine holds at length art driven,
Where not a torrent murmurs heard by thee.
Of one deep bliss thine ear hath been bereft;
Then cleave, O cleave to that which still is left;
For, high-soul'd Maid, what sorrow would it be
That Mountain floods should thunder as before,
And Ocean bellow from his rocky shore,
And neither awful Voice be heard by Thee!

William Wordsworth

1   **On the Extinction of the Venetian Republic**

Once did She hold the gorgeous East in fee,
And was the safeguard of the West; the worth
Of Venice did not fall below her birth,
Venice, the eldest child of liberty.
She was a maiden city, bright and free;
No guile seduced, no force could violate;
And when she took unto herself a mate,
She must espouse the everlasting Sea.
And what if she had seen those glories fade,
Those titles vanish, and that strength decay,—
Yet shall some tribute of regret be paid
When her long life hath reach'd its final day:
Men are we, and must grieve when even the shade
Of that which once was great is pass'd away.

William Wordsworth

2   **London, 1802**

O Friend! I know not which way I must look
For comfort, being, as I am, opprest
To think that now our life is only drest
For show; mean handiwork of craftsman, cook,
Or groom!—We must run glittering like a brook
In the open sunshine, or we are unblest;
The wealthiest man among us is the best:
No grandeur now in Nature or in book.
Delights us. Rapine, avarice, expense,
This is idolatry; and these we adore:
Plain living and high thinking are no more:
The homely beauty of the good old cause
Is gone; our peace, our fearful innocence,
And pure religion breathing household laws.

William Wordsworth

213   **The Same**

Milton! thou shouldst be living at this hour:
England hath need of thee: she is a fen
Of stagnant waters: altar, sword, and pen,
Fireside, the heroic wealth of hall and bower,
Have forfeited their ancient English dower
Of inward happiness. We are selfish men:
O! raise us up, return to us again;
And give us manners, virtue, freedom, power.
Thy soul was like a Star, and dwelt apart:
Thou hadst a voice whose sound was like the sea,
Pure as the naked heavens, majestic, free;
So didst thou travel on life's common way
In cheerful godliness, and yet thy heart
The lowliest duties on herself did lay.

William Wordsworth

214

When I have borne in memory what has tamed
Great nations; how ennobling thoughts depart
When men change swords for ledgers, and desert
The student's bower for gold,—some fears unnamed
I had, my Country!—am I to be blamed?
Now, when I think of thee, and what thou art,
Verily, in the bottom of my heart
Of those unfilial fears I am ashamed.
For dearly must we prize thee; we who find
In thee a bulwark for the cause of men;
And I by my affection was beguiled:
What wonder if a Poet now and then,
Among the many movements of his mind,
Felt for thee as a lover or a child!

William Wordsworth

215   **Hohenlinden**

On Linden, when the sun was low,
All bloodless lay the untrodden snow;
And dark as winter was the flow
    Of Iser, rolling rapidly.

But Linden saw another sight,
When the drum beat at dead of night,
Commanding fires of death to light
    The darkness of her scenery.

By torch and trumpet fast array'd
Each horseman drew his battle blade
And furious every charger neigh'd
    To join the dreadful revelry.

Then shook the hills with thunder riven,
Then rush'd the steed, to battle driven,
And louder than the bolts of Heaven
    Far flash'd the red artillery.

But redder yet that light shall glow
On Linden's hills of stainéd snow;
And bloodier yet the torrent flow
    Of Iser, rolling rapidly.

'Tis morn; but scarce yon level sun
Can pierce the war-clouds, rolling dun,
Where furious Frank and fiery Hun
    Shout in their sulphurous canopy.

The combat deepens. On, ye brave
Who rush to glory, or the grave!
Wave, Munich, all thy banners wave,
    And charge with all thy chivalry!

Few, few shall part, where many meet!
The snow shall be their winding-sheet,
And every turf beneath their feet
    Shall be a soldier's sepulchre.

Thomas Campbell

216

After Blenheim

It was a summer evening,
    Old Kaspar's work was done,
And he before his cottage door
    Was sitting in the sun;
And by him sported on the green
His little grandchild Wilhelmine.

She saw her brother Peterkin
    Roll something large and round
Which he beside the rivulet
    In playing there had found;
He came to ask what he had found
That was so large and smooth and round.

Old Kaspar took it from the boy
   Who stood expectant by;
And then the old man shook his head,
   And with a natural sigh
' 'Tis some poor fellow's skull,' said he,
'Who fell in the great victory.

'I find them in the garden,
   For there's many here about;
And often when I go to plough
   The ploughshare turns them out.
For many thousand men,' said he,
'Were slain in that great victory.'

'Now tell us what 'twas all about,'
   Young Peterkin he cries;
And little Wilhelmine looks up
   With wonder-waiting eyes;
'Now tell us all about the war,
And what they fought each other for.'

'It was the English,' Kaspar cried,
   'Who put the French to rout;
But what they fought each other for
   I could not well make out.
But everybody said,' quoth he,
'That 'twas a famous victory.

'My father lived at Blenheim then,
   Yon little stream hard by;
They burnt his dwelling to the ground,
   And he was forced to fly:
So with his wife and child he fled,
Nor had he where to rest his head.

'With fire and sword the country round
   Was wasted far and wide,
And many a childing mother then
   And new-born baby died:
But things like that, you know, must be
At every famous victory.

'They say it was a shocking sight
   After the field was won;
For many thousand bodies here
   Lay rotting in the sun:

But things like that, you know, must be
   After a famous victory.

'Great praise the Duke of Marlbro' won
   And our good Prince Eugene;'
'Why, 'twas a very wicked thing!'
   Said little Wilhelmine;
'Nay . . nay . . my little girl,' quoth he,
'It was a famous victory.

'And everybody praised the Duke
   Who this great fight did win.'
'But what good came of it at last?'
   Quoth little Peterkin:—
'Why, that I cannot tell,' said he,
'But 'twas a famous victory!'

Robert Southey

17   Pro Patria Mori

When he who adores thee has left but the name
   Of his fault and his sorrows behind,
O! say wilt thou weep, when they darken the fame
   Of a life that for thee was resign'd?
Yes, weep, and however my foes may condemn,
   Thy tears shall efface their decree;
For, Heaven can witness, though guilty to them,
   I have been but too faithful to thee.

With thee were the dreams of my earliest love,
   Every thought of my reason was thine:
In my last humble prayer to the Spirit above
   Thy name shall be mingled with mine!
O! blest are the lovers and friends who shall live
   The day of thy glory to see;
But the next dearest blessing that Heaven can give
   Is the pride of thus dying for thee.

Thomas Moore

18   The Burial of Sir John Moore at Corunna

Not a drum was heard, not a funeral note,
   As his corse to the rampart we hurried;
Not a soldier discharged his farewell shot
   O'er the grave where our Hero we buried.

We buried him darkly at dead of night,
   The sods with our bayonets turning;
By the struggling moonbeam's misty light
   And the lantern dimly burning.

No useless coffin enclosed his breast,
   Not in sheet or in shroud we wound him;
But he lay like a Warrior taking his rest
   With his martial cloak around him.

Few and short were the prayers we said,
   And we spoke not a word of sorrow;
But we steadfastly gaz'd on the face that was dead,
   And we bitterly thought of the morrow.

We thought, as we hollow'd his narrow bed
   And smooth'd down his lonely pillow,
That the Foe and the Stranger would tread o'er his head,
   And we far away on the billow!

Lightly they'll talk of the Spirit that's gone
   And o'er his cold ashes upbraid him,—
But little he'll reck, if they let him sleep on
   In the grave where a Briton has laid him.

But half of our heavy task was done
   When the clock struck the hour for retiring:
And we heard the distant and random gun
   That the foe was sullenly firing.

Slowly and sadly we laid him down,
   From the field of his fame fresh and gory;
We carved not a line, and we raised not a stone—
   But we left him alone with his glory.

Charles Wolfe

219   **Simon Lee the Old Huntsman**

In the sweet shire of Cardigan,
   Not far from pleasant Ivor Hall,
An old man dwells, a little man,—
   'Tis said he once was tall.
Full five-and-thirty years he lived
   A running huntsman merry;
And still the centre of his cheek
   Is red as a ripe cherry.

No man like him the horn could sound,
    And hill and valley rang with glee
When Echo bandied round and round
    The halloo of Simon Lee.
In those proud days he little cared
    For husbandry or tillage;
To blither tasks did Simon rouse
    The sleepers of the village.

He all the country could outrun,
    Could leave both man and horse behind;
And often, ere the chase was done,
    He reeled and was stone-blind.
And still there's something in the world
    At which his heart rejoices;
For when the chiming hounds are out,
    He dearly loves their voices!

But O the heavy change!—bereft
    Of health, strength, friends, and kindred, see!
Old Simon to the world is left
    In liveried poverty:
His master's dead, and no one now
    Dwells in the Hall of Ivor;
Men, dogs, and horses, all are dead;
    He is the sole survivor.

And he is lean and he is sick;
    His body, dwindled and awry,
Rests upon ankles swoln and thick;
    His legs are thin and dry.
One prop he has, and only one,
    His wife, an aged woman,
Lives with him, near the waterfall,
    Upon the village common.

Beside their moss-grown hut of clay,
    Not twenty paces from the door,
A scrap of land they have, but they
    Are poorest of the poor.
This scrap of land he from the heath
    Enclosed when he was stronger;
But what to them avails the land
    Which he can till no longer?

Oft, working by her husband's side,
    Ruth does what Simon cannot do;

For she, with scanty cause for pride,
  Is stouter of the two.
And, though you with your utmost skill
  From labour could not wean them,
'Tis little, very little, all
  That they can do between them.

Few months of life has he in store
  As he to you will tell,
For still, the more he works, the more
  Do his weak ankles swell.
My gentle reader, I perceive
  How patiently you've waited,
And now I fear that you expect
  Some tale will be related.

O reader! had you in your mind
  Such stores as silent thought can bring,
O gentle reader! you would find
  A tale in every thing.
What more I have to say is short,
  And you must kindly take it:
It is no tale; but, should you think,
  Perhaps a tale you'll make it.

One summer-day I chanced to see
  This old man doing all he could
To unearth the root of an old tree,
  A stump of rotten wood.
The mattock totter'd in his hand;
  So vain was his endeavour
That at the root of the old tree
  He might have worked for ever.

'You're overtask'd, good Simon Lee,
  Give me your tool,' to him I said;
And at the word right gladly he
  Received my proffer'd aid.
I struck, and with a single blow
  The tangled root I sever'd,
At which the poor old man so long
  And vainly had endeavour'd

The tears into his eyes were brought,
  And thanks and praises seem'd to run
So fast out of his heart, I thought
  They never would have done.

—I've heard of hearts unkind, kind deeds
  With coldness still returning;
Alas! the gratitude of men
  Hath oftener left me mourning.

William Wordsworth

220   The Old Familiar Faces

I have had playmates, I have had companions
In my days of childhood, in my joyful school-days;
  All, all are gone, the old familiar faces.

I have been laughing, I have been carousing,
Drinking late, sitting late, with my bosom cronies;
  All, all are gone, the old familiar faces.

I loved a love once, fairest among women:
Closed are her doors on me, I must not see her—
  All, all are gone, the old familiar faces.

I have a friend, a kinder friend has no man:
Like an ingrate, I left my friend abruptly;
  Left him, to muse on the old familiar faces.

Ghost-like I paced round the haunts of my childhood,
Earth seem'd a desert I was bound to traverse,
  Seeking to find the old familiar faces.

Friend of my bosom, thou more than a brother,
Why wert not thou born in my father's dwelling?
  So might we talk of the old familiar faces.

How some they have died, and some they have left me,
And some are taken from me; all are departed;
  All, all are gone, the old familiar faces.

Charles Lamb

221   The Journey Onwards

As slow our ship her foamy track
  Against the wind was cleaving,
Her trembling pennant still look'd back
  To that dear isle 'twas leaving.
So loth we part from all we love,
  From all the links that bind us;
So turn our hearts, as on we rove,
  To those we've left behind us!

When, round the bowl, of vanish'd years
    We talk with joyous seeming—
With smiles that might as well be tears,
    So faint, so sad their beaming;
While memory brings us back again
    Each early tie that twined us,
O, sweet's the cup that circles then
    To those we've left behind us!

And when in other climes we meet
    Some isle or vale enchanting,
Where all looks flowery, wild, and sweet,
    And nought but love is wanting;
We think how great had been our bliss
    If Heaven had but assign'd us
To live and die in scenes like this,
    With some we've left behind us!

As travellers oft look back at eve
    When eastward darkly going,
To gaze upon that light they leave
    Still faint behind them glowing,—
So, when the close of pleasure's day
    To gloom hath near consign'd us,
We turn to catch one fading ray
    Of joy that's left behind us.

Thomas Moore

222   **Youth and Age**

There's not a joy the world can give like that it takes away,
When the glow of early thought declines in feeling's dull decay;
'Tis not on youth's smooth cheek the blush alone which fades
    so fast,
But the tender bloom of heart is gone, ere youth itself be past.
Then the few whose spirits float above the wreck of happiness
Are driven o'er the shoals of guilt or ocean of excess:
The magnet of their course is gone, or only points in vain
The shore to which their shiver'd sail shall never stretch again
Then the mortal coldness of the soul like death itself comes
    down;
It cannot feel for others' woes, it dare not dream its own;
That heavy chill has frozen o'er the fountain of our tears,
And though the eye may sparkle still, 'tis where the ice appears.
Though wit may flash from fluent lips, and mirth distract the
    breast,

Through midnight hours that yield no more their former hope
    of rest;
'Tis but as ivy-leaves around the ruin'd turret wreathe,
All green and wildly fresh without, but worn and grey beneath.
O could I feel as I have felt, or be what I have been,
Or weep as I could once have wept o'er many a vanish'd
    scene,—
As springs in deserts found seem sweet, all brackish though
    they be,
So midst the wither'd waste of life, those tears would flow to
    me!

George Gordon, Lord Byron

223

A Lesson

There is a flower, the Lesser Celandine,
    That shrinks like many more from cold and rain,
And, the first moment that the sun may shine,
    Bright as the sun himself, 'tis out again!

When hailstones have been falling, swarm on swarm,
    Or blasts the green field and the trees distrest,
Oft have I seen it muffled up from harm
    In close self-shelter, like a thing at rest.

But lately, one rough day, this flower I past,
    And recognized it, though an alter'd form,
Now standing forth an offering to the blast,
    And buffeted at will by rain and storm.

I stopp'd and said, with inly-mutter'd voice,
    'It doth not love the shower, nor seek the cold;
This neither is its courage nor its choice,
    But its necessity in being old.

'The sunshine may not cheer it, nor the dew;
    It cannot help itself in its decay;
Stiff in its members, wither'd, changed of hue.'
    And, in my spleen, I smiled that it was grey.

To be a prodigal's favourite—then, worse truth,
    A miser's pensioner—behold our lot!
O Man! that from thy fair and shining youth
    Age might but take the things Youth needed not!

William Wordsworth

224   **Past and Present**

I remember, I remember
    The house where I was born,
The little window where the sun
    Came peeping in at morn;
He never came a wink too soon
    Nor brought too long a day;
But now, I often wish the night
    Had borne my breath away.

I remember, I remember
    The roses, red and white,
The violets, and the lily-cups—
    Those flowers made of light!
The lilacs where the robin built,
    And where my brother set
The laburnum on his birth-day,—
    The tree is living yet!

I remember, I remember
    Where I was used to swing,
And thought the air must rush as fresh
    To swallows on the wing;
My spirit flew in feathers then
    That is so heavy now,
And summer pools could hardly cool
    The fever on my brow.

I remember, I remember
    The fir trees dark and high;
I used to think their slender tops
    Were close against the sky:
It was a childish ignorance,
    But now 'tis little joy
To know I'm farther off from Heaven
    Than when I was a boy.

                                    Thomas Hood

225   **The Light of Other Days**

Oft in the stilly night,
    Ere slumber's chain has bound me,
Fond Memory brings the light
    Of other days around me:
        The smiles, the tears

Of boyhood's years,
The words of love then spoken;
The eyes that shone,
Now dimm'd and gone,
The cheerful hearts now broken!
Thus in the stilly night,
Ere slumber's chain has bound me,
Sad memory brings the light
Of other days around me.

When I remember all
The friends so link'd together
I've seen around me fall
Like leaves in wintry weather,
I feel like one
Who treads alone
Some banquet-hall deserted,
Whose lights are fled
Whose garlands dead,
And all but he departed!
Thus in the stilly night,
Ere slumber's chain has bound me,
Sad Memory brings the light
Of other days around me. *Thomas Moore*

226

Invocation

Rarely, rarely, comest thou,
Spirit of Delight!
Wherefore hast thou left me now
Many a day and night?
Many a weary night and day
'Tis since thou art fled away.

How shall ever one like me
Win thee back again?
With the joyous and the free
Thou wilt scoff at pain.
Spirit false! thou hast forgot
All but those who need thee not.

As a lizard with the shade
Of a trembling leaf,
Thou with sorrow art dismay'd;
Even the sighs of grief
Reproach thee, that thou art not near,
And reproach thou wilt not hear.

Let me set my mournful ditty
    To a merry measure;
Thou wilt never come for pity,
    Thou wilt come for pleasure;
Pity then will cut away
Those cruel wings, and thou wilt stay.

I love all that thou lovest,
    Spirit of Delight!
The fresh Earth in new leaves drest
    And the starry night;
Autumn evening, and the morn
When the golden mists are born.

I love snow and all the forms
    Of the radiant frost;
I love waves, and winds, and storms,
    Everything almost
Which is Nature's, and may be
Untainted by man's misery.

I love tranquil solitude,
    And such society
As is quiet, wise, and good;
    Between thee and me
What diff'rence? but thou dost possess
The things I seek, not love them less.

I love Love—though he has wings,
    And like light can flee,
But above all other things,
    Spirit, I love thee—
Thou art love and life! O come!
Make once more my heart thy home!

                              Percy Bysshe Shelley

227   **Stanzas Written in Dejection Near Naples**

The sun is warm, the sky is clear,
    The waves are dancing fast and bright,
Blue isles and snowy mountains wear
    The purple noon's transparent might:
    The breath of the moist earth is light
Around its unexpanded buds;
    Like many a voice of one delight—
The winds, the birds, the ocean-floods—
The City's voice itself is soft like Solitude's.

I see the Deep's untrampled floor
   With green and purple seaweeds strown;
I see the waves upon the shore,
   Like light dissolved in star-showers, thrown:
I sit upon the sands alone;
The lightning of the noontide ocean
   Is flashing round me, and a tone
Arises from its measured motion—
How sweet! did any heart now share in my emotion.

Alas! I have nor hope nor health,
   Nor peace within nor calm around,
Nor that content, surpassing wealth,
   The sage in meditation found,
   And walked with inward glory crowned—
Nor fame, nor power, nor love, nor leisure;
   Others I see whom these surround—
Smiling they live, and call life pleasure;
To me that cup has been dealt in another measure.

Yet now despair itself is mild
   Even as the winds and waters are;
I could lie down like a tired child,
   And weep away the life of care
   Which I have borne, and yet must bear,
Till death like sleep might steal on me,
   And I might feel in the warm air
My cheek grow cold, and hear the sea
Breathe o'er my dying brain its last monotony.

Percy Bysshe Shelley

228   **The Scholar**

My days among the Dead are past;
   Around me I behold,
Where'er these casual eyes are cast,
   The mighty minds of old:
My never-failing friends are they,
With whom I converse day by day.

With them I take delight in weal
   And seek relief in woe;
And while I understand and feel
   How much to them I owe,
My cheeks have often been bedew'd
With tears of thoughtful gratitude.

My thoughts are with the Dead; with them
   I live in long-past years,
Their virtues love, their faults condemn,
   Partake their hopes and fears,
And from their lessons seek and find
Instruction with an humble mind.

My hopes are with the Dead; anon
   My place with them will be,
And I with them shall travel on
   Through all Futurity;
Yet leaving here a name, I trust,
That will not perish in the dust.

Robert Southey

229   The Mermaid Tavern

Souls of Poets dead and gone,
What Elysium have ye known,
Happy field or mossy cavern,
Choicer than the Mermaid Tavern?
Have ye tippled drink more fine
Than mine host's Canary wine?
Or are fruits of Paradise
Sweeter than those dainty pies
Of venison? O generous food!
Drest as though bold Robin Hood
Would, with his Maid Marian,
Sup and bowse from horn and can.

I have heard that on a day
Mine host's signboard flew away
Nobody knew whither, till
An astrologer's old quill
To a sheepskin gave the story—
Said he saw you in your glory
Underneath a new-old Sign
Sipping beverage divine,
And pledging with contented smack
The Mermaid in the Zodiac.

Souls of Poets dead and gone,
What Elysium have ye known—
Happy field or mossy cavern—
Choicer than the Mermaid Tavern?

John Keats

The Pride of Youth

Proud Maisie is in the wood,
　　Walking so early;
Sweet Robin sits on the bush
　　Singing so rarely.

'Tell me, thou bonny bird,
　　When shall I marry me?'
—'When six braw gentlemen
　　Kirkward shall carry ye.'

'Who makes the bridal bed,
　　Birdie, say truly?'
—'The grey-headed sexton
　　That delves the grave duly.

'The glow-worm o'er grave and stone
　　Shall light thee steady;
The owl from the steeple sing
　　Welcome, proud lady.'

Sir Walter Scott

231　　　　**The Bridge of Sighs**

One more Unfortunate
Weary of breath,
Rashly importunate,
Gone to her death!
Take her up tenderly,
Lift her with care;
Fashion'd so slenderly,
Young, and so fair!
Look at her garments
Clinging like cerements,
Whilst the wave constantly
Drips from her clothing;
Take her up instantly,
Loving, not loathing.
Touch her not scornfully;
Think of her mournfully,
Gently and humanly;
Not of the stains of her—
All that remains of her
Now is pure womanly.
Make no deep scrutiny

Into her mutiny
Rash and undutiful:
Past all dishonour,
Death has left on her
Only the beautiful.
Still, for all slips of hers,
One of Eve's family—
Wipe those poor lips of hers
Oozing so clammily.
Loop up her tresses
Escaped from the comb,
Her fair auburn tresses;
Whilst wonderment guesses
Where was her home?
Who was her father?
Who was her mother?
Had she a sister?
Had she a brother?
Or was there a dearer one
Still, and a nearer one
Yet, than all other?

Alas! for the rarity
Of Christian charity
Under the sun!
O! it was pitiful!
Near a whole city full,
Home she had none.
Sisterly, brotherly,
Fatherly, motherly
Feelings had changed:
Love, by harsh evidence,
Thrown from its eminence,
Even God's providence
Seeming estranged.
Where the lamps quiver
So far in the river,
With many a light
From window and casement,
From garret to basement,
She stood, with amazement,
Houseless by night.
The bleak wind of March
Made her tremble and shiver;
But not the dark arch,
Or the black flowing river:
Mad from life's history,
Glad to death's mystery,
Swift to be hurl'd—
Any where, any where
Out of the world!
In she plunged boldly,
No matter how coldly
The rough river ran,

Over the brink of it,—
Picture it, think of it,
Dissolute Man!
Lave in it, drink of it
Then, if you can!
Take her up tenderly,
Lift her with care;
Fashion'd so slenderly,
Young, and so fair!
Ere her limbs frigidly
Stiffen too rigidly,
Decently, kindly,
Smooth and compose them;
And her eyes, close them,
Staring so blindly!
Dreadfully staring
Thro' muddy impurity,
As when with the daring
Last look of despairing
Fix'd on futurity
Perishing gloomily,
Spurr'd by contumely,
Cold inhumanity,
Burning insanity,
Into her rest.
—Cross her hands humbly,
As if praying dumbly,
Over her breast!
Owning her weakness,
Her evil behaviour,
And leaving, with meekness,
Her sins to her Saviour!

Thomas Hood

232   **Elegy**

O snatch'd away in beauty's bloom!
On thee shall press no ponderous tomb;
 But on thy turf shall roses rear
 Their leaves, the earliest of the year,
And the wild cypress wave in tender gloom:

And oft by yon blue gushing stream
 Shall Sorrow lean her drooping head,
And feed deep thought with many a dream,
 And lingering pause and lightly tread;
Fond wretch! as if her step disturb'd the dead!

Away! we know that tears are vain,
 That Death nor heeds nor hears distress:
Will this unteach us to complain?
 Or make one mourner weep the less?
And thou, who tell'st me to forget,
Thy looks are wan, thine eyes are wet.

George Gordon, Lord Byron

233   **Hester**

When maidens such as Hester die,
Their place ye may not well supply,
Though ye among a thousand try
  With vain endeavour.
A month or more hath she been dead,
Yet cannot I by force be led
To think upon the wormy bed
  And her together.

A springy motion in her gait,
A rising step, did indicate
Of pride and joy no common rate
  That flush'd her spirit:
I know not by what name beside
I shall it call: if 'twas not pride,
It was a joy to that allied
  She did inherit.

Her parents held the Quaker rule,
Which doth the human feeling cool;
But she was train'd in Nature's school,
  Nature had blest her.
A waking eye, a prying mind,
A heart that stirs, is hard to bind;
A hawk's keen sight ye cannot blind,
  Ye could not Hester.

My sprightly neighbour! gone before
To that unknown and silent shore,
Shall we not meet, as heretofore
  Some summer morning—
When from thy cheerful eyes a ray
Hath struck a bliss upon the day,
A bliss that would not go away,
  A sweet fore-warning?

Charles Lamb

234   **Coronach**

He is gone on the mountain,
    He is lost to the forest,
Like a summer-dried fountain,
    When our need was the sorest.
The font reappearing
    From the raindrops shall borrow,
But to us comes no cheering,
    To Duncan no morrow!

The hand of the reaper
    Takes the ears that are hoary,
But the voice of the weeper
    Wails manhood in glory.
The autumn winds rushing
    Waft the leaves that are serest,
But our flower was in flushing
    When blighting was nearest.

Fleet foot on the correi,
    Sage counsel in cumber,
Red hand in the foray,
    How sound is thy slumber!
Like the dew on the mountain,
    Like the foam on the river,
Like the bubble on the fountain,
    Thou art gone, and for ever!

                                    Sir Walter Scott

235   **The Death-Bed**

We watch'd her breathing thro' the night,
    Her breathing soft and low,
As in her breast the wave of life
    Kept heaving to and fro.

But when the morn came dim and sad
    And chill with early showers,
Her quiet eyelids closed—she had
    Another morn than ours.

                                    Thomas Hood

236   **Rosabelle**

O listen, listen, ladies gay!
    No haughty feat of arms I tell;

Soft is the note, and sad the lay
    That mourns the lovely Rosabelle.

Moor, moor the barge, ye gallant crew!
    And, gentle ladye, deign to stay!
Rest thee in Castle Ravensheuch,
    Nor tempt the stormy firth to-day.

'The blackening wave is edged with white;
    To inch and rock the sea-mews fly;
The fishers have heard the Water-Sprite,
    Whose screams forebode that wreck is nigh.

'Last night the gifted Seer did view
    A wet shroud swathed round ladye gay;
Then stay thee, Fair, in Ravensheuch;
    Why cross the gloomy firth to-day?'

' 'Tis not because Lord Lindesay's heir
    Tonight at Roslin leads the ball,
But that my ladye-mother there
    Sits lonely in her castle-hall.

' 'Tis not because the ring they ride,
    And Lindesay at the ring rides well,
But that my sire the wine will chide
    If 'tis not fill'd by Rosabelle.'

—O'er Roslin all that dreary night
    A wondrous blaze was seen to gleam;
'Twas broader than the watch-fire's light,
    And redder than the bright moonbeam.

It glared on Roslin's castled rock,
    It ruddied all the copse-wood glen;
'Twas seen from Dryden's groves of oak,
    And seen from cavern'd Hawthornden.

Seem'd all on fire that chapel proud,
    Where Roslin's chiefs uncoffin'd lie,
Each Baron, for a sable shroud,
    Sheath'd in his iron panoply.

Seem'd all on fire within, around,
    Deep sacristy and altar's pale;
Shone every pillar foliage-bound,
    And glimmer'd all the dead men's mail.

Blazed battlement and pinnet high,
  Blazed every rose-carved buttress fair—
So still they blaze, when fate is nigh
  The lordly line of high St. Clair.

There are twenty of Roslin's barons bold
  Lie buried within that proud chapelle;
Each one the holy vault doth hold,
  But the sea holds lovely Rosabelle!

And each St. Clair was buried there
  With candle, with book, and with knell;
But the sea-caves rung, and the wild winds sung
  The dirge of lovely Rosabelle.

                         Sir Walter Scott

237   **On an Infant Dying as Soon as Born**

I saw where in the shroud did lurk
A curious frame of Nature's work;
A flow'ret crushéd in the bud,
A nameless piece of Babyhood,
Was in her cradle-coffin lying;
Extinct, with scarce the sense of dying:
So soon to exchange the imprisoning womb
For darker closets of the tomb!
She did but ope an eye, and put
A clear beam forth, then straight up shut
For the long dark: ne'er more to see
Through glasses of mortality.
Riddle of destiny, who can show
What thy short visit meant, or know
What thy errand here below?
Shall we say, that Nature blind
Check'd her hand, and changed her mind,
Just when she had exactly wrought
A finish'd pattern without fault?
Could she flag, or could she tire,
Or lack'd she the Promethean fire
(With her nine moons' long workings sicken'd)
That should thy little limbs have quicken'd?
Limbs so firm, they seem'd to assure
Life of health, and days mature;
Woman's self in miniature!
Limbs so fair, they might supply
(Themselves now but cold imagery)
The sculptor to make Beauty by.

Or did the stern-eyed Fate descry
That babe or mother, one must die;
So in mercy left the stock
And cut the branch; to save the shock
Of young years widow'd, and the pain
When Single State comes back again
To the lone man who, 'reft of wife,
Thenceforward drags a maiméd life?
The economy of Heaven is dark,
And wisest clerks have miss'd the mark,
Why human buds, like this, should fall
More brief than fly ephemeral
That has his day; while shrivell'd crones
Stiffen with age to stocks and stones;
And crabbéd use the conscience sears
In sinners of an hundred years.
—Mother's prattle, mother's kiss,
Baby fond, thou ne'er wilt miss:
Rites, which custom does impose,
Silver bells, and baby clothes;
Coral redder than those lips
Which pale death did late eclipse;
Music framed for infants' glee,
Whistle never tuned for thee;
Though thou want'st not, thou shalt have them,
Loving hearts were they which gave them.
Let not one be missing; nurse,
See them laid upon the hearse
Of infant slain by doom perverse.
Why should kings and nobles have
Pictured trophies to their grave,
And we, churls, to thee deny
Thy pretty toys with thee to lie—
A more harmless vanity?

Charles Lamb

The Affliction of Margaret

Where art thou, my beloved Son,
   Where art thou, worse to me than dead?
O find me, prosperous or undone!
   Or, if the grave be now thy bed,
Why am I ignorant of the same
That I may rest; and neither blame
Nor sorrow may attend thy name?

238

Seven years, alas! to have received
  No tidings of an only child;
To have despaired, have hoped, believed,
  And been for evermore beguiled,—
Sometimes with thoughts of very bliss!
I catch at them, and then I miss;
Was ever darkness like to this?

He was among the prime in worth,
  An object beauteous to behold;
Well born, well bred; I sent him forth
  Ingenuous, innocent, and bold:
If things ensued that wanted grace,
As hath been said, they were not base;
And never blush was on my face.

Ah! little doth the young one dream,
  When full of play and childish cares,
What power is in his wildest scream
  Heard by his mother unawares!
He knows it not, he cannot guess:
Years to a mother bring distress;
But do not make her love the less.

Neglect me! no, I suffered long
  From that ill thought; and being blind
Said, 'Pride shall help me in my wrong:
  Kind mother have I been, as kind
As ever breathed:' and that is true;
I've wet my path with tears like dew,
Weeping for him when no one knew.

My Son, if thou be humbled, poor,
  Hopeless of honour and of gain,
O! do not dread thy mother's door;
  Think not of me with grief and pain:
I now can see with better eyes;
And worldly grandeur I despise,
And fortune with her gifts and lies.

Alas! the fowls of heaven have wings,
  And blasts of heaven will aid their flight;
They mount—how short a voyage brings
  The wanderers back to their delight!
Chains tie us down by land and sea;
And wishes, vain as mine, may be
All that is left to comfort thee.

Perhaps some dungeon hears thee groan,
　Maim'd, mangled by inhuman men;
Or thou upon a desert thrown
　Inheritest the lion's den;
Or hast been summon'd to the deep,
Thou, thou, and all thy mates, to keep
An incommunicable sleep.

I look for ghosts; but none will force
　Their way to me: 'tis falsely said
That there was ever intercourse
　Between the living and the dead;
For surely then I should have sight
Of him I wait for day and night
With love and longings infinite.

My apprehensions come in crowds;
　I dread the rustling of the grass;
The very shadows of the clouds
　Have power to shake me as they pass:
I question things, and do not find
One that will answer to my mind;
And all the world appears unkind.

Beyond participation lie
　My troubles, and beyond relief:
If any chance to heave a sigh,
　They pity me, and not my grief.
Then come to me, my Son, or send
Some tidings, that my woes may end;
I have no other earthly friend.

William Wordsworth

239　　　　　　**Hunting Song**

Waken, lords and ladies gay!
On the mountain dawns the day;
All the jolly chase is here
With hawk and horse and hunting-spear;
Hounds are in their couples yelling,
Hawks are whistling, horns are knelling,
Merrily merrily mingle they,
'Waken, lords and ladies gay!'

Waken, lords and ladies gay!
The mist has left the mountain grey,

Springlets in the dawn are steaming,
Diamonds on the brake are gleaming;
And foresters have busy been
To track the buck in thicket green;
Now we come to chant our lay,
'Waken, lords and ladies gay!'

Waken, lords and ladies gay!
To the greenwood haste away;
We can show you where he lies,
Fleet of foot and tall of size;
We can show the marks he made
When 'gainst the oak his antlers fray'd;
You shall see him brought to bay;
'Waken, lords and ladies gay!'

Louder, louder chant the lay,
Waken, lords and ladies gay!
Tell them youth and mirth and glee
Run a course as well as we;
Time, stern huntsman! who can balk,
Stanch as hound and fleet as hawk;
Think of this, and rise with day,
Gentle lords and ladies gay!

Sir Walter Scott

240   **To the Skylark**

Ethereal minstrel! pilgrim of the sky!
    Dost thou despise the earth where cares abound?
Or, while the wings aspire, are heart and eye
    Both with thy nest upon the dewy ground?
Thy nest which thou canst drop into at will,
Those quivering wings composed, that music still!

To the last point of vision, and beyond,
    Mount, daring warbler!—the love-prompted strain
('Twixt thee and thine a never-failing bond),
    Thrills not the less the bosom of the plain:
Yet might'st thou seem, proud privilege! to sing
All independent of the leafy spring.

Leave to the nightingale her shady wood;
    A privacy of glorious light is thine,
Whence thou dost pour upon the world a flood
    Of harmony, with instinct more divine;
Type of the wise, who soar, but never roam—
True to the kindred points of Heaven and Home!

William Wordsworth

To a Skylark

Hail to thee, blithe Spirit!
  Bird thou never wert,
That from heaven, or near it,
  Pourest thy full heart
In profuse strains of unpremeditated art.

Higher still and higher
  From the earth thou springest
Like a cloud of fire;
  The blue deep thou wingest,
And singing still dost soar, and soaring ever singest.

In the golden lightning
  Of the sunken sun,
O'er which clouds are brightening,
  Thou dost float and run,
Like an unbodied joy whose race is just begun.

The pale purple even
  Melts around thy flight;
Like a star of heaven
  In the broad daylight
Thou art unseen, but yet I hear thy shrill delight:

Keen as are the arrows
  Of that silver sphere,
Whose intense lamp narrows
  In the white dawn clear
Until we hardly see, we feel that it is there.

All the earth and air
  With thy voice is loud,
As, when night is bare,
  From one lonely cloud
The moon rains out her beams, and heaven is overflow'd.

What thou art we know not;
  What is most like thee?
From rainbow clouds there flow not
  Drops so bright to see
As from thy presence shower a rain of melody.

Like a poet hidden
  In the light of thought,
Singing hymns unbidden,
  Till the world is wrought
To sympathy with hopes and fears it heeded not:

Like a high-born maiden
      In a palace tower,
Soothing her love-laden
      Soul in secret hour
With music sweet as love, which overflows her bower:

Like a glow-worm golden
      In a dell of dew,
Scattering unbeholden
      Its aerial hue
Among the flowers and grass, which screen it from the view

Like a rose embower'd
      In its own green leaves,
By warm winds deflower'd,
      Till the scent it gives
Makes faint with too much sweet these heavy-wingéd thieve

Sound of vernal showers
      On the twinkling grass,
Rain-awaken'd flowers,
      All that ever was
Joyous, and clear, and fresh, thy music doth surpass.

Teach us, sprite or bird,
      What sweet thoughts are thine:
I have never heard
      Praise of love or wine
That panted forth a flood of rapture so divine.

Chorus hymeneal,
      Or triumphal chant,
Match'd with thine would be all
      But an empty vaunt—
A thing wherein we feel there is some hidden want.

What objects are the fountains
      Of thy happy strain?
What fields, or waves, or mountains?
      What shapes of sky or plain?
What love of thine own kind? what ignorance of pain?

With thy clear keen joyance
      Languor cannot be:
Shadow of annoyance
      Never came near thee:
Thou lovest; but ne'er knew loves sad satiety.

Waking or asleep
　　Thou of death must deem
Things more true and deep
　　Than we mortals dream,
Or how could thy notes flow in such a crystal stream?

We look before and after,
　　And pine for what is not:
Our sincerest laughter
　　With some pain is fraught:
Our sweetest songs are those that tell of saddest thought.

Yet if we could scorn
　　Hate, and pride, and fear;
If we were things born
　　Not to shed a tear,
I know not how thy joy we ever should come near.

Better than all measures
　　Of delightful sound,
Better than all treasures
　　That in books are found,
Thy skill to poet were, thou scorner of the ground!

Teach me half the gladness
　　That thy brain must know,
Such harmonious madness
　　From my lips would flow
The world should listen then, as I am listening now!
　　　　　　　　　　　　Percy Bysshe Shelley

242　　　　　　　**The Green Linnet**

Beneath these fruit-tree boughs that shed
Their snow-white blossoms on my head,
With brightest sunshine round me spread
　　Of spring's unclouded weather,
In this sequestered nook how sweet
To sit upon my orchard-seat!
And birds and flowers once more to greet,
　　My last year's friends together.

One have I marked, the happiest guest
In all this covert of the blest:
Hail to Thee, far above the rest
　　In joy of voice and pinion!

Thou, Linnet! in thy green array,
Presiding Spirit here to-day,
Dost lead the revels of the May,
    And this is thy dominion.

While birds, and butterflies, and flowers,
Make all one band of paramours,
Thou, ranging up and down the bowers,
    Art sole in thy employment;
A Life, a Presence like the Air,
Scattering thy gladness without care,
Too blest with any one to pair,
    Thyself thy own enjoyment.

Amid yon tuft of hazel trees,
That twinkle to the gusty breeze,
Behold him perch'd in ecstasies,
    Yet seeming still to hover;
There! where the flutter of his wings
Upon his back and body flings
Shadows and sunny glimmerings,
    That cover him all over.

My dazzled sight he oft deceives—
A Brother of the dancing leaves;
Then flits, and from the cottage-eaves
    Pours forth his song in gushes;
As if by that exulting strain
He mocked and treated with disdain
The voiceless Form he chose to feign,
    While fluttering in the bushes.

                              William Wordsworth

243   **To the Cuckoo**

O blithe newcomer! I have heard,
    I hear thee and rejoice:
O Cuckoo! shall I call thee Bird,
    Or but a wandering Voice?

While I am lying on the grass
    Thy twofold shout I hear;
From hill to hill it seems to pass,
    And once far off and near.

Though babbling only to the vale
    Of sunshine and of flowers,

Thou bringest unto me a tale
   Of visionary hours.

Thrice welcome, darling of the Spring!
   Even yet thou art to me
No bird, but an invisible thing,
   A voice, a mystery;

The same whom in my school-boy days
   I listen'd to; that Cry
Which made me look a thousand ways
   In bush, and tree, and sky.

To seek thee did I often rove
   Through woods and on the green;
And thou wert still a hope, a love;
   Still longed for, never seen.

And I can listen to thee yet;
   Can lie upon the plain
And listen, till I do beget
   That golden time again.

O blessèd Bird! the earth we pace
   Again appears to be
An unsubstantial, fairy place,
   That is fit home for Thee!

                 William Wordsworth

244   **Ode to a Nightingale**

My heart aches, and a drowsy numbness pains
   My sense, as though of hemlock I had drunk,
Or emptied some dull opiate to the drains
   One minute past, and Lethe-wards had sunk:
'Tis not through envy of thy happy lot,
   But being too happy in thine happiness,—
      That thou, light-wingèd Dryad of the trees,
        In some melodious plot
   Of beechen green, and shadows numberless,
    Singest of summer in full-throated ease.

O for a draught of vintage! that hath been
   Cool'd a long age in the deep-delvèd earth,
Tasting of Flora and the country green,
   Dance, and Provençal song, and sunburnt mirth!

O for a beaker full of the warm South,
  Full of the true, the blushful Hippocrene,
    With beaded bubbles winking at the brim,
      And purple-stainèd mouth;
  That I might drink, and leave the world unseen,
    And with thee fade away into the forest dim:

Fade far away, dissolve, and quite forget
  What thou among the leaves hast never known,
The weariness, the fever, and the fret
  Here, where men sit and hear each other groan;
Where palsy shakes a few, sad, last grey hairs,
  Where youth grows pale, and spectre-thin, and dies;
    Where but to think is to be full of sorrow
      And leaden-eyed despairs;
  Where Beauty cannot keep her lustrous eyes,
    Or new Love pine at them beyond to-morrow.

Away! away! for I will fly to thee,
  Not charioted by Bacchus and his pards,
But on the viewless wings of Poesy,
  Though the dull brain perplexes and retards:
Already with thee! tender is the night,
  And haply the Queen-Moon is on her throne,
    Cluster'd around by all her starry Fays;
      But here there is no light,
  Save what from heaven is with the breezes blown
    Through verdurous glooms and winding mossy ways.

I cannot see what flowers are at my feet,
  Nor what soft incense hangs upon the boughs,
But, in embalmed darkness, guess each sweet
  Wherewith the seasonable month endows
The grass, the thicket, and the fruit-tree wild;
  White hawthorn, and the pastoral eglantine;
    Fast-fading violets cover'd up in leaves;
      And mid-May's eldest child
  The coming musk-rose, full of dewy wine,
    The murmurous haunt of flies on summer eves.

Darkling I lisent; and, for many a time
  I have been half in love with easeful Death,
Call'd him soft names in many a musèd rhyme,
  To take into the air my quiet breath;
Now more than ever seems it rich to die,
  To cease upon the midnight with no pain,

While thou art pouring forth thy soul abroad
　　In such an ecstasy!
Still wouldst thou sing, and I have ears in vain—
　　To thy high requiem become a sod.

Thou wast not born for death, immortal Bird!
　　No hungry generations tread thee down;
The voice I hear this passing night was heard
　　In ancient days by emperor and clown:
Perhaps the self-same song that found a path
　　Through the sad heart of Ruth, when, sick for home,
　　　　She stood in tears amid the alien corn;
　　　　　　The same that oft-times hath
　　Charm'd magic casements, opening on the foam
　　　　Of perilous seas, in faery lands forlorn.

Forlorn! the very word is like a bell
　　To toll me back from thee to my sole self!
Adieu! the fancy cannot cheat so well
　　As she is famed to do, deceiving elf.
Adieu! adieu! thy plaintive anthem fades
　　Past the near meadows, over the still stream,
　　　　Up the hill-side; and now 'tis buried deep
　　　　　　In the next valley-glades:
　　Was it a vision, or a waking dream?
　　　　Fled is that music:—do I wake or sleep?

John Keats

245　　　　　　**Upon Westminster Bridge**

Earth has not anything to show more fair:
Dull would he be of soul who could pass by
A sight so touching in its majesty:
This City now doth like a garment wear
The beauty of the morning: silent, bare,
Ships, towers, domes, theatres, and temples lie
Open unto the fields, and to the sky,
All bright and glittering in the smokeless air.
Never did sun more beautifully steep
In his first splendour valley, rock, or hill;
Ne'er saw I, never felt, a calm so deep!
The river glideth at his own sweet will:
Dear God! the very houses seem asleep;
And all that mighty heart is lying still!

William Wordsworth

246 ### Ozymandias of Egypt

I met a traveller from an antique land
Who said: Two vast and trunkless legs of stone
Stand in the desert. Near them on the sand,
Half sunk, a shatter'd visage lies, whose frown
And wrinkled lip and sneer of cold command
Tell that its sculptor well those passions read
Which yet survive, stamp'd on these lifeless things,
The hand that mock'd them and the heart that fed;
And on the pedestal these words appear:
'My name is Ozymandias, king of kings:
Look on my works, ye Mighty, and despair!'
Nothing beside remains. Round the decay
Of that colossal wreck, boundless and bare,
The lone and level sands stretch far away.

Percy Bysshe Shelley

247 ### Composed at Neidpath Castle, the Property of Lord Queensberry: 1803

Degenerate Douglas! O the unworthy lord!
Whom were despite of heart could so far please
And love of havoc, (for with such disease
Fame taxes him,) that he could send forth word
To level with the dust a noble horde,
A brotherhood of venerable trees,
Leaving an ancient dome, and towers like these,
Beggar'd and outraged!—Many hearts deplored
The fate of those old trees; and oft with pain
The traveller at this day will stop and gaze
On wrongs, which Nature scarcely seems to heed:
For sheltered places, bosoms, nooks, and bays,
And the pure mountains, and the gentle Tweed,
And the green silent pastures, yet remain.

William Wordsworth

248 ### Admonition to a Traveller

Yes, there is holy pleasure in thine eye!
The lovely cottage in the guardian nook
Hath stirr'd thee deeply; with its own dear brook,
Its own small pasture, almost its own sky!
But covet not the abode; forbear to sigh
As many do, repining while they look;
Intruders who would tear from Nature's book

This precious leaf with harsh impiety:
Think what the home must be if it were thine,
Even thine, though few thy wants! Roof, window, door,
The very flowers are sacred to the Poor,
The roses to the porch which they entwine:
Yea, all that now enchants thee, from the day
On which it should be touch'd, would melt away!

William Wordsworth

249   **To the Highland Girl of Inversneyde**

Sweet Highland Girl, a very shower
Of beauty is thy earthly dower!
Twice seven consenting years have shed
Their utmost bounty on thy head:
And these grey rocks; that household lawn;
Those trees—a veil just half withdrawn;
This fall of water that doth make
A murmur near the silent lake;
This little bay; a quiet road
That holds in shelter thy abode;
In truth together do ye seem
Like something fashion'd in a dream;
Such forms as from their covert peep
When earthly cares are laid asleep!
But O fair Creature! in the light
Of common day, so heavenly bright,
I bless Thee, Vision as thou art,
I bless thee with a human heart:
God shield thee to thy latest years!
Thee, neither know I, nor thy peers;
And yet my eyes are fill'd with tears.

With earnest feeling I shall pray
For thee when I am far away;
For never saw I mien or face
In which more plainly I could trace
Benignity and home-bred sense
Ripening in perfect innocence.
Here scattered like a random seed,
Remote from men, Thou dost not need
The embarrassed look of shy distress,
And maidenly shamefacedness:
Thou wear'st upon thy forehead clear
The freedom of a mountaineer:
A face with gladness overspread;

Soft smiles, by human kindness bred;
And seemliness complete, that sways
Thy courtesies, about thee plays;
With no restraint, but such as springs
From quick and eager visitings
Of thoughts that lie beyond the reach
Of thy few words of English speech:
A bondage sweetly brook'd, a strife
That gives thy gestures grace and life!
So have I, not unmoved in mind,
Seen birds of tempest-loving kind
Thus beating up against the wind.

What hand but would a garland cull
For thee who art so beautiful?
O happy pleasure! here to dwell
Beside thee in some heathy dell;
Adopt your homely ways and dress,
A shepherd, thou a shepherdess!
But I could frame a wish for thee
More like a grave reality:
Thou art to me but as a wave
Of the wild sea: and I would have
Some claim upon thee, if I could,
Though but of common neighbourhood,
What joy to hear thee, and to see!
Thy elder brother I would be,
Thy father—anything to thee!

Now thanks to Heaven! that of its grace
Hath led me to this lonely place.
Joy have I had; and going hence
I bear away my recompense.
In spots like these it is we prize
Our memory, feel that she hath eyes:
Then why should I be loth to stir?
I feel this place was made for her;
To give new pleasure like the past,
Continued long as life shall last.
Nor am I loth, though pleased at heart,
Sweet Highland Girl! from thee to part;
For I, methinks, till I grow old,
As fair before me shall behold
As I do now, the cabin small,
The lake, the bay, the waterfall;
And Thee, the Spirit of them all!

William Wordsworth

The Reaper

Behold her, single in the field,
   Yon solitary Highland Lass!
Reaping and singing by herself;
   Stop here, or gently pass!
Alone she cuts and binds the grain,
And sings a melancholy strain;
O listen! for the vale profound
Is overflowing with the sound.

No nightingale did ever chant
   More welcome notes to weary bands
Of travellers in some shady haunt,
   Among Arabian sands:
A voice so thrilling ne'er was heard
In spring-time from the cuckoo-bird,
Breaking the silence of the seas
Among the farthest Hebrides.

Will no one tell me what she sings?
   Perhaps the plaintive numbers flow
For old, unhappy, far-off things,
   And battles long ago:
Or is it some more humble lay,
Familiar matter of to-day?
Some natural sorrow, loss, or pain,
That has been, and may be again?

Whate'er the theme, the maiden sang
   As if her song could have no ending;
I saw her singing at her work,
   And o'er the sickle bending;
I listen'd, motionless and still;
And, as I mounted up the hill,
The music in my heart I bore,
Long after it was heard no more.

William Wordsworth

The Reverie of Poor Susan

At the corner of Wood Street, when daylight appears,
Hangs a Thrush that sings loud, it has sung for three years;
Poor Susan has pass'd by the spot, and has heard
In the silence of morning the song of the bird.

'Tis a note of enchantment; what ails her? She sees
A mountain ascending, a vision of trees;

Bright volumes of vapour through Lothbury glide,
And a river flows on through the vale of Cheapside.

Green pastures she views in the midst of the dale,
Down which she so often has tripp'd with her pail;
And a single small cottage, a nest like a dove's,
The one only dwelling on earth that she loves.

She looks, and her heart is in heaven: but they fade,
The mist and the river, the hill and the shade;
The stream will not flow, and the hill will not rise,
And the colours have all pass'd away from her eyes!

William Wordsworth

252   **To a Lady, with a Guitar**

Ariel to Miranda:—Take
This slave of Music, for the sake
Of him who is the slave of thee;
And teach it all the harmony
In which thou canst, and only thou,
Make the delighted spirit glow,
Till joy denies itself again
And, too intense, is turn'd to pain.
For by permission and command
Of thine own Prince Ferdinand,
Poor Ariel sends this silent token
Of more than ever can be spoken;
Your guardian spirit, Ariel, who
From life to life must still pursue
Your happiness; for thus alone
Can Ariel ever find his own.
From Prospero's enchanted cell,
As the mighty verses tell,
To the throne of Naples he
Lit you o'er the trackless sea,
Flitting on, your prow before,
Like a living meteor.
When you die, the silent Moon
In her interlunar swoon
Is not sadder in her cell
Than deserted Ariel.
When you live again on earth,
Like an unseen star of birth
Ariel guides you o'er the sea
Of life from your nativity.

Many changes have been run
Since Ferdinand and you begun
Your course of love, and Ariel still
Has tracked your steps and served your will.
Now in humbler, happier lot,
This is all remember'd not;
And now, alas! the poor sprite is
Imprisoned for some fault of his
In a body like a grave;—
From you he dares to crave,
For his service and his sorrow,
A smile to-day, a song to-morrow.

The artist who this idol wrought
To echo all harmonious thought,
Felled a tree, while on the steep
The woods were in their winter sleep,
Rocked in that repose divine
On the wind-swept Apennine;
And dreaming, some of Autumn past,
And some of Spring approaching fast,
And some of April buds and showers,
And some of songs in July bowers,
And all of love; and so this tree,—
O that such our death may be!—
Died in sleep, and felt no pain,
To live in happier form again:
From which, beneath Heaven's fairest star,
The artist wrought this loved Guitar;
And taught it justly to reply
To all who question skilfully
In language gentle as thine own;
Whispering in enamoured tone
Sweet oracles of woods and dells,
And summer winds in sylvan cells;
—For it had learnt all harmonies
Of the plains and of the skies,
Of the forests and the mountains,
And the many-voicéd fountains;
The clearest echoes of the hills,
The softest notes of falling rills,
The melodies of birds and bees,
The murmuring of summer seas,
And pattering rain, and breathing dew,
And airs of evening; and it knew
That seldom-heard mysterious sound
Which, driven on its diurnal round,

As it floats through boundless day,
Our world enkindles on its way:
—All this it knows, but will not tell
To those who cannot question well
The Spirit that inhabits it;
It talks according to the wit
Of its companions; and no more
Is heard than has been felt before
By those who tempt it to betray
These secrets of an elder day.
But, sweetly as its answers will
Flatter hands of perfect skill,
It keeps its highest holiest tone
For our belovéd friend alone.

Percy Bysshe Shelley

253   The Daffodils

I wandered lonely as a cloud
    That floats on high o'er vales and hills,
When all at once I saw a crowd,
    A host, of golden daffodils,
Beside the lake, beneath the trees,
Fluttering and dancing in the breeze.

Continuous as the stars that shine
    And twinkle on the milky way,
They stretched in never-ending line
    Along the margin of a bay:
Ten thousand saw I at a glance
Tossing their heads in sprightly dance.

The waves beside them danced, but they
    Out-did the sparkling waves in glee:
A Poet could not but be gay
    In such a jocund company!
I gazed—and gazed—but little thought
What wealth the show to me had brought:

For oft, when on my couch I lie
    In vacant or inpensive mood,
They flash upon that inward eye
    Which is the bliss of solitude;
And then my heart with pleasure fills,
And dances with the daffodils.

William Wordsworth

To the Daisy

With little here to do or see
Of things that in the great world be,
Daisy! again I talk to thee,
        For thou art worthy,
Thou unassuming Commonplace
Of Nature, with that homely face,
And yet with something of a grace
        Which love makes for thee!

Oft on the dappled turf at ease
I sit and play with similes,
Loose types of things through all degrees,
        Thoughts of thy raising;
And many a fond and idle name
I give to thee, for praise or blame,
As is the humour of the game,
        While I am gazing.

A nun demure, of lowly port;
Or sprightly maiden, of Love's court,
In thy simplicity the sport
        Of all temptations;
A queen in crown of rubies drest;
A starveling in a scanty vest;
Are all, as seems to suit thee best,
        Thy appellations.

A little Cyclops, with one eye
Staring to threaten and defy,
That thought comes next—and instantly
        The freak is over.
The shape will vanish, and behold!
A silver shield with boss of gold
That spreads itself, some fairy bold
        In fight to cover.

I see thee glittering from afar—
And then thou art a pretty star,
Not quite so fair as many are
        In heaven above thee!
Yet like a star, with glittering crest,
Self-poised in air thou seem'st to rest—
May peace come never to his nest
        Who shall reprove thee!

Sweet Flower! for by that name at last
When all my reveries are past

I call thee, and to that cleave fast,
    Sweet silent creature!
That breath'st with me in sun and air,
Do thou, as thou are wont, repair
My heart with gladness, and a share
    Of thy meek nature!

William Wordsworth

255   Ode to Autumn

Season of mists and mellow fruitfulness,
    Close bosom-friend of the maturing sun;
Conspiring with him how to load and bless
    With fruit the vines that round the thatch-eaves run;
To bend with apples the moss'd cotttage-trees,
    And fill all fruit with ripeness to the core;
      To swell the gourd, and plump the hazel shells
    With a sweet kernel; to set budding more,
And still more, later flowers for the bees,
Until they think warm days will never cease;
      For Summer has o'erbrimm'd their clammy cells.

Who hath not seen thee oft amid thy store?
    Sometimes whoever seeks abroad may find
Thee sitting careless on a granary floor,
    Thy hair soft-lifted by the winnowing wind;
Or on a half-reap'd furrow sound asleep,
    Drowns'd with the fume of poppies, while thy hook
      Spares the next swath and all its twinéd flowers;
And sometimes like a gleaner thou dost keep
    Steady thy laden head across a brook;
    Or by a cider-press, with patient look,
      Thou watchest the last oozings, hours by hours.

Where are the songs of Spring? Aye, where are they?
    Think not of them,—thou hast thy music too,
While barréd clouds bloom the soft-dying day
    And touch the stubble-plains with rosy hue;
Then in a wailful choir the small gnats mourn
    Among the river sallows, borne aloft
      Or sinking as the light wind lives or dies;
And full-grown lambs loud bleat from hilly bourn;
    Hedge-crickets sing, and now with treble soft
    The redbreast whistles from a garden-croft,
      And gathering swallows twitter in the skies.

John Keats

Ode to Winter

When first the fiery-mantled Sun
His heavenly race began to run,
Round the earth and ocean blue
His children four the Seasons flew:—
   First, in green apparel dancing,
The young Spring smiled with angel-grace;
   Rosy Summer, next advancing,
Rush'd into her sire's embrace—
Her bright-hair'd sire, who bade her keep
   For ever nearest to his smiles.
On Calpe's olive-shaded steep
   Or India's citron-cover'd isles.
More remote, and buxom-brown,
   The Queen of vintage bow'd before his throne;
A rich pomegranate gemm'd her crown,
   A ripe sheaf bound her zone.

But howling Winter fled afar
To hills that prop the polar star;
And loves on deer-borne car to ride
With barren darkness at his side,
   Round the shore where loud Lofoden
   Whirls to death the roaring whale,
   Round the hall where Runic Odin
   Howls his war-song to the gale—
Save when adown the ravaged globe
   He travels on his native storm,
Deflowering Nature's grassy robe
   And trampling on her faded form;
Till light's returning lord assume
   The shaft that drives him to his polar field,
Of power to pierce his raven plume
   And crystal-cover'd shield.

O sire of storms! whose savage ear
The Lapland drum delights to hear,
When Frenzy with her bloodshot eye
Implores thy dreadful deity—
   Archangel! power of desolation!
   Fast descending as thou art,
Say hath mortal invocation
   Spells to touch thy stony heart?
Then, sullen Winter! hear my prayer
And gently rule the ruin'd year;
Nor chill the wanderer's bosom bare,

Nor freeze the wretch's falling tear:
To shuddering Want's unmantled bed
    Thy horror-breathing agues cease to lend,
And gently on the orphan head
    Of innocence descend.

But chiefly spare, O king of clouds!
The sailor on his airy shrouds,
When wrecks and beacons strew the steep
And spectres walk along the deep.
Milder yet thy snowy breezes
    Pour on yonder tented shores,
Where the Rhine's broad billow freezes,
    Or the dark-brown Danube roars.
Or winds of Winter! list ye there
    To many a deep and dying groan?
Or start, ye demons of the midnight air,
    At shrieks and thunders louder than your own?
Alas! e'en your unhallow'd breath
    May spare the victim fallen low;
But man will ask no truce to death,
    No bounds to human woe.

                                Thomas Campbell

257   **Yarrow Unvisited: 1803**

From Stirling Castle we had seen
    The mazy Forth unravell'd,
Had trod the banks of Clyde and Tay,
    And with the Tweed had travell'd;
And when we came to Clovenford,
    Then said my 'winsome Marrow,'
'Whate'er betide, we'll turn aside,
    And see the Braes of Yarrow.'

'Let Yarrow folk, frae Selkirk town,
    Who have been buying, selling,
Go back to Yarrow, 'tis their own,
    Each maiden to her dwelling!
On Yarrow's banks let herons feed,
    Hares couch, and rabbits burrow,
But we will downward with the Tweed,
    Nor turn aside to Yarrow.

'There's Galla Water, Leader Haughs,
    Both lying right before us:

And Dryburgh, where with chiming Tweed
    The lintwhites sing in chorus;
There's pleasant Tiviot-dale, a land
    Made blithe with plough and harrow;
Why throw away a needful day
    To go in search of Yarrow?

'What's Yarrow but a river bare
    That glides the dark hills under?
There are a thousand such elsewhere
    As worthy of your wonder.'
—Strange words they seem'd of slight and scorn;
    My True-love sigh'd for sorrow,
And look'd me in the face, to think
    I thus could speak of Yarrow!

'O green,' said I, 'are Yarrow's holms,
    And sweet is Yarrow flowing!
Fair hangs the apple frae the rock,
    But we will leave it growing.
O'er hilly path and open Strath
    We'll wander Scotland thorough;
But, though so near, we will not turn
    Into the dale of Yarrow.

'Let beeves and home-bred kine partake
    The sweets of Burn-mill meadow;
The swan on still St. Mary's Lake
    Float double, swan and shadow!
We will not see them; will not go
    To-day, nor yet to-morrow;
Enough if in our hearts we know
    There's such a place as Yarrow.

'Be Yarrow stream unseen, unknown!
    It must, or we shall rue it:
We have a vision of our own,
    Ah! why should we undo it?
The treasured dreams of times long past,
    We'll keep them, winsome Marrow!
For when we're there, although 'tis fair,
    'Twill be another Yarrow!

'If Care with freezing years should come,
    And wandering seem but folly,—
Should we be loth to stir from home,
    And yet be melancholy;

Should life be dull, and spirits low,
  'Twill soothe us in our sorrow
That earth has something yet to show,
  The bonny holms of Yarrow!'

William Wordsworth

258   **Yarrow Visited: 1814**

And is this—Yarrow?—*This* the Stream
  Of which my fancy cherish'd
So faithfully, a waking dream,
  An image that hath perish'd?
O that some Minstrel's harp were near
  To utter notes of gladness
And chase this silence from the air,
  That fills my heart with sadness!

Yet why?—a silvery current flows
  With uncontroll'd meanderings;
Nor have these eyes by greener hills
  Been soothed, in all my wanderings.
And, through her depths, St. Mary's Lake
  Is visibly delighted;
For not a feature of those hills
  Is in the mirror slighted.

A blue sky bends o'er Yarrow Vale,
  Save where that pearly whiteness
Is round the rising sun diffused,
  A tender hazy brightness;
Mild dawn of promise! that excludes
  All profitless dejection;
Though not unwilling here to admit
  A pensive recollection.

Where was it that the famous Flower
  Of Yarrow Vale lay bleeding?
His bed perchance was yon smooth mound
  On which the herd is feeding:
And haply from this crystal pool,
  Now peaceful as the morning,
The Water-wraith ascended thrice,
  And gave his doleful warning.

Delicious is the Lay that sings
  The haunts of happy lovers,

The path that leads them to the grove,
   The leafy grove that covers:
And pity sanctifies the verse
   That paints, by strength of sorrow,
The unconquerable strength of love;
   Bear witness, rueful Yarrow!

But thou, that didst appear so fair
   To fond imagination,
Dost rival in the light of day
   Her delicate creation:
Meek loveliness is round thee spread,
   A softness still and holy:
The grace of forest charms decay'd,
   And pastoral melancholy.

That region left, the vale unfolds,
   Rich groves of lofty stature,
With Yarrow winding through the pomp
   Of cultivated nature;
And, rising from those lofty groves,
   Behold a ruin hoary,
The shatter'd front of Newark's Towers,
   Renown'd in Border story.

Fair scenes for childhood's opening bloom,
   For sportive youth to stray in,
For manhood to enjoy his strength,
   And age to wear away in!
Yon cottage seems a bower of bliss,
   A covert for protection
Of tender thoughts, that nestle there—
   The brood of chaste affection.

How sweet on this autumnal day
   The wild-wood fruits to gather,
And on my True-love's forehead plant
   A crest of blooming heather!
And what if I enwreathed my own?
   'Twere no offence to reason;
The sober hills thus deck their brows
   To meet the wintry season.

I see—but not by sight alone,
   Loved Yarrow, have I won thee;
A ray of Fancy still survives—
   Her sunshine plays upon thee!

Thy ever-youthful waters keep
    A course of lively pleasure;
And gladsome notes my lips can breathe
    Accordant to the measure.

The vapours linger round the heights,
    They melt, and soon must vanish;
One hour is theirs, nor more is mine—
    Sad thought! which I would banish,
But that I know, where'er I go,
    Thy genuine image, Yarrow!
Will dwell with me—to heighten joy,
    And cheer my mind in sorrow.

                         William Wordsworth

259   **The Invitation**

Best and brightest, come away,
Fairer far than this fair Day,
Which, like thee to those in sorrow,
Comes to bid a sweet good-morrow
To the rough Year just awake
In its cradle on the brake.
The brightest hour of unborn Spring
Through the winter wandering,
Found, it seems, the halcyon Morn
To hoar February born;
Bending from Heaven, in azure mirth,
It kiss'd the forehead of the Earth,
And smiled upon the silent sea,
And bade the frozen streams be free,
And waked to music all their fountains,
And breathed upon the frozen mountains,
And like a prophetess of May
Strew'd flowers upon the barren way,
Making the wintry world appear
Like one on whom thou smilest, dear.

Away, away, from men and towns,
To the wild wood and the downs—
To the silent wilderness
Where the soul need not repress
Its music, lest it should not find
An echo in another's mind,
While the touch of Nature's art
Harmonizes heart to heart.

Radiant Sister of the Day
Awake! arise! and come away!
To the wild woods and the plains,
And the pools where winter rains
Image all their roof of leaves,
Where the pine its garland weaves
Of sapless green and ivy dun
Round stems that never kiss the sun;
Where the lawns and pastures be
And the sandhills of the sea;
Where the melting hoar-frost wets
The daisy-star that never sets,
And wind-flowers and violets,
Which yet join not scent to hue,
Crown the pale year weak and new;
When the night is left behind
In the deep east, dun and blind,
And the blue noon is over us,
And the multitudinous
Billows murmur at our feet,
Where the earth and ocean meet,
And all things seem only one
In the universal sun.

Percy Bysshe Shelley

260   **The Recollection**

Now the last day of many days,
    All beautiful and bright as thou,
        The loveliest and the last, is dead,
Rise, Memory, and write its praise!
Up,—to thy wonted work! come, trace
        The epitaph of glory fled,
For now the Earth has changed its face,
    A frown is on the Heaven's brow.

We wander'd to the Pine Forest
    That skirts the Ocean's foam;
The lightest wind was in its nest,
    The tempest in its home.
The whispering waves were half asleep,
    The clouds were gone to play,
And on the bosom of the deep
    The smile of Heaven lay;
It seem'd as if the hour were one
    Sent from beyond the skies

Which scatter'd from above the sun
   A light of Paradise.

We paused amid the pines that stood
   The giants of the waste,
Tortured by storms to shapes as rude
   As serpents interlaced,
And soothed by every azure breath
   That under Heaven is blown
To harmonies and hues beneath,
   As tender as its own:
Now all the tree-tops lay asleep
   Like green waves on the sea,
As still as in the silent deep
   The ocean woods may be.

How calm it was!—the silence there
   By such a chain was bound,
That even the busy woodpecker
   Made stiller by her sound
The inviolable quietness;
   The breath of peace we drew
With its soft motion made not less
   The calm that round us grew.
There seem'd from the remotest seat
   Of the wide mountain waste,
To the soft flower beneath our feet
   A magic circle traced,—
A spirit interfused around,
   A thrilling silent life;
To momentary peace it bound
   Our mortal nature's strife;—
And still I felt the centre of
   The magic circle there
Was one fair form that fill'd with love
   The lifeless atmosphere.

We paused beside the pools that lie
   Under the forest bough;
Each seem'd as 'twere a little sky
   Gulf'd in a world below;
A firmament of purple light
   Which in the dark earth lay,
More boundless than the depth of night,
   And purer than the day—
In which the lovely forests grew

As in the upper air,
More perfect both in shape and hue
  Than any spreading there.
There lay the glade and neighbouring lawn,
  And through the dark green wood
The white sun twinkling like the dawn
  Out of a speckled cloud.
Sweet views which in our world above
  Can never well be seen
Were imaged by the water's love
  Of that fair forest green:
And all was interfused beneath
  With an Elysian glow,
An atmosphere without a breath,
  A softer day below.
Like one beloved, the scene had lent
  To the dark water's breast
Its every leaf and lineament
  With more than truth exprest;
Until an envious wind crept by,
  Like an unwelcome thought
Which from the mind's too faithful eye
  Blots one dear image out.
Though thou art ever fair and kind,
  The forests ever green,
Less oft is peace in Shelley's mind
  Than calm in waters seen.

Percy Bysshe Shelley

261

By the Sea

It is a beauteous evening, calm and free;
The holy time is quiet as a Nun
Breathless with adoration; the broad sun
Is sinking down in its tranquillity;
The gentleness of heaven broods o'er the Sea:
Listen! the mighty Being is awake,
And doth with his eternal motion make
A sound like thunder—everlastingly.
Dear child! dear girl! that walkest with me here,
If thou appear untouch'd by solemn thought
Thy nature is not therefore less divine:
Thou liest in Abraham's bosom all the year,
And worshipp'st at the Temple's inner shrine,
God being with thee when we know it not.

William Wordsworth

262
To the Evening Star

Star that bringest home the bee,
And sett'st the weary labourer free!
   If any star shed peace, 'tis thou,
    That send'st it from above,
   Appearing when Heaven's breath and brow
    Are sweet as hers we love.

Come to the luxuriant skies,
Whilst the landscape's odours rise,
   Whilst far-off lowing herds are heard,
    And songs when toil is done,
   From cottages whose smoke unstirr'd
    Curls yellow in the sun.

Star of love's soft interviews,
Parted lovers on thee muse;
   Their remembrancer in Heaven
    Of thrilling vows thou art,
   Too delicious to be riven
    By absence from the heart.

Thomas Campbell

263
Datur Hora Quieti

The sun upon the lake is low,
   The wild birds hush their song,
The hills have evening's deepest glow,
   Yet Leonard tarries long.
Now all whom varied toil and care
   From home and love divide,
In the calm sunset may repair
   Each to the loved one's side.

The noble dame on turret high,
   Who waits her gallant knight,
Looks to the western beam to spy
   The flash of armour bright.
The village maid, with hand on brow
   The level ray to shade,
Upon the footpath watches now
   For Colin's darkening plaid.

Now to their mates the wild swans row,
   By day they swam apart,

And to the thicket wanders slow
  The hind beside the hart.
The woodlark at his partner's side
  Twitters his closing song—
All meet whom day and care divide,
  But Leonard tarries long!

Sir Walter Scott

264 ### To the Moon

Art thou pale for weariness
Of climbing heaven, and gazing on the earth,
  Wandering companionless
Among the stars that have a different birth,—
And ever-changing, like a joyless eye
That finds no object worth its constancy?

Percy Bysshe Shelley

265

A widow bird sate mourning for her love
  Upon a wintry bough;
The frozen wind crept on above,
  The freezing stream below.

There was no leaf upon the forest bare,
  No flower upon the ground,
And little motion in the air
  Except the mill-wheel's sound.

Percy Bysshe Shelley

266 ### To Sleep

A flock of sheep that leisurely pass by,
One after one; the sound of rain, and bees
Murmuring; the fall of rivers, winds and seas,
Smooth fields, white sheets of water, and pure sky;
I have thought of all by turns, and yet do lie
Sleepless; and soon the small birds' melodies
Must hear, first uttered from my orchard trees,
And the first cuckoo's melancholy cry.
Even thus last night, and two nights more, I lay,
And could not win thee, Sleep! by any stealth:
So do not let me wear to-night away:
Without Thee what is all the morning's wealth?
Come, blessèd barrier between day and day,
Dear mother of fresh thoughts and joyous health!

William Wordsworth

267   **The Soldier's Dream**

Our bugles sang truce, for the night-cloud had lower'd,
 And the sentinel stars set their watch in the sky;
And thousands had sunk on the ground overpowere'd,
 The weary to sleep, and the wounded to die.

When reposing that night on my pallet of straw
 By the wolf-scaring faggot that guarded the slain,
At the dead of the night a sweet vision I saw;
 And thrice ere the morning I dreamt it again.

Methought from the battle-field's dreadful array
 Far, far I had roam'd on a desolate track:
'Twas autumn,—and sunshine arose on the way
 To the home of my fathers, that welcomed me back.

I flew to the pleasant fields traversed so oft
 In life's morning march, when my bosom was young;
I heard my own mountain-goats bleating aloft,
 And knew the sweet strain that the corn-reapers sung.

Then pledged we the wine-cup, and fondly I swore
 From my home and my weeping friends never to part;
My little ones kiss'd me a thousand times o'er,
 And my wife sobb'd aloud in her fullness of heart.

'Stay—stay with us!—rest!—thou art weary and worn!'—
 And fain was their war-broken soldier to stay;—
But sorrow return'd with the dawning of morn,
 And the voice in my dreaming ear melted away.
        Thomas Campbell

268   **A Dream of the Unknown**

I dream'd that as I wander'd by the way
 Bare Winter suddenly was changed to Spring,
And gentle odours led my steps astray,
 Mix'd with a sound of waters murmuring
Along a shelving bank of turf, which lay
 Under a copse, and hardly dared to fling
Its green arms round the bosom of the stream,
But kiss'd it and then fled, as thou mightest in dream.

There grew pied wind-flowers and violets,
 Daisies, those pearl'd Arcturi of the earth,

The constellated flower that never sets;
  Faint oxlips; tender blue-bells, at whose birth
The sod scarce heaved; and that tall flower that wets—
  Like a child, half in tenderness and mirth—
Its mother's face with heaven's collected tears,
When the low wind, its playmate's voice, it hears.

And in the warm hedge grew lush eglantine,
  Green cow-bind and the moonlight-colour'd may,
And cherry-blossoms, and white cups, whose wine
  Was the bright dew yet drain'd not by the day;
And wild roses, and ivy serpentine
  With its dark buds and leaves, wandering astray;
And flowers azure, black and streak'd with gold,
Fairer than any waken'd eyes behold.

And nearer to the river's trembling edge
  There grew broad flag-flowers, purple prank with white,
And starry river buds among the sedge,
  And floating water-lilies, broad and bright,
Which lit the oak that overhung the hedge
  With moonlight beams of their own watery light;
And bulrushes, and reeds of such deep green
As soothed the dazzled eye with sober sheen.

Methought that of these visionary flowers
  I made a nosegay, bound in such a way
That the same hues, which in their natural bowers
  Were mingled or opposed, the like array
Kept these imprison'd children of the Hours
  Within my hand,—and then, elate and gay,
I hasten'd to the spot whence I had come,
That I might there present it—O! to Whom?

Percy Bysshe Shelley

69   The Inner Vision

Most sweet it is with unuplifted eyes
To pace the ground, if path be there or none,
While a fair region round the traveller lies
Which he forbears again to look upon;
Pleased rather with some soft ideal scene,
The work of Fancy, or some happy tone
Of meditation, slipping in between
The beauty coming and the beauty gone.
If Thought and Love desert us, from that day

Let us break off all commerce with the Muse:
With Thought and Love companions of our way—
Whate'er the senses take or may refuse,—
The Mind's internal heaven shall shed her dews
Of inspiration on the humblest lay.

William Wordswor.

270   **The Realm of Fancy**

Ever let the Fancy roam!
Pleasure never is at home:
At a touch sweet Pleasure melteth,
Like to bubbles when rain pelteth;
Then let wingéd Fancy wander
Through the thought still spread beyond her:
Open wide the mind's cage-door,
She'll dart forth, and cloudward soar.
O sweet Fancy! let her loose;
Summer's joys are spoilt by use,
And the enjoying of the Spring
Fades as does its blossoming:
Autumn's red-lipp'd fruitage too,
Blushing through the mist and dew,
Cloys with tasting: What do then?
Sit thee by the ingle, when
The sear faggot blazes bright,
Spirit of a winter's night;
When the soundless earth is muffled,
And the cakéd snow is shuffled
From the ploughboy's heavy shoon;
When the Night doth meet the Noon
In a dark conspiracy
To banish Even from her sky.
—Sit thee there, and send abroad,
With a mind self-overawed,
Fancy, high-commission'd:—send her!
She has vassals to attend her;
She will bring, in spite of frost,
Beauties that the earth hath lost;
She will bring thee, all together,
All delights of summer weather;
All the buds and bells of May
From dewy sward or thorny spray;
All the heapéd Autumn's wealth,
With a still, mysterious stealth;
She will mix these pleasures up

Like three fit wines in a cup,
And thou shalt quaff it;—thou shalt hear
Distant harvest-carols clear;
Rustle of the reapéd corn;
Sweet birds antheming the morn:
And in the same moment—hark!
'Tis the early April lark,
Or the rooks, with busy caw,
Foraging for sticks and straw.
Thou shalt, at one glance, behold
The daisy and the marigold;
White-plumed lilies, and the first
Hedge-grown primrose that hath burst;
Shaded hyacinth, alay
Sapphire queen of the mid-May;
And every leaf, and every flower
Pearléd with the self-same shower.
Thou shalt see the field-mouse peep
Meagre from its celléd sleep;
And the snake all winter-thin
Cast on sunny bank its skin;
Freckled nest-eggs thou shalt see
Hatching in the hawthorn-tree,
When the hen-bird's wing doth rest
Quiet on her mossy nest;
Then the hurry and alarm
When the bee-hive casts its swarm;
Acorns ripe down-pattering
While the autumn breezes sing.

O sweet Fancy! let her loose;
Everything is spoilt by use:
Where's the cheek that doth not fade,
Too much gazed at? Where's the maid
Whose lip mature is ever new?
Where's the eye, however blue,
Doth not weary? Where's the face
One would meet in every place?
Where's the voice, however soft,
One would hear so very oft?
At a touch sweet Pleasure melteth.
Like to bubbles when rain pelteth.
Let them wingéd Fancy find
Thee a mistress to thy mind:
Dulcet-eyed as Ceres' daughter,
Ere the God of Torment taught her
How to frown and how to chide;

With a waist and with a side
White as Hebe's, when her zone
Slipt its golden clasp, and down
Fell her kirtle to her feet,
While she held the goblet sweet,
And Jove grew languid.—Break the mesh
Of the Fancy's silken leash;
Quickly break her prison-string,
And such joys as these she'll bring.
—Let the wingèd Fancy roam!
Pleasure never is at home.

John Keats

271   Hymn to the Spirit of Nature

Life of Life! thy lips enkindle
    With their love the breath between them;
And thy smiles before they dwindle
    Make the cold air fire; then screen them
In those looks, where whoso gazes
Faints, entangled in their mazes.

Child of Light! thy limbs are burning
    Through the vest which seems to hide them,
As the radiant lines of morning
    Through the clouds, ere they divide them;
And this atmosphere divinest
Shrouds thee wheresoe'er thou shinest.

Fair are others: none beholds thee;
    But thy voice sounds low and tender
Like the fairest, for it folds thee
    From the sight, that liquid spendour;
And all feel, yet see thee never,—
As I feel now, lost for ever!

Lamp of Earth! where'er thou movest
    Its dim shapes are clad with brightness.
And the souls of whom thou lovest
    Walk upon the winds with lightness
Till they fail, as I am failing,
Dizzy, lost, yet unbewailing!

Percy Bysshe Shelley

Written in Early Spring

I heard a thousand blended notes
　　While in a grove I sat reclined,
In that sweet mood when pleasant thoughts
　　Bring sad thoughts to the mind.

To her fair works did Nature link
　　The human soul that through me ran;
And much it grieved my heart to think
　　What man has made of man.

Through primrose tufts, in that green bower,
　　The periwinkle trail'd its wreaths;
And 'tis my faith that every flower
　　Enjoys the air it breathes.

The birds around me hopp'd and play'd,
　　Their thoughts I cannot measure—
But the least motion which they made
　　It seem'd a thrill of pleasure.

The budding twigs spread out their fan
　　To catch the breezy air;
And I must think, do all I can,
　　That there was pleasure there.

If this belief from heaven be sent,
　　If such be Nature's holy plan,
Have I not reason to lament
　　What man has made of man?

William Wordsworth

Ruth: Or the Influences of Nature

When Ruth was left half desolate
Her father took another mate;
　　And Ruth, not seven years old,
A slighted child, at her own will
Went wandering over dale and hill,
　　In thoughtless freedom, bold.
And she had made a pipe of straw,
And music from that pipe could draw
　　Like sounds of winds and floods;
Had built a bower upon the green,
As if she from her birth had been

An infant of the woods.
Beneath her father's roof, alone
She seem'd to live; her thoughts her own;
    Herself her own delight:
Pleased with herself, nor sad nor gay,
And, passing thus the live-long day,
    She grew to woman's height.

There came a youth from Georgia's shore—
A military casque he wore
    With splendid feathers drest;
He brought them from the Cherokees;
The feathers nodded in the breeze
    And made a gallant crest.

From Indian blood you deem him sprung:
But no! he spake the English tongue
    And bore a soldier's name;
And, when America was free
From battle and from jeopardy,
    He 'cross the ocean came.

With hues of genius on his cheek,
In finest tones the youth could speak:
    —While he was yet a boy
The moon, the glory of the sun,
And streams that murmur as they run,
    Had been his dearest joy.

He was a lovely youth! I guess
The panther in the wilderness
    Was not so fair as he;
And when he chose to sport and play,
No dolphin ever was so gay
    Upon the tropic sea.

Among the Indians he had fought;
And with him many tales he brought
    Of pleasure and of fear;
Such tales as, told to any maid
By such a youth, in the green shade,
    Were perilous to hear.

He told of girls, a happy rout!
Who quit their fold with dance and shout,
    Their pleasant Indian town,
To gather strawberries all day long;
Returning with a choral song
    When daylight is gone down.

He spake of plants that hourly change
Their blossoms, through a boundless range
    Of intermingling hues;
With budding, fading, faded flowers,

They stand the wonder of the bowers
  From morn to evening dews.
He told of the magnolia, spread
High as a cloud, high over head!
  The cypress and her spire;
—Of flowers that with one scarlet gleam
Cover a hundred leagues, and seem
  To set the hills on fire.
The youth of green savannahs spake,
And many an endless, endless lake
  With all its fairy crowds
Of islands, that together lie
As quietly as spots of sky
  Among the evening clouds.
'How pleasant,' then he said, 'it were
A fisher or a hunter there,
  In sunshine or in shade
To wander with an easy mind,
And build a household fire, and find
  A home in every glade!
What days and what bright years! Ah me!
Our life were life indeed, with thee
  So pass'd in quiet bliss;
And all the while,' said he, 'to know
That we were in a world of woe,
  On such an earth as this!'
And then he sometimes interwove
Fond thoughts about a father's love,
  'For there,' said he, 'are spun
Around the heart such tender ties,
That our own children to our eyes
  Are dearer than the sun.
Sweet Ruth! and could you go with me
My helpmate in the woods to be,
  Our shed at night to rear;
Or run, my own adopted bride,
A sylvan huntress at my side,
  And drive the flying deer!
Beloved Ruth!'—No more he said.
The wakeful Ruth at midnight shed
  A solitary tear:
She thought again—and did agree
With him to sail across the sea,
  And drive the flying deer.
'And now, as fitting is and right,
We in the church our faith will plight,
  A husband and a wife.'

Even so they did; and I may say
That to sweet Ruth that happy day
   Was more than human life.
Through dream and vision did she sink,
Delighted all the while to think
   That, on those lonesome floods
And green savannahs, she should share
His board with lawful joy, and bear
   His name in the wild woods.

But, as you have before been told,
This Stripling, sportive, gay, and bold,
   And with his dancing crest
So beautiful, through savage lands
Had roam'd about, with vagrant bands
   Of Indians in the West.

The wind, the tempest roaring high,
The tumult of a tropic sky
   Might well be dangerous food
For him, a youth to whom was given
So much of earth—so much of heaven,
   And such impetuous blood.

Whatever in those climes he found
Irregular in sight or sound
   Did to his mind impart
A kindred impulse, seem'd allied
To his own powers, and justified
   The workings of his heart.

Nor less, to feed voluptuous thought,
The beauteous forms of Nature wrought,—
   Fair trees and gorgeous flowers;
The breezes their own languor lent;
The stars had feelings, which they sent
   Into those favour'd bowers.

Yet, in his worst pursuits, I ween
That sometimes there did intervene
   Pure hopes of high intent:
For passions, link'd to forms so fair
And stately, needs must have their share
   Of noble sentiment.

But ill he lived, much evil saw,
With men to whom no better law
   Nor better life was known;
Deliberately and undeceived
Those wild men's vices he received,
   And gave them back his own.

His genius and his moral frame
Were thus impair'd, and he became

The slave of low desires:
A man who without self-control
Would seek what the degraded soul
   Unworthily admires.
And yet he with no feign'd delight
Had woo'd the maiden, day and night
   Had loved her, night and morn:
What could he less than love a maid
Whose heart with so much nature play'd—
   So kind and so forlorn?
Sometimes most earnestly he said,
'O Ruth! I have been worse than dead;
   False thoughts, thoughts bold and vain
Encompass'd me on every side
When I, in confidence and pride,
   Had cross'd the Atlantic main.
Before me shone a glorious world
Fresh as a banner bright, unfurl'd
   To music suddenly:
I looked upon those hills and plains,
And seem'd as if let loose from chains
   To live at liberty.
No more of this—for now, by thee,
Dear Ruth! more happily set free,
   With nobler zeal I burn;
My soul from darkness is released
Like the whole sky when to the east
   The morning doth return.'
Full soon that better mind was gone;
No hope, no wish remain'd, not one,—
   They stirr'd him now no more;
New objects did new pleasure give,
And once again he wish'd to live
   As lawless as before.
Meanwhile, as thus with him it fared,
They for the voyage were prepared,
   And went to the sea-shore:
But, when they thither came, the youth
Deserted his poor bride, and Ruth
   Could never find him more.
God help thee, Ruth!—Such pains she had,
That she in half a year was mad,
   And in a prison housed;
And there, with many a doleful song
Made of wild words, her cup of wrong
   She fearfuly caroused.
Yet sometimes milder hours she knew,

Nor wanted sun, nor rain, nor dew,
　Nor pastimes of the May,
—They all were with her in her cell;
And a clear brook with cheerful knell
　Did o'er the pebbles play.

When Ruth three seasons thus had lain,
There came a respite to her pain;
　She from her prison fled;
But of the Vagrant none took thought;
And where it liked her best she sought
　Her shelter and her bread.

Among the fields she breathed again:
The master-current of her brain
　Ran permanent and free;
And, coming to the banks of Tone,
There did she rest; and dwell alone
　Under the greenwood tree.

The engines of her pain, the tools
That shaped her sorrow, rocks and pools,
　And airs that gently stir
The vernal leaves—she loved them still,
Nor ever tax'd them with the ill
　Which had been done to her.

A barn her winter bed supplies;
But, till the warmth of summer skies
　And summer days is gone,
(And all do in this tale agree)
She sleeps beneath the greenwood tree,
　And other home hath none.

An innocent life, yet far astray!
And Ruth will, long before her day,
　Be broken down and old.
Sore aches she needs must have! but less
Of mind, than body's wretchedness,
　From damp, and rain, and cold.

If she is prest by want of food
She from her dwelling in the wood
　Repairs to a road-side;
And there she begs at one steep place,
Where up and down with easy pace
　The horsemen-travellers ride.

That oaten pipe of hers is mute
Or thrown away: but with a flute
　Her loneliness she cheers;
This flute, made of a hemlock stalk,
At evening in his homeward walk
　The Quantock woodman hears.

I, too, have pass'd her on the hills
Setting her little water-mills
   By spouts and fountains wild—
Such small machinery as she turn'd
Ere she had wept, ere she had mourn'd,
   A young and happy child!
Farewell! and when thy days are told,
Ill-fated Ruth! in hallow'd mould
   Thy corpse shall buried be;
For thee a funeral bell shall ring,
And all the congregation sing
   A Christian psalm for thee.

William Wordsworth

274   **Written in the Euganean Hills, North Italy**

Many a green isle needs must be
In the deep wide sea of misery,
Or the mariner, worn and wan,
Never thus could voyage on
Day and night, and night and day,
Drifting on his dreary way,
With the solid darkness black
Closing round his vessel's track;
Whilst above, the sunless sky,
Big with clouds, hangs heavily,
And behind, the tempest fleet
Hurries on with lightning feet,
Riving sail, and cord, and plank,
Till the ship has almost drank
Death from the o'er-brimming deep;
And sinks down, down, like that sleep
When the dreamer seems to be
Weltering through eternity;
And the dim low line before
Of a dark and distant shore
Still recedes, as ever still
Longing with divided will,
But no power to seek or shun,
He is ever drifted on
O'er the unreposing wave,
To the haven of the grave.

Aye, many flowering islands lie
In the waters of wide Agony:
To such a one this morn was led

My bark, by soft winds piloted.
—'Mid the mountains Euganean
I stood listening to the paean
With which the legion'd rooks did hail
The sun's uprise majestical:
Gathering round with wings all hoar,
Through the dewy mist they soar
Like gray shades, till the eastern heaven
Bursts, and then,—as clouds of even,
Fleck'd with fire and azure, lie
In the unfathomable sky,—
So their plumes of purple grain
Starr'd with drops of golden rain
Gleam above the sunlight woods,
As in silent multitudes
On the morning's fitful gale
Through the broken mist they sail;
And the vapours cloven and gleaming
Follow down the dark steep streaming,
Till all is bright, and clear, and still
Round the solitary hill.

Beneath its spread like a green sea
The waveless plain of Lombardy,
Bounded by the vaporous air,
Islanded by cities fair;
Underneath Day's azure eyes,
Ocean's nursling, Venice lies,—
A peopled labyrinth of walls,
Amphitrite's destined halls,
Which her hoary sire now paves
With his blue and beaming waves.
Lo! the sun upsprings behind,
Broad, red, radiant, half-reclined
On the level quivering line
Of the waters crystalline;
And before that chasm of light,
As within a furnace bright,
Column, tower, and dome, and spire,
Shine like obelisks of fire,
Pointing with inconstant motion
From the altar of dark ocean
To the sapphire-tinted skies;
As the flames of sacrifice
From the marble shrines did rise,
As to pierce the dome of gold
Where Apollo spoke of old.

Sun-girt City! thou hast been
Ocean's child, and then his queen;
Now is come a darker day,
And thou soon must must be his prey,
If the power that raised thee here
Hallow so thy watery bier.
A less drear ruin then than now,
With thy conquest-branded brow
Stooping to the slave of slaves
From thy throne, among the waves
Wilt thou be,—when the sea-mew
Flies, as once before it flew,
O'er thine isles depopulate,
And all is in its ancient state,
Save where many a palace gate,
With green sea-flowers overgrown
Like a rock of ocean's own,
Topples o'er the abandon'd sea
As the tides change sullenly.
The fisher on his watery way
Wandering at the close of day,
Will spread his sail and seize his oar
Till he pass the gloomy shore,
Lest thy dead should, from their sleep
Bursting o'er the starlight deep,
Lead a rapid masque of death
O'er the waters of his path.

Noon descends around me now:
'Tis the noon of autumn's glow,
When a soft and purple mist
Like a vaporous amethyst,
Or an air-dissolvéd star
Mingling light and fragrance, far
From the curved horizon's bound
To the point of Heaven's profound,
Fills the overflowing sky;
And the plains that silent lie
Underneath; the leaves unsodden
Where the infant Frost has trodden
With his morning-wingéd feet
Whose bright print is gleaming yet;
And the red and golden vines
Piercing with their trellised lines
The rough, dark-skirted wilderness;
The dun and bladed grass no less,
Pointing from this hoary tower

In the windless air; the flower
Glimmering at my feet; the line
Of the olive-sandall'd Apennine
In the south dimly islanded;
And the Alps, whose snows are spread
High between the clouds and sun;
And of living things each one;
And my spirit, which so long
Darken'd this swift stream of song,—
Interpenetrated lie
By the glory of the sky;
Be it love, light, harmony,
Odour, or the soul of all
Which from Heaven like dew doth fall,
Or the mind which feeds this verse
Peopling the lone universe.

Noon descends, and after noon
Autumn's evening meets me soon.
Leading the infantine moon
And that one star, which to her
Almost seems to minister
Half the crimson light she brings
From the sunset's radiant springs:
And the soft dreams of the morn
(Which like wingéd winds had borne
To silent isle, which lies
'Mid remember'd agonies,
The frail bark of this lone being),
Pass, to other sufferers fleeing,
And its ancient pilot, Pain,
Sits beside the helm again.

Other flowering isles must be
In the sea of Life and Agony:
Other spirits float and flee
O'er that gulf: even now, perhaps,
On some rock the wild wave wraps,
With folding wings they waiting sit
For my bark, to pilot it
To some calm and blooming cove,
Where for me, and those I love,
May a windless bower be built,
Far from passion, pain, and guilt,
In a dell 'mid lawny hills
Which the wild sea-murmur fills,
And soft sunshine, and the sound

Of old forests echoing round,
And the light and smell divine,
Of all flowers that breathe and shine.
—We may live so happy there,
That the Spirits of the Air
Envying us, may even entice
To our healing Paradise
The polluting multitude;
But their rage would be subdued
By that clime divine and calm,
And the winds whose wings rain balm
On the uplifted soul, and leaves
Under which the bright sea heaves;
While each breathless interval
In their whisperings musical
The inspired soul supplies
With its own deep melodies;
And the love which heals all strife
Circling, like the breath of life,
All things in that sweet abode
With its own mild brotherhood.
They, not it, would change; and soon
Every sprite beneath the moon
Would repent its envy vain,
And the earth grow young again.

                    Percy Bysshe Shelley

275   Ode to the West Wind

O wild West Wind, thou breath of Autumn's being,
Thou, from whose unseen presence the leaves dead
Are driven, like ghosts from an enchanter fleeing,
Yellow, and black, and pale, and hectic red,
Pestilence-stricken multitudes: O thou
Who chariotest to their dark wintry bed
The wingéd seeds, where they lie cold and low,
Each like a corpse within its grave, until
Thine azure sister of the Spring shall blow
Her clarion o'er the dreaming earth, and fill
(Driving sweet buds like flocks to feed in air)
With living hues and odours plain and hill:
Wild Spirit, which art moving everywhere;
Destroyer and Preserver; hear, oh, hear!

Thou on whose stream, mid the steep sky's commotion,
Loose clouds like earth's decaying leaves are shed,

Shook from the tangled boughs of Heaven and Ocean,
Angels of rain and lightning: there are spread
On the blue surface of thine airy surge,
Like the bright hair uplifted from the head
Of some fierce Maenad, even from the dim verge
Of the horizon to the zenith's height,
The locks of the approaching storm. Thou dirge
Of the dying year, to which this closing night
Will be the dome of a vast sepulchre,
Vaulted with all thy congregated might
Of vapours, from whose solid atmosphere
Black rain, and fire, and hail, will burst: oh, hear!

Thou who didst waken from his summer dreams
The blue Mediterranean, where he lay,
Lull'd by the coil of his crystalline streams,
Beside a pumice isle in Baiae's bay,
And saw in sleep old palaces and towers
Quivering within the wave's intenser day,
All overgrown with azure moss and flowers
So sweet, the sense faints picturing them! Thou
For whose path the Atlantic's level powers
Cleave themselves into chasms, while far below
The sea-blooms and the oozy woods which wear
The sapless foliage of the ocean, know
Thy voice, and suddenly grow grey with fear,
And tremble and despoil themselves: oh, hear!

If I were a dead leaf thou mightest bear;
If I were a swift cloud to fly with thee;
A wave to pant beneath thy power, and share
The impulse of thy strength, only less free
Than thou, O uncontrollable! If even
I were as in my boyhood, and could be
The comrade of thy wanderings over Heaven,
As then, when to outstrip thy skyey speed
Scarce seemed a vision, I would ne'er have striven
As thus with thee in prayer in my sore need.
Oh, lift me as a wave, a leaf, a cloud!
I fall upon the thorns of life! I bleed!
A heavy weight of hours has chained and bowed
One too like thee: tameless, and swift, and proud.

Make me thy lyre, even as the forest is:
What if my leaves are falling like its own!
The tumult of thy mighty harmonies
Will take from both a deep, autumnal tone,

Sweet though in sadness. Be thou, Spirit fierce,
My spirit! Be thou me, impetuous one!
Drive my dead thoughts over the universe
Like withered leaves to quicken a new birth!
And, by the incantation of this verse,
Scatter, as from an unextinguished hearth
Ashes and sparks, my words among mankind!
Be through my lips to unawakened earth
The trumpet of a prophecy! O Wind,
If Winter comes, can Spring be far behind?

Percy Bysshe Shelley

276   **Nature and the Poet**

*Suggested by a Picture of Peele Castle in a Storm,
Painted by Sir George Beaumont*

I was thy neighbour once, thou rugged Pile!
    Four summer weeks I dwelt in sight of thee:
I saw thee every day; and all the while
    Thy Form was sleeping on a glassy sea.

So pure the sky, so quiet was the air!
    So like, so very like, was day to day!
Whene'er I look'd, thy image still was there;
    It trembled, but it never pass'd away.

How perfect was the calm! It seem'd no sleep,
    No mood, which season takes away, or brings:
I could have fancied that the mighty Deep
    Was even the gentlest of all gentle things.

Ah! then if mine had been the Painter's hand
    To express what then I saw; and add the gleam,
The light that never was on sea or land,
    The consecration, and the Poet's dream,—

I would have planted thee, thou hoary Pile,
    Amid a world how different from this!
Beside a sea that could not cease to smile;
    On tranquil land, beneath a sky of bliss.

A picture had it been of lasting ease,
    Elysian quiet, without toil or strife;
No motion but the moving tide, a breeze,
    Or merely silent Nature's breathing life.

Such, in the fond illusion of my heart,
  Such picture would I at that time have made;
And seen the soul of truth in every part,
  A steadfast peace that might not be betray'd.

So once it would have been,—'tis so no more;
  I have submitted to a new control:
A power is gone, which nothing can restore;
  A deep distress hath humanized my soul.

Not for a moment could I now behold
  A smiling sea, and be what I have been:
The feeling of my loss will ne'er be old;
  This, which I know, I speak with mind serene.

Then, Beaumont, Friend! who would have been the Friend
  If he had lived, of him whom I deplore,
This work of thine I blame not, but commend
  This sea in anger, and that dismal shore.

O 'tis a passionate work!—yet wise and well,
  Well chosen is the spirit that is here;
That hulk which labours in the deadly swell,
  This rueful sky, this pageantry of fear!

And this huge Castle, standing here sublime,
  I love to see the look with which it braves,
—Cased in the unfeeling armour of old time—
  The lightning, the fierce wind, and trampling waves.

Farewell, farewell the heart that lives alone,
  Housed in a dream, at distance from the Kind!
Such happiness, whenever it be known,
  Is to be pitied; for 'tis surely blind.

But welcome fortitude, and patient cheer,
  And frequent sights of what is to be borne!
Such sights, or worse, as are before me here:—
  Not without hope we suffer and we mourn.

                                   William Wordsworth.

277   **The Poet's Dream**

        On a poet's lips I slept
        Dreaming like a love-adept
        In the sound his breathing kept;
        Nor seeks nor finds he mortal blisses,

But feeds on the aerial kisses
Of shapes that haunt thought's wildernesses.
He will watch from dawn to gloom
The lake-reflected sun illume
The yellow bees in the ivy-bloom,
   Nor heed nor see what things they be;
But from these create he can
Forms more real than living man,
   Nurslings of immortality!

Percy Bysshe Shelley

278

The world is too much with us; late and soon,
Getting and spending, we lay waste our powers:
Little we see in Nature that is ours;
We have given our hearts away, a sordid boon!
This Sea that bares her bosom to the moon,
The winds that will be howling at all hours
And are up-gather'd now like sleeping flowers,
For this, for everything, we are out of tune;
It moves us not.—Great God! I'd rather be
A Pagan suckled in a creed outworn,
So might I, standing on this pleasant lea,
Have glimpses that would make me less forlorn;
Have sight of Proteus rising from the sea;
Or hear old Triton blow his wreathèd horn.

William Wordsworth

279   **Within King's College Chapel, Cambridge**

Tax not the royal Saint with vain expense,
With ill-match'd aims the Architect who plann'd
(Albeit labouring for a scanty band
Of white-robed Scholars only) this immense
And glorious work of fine intelligence!
Give all thou canst; high Heaven rejects the lore
Of nicely-calculated less or more:
So deem'd the man who fashion'd for the sense
These lofty pillars, spread that branching roof
Self-poised, and scoop'd into ten thousand cells,
Where light and shade repose, where music dwells
Lingering—and wandering on as loth to die;
Like thoughts whose very sweetness yieldeth proof
That they were born for immortality.

William Wordsworth

Youth and Age

Verse, a breeze 'mid blossoms straying,
   Where Hope clung feeding, like a bee—
Both were mine! Life went a-maying
     With Nature, Hope, and Poesy,
       When I was young!

When I was young?—Ah, woeful When!
Ah! for the change 'twixt Now and Then!
This breathing house not built with hands,
   This body that does me grievous wrong,
O'er aery cliffs and glittering sands
   How lightly then it flash'd along:
Like those trim skiffs, unknown of yore,
   On winding lakes and rivers wide,
That ask no aid of sail or oar,
   That fear no spite of wind or tide!
Nought cared this body for wind or weather
When Youth and I lived in't together.

Flowers are lovely; Love is flower-like;
   Friendship is a sheltering tree;
O! the joys, that came down shower-like,
     Of Friendship, Love, and Liberty,
       Ere I was old!

Ere I was old? Ah, woeful Ere,
Which tells me, Youth's no longer here!
O Youth! for years so many and sweet
   'Tis known that Thou and I were one,
I'll think it but a fond conceit—
   It cannot be that thou art gone!
Thy vesper bell hath not yet toll'd:—
And thou wert ay a masker bold!
What strange disguise hast now put on
To make believe that thou art gone?
I see these locks in silvery slips,
   This drooping gait, this alter'd size:
But Springtide blossoms on thy lips,
   And tears take sunshine from thine eyes!
Life is but thought: so think I will
The Youth and I are houesemates still.

Dew-drops are the gems of morning,
   But the tears of mournful eve!
Where no hope is, life's a warning
     That only serves to make us grieve,
       When we are old:

—That only serves to make us grieve
  With oft and tedious taking-leave,
Like some poor nigh-related guest
That may not rudely be dismist,
Yet hath outstay'd of his welcome while,
And tells the jest without the smile.
                    Samuel Taylor Coleridge

281   **The Two April Mornings**

We walk'd along, while bright and red
    Uprose the morning sun;
And Matthew stopp'd, he look'd, and said,
    'The will of God be done!'

A village schoolmaster was he,
    With hair of glittering grey;
As blithe a man as you could see
    On a spring holiday.

And on that morning, through the grass
    And by the steaming rills
We travell'd merrily, to pass
    A day among the hills.

'Our work,' said I, 'was well begun;
    Then, from thy breast what thought,
Beneath so beautiful a sun,
    So sad a sigh has brought?'

A second time did Matthew stop;
    And fixing still his eye
Upon the eastern mountain-top,
    To me he made reply:

'Yon cloud with that long purple cleft
    Brings fresh into my mind
A day like this, which I have left
    Full thirty years behind.

'And just above yon slope of corn
    Such colours, and no other,
Were in the sky, that April morn,
    Of this the very brother.

'With rod and line I sued the sport
    Which that swet season gave,
And, to the churchyard come, stopp'd short
    Beside my daughter's grave.

'Nine summers had she scarcely seen,
    The pride of all the vale;
And then she sang;—she would have been
    A very nightingale.

'Six feet in earth my Emma lay;
    And yet I loved her more—
For so it seem'd,—than till that day
    I e'er had loved before.

'And turning from her grave, I met
    Beside the churchyard yew
A blooming Girl, whose hair was wet
    With points of morning dew.

'A basket on her head she bare;
    Her brow was smooth and white:
To see a child so very fair,
    It was a pure delight!

'No fountain from its rocky cave
    E'er tripp'd with foot so free;
She seem'd as happy as a wave
    That dances on the sea.

'There came from me a sigh of pain
    Which I could ill confine;
I looked at her, and looked again:
    And did not wish her mine!'

—Matthew is in his grave, yet now
    Methinks I see him stand
As at that moment, with a bough
    Of wilding in his hand.

                        William Wordsworth

282   **The Fountain: A Conversation**

We talk'd with open heart, and tongue
    Affectionate and true,
A pair of friends, though I was young,
    And Matthew seventy-two.

We lay beneath a spreading oak,
    Beside a mossy seat;
And from the turf a fountain broke
    And gurgled at our feet.

'Now, Matthew!' said I, 'let us match
    This water's pleasant tune
With some old border-song, or catch
    That suits a summer's noon;

'Or of the church-clock and the chimes
   Sing here beneath the shade
That half-mad thing of witty rhymes
   Which you last April made!'

In silence Matthew lay, and eyed
   The spring beneath the tree:
And thus the dear old man replied,
   The grey-hair'd man of glee:

'No check, no stay, this Streamlet fears,
   How merrily it goes!
'Twill murmur on a thousand years
   And flow as now it flows.

'And here, on this delightful day,
   I cannot choose but think
How oft, a vigorous man, I lay
   Beside this fountain's brink.

'My eyes are dim with childish tears,
   My heart is idly stirr'd,
For the same sound is in my ears
   Which in those days I heard.

'Thus fares it still in our decay:
   And yet the wiser mind
Mourns less for what age takes away,
   Than what it leaves behind.

'The blackbird amid leafy trees,
   The lark above the hill,
Let loose their carols when they please,
   Are quiet when they will.

'With Nature never do they wage
   A foolish strife; they see
A happy youth, and their old age
   Is beautiful and free:

'But we are press'd by heavy laws;
   And often, glad no more,
We wear a face of joy, because
   We have been glad of yore.

'If there be one who need bemoan
   His kindred laid in earth,
The household hearts that were his own,—
   It is the man of mirth.

'My days, my friend, are almost gone,
   My life has been approved,
And many love me; but by none
   Am I enough beloved.'

'Now both himself and me he wrongs,
  The man who thus complains!
I live and sing my idle songs
  Upon these happy plains:

'And, Matthew, for thy children dead
  I'll be a son to thee!'
At this he grasp'd my hand and said,
  'Alas! that cannot be.'

We rose up from the fountain-side;
  And down the smooth descent
Of the green sheep-track did we glide;
  And through the wood we went;

And, ere we came to Leonard's rock,
  He sang those witty rhymes
About the crazy old church-clock
  And the bewilder'd chimes.

William Wordsworth

283   **The River of Life**

The more we live, more brief appear
  Our life's succeeding stages:
A day to childhood seems a year,
  And years like passing ages.

The gladsome current of our youth,
  Ere passion yet disorders,
Steals lingering like a river smooth
  Along its grassy borders.

But as the careworn cheek grows wan,
  And sorrow's shafts fly thicker,
Ye stars, that measure life to man,
  Why seem your courses quicker?

When joys have lost their bloom and breath,
  And life itself is vapid,
Why, as we reach the Falls of death,
  Feel we its tide more rapid?

It may be strange—yet who would change
  Time's course to slower speeding,
When one by one our friends have gone
  And left our bosoms bleeding?

Heaven gives our years of fading strength
   Indemnifying fleetness;
And those of youth, a seeming length,
   Proportion'd to their sweetness.

Thomas Campbell

84   **The Human Seasons**

Four seasons fill the measure of the year;
There are four seasons in the mind of man:
He has his lusty Spring, when fancy clear
Takes in all beauty with an easy span:
He has his Summer, when luxuriously
Spring's honey'd cud of youthful thought he loves
To ruminate, and by such dreaming nigh
His nearest unto heaven: quiet coves
His soul has in its Autumn, when his wings
He furleth close: contented so to look
On mists in idleness—to let fair things
Pass by unheeded as a threshold brook:
He has his Winter too of pale misfeature,
Or else he would forgo his mortal nature.

John Keats

85   **A Lament**

O World! O Life! O Time!
On whose last steps I climb,
   Trembling at that where I had stood before;
When will return the glory of your prime?
     No more—Oh, never more!

Out of the day and night
A joy has taken flight:
   Fresh spring, and summer, and winter hoar
Move my faint heart with grief, but with delight
     No more—Oh, never more!

Percy Bysshe Shelley

286

     My heart leaps up when I behold
       A rainbow in the sky:
     So was it when my life began,
     So is it now I am a man,
     So be it when I shall grow old,

Or let me die!
The Child is father of the Man:
And I could wish my days to be
Bound each to each by natural piety.
William Wordswor

287   **Ode on Intimations of Immortality
from Recollections of Early Childhood**

There was a time when meadow, grove, and stream,
The earth, and every common sight,
To me did seem
Apparell'd in celestial light,
The glory and the freshness of a dream.
It is not now as it hath been of yore;—
Turn wheresoe'er I may,
By night or day,
The things which I have seen I now can see no more.

The rainbow comes and goes,
And lovely is the rose;
The moon doth with delight
Look round her when the heavens are bare;
Waters on a starry night
Are beautiful and fair;
The sunshine is a glorious birth;
But yet I know, where'er I go,
That there hath pass'd away a glory from the earth.

Now, while the birds thus sing a joyous song,
And while the young lambs bound
As to the tabor's sound,
To me alone there came a thought of grief:
A timely utterance gave that thought relief,
And I again am strong.
The cataracts blow their trumpets from the steep,—
No more shall grief of mine the season wrong:
I hear the echoes through the mountains throng,
The winds come to me from the fields of sleep,
And all the earth is gay;
Land and sea
Give themselves up to jollity,
And with the heart of May
Doth every beast keep holiday;—
Thou child of joy,
Shout round me, let me hear thy shouts, thou happy Shepherd
boy!

Ye blessèd Creatures, I have heard the call
    Ye to each other make; I see
The heavens laugh with you in your jubilee;
    My heart is at your festival,
    My head hath its coronal,
The fulness of your bliss, I feel—I feel it all.
       O evil day! if I were sullen
       While Earth herself is adorning
         This sweet May-morning;
       And the children are culling
         On every side
In a thousand valleys far and wide
Fresh flowers; while the sun shines warm,
And the babe leaps up on his mother's arm:—
       I hear, I hear, with joy I hear!
    —But there's a tree, of many, one,
A single field which I have look'd upon,
Both of them speak of something that is gone:
       The pansy at my feet
       Doth the same tale repeat:
Whither is fled the visionary gleam?
Where is it now, the glory and the dream?

Our birth is but a sleep and a forgetting;
The Soul that rises with us, our life's Star,
       Hath had elsewhere its setting,
         And cometh from afar;
       Not in entire forgetfulness,
       And not in utter nakedness,
But trailing clouds of glory do we come
       From God, who is our home:
Heaven lies about us in our infancy!
Shades of the prison-house begin to close
       Upon the growing Boy,
But he beholds the light, and whence it flows,
       He sees it in his joy;
The Youth, who daily farther from the east
     Must travel, still is Nature's priest,
       And by the vision splendid
       Is on his way attended;
At length the Man perceives it die away,
And fade into the light of common day.

Earth fills her lap with pleasures of her own;
Yearnings she hath in her own natural kind,
And, even with something of a mother's mind
       And no unworthy aim,

The homely nurse doth all she can
To make her foster-child, her inmate, Man,
        Forget the glories he hath known,
And that imperial palace whence he came.

Behold the Child among his new-born blisses,
    A six years' darling of a pigmy size!
    See, where 'mid work of his own hand he lies,
Fretted by sallies of his mother's kisses,
    With light upon him from his father's eyes!
See, at his feet, some little plan or chart,
Some fragment from his dream of human life,
Shaped by himself with newly-learnéd art;
            A wedding or a festival,
            A mourning or a funeral;
                And this hath now his heart,
            And unto this he frames his song:
                Then will he fit his tongue
To dialogues of business, love, or strife;
            But it will not be long
            Ere this be thrown aside,
            And with new joy and pride
The little actor cons another part;
Filling from time to time his 'humorous stage'
With all the Persons, down to palsied Age,
That life brings with her in her equipage;
            As if his whole vocation
            Were endless imitation.

Thou, whose exterior semblance doth belie
            Thy soul's immensity;
Thou best Philosopher, who yet dost keep
Thy heritage, thou Eye among the blind,
That, deaf and silent, read'st the eternal deep,
Haunted for ever by the eternal Mind,—
            Mighty Prophet! Seer blest!
            On whom those truths do rest
Which we are toiling all our lives to find,
In darkness lost, the darkness of the grave;
Thou, over whom thy Immortality
Broods like the Day, a Master o'er a Slave,
A Presence which is not to be put by;
Thou little Child, yet glorious in the might
Of heaven-born freedom on thy being's height,
Why with such earnest pains dost thou provoke
The years to bring the inevitable yoke,
Thus blindly with thy blessedness at strife?

Full soon thy Soul shall have her earthly freight,
And custom lie upon thee with a weight
Heavy as frost, and deep almost as life!

       O joy! that in our embers
         Is something that doth live,
       That Nature yet remembers
         What was so fugitive!
The thought of our past years in me doth breed
Perpetual benediction: not indeed
For that which is most worthy to be blest,
Delight and liberty, the simple creed
Of Childhood, whether busy or at rest,
With new-fledged hope still fluttering in his breast:
       —Not for these I raise
         The song of thanks and praise;
   But for those obstinate questionings
     Of sense and outward things,
     Fallings from us, vanishings,
     Blank misgivings of a creature
Moving about in worlds not realized,
High instincts, before which our mortal nature
Did tremble like a guilty thing surprised:
       But for those first affections,
       Those shadowy recollections,
         Which, be they what they may,
Are yet the fountain-light of all our day,
Are yet a master-light of all our seeing;
       Uphold us, cherish, and have power to make
Our noisy years seem moments in the being
     Of the eternal silence: truths that wake,
         To perish never;
Which neither listlessness, nor mad endeavour,
        Nor man nor boy
Nor all that is at enmity with joy,
Can utterly abolish or destroy!
   Hence in a season of calm weather
        Though inland far we be,
Our souls have sight of that immortal sea
        Which brought us hither;
        Can in a moment travel thither—
And see the children sport upon the shore,
And hear the mighty waters rolling evermore.

Then, sing ye birds, sing, sing a joyous song!
        And let the young lambs bound
        As to the tabor's sound!

We, in thought, will join your throng
    Ye that pipe and ye that play,
    Ye that through your hearts to-day
    Feel the gladness of the May!
What though the radiance which was once so bright
Be now for ever taken from my sight,
    Though nothing can bring back the hour
Of splendour in the grass, of glory in the flower;
    We will grieve not, rather find
    Strength in what remains behind;
    In the primal sympathy
    Which having been must ever be;
    In the soothing thoughts that spring
    Out of human suffering;
    In the faith that looks through death,
In years that bring the philosophic mind.

And O, ye Fountains, Meadows, Hills, and Groves,
Forbode not any severing of our loves!
Yet in my heart of hearts I feel your might;
I only have relinquish'd one delight
To live beneath your more habitual sway;
I love the brooks which down their channels fret,
Even more than when I tripp'd lightly as they;
The innocent brightness of a new-born day
    Is lovely yet;
The clouds that gather round the setting sun
Do take a sober colouring from an eye
That hath kept watch o'er man's mortality;
Another race hath been, and other palms are won.
Thanks to the human heart by which we live,
Thanks to its tenderness, its joys, and fears,
To me the meanest flower that blows can give
Thoughts that do often lie too deep for tears.

                        William Wordsworth

288   Music, when soft voices die,
          Vibrates in the memory—
          Odours, when sweet violets sicken,
          Live within the sense they quicken.

          Rose leaves, when the rose is dead,
          Are heaped for the beloved's bed;
          And so thy thoughts, when thou are gone,
          Love itself shall slumber on.

                      Percy Bysshe Shelley

289   **The Poetry of Earth**

The poetry of earth is never dead:
When all the birds are faint with the hot sun,
And hide in cooling trees, a voice will run
From hedge to hedge about the new-mown mead;
That is the Grasshopper's—he takes the lead
In summer luxury,—he has never done
With his delights; for when tired out with fun
He rests at ease beneath some pleasant weed.

The poetry of earth is ceasing never:
On a lone winter evening, when the frost
Has wrought a silence, from the stove there shrills
The Cricket's song, in warmth increasing ever,
And seems to one in drowsiness half lost,
The Grasshopper's among some grassy hills.

John Keats

290   **To One Who Has Been Long in City Pent**

To one who has been long in city pent,
'Tis very sweet to look into the fair
And open face of heaven,—to breathe a prayer
Full in the smile of the blue firmament.
Who is more happy, when, with heart's content,
Fatigued he sinks into some pleasant lair
Of wavy grass, and reads a debonair
And gentle tale of love and languishment?

Returning home at evening, with an ear
Catching the notes of Philomel,—an eye
Watching the sailing cloudlet's bright career,
He mourns that day so soon has glided by:
E'en like the passage of an angel's tear
That falls through the clear ether silently.

John Keats

291   **On the Sea**

It keeps eternal whisperings around
    Desolate shores, and with its mighty swell
Gluts twice ten thousand Caverns, till the spell
    Of Hecate leaves them their old shadowy sound.
Often 'tis in such gentle temper found,
    That scarcely will the very smallest shell
Be moved for days from where it sometime fell,
    When last the winds of Heaven were unbound.
Oh ye! who have your eye-balls vexed and tired,
    Feast them upon the wideness of the Sea;
Oh ye! whose ears are dinned with uproar rude,
    Or fed too much with cloying melody—
Sit ye near some old Cavern's Mouth, and brood
    Until ye start, as if the sea-nymphs quired!

                                    John Keat

292   **The Cloud**

I bring fresh showers for the thirsting flowers,
    From the seas and the streams;
I bear light shade for the leaves when laid
    In their noonday dreams.
From my wings are shaken the dews that waken
    The sweet buds every one,
When rocked to rest on their mother's breast,
    As she dances about the sun.
I wield the flail of the lashing hail,
    And whiten the green plains under,
And then again I dissolve it in rain,
    And laugh as I pass in thunder.
I sift the snow on the mountains below,
    And their great pines groan aghast;
And all the night 'tis my pillow white,
    While I sleep in the arms of the blast.

Sublime on the towers of my skyey bowers,
    Lightning my pilot sits;
In a cavern under is fettered the thunder,
    It struggles and howls at fits;
Over earth and ocean, with gentle motion,
    This pilot is guiding me,
Lured by the love of the genii that move
    In the depths of the purple sea;
Over the rills, and the crags, and the hills,
    Over the lakes and the plains,

Wherever he dream, under mountain or stream,
   The Spirit he loves remains;
And I all the while bask in Heaven's blue smile,
   Whilst he is dissolving in rains.

The sanguine Sunrise, with his meteor eyes,
   And his burning plumes outspread,
Leaps on the back of my sailing rack,
   When the morning star shines dead;
As on the jag of a mountain crag,
   Which an earthquake rocks and swings,
An eagle alit one moment may sit
   In the light of its golden wings.
And when Sunset may breathe, from the lit sea beneath,
   Its ardours of rest and of love,
And the crimson pall of eve may fall
   From the depth of Heaven above,
With wings folded I rest, on mine aëry nest,
   As still as a brooding dove.

That orbèd maiden with white fire laden,
   Whom mortals call the Moon,
Glides glimmering o'er my fleece-like floor,
   By the midnight breezes strewn;
And wherever the beat of her unseen feet,
   Which only the angels hear,
May have broken the woof of my tent's thin roof,
   The stars peep behind her and peer;
And I laugh to see them whirl and flee,
   Like a swarm of golden bees,
When I widen the rent in my wind-built tent,
   Till the calm rivers, lakes, and seas,
Like strips of the sky fallen through me on high,
   Are each paved with the moon and these.

I bind the Sun's throne with a burning zone,
   And the Moon's with a girdle of pearl;
The volcanoes are dim, and the stars red and swim,
   When the whirlwinds my banner unfurl.
From cape to cape, with a bridge-like shape,
   Over a torrent sea,
Sunbeam-proof, I hang like a roof,—
   The mountains its columns be.
The triumphal arch through which I march
   With hurricane, fire, and snow,
When the Powers of the air are chained to my chair,
   Is the million-coloured bow;

The sphere-fire above its soft colours wove,
　　While the moist Earth was laughing below.

I am the daughter of Earth and Water,
　　And the nursling of the Sky;
I pass through the pores of the ocean and shores:
　　I change, but I cannot die.
For after the rain when with never a stain
　　The pavilion of Heaven is bare,
And the winds and sunbeams with their convex gleams
　　Build up the blue dome of air,
I silently laugh at my own cenotaph,
　　And out of the caverns of rain,
Like a child from the womb, like a ghost from the tomb,
　　I arise and unbuild it again.

Percy Bysshe Shelley

293   ### Ah! Sun-flower

　　Ah, Sun-flower! weary of time,
　　Who countest the steps of the sun;
　　Seeking after that sweet golden clime,
　　Where the traveller's journey is done;

　　Where the Youth pined away with desire,
　　And the pale Virgin shrouded in snow,
　　Arise from their graves, and aspire
　　Where my Sun-flower wishes to go.

William Blake

294   ### Auguries of Innocence

To see a World in a grain of sand,
And a Heaven in a wild flower,
Hold Infinity in the palm of your hand,
And Eternity in an hour.
A robin redbreast in a cage
Puts all Heaven in a rage.
A dove-house fill'd with doves and pigeons
Shudders Hell thro' all its regions.
A dog starv'd at his master's gate
Predicts the ruin of the State.
A horse misus'd upon the road
Calls to Heaven for human blood.
Each outcry of the hunted hare

A fibre from the brain does tear.
A skylark wounded in the wing,
A cherubim does cease to sing.
The game-cock clipt and arm'd for fight
Does the rising sun affright.
Every wolf's and lion's howl
Raises from Hell a Human soul.
The wild deer, wandering here and there,
Keeps the Human soul from care.
The lamb misus'd breeds public strife,
And yet forgives the butcher's knife.
The bat that flits at close of eve
Has left the brain that won't believe.
The owl that calls upon the night
Speaks the unbeliever's fright.
He who shall hurt the little wren
Shall never be belov'd by men.
He who the ox to wrath has mov'd
Shall never be by woman lov'd.
The wanton boy that kills the fly
Shall feel the spider's enmity.
He who torments the chafer's sprite
Weaves a bower in endless night.
The caterpillar on the leaf
Repeats to thee thy mother's grief.
Kill not the moth nor butterfly,
For the Last Judgment draweth nigh.
He who shall train the horse to war
Shall never pass the polar bar.
The beggar's dog and widow's cat
Feed them, and thou wilt grow fat.
The gnat that sings his summer's song
Poison gets from Slander's tongue.
The poison of the snake and newt
Is the sweat of Envy's foot.
The poison of the honey-bee
Is the artist's jealousy.
The prince's robes and beggar's rags
Are toadstools on the miser's bags.
A truth that's told with bad intent
Beats all the lies you can invent.
It is right it should be so;
Man was made for joy and woe;
And when this we rightly know,
Thro' the world we safely go.
Joy and woe are woven fine,
A clothing for the soul divine;

Under every grief and pine
Runs a joy with silken twine.
The babe is more than swaddling-bands;
Throughout all these human lands
Tools were made, and born were hands,
Every farmer understands.
Every tear from every eye
Becomes a babe in Eternity;
This is caught by Females bright,
And return'd to its own delight.
The bleat, the bark, bellow, and roar
Are waves that beat on Heaven's shore.
The babe that weeps the rod beneath
Writes revenge in realms of death.
The beggar's rags, fluttering in air,
Does to rags the heavens tear.
The soldier, arm'd with sword and gun,
Palsied strikes the summer's sun.
The poor man's farthing is worth more
Than all the gold on Afric's shore.
One mite wrung from the labourer's hands
Shall buy and sell the miser's lands:
Or, if protected from on high,
Does that whole nation sell and buy.
He who mocks the infant's faith
Shall be mock'd in Age and Death.
He who shall teach the child to doubt
The rotting grave shall ne'er get out.
He who repeats the infant's faith
Triumphs over Hell and Death.
The child's toys and the old man's reasons
Are the fruits of the two seasons.
The questioner, who sits so sly,
Shall never know how to reply.
He who replies to words of Doubt
Doth put the light of knowledge out.
The strongest poison ever known
Came from Caesar's laurel crown.
Nought can deform the human race
Like to the armour's iron brace.
When gold and gems adorn the plough
To peaceful arts shall Envy bow.
A riddle, or the cricket's cry,
Is to Doubt a fit reply.
The emmet's inch and eagle's mile
Make lame Philosophy to smile.
He who doubts from what he sees

Will ne'er believe, do what you please.
If the Sun and Moon should doubt,
They'd immediately go out.
To be in a passion you good may do,
But no good if a passion is in you.
The whore and gambler, by the state
Licensed, build that nation's fate.
The harlot's cry from street to street
Shall weave Old England's winding-sheet.
The winner's shout, the loser's curse,
Dance before dead England's hearse.
Every night and every morn
Some to misery are born.
Every morn and every night
Some are born to sweet delight.
Some are born to sweet delight,
Some are born to endless night.
We are told to believe a lie
When we see not thro' the eye,
Which was born in a night, to perish in a night,
When the Soul slept in beams of light.
God appears, and God is Light,
To those poor souls who dwell in Night;
But does a Human Form display
To those who dwell in realms of Day.

William Blake

295   **Ode on a Grecian Urn**

Thou still unravished bride of quietness,
    Thou foster-child of silence and slow time,
Sylvan historian, who canst thus express
    A flowery tale more sweetly than our rhyme:
What leaf-fringed legend haunts about thy shape
    Of deities or mortals, or of both,
        In Tempe or the dales of Arcady?
What men or gods are these? What maidens loth?
    What mad pursuit? What struggle to escape?
        What pipes and timbrels? What wild ecstasy?

Heard melodies are sweet, but those unheard
    Are sweeter; therefore, ye soft pipes, play on;
Not to the sensual ear, but, more endeared,
    Pipe to the spirit ditties of no tone:
Fair youth, beneath the trees, thou canst not leave

Thy song, nor ever can those trees be bare;
　　Bold Lover, never, never canst thou kiss,
Though winning near the goal—yet, do not grieve;
　　She cannot fade, though thou hast not thy bliss,
　　　For ever wilt thou love, and she be fair!

Ah, happy, happy boughs! that cannot shed
　　Your leaves, nor ever bid the Spring adieu;
And, happy melodist, unwearièd,
　　For ever piping songs for ever new;
More happy love! more happy, happy love!
　　For ever warm and still to be enjoyed,
　　　For ever panting, and for ever young;
All breathing human passion far above,
　　That leaves a heart high-sorrowful and cloyed,
　　　A burning forehead, and a parching tongue.

Who are these coming to the sacrifice?
　　To what green altar, O mysterious priest,
Lead'st thou that heifer lowing at the skies,
　　And all her silken flanks with garlands dressed?
What little town by river or sea shore,
　　Or mountain-built with peaceful citadel,
　　　Is emptied of its folk, this pious morn?
And, little town, thy streets for evermore
　　Will silent be; and not a soul, to tell
　　　Why thou art desolate, can e'er return.

O Attic shape! Fair attitude! with brede
　　Of marble men and maidens overwrought,
With forest branches and the trodden weed;
　　Thou, silent form, dost tease us out of thought
As doth eternity: Cold Pastoral!
　　When old age shall this generation waste,
　　　Thou shalt remain, in midst of other woe
Than ours, a friend to man, to whom thou say'st,
　　"Beauty is truth, truth beauty,"—that is all
　　　Ye know on earth, and all ye need to know.

John Keats

296　　　　**Riddle of the World**

Know then thyself, presume not God to scan,
The proper study of Mankind is Man.
Plac'd on this isthmus of a middle state,
A Being darkly wise, and rudely great:

With too much knowledge for the Sceptic side,
With too much weakness for the Stoic's pride,
He hangs between; in doubt to act, or rest;
In doubt to deem himself a God, or Beast;
In doubt his Mind or Body to prefer;
Born but to die, and reas'ning but to err;
Alike in ignorance, his reason such,
Whether he thinks too little, or too much:
Chaos of Thought and Passion, all confus'd;
Still by himself abus'd, or disabus'd;
Created half to rise, and half to fall;
Great Lord of all things, yet a prey to all;
Sole judge of truth, in endless error hurl'd:
The glory, jest, and riddle of the world!

Alexander Pope

297

Kubla Khan

In Xanadu did Kubla Khan
A stately pleasure-dome decree:
Where Alph, the sacred river, ran
Through caverns measureless to man
  Down to a sunless sea.
So twice five miles of fertile ground
With walls and towers were girdled round:
And there were gardens bright with sinuous rills,
Where blossomed many an incense-bearing tree;
And here were forests ancient as the hills,
Enfolding sunny spots of greenery.

But oh! that deep romantic chasm which slanted
Down the green hill athwart a cedarn cover!
A savage place! as holy and enchanted
As e'er beneath a waning moon was haunted
By woman wailing for her demon-lover!
And from this chasm, with ceaseless turmoil seething,
As if this earth in fast thick pants were breathing,
A mighty fountain momently was forced:
Amid whose swift half-intermitted burst
Huge fragments vaulted like rebounding hail,
Or chaffy grain beneath the thresher's flail:
And 'mid these dancing rocks at once and ever
It flung up momently the sacred river.
Five miles meandering with a mazy motion
Through wood and dale the sacred river ran,
Then reached the caverns measureless to man,

And sank in tumult to a lifeless ocean:
And 'mid this tumult Kubla heard from far
Ancestral voices prophesying war!
   The shadow of the dome of pleasure
   Floated midway on the waves;
   Where was heard the mingled measure
   From the fountain and the caves.
It was a miracle of rare device,
A sunny pleasure-dome with caves of ice!

   A damsel with a dulcimer
   In a vision once I saw:
   It was an Abyssinian maid,
   And on her dulcimer she played,
   Singing of Mount Abora.
   Could I revive within me
   Her symphony and song,
   To such a deep delight 'twould win me,
That with music loud and long,
I would build that dome in air,
That sunny dome! those caves of ice!
And all who heard should see them there,
And all should cry, Beware! Beware!
His flashing eyes, his floating hair!
Weave a circle round him thrice,
And close your eyes with holy dread,
For he on honey-dew hath fed,
And drunk the milk of Paradise.

Samuel Taylor Coleridge

298   **To Night**

Mysterious Night! when our first parent knew
Thee from report divine, and heard thy name,
Did he not tremble for this lovely frame,
This glorious canopy of light and blue?
Yet 'neath a curtain of translucent dew,
Bathed in the rays of the great setting flame,
Hesperus with the host of heaven came,
And lo! Creation widened in man's view.
Who could have thought such darkness lay concealed
Within thy beams, O sun! or who could find,
Whilst fly and leaf and insect stood revealed,
That to such countless orbs thou mad'st us blind!
Why do we then shun death with anxious strife?
If Light can thus deceive, wherefore not Life?

Joseph Blanco White

To Sleep

O soft embalmer of the still midnight,
Shutting, with careful fingers and benign,
Our gloom-pleas'd eyes, embower'd from the light,
Enshaded in forgetfulness divine:
O soothest Sleep! if so it please thee, close,
In midst of this thine hymn, my willing eyes,
Or wait the amen, ere thy poppy throws
Around my bed its lulling charities.
Then save me, or the passèd day will shine
Upon my pillow, breeding many woes;
Save me from curious conscience, that still lords
Its strength for darkness, burrowing like a mole;
Turn the key deftly in the oilèd wards,
And seal the hushèd casket of my soul.

John Keats

To Be, or Not to Be

To be, or not to be: that is the question:
Whether 'tis nobler in the mind to suffer
The slings and arrows of outrageous fortune,
Or to take arms against a seat of troubles,
And by opposing end them? To die: to sleep;
No more; and, by a sleep to say we end
The heart-ache and the thousand natural shocks
That flesh is heir to, 'tis a consummation
Devoutly to be wished. To die, to sleep;
To sleep: perchance to dream: aye, there's the rub;
For in that sleep of death what dreams may come
When we have shuffled off this mortal coil,
Must give us pause. There's the respect
That makes calamity of so long life;
For who would bear the whips and scorns of time,
The oppressor's wrong, the proud man's contumely,
The pangs of disprized love, the law's delay,
The insolence of office, and the spurns
That patient merit of the unworthy takes,
When he himself might his quietus make
With a bare bodkin? who would fardels bear,
To grunt and sweat under a weary life,
But that the dread of something after death,
The undiscovered country from whose bourn
No traveller returns, puzzles the will,
And makes us rather bear those ills we have
Than fly to others that we know not of?

Thus conscience does make cowards of us all;
And thus the native hue of resolution
Is sicklied o'er with the pale cast of thought,
And enterprises of great pith and moment
With this regard their currents turn awry,
And lose the name of action.

William Shakespeare

301   **I Am**

I am; yet what I am none cares or knows,
    My friends forsake me like a memory lost;
I am the self-consumer of my woes,
    They rise and vanish in oblivious host,
Like shades in love and death's oblivion lost;
And yet I am, and live with shadows tost

Into the nothingness of scorn and noise,
    Into the living sea of waking dreams,
Where there is neither sense of life nor joys,
    But the vast shipwreck of my life's esteems;
And e'en the dearest—that I loved the best—
Are strange—nay, rather stranger than the rest.

I long for scenes where man has never trod;
    A place where woman never smiled or wept;
There to abide with my Creator, God,
    And sleep as I in childhood sweetly slept:
Untroubling and untroubled where I lie;
The grass below—above the vaulted sky.

John Clare

302   **Written on the Eve of Execution**

My prime of youth is but a frost of cares,
    My feast of joy is but a dish of pain,
My crop of corn is but a field of tares,
    And all my good is but vain hope of gain;
My life is fled, and yet I saw no sun;
And now I live, and now my life is done.

My tale was heard, and yet it was not told;
    My fruit is fallen, and yet my leaves are green;
My youth is spent, and yet I am not old;
    I saw the world, and yet I was not seen;
My thread is cut, and yet it is not spun;
And now I live, and now my life is done.

I sought my death and I found it in the womb,
   I lookt for life and saw it was a shade,
I trod the earth and knew it was my tomb,
   And now I die, and now I was but made;
My glass is full, and now my glass is run,
And now I live, and now my life is done.

                    Chidiock Tichbourne

Alps on Alps

A little learning is a dang'rous thing;
Drink deep, or taste not the Pierian spring:
There shallow draughts intoxicate the brain,
And drinking largely sobers us again.
Fir'd at first sight with what the Muse imparts,
In fearless youth we tempt the heights of Arts,
While from the bounded level of our mind,
Short views we take, nor see the lengths behind;
But more advanc'd, behold with strange surprise
New distant scenes of endless science rise!
So pleas'd at first the tow'ring Alps we try,
Mount o'er the vales, and seem to tread the sky,
Th' eternal snows appear already past,
And the first clouds and mountains seem the last:
But, those attain'd, we tremble to survey
The growing labours of the lengthen'd way,
Th' increasing prospect tires our wand'rings eyes.
Hills peep o'er hills, and Alps on Alps arise!

                    Alexander Pope

The Expense of Spirit

The expense of spirit in a waste of shame
Is lust in action; and till action, lust
Is perjur'd, murd'rous, bloody, full of blame,
Savage, extreme, rude, cruel, not to trust:
Enjoy'd no sooner but despised straight;
Past reason hunted, and no sooner had,
Past reason hated, as a swallow'd bait
On purpose laid to make the taker mad:
Mad in pursuit and in possession so;
Had, having, and in quest to have, extreme;
A bliss in proof, and prov'd, a very woe;
Before, a joy propos'd; behind, a dream.
All this the world well knows; yet none knows well
To shun the heaven that leads men to this hell.

                    William Shakespeare

305

Ode on Melancholy

No, no, go not to Lethe, neither twist
 Wolf's-bane, tight-rooted, for its poisonous wine;
Nor suffer thy pale forehead to be kiss'd
 By nightshade, ruby grape of Proserpine;
Makes not your rosary of yew-berries,
 Nor let the beetle, nor the death-moth be
  Your mournful Psyche, nor the downy owl
A partner in your sorrow's mysteries;
 For shade to shade will come too drowsily,
  And drown the wakeful anguish of the soul.

But when the melancholy fit shall fall
 Sudden from heaven like a weeping cloud,
That fosters the droop-headed flowers all,
 And hides the green hill in an April shroud;
Then glut thy sorrow on a morning rose,
 Or on the rainbow of the salt sand-wave,
  Or on the wealth of the globèd peonies;
Or if thy mistress some rich anger shows,
 Emprison her soft hand, and let her rave,
  And feed deep, deep upon her peerless eyes.

She dwells with Beauty—Beauty that must die;
 And Joy, whose hand is ever at his lips
Bidding adieu; and aching Pleasure nigh,
 Turning to poison while the bee-mouth sips:
Ay, in the very temple of Delight
 Veil'd Melancholy has her sovereign shrine,
  Though seen of none save him whose strenuous tongu
Can burst Joy's grape against his palate fine;
 His soul shall taste the sadness of her might,
  And be among her cloudy trophies hung.

John Kea

306

Ode to Psyche

O Goddess! hear these tuneless numbers, wrung
 By sweet enforcement and remembrance dear,
And pardon that thy secrets should be sung
 Even into thine own soft-conchèd ear:
Surely I dreamt to-day, or did I see
 The wingèd Psyche with awaken'd eyes?
I wandered in a forest thoughtlessly,
 And, on the sudden, fainting with surprise,

Saw two fair creatures, couched side by side
　　In deepest grass, beneath the whisp'ring roof
　　Of leaves and trembled blossoms, where there ran
　　　　A brooklet, scarce espied:
'Mid hushed, cool-rooted flowers, fragrant-eyed,
　　Blue, silver-white, and budded Tyrian,
They lay calm-breathing on the bedded grass;
　　Their arms embraced, and their pinions too;
　　Their lips touch'd not, but had not bade adieu,
As if disjoined by soft-handed slumber,
And ready still past kisses to outnumber
　　At tender eye-dawn of aurorean love:
　　　　The winged boy I knew;
But who wast thou, O happy, happy dove?
　　　　His Psyche true!

O latest born and loveliest vision far
　　Of all Olympus' faded hierarchy!
Fairer than Phoebe's sapphire-region'd star,
　　Or Vesper, amorous glow-worm of the sky;
Fairer than these, though temple thou hast none,
　　　　Nor altar heap'd with flowers;
Nor virgin-choir to make delicious moan
　　　　Upon the midnight hours;
No voice, no lute, no pipe, no incense sweet
　　From chain-swung censer teeming;
No shrine, no grove, no oracle, no heat
　　Of pale-mouth'd prophet dreaming.

O brightest! though too late for antique vows,
　　Too, too late for the fond believing lyre,
When holy were the haunted forest boughs,
　　Holy the air, the water, and the fire;
Yet even in these days so far retir'd
　　From happy pieties, thy lucent fans,
　　Fluttering among the faint Olympians,
I see, and sing, by my own eyes inspired.
So let me be thy choir, and make a moan
　　　　Upon the midnight hours;
Thy voice, thy lute, thy pipe, thy incense sweet
　　From swinged censer teeming;
Thy shrine, thy grove, thy oracle, thy heat
　　Of pale-mouth'd prophet dreaming.

　　Yes, I will be thy priest, and build a fane
　　　　In some untrodden region of my mind

Where branched thoughts, new grown with pleasant
    pain
    Instead of pines shall murmur in the wind:
Far, far around shall those dark-cluster'd trees
    Fledge the wild-ridged mountains steep by steep;
And there by zephyrs, streams, and birds, and bees,
    The moss-lain Dryads shall be lull'd to sleep;
And in the midst of this wide quietness
A rosy sanctuary will I dress
With the wreath'd trellis of a working brain,
    With buds, and bells, and stars without a name,
With all the gardener Fancy e'er could feign,
    Who breeding flowers, will never breed the same:
And there shall be for thee all soft delight
    That shadowy thought can win,
A bright torch, and a casement ope at night,
    To let the warm Love in!

John Kea

307   **Ode on Indolence**

They toil not, neither do they spin.

One morn before me were three figures seen,
    With bowed necks, and joined hands, side-fac'd;
And one behind the other stepp'd serene,
    In placid sandals, and in white robes grac'd;
They pass'd, like figures on a marble urn,
    When shifted round to see the other side;
    They came again; as when the urn once more
Is shifted round, the first seen shades return;
    And they were strange to me, as may betide
    With vases, to one deep in Phidian lore.

How is it, shadows! that I knew ye not?
    How came ye muffled in so hush a mask?
Was it a silent deep-disguisèd plot
    To steal away, and leave without a task
My idle days? Ripe was the drowsy hour;
    The blissful cloud of summer-indolence
    Benumb'd my eyes; my plus grew less and less;
Pain had no sting, and pleasure's wreath no flower:
    O, why did ye not melt, and leave my sense
    Unhaunted quite of all but—nothingness?

A third time pass'd they by, and, passing, turn'd
    Each one the face a moment whiles to me;

Then faded, and to follow them I burn'd
 And ach'd for wings because I knew the three;
The first was a fair maid, and Love her name;
 The second was Ambition, pale of cheek,
  And ever watchful with fatiguèd eye;
The last, whom I love more, the more of blame
 Is heap'd upon her, maiden most unmeek,—
  I knew to be my demon Poesy.

They faded, and, forsooth! I wanted wings:
 O folly! What is Love? and where is it?
And for that poor Ambition! it springs
 From a man's little heart's short fever-fit;
For Poesy!—no,—she has not a joy,—
 At least for me,—so sweet as drowsy noons,
  And evenings steep'd in honied indolence;
O, for an age so shelter'd from annoy,
 That I may never know how change the moons,
  Or hear the voice of busy common-sense!

And once more came they by;—alas! wherefore?
 My sleep had been embroider'd with dim dreams;
My soul had been a lawn besprinkled o'er
 With flowers, and stirring shades, and baffled beams:
The morn was clouded, but no shower fell,
 Tho' in her lids hung the sweet tears of May;
  The open casement press'd a new-leav'd vine,
Let in the budding warmth and throstle's lay;
O shadows! 'twas a time to bid farewell!
  Upon your skirts had fallen no tears of mine.

So, ye three ghosts, adieu! Ye cannot raise
 My head cool-bedded in the flowery grass;
For I would not be dieted with praise,
 A pet-lamb in a sentimental farce!
Fade softly from my eyes, and be once more
 In masque-like figures on the dreamy urn;
  Farewell! I yet have visions for the night,
And for the day faint visions there is store;
 Vanish, ye phantoms! from my idle spright,
  Into the clouds, and nevermore return!

                                   John Keats

A Man's a Man for A' That

Is there for honest poverty
    That hangs his head, an' a' that;
The coward slave—we pass him by,
    We dare be poor for a' that!
For a' that, an' a' that,
    Our toils obscure an' a' that,
The rank is but the guinea's stamp,
    The man's the gowd for a' that.

What though on hamely fare we dine,
    Wear hoddin grey, an' a' that?
Gie fools their silks, and knaves their wine,
    A man's a man for a' that.
For a' that, an' a' that,
    Their tinsel show an' a' that,
The honest man, tho' e'er sae poor,
    Is king o' men for a' that.

Ye see yon birkie ca'd a lord,
    Wha struts, an' stares, an' a' that;
Tho' hundreds worship at his word,
    He's but a coof for a' that,
For a' that, an' a' that,
    His ribband, star, an' a' that,
The man o' independent mind
    He looks an' laughs at a' that.

A prince can mak a belted knight,
    A marquis, duke, an' a' that;
But an honest man's aboon his might,
    Gude faith, he maunna fa' that!
For a' that, an' 'a' that,
    Their dignities an' a' that,
The pith o' sense, an' pride o' worth,
    Are higher rank than a' that.

Then let us pray that come it may,
    (As come it will for a' that,)
That Sense and Worth, o'er a' the earth,
    Shall bear the gree, an' a' that.
For a' that, an' a' that,
    It's coming yet for a' that,
That man to man, the world o'er,
    Shall brithers be for a' that.

Robert Burns

The Golden Treasury

William Shakespeare

John Donne

Edmund Spenser

John Milton

Ben Jonson

George Herbert

Sir Walter Raleigh

Sir Thomas Wyatt

Sir Philip Sidney

Alexander Pope

Andrew Marvell

Thomas Gray

Portraits of the Poets

John Dryden

Christopher Smart

William Blake

Robert Herrick

Walter Savage Landor

Oliver Goldsmith

John Clare

William Wordsworth

Samuel Taylor Coleridg

Percy Bysshe Shelley

John Keats

Lord Byron

The Golden Treasury

Emily Brontë

Thomas Moore

Christina Rossetti

Ralph Waldo Emerson

H. W. Longfellow

James Russell Lowell

Henry David Thoreau

William Cullen Bryant

Herman Melville

Robert Burns

Thomas Hood

Edward Fitzgerald

Portraits of the Poets

Alfred, Lord Tennyson

Walt Whitman

Emily Dickinson

Elizabeth B. Browning

Robert Browning

A. C. Swinburne

George Meredith

Matthew Arnold

Francis Thompson

Robert Bridges

Walter da la Mare

Edgar Allan Poe

The Golden Treasury

Gerard Manley Hopkins

W. B. Yeats

Thomas Hardy

D. H. Lawrence

A. E. Housman

John Masefield

Robert Frost

Wallace Stevens

E. A. Robinson

Wilfred Owen

Rupert Brooke

Rudyard Kipling

Portraits of the Poets

John Crowe Ransom

Edwin Muir

Robert Graves

William Carlos Williams

E. E. Cummings

Hart Crane

Archibald MacLeish

Robinson Jeffers

Conrad Aiken

Elinor Wylie

Vachel Lindsay

Edna St. Vincent Millay

The Golden Treasury

Ezra Pound

Marianne Moore

T. S. Eliot

William Empson

W. H. Auden

F. R. Higgins

Robert Penn Warren

Theodore Roethke

Stephen Spender

C. Day Lewis

W. R. Rodgers

Louis MacNeice

Portraits of the Poets

Dylan Thomas

George Barker

Vernon Watkins

Oscar Williams

Gene Derwood

Robert Lowell

Elizabeth Bishop

Richard Eberhart

Delmore Schwartz

Richard Wilbur

James Wright

Ted Hughes

309 Money, thou bane of bliss and source of woe,
Whence com'st thou, that thou art so fresh and fine?
I know thy parentage is base and low:
Man found thee poor and dirty in a mine.
Surely thou didst so little contribute
To this great kingdom which thou now hast got,
That he was fain, when thou wert destitute,
To dig thee out of thy dark cave and grot:
Thus forcing thee, by fire he made thee bright:
Nay, thou hast got the face of man; for we
Have with our stamp and seal transferred our right:
Thou art the man, and man but dross to thee.
Man calleth thee his wealth, who made thee rich,
And while he digs thee out, falls in the ditch.

George Herbert

310   **If There Were Dreams to Sell**

If there were dreams to sell,
      What would you buy?
Some cost a passing bell;
      Some a light sigh,
That shakes from Life's fresh crown
Only a rose-leaf down.
If there were dreams to sell,
Merry and sad to tell,
And the crier rang the bell,
      What would you buy?

A cottage lone and still,
      With bowers nigh,
Shadowy, my woes to still,
      Until I die.
Such pearl from Life's fresh crown
Fain would I shake me down.
Were dreams to have at will,
This would best heal my ill,
      This would I buy.

Thomas Lovell Beddoes

311   **The Call**

Sound, sound the clarion, fill the fife!
      Throughout the sensual world proclaim,
One crowded hour of glorious life
      Is worth an age without a name.

Thomas Osbert Mordaunt

All, all of a piece throughout:
Thy chase had a beast in view;
Thy wars brought nothing about;
Thy lovers were all untrue.
'Tis well an old age is out,
And time to begin a new.   *John Dryden*

313   The Seven Ages of Man

All the world's a stage,
And all the men and women merely players:
They have their exits and their entrances;
And one man in his time plays many parts,
His acts being seven ages. At first the infant,
Mewling and puking in the nurse's arms.
And then the whining school-boy, with his satchel,
And shining morning face, creeping like snail
Unwillingly to school. And then the lover
Sighing like a furnace, with a woeful ballad
Made to his mistress' eyebrow. Then a soldier,
Full of strange oaths, and bearded like the pard,
Jealous in honour, sudden and quick in quarrel,
Seeking the bubble reputation
Even in the cannon's mouth. And then the justice,
In fair round belly with good capon lin'd,
With eyes severe, and beard of formal cut,
Full of wise saws and modern instances;
And so he plays his part. The sixth age shifts
Into the lean and slipper'd pantaloon,
With spectacles on nose and pouch on side,
His youthful hose well sav'd a world too wide
For his shrunk shank; and his big manly voice,
Turning again toward childish treble, pipes
And whistles in his sound. Last scene of all,
That ends this strange eventful history,
Is second childishness and mere oblivion,
Sans teeth, sans eyes, sans taste, sans everything.
                        William Shakespeare

314   On a Fly Drinking from His Cup

Busy, curious, thirsty fly!
Drink with me and drink as I:
Freely welcome to my cup,
Couldst thou sip and sip it up:
Make the most of life you may,
Life is short and wears away.

Just alike, both mine and thine,
Hasten quick to their decline:
Thine's a summer, mine no more,
Though repeated to three-score.
Three-score summers, when they're gone,
Will appear as short as one!

William Oldys

15   Even Such Is Time

Even such is Time, which takes in trust
   Our youth, and joys, and all we have;
And pays us but with age and dust,
   Which, in the dark and silent grave,
When we have wandered all our ways,
Shuts up the story of our days:
   And from which earth and grave and dust
   The Lord shall raise me up, I trust.

Sir Walter Raleigh

16   On Time

Fly envious Time, till thou run out thy race,
Call on the lazy leaden-stepping hours,
Whose speed is but the heavy Plummet's pace;
And glut thy self with what thy womb devours,
Which is no more than what is false and vain,
And merely mortal dross;
So little is our loss,
So little is thy gain.
For when as each thing bad thou hast entomb'd,
And last of all, thy greedy self consum'd,
Then long Eternity shall greet our bliss
With an individual kiss;
And Joy shall overtake us as a flood,
When every thing that is sincerely good
And perfectly divine,
With Truth, and Peace, and Love shall ever shine
About the supreme Throne
Of him, t'whose happy-making sight alone,
When once our heav'nly-guided soul shall climb,
Then all this Earthy grossness quit,
Attir'd with Stars, we shall for ever sit,
Triumphing over Death, and Chance, and thee O Time.

John Milton

317   How soon hath Time the subtle thief of youth,
         Stol'n on his wing my three and twentieth year!
         My hasting days fly on with full career,
         But my late spring no bud or blossom shew'th.
         Perhaps my semblance might deceive the truth,
         That I to manhood am arriv'd so near,
         And inward ripeness doth much less appear,
         That some more timely-happy spirits endu'th.
         Yet be it less or more, or soon or slow,
         It shall be still in strictest measure ev'n,
         To that same lot, however mean, or high,
         Toward which Time leads me, and the will of Heav'n
         All is, if I have grace to use it so,
         As ever in my great Task-Master's eye.

                                              John Milton

318   **On Seeing the Elgin Marbles**

         My spirit is too weak—mortality
         Weighs heavily on me like unwilling sleep,
         And each imagined pinnacle and steep
         Of godlike hardship, tells me I must die
         Like a sick Eagle looking at the sky.
         Yet 'tis a gentle luxury to weep
         That I have not the cloudy winds to keep,
         Fresh for the opening of the morning's eye.
         Such dim-conceivèd glories of the brain
         Bring round the heart an undescribable feud;
         So do these wonders a most dizzy pain,
         That mingles Grecian grandeur with the rude
         Wasting of old Time—with a billowy main—
         A sun—a shadow of a magnitude.

                                              John Keats

319   **Vital Spark of Heavenly Flame**

              Vital spark of heavenly flame!
              Quit, O quit this mortal frame:
                 Trembling, hoping, lingering, flying,
                 O the pain, the bliss of dying!
              Cease, fond Nature, cease thy strife,
              And let me languish into life.

                 Hark! they whisper; angels say,
                 Sister Spirit, come away!

What is this absorbs me quite?
Steals my senses, shuts my sight,
Drowns my spirits, draws my breath?
Tell me, my soul, can this be death?

The world recedes; it disappears!
Heav'n opens on my eyes! my ears
With sounds seraphic ring!
Lend, lend your wings! I mount! I fly!
O Grave! where is thy victory?
O Death! where is thy sting!

Alexander Pope

20   On His Deceased Wife

Methought I saw my espousèd Saint
Brought to me like Alcestis from the grave,
Whom Jove's great Son to her glad Husband gave,
Rescued from death by force though pale and faint.
Mine as whom washed from spot of child-bed taint,
Purification in the old Law did save,
And such, as yet once more I trust to have
Full sight of her in Heaven without restraint,
Came vested all in white, pure as her mind:
Her face was veiled, yet to my fancied sight,
Love, sweetness, goodness, in her person shined
So clear, as in no face with more delight.
But O as to embrace me she inclined
I waked, she fled, and day brought back my night.

John Milton

21   Death, Be Not Proud

Death, be not proud, though some have callèd thee
Mighty and dreadful, for thou art not so;
For those whom thou think'st thou dost overthrow
Die not, poor Death; nor yet canst thou kill me.
From rest and sleep, which but thy pictures be,
Much pleasure; then from thee much more must flow;
And soonest our best men with thee do go—
Rest of their bones and souls' delivery!
Thou'rt slave to fate, chance, kings, and desperate men,
And dost with poison, war, and sickness dwell;
And poppy or charms can make us sleep as well
And better than thy stroke. Why swell'st thou then?
One short sleep past, we wake eternally,
And Death shall be no more: Death, thou shalt die.

John Donne

322 **They Are All Gone**

They are all gone into the world of light!
  And I alone sit lingering here;
Their very memory is fair and bright,
    And my sad thoughts doth clear.

It glows and glitters in my cloudy breast,
  Like stars upon some gloomy grove,
Or those faint beams in which this hill is dressed,
    After the sun's remove.

I see them walking in an air of glory,
  Whose light doth trample on my days;
My days, which are at best but dull and hoary,
    Mere glimmering and decays.

O holy Hope! and high Humility!
  High as the heavens above!
These are your walks, and you have showed them me,
    To kindle my cold love.

Dear beauteous Death! the jewel of the just,
  Shining nowhere but in the dark;
What mysteries do lie beyond thy dust,
    Could man outlook that mark!

He that hath found some fledged bird's nest may know
  At first sight if the bird be flown;
But what fair well or grove he sings in now,
    That is to him unknown.

And yet, as angels in some brighter dreams
  Call to the soul when man doth sleep,
So some strange thoughts transcend our wonted themes,
    And into glory peep.

If a star were confined into a tomb,
  Her captive flames must needs burn there;
But when the hand that locked her up gives room,
    She'll shine through all the sphere.

O Father of eternal life, and all
  Created glories under Thee!
Resume Thy spirit from this world of thrall
    Into true liberty.

Either disperse these mists, which blot and fill
   My perspective still as they pass;
Or else remove me hence unto that hill
    Where I shall need no glass.

Henry Vaughan

23   **When as Man's Life**

When as Man's life, the light of human lust,
In socket of his earthly lanthorne burns,
That all this glory unto ashes must,
And generation to corruption turns—
   Then fond desires that only fear their end,
   Do vainly wish for life, but to amend.

But when this life is from the body fled,
To see itself in that *eternal Glass,*
Where time doth end, and thoughts accuse the dead,
Where all to come is one with all that was;
   Then living men ask how he left his breath,
   That while he lived never thought of death.

Fulke Greville, Lord Brooke

24   **Like to the Falling of a Star**

    Like to the falling of a star,
    Or as the flights of eagles are,
    Or like the fresh spring's gaudy hue,
    Or silver drops of morning dew,
    Or like a wind that chafes the flood,
    Or bubbles which on water stood:
    Even such is man, whose borrowed light
    Is straight called in and paid to night:
    The wind blows out, the bubble dies,
    The spring intombed in autumn lies:
    The dew's dried up, the star is shot,
    The flight is past, and man forgot.

Henry King

25   **Times Go by Turns**

The loppèd tree in time may grow again,
Most naked plants renew both fruit and flower;
The sorriest wight may find release of pain,
The driest soil suck in some moistening shower;

Times go by turns, and chances change by course,
From foul to fair, from better hap to worse.

The sea of Fortune doth not ever flow,
She draws her favours to the lowest ebb;
Her tides have equal times to come and go,
Her loom doth weave the fine and coarsest web;
No joy so great but runneth to an end,
No hap so hard but may in fine amend.

Not always fall of leaf, nor ever spring,
No endless night, yet not eternal day;
The saddest birds a season find to sing,
The roughest storm a calm may soon allay:
Thus, with succeeding turn, God tempereth all,
That man may hope to rise, yet fear to fall.

A chance may win that by mischance was lost;
That net that holds no great, takes little fish;
In some things all, in all things none are crossed;
Few all they need, but none have all they wish.
Unmingled joys here to no man befall;
Who least, hath some; who most, hath never all.

Robert Southwell

326   **All the Flowers of the Spring**

All the flowers of the spring
Meet to perfume our burying;
These have but their growing prime,
And man doth flourish but his time:
Survey our progress from our birth;
We are set, we grow, we turn to earth.
Courts adieu, and all delights,
All bewitching appetites.
Sweetest breath and clearest eye,
Like perfumes, go out and die;
And consequently this is done
As shadows wait upon the sun.
Vain the ambition of kings
Who seek by trophies and dead things
To leave a living name behind,
And weave but nets to catch the wind.

John Webster

Upon a Wasp Chilled with Cold

The bear that breathes the northern blast
Did numb, torpedo-like, a wasp
Whose stiffened limbs encrampt, lay bathing
In Sol's warm breath and shine as saving,
Which with her hands she chafes and slams
Rubbing her legs, shanks, thighs, and hands.
Her petty toes, and fingers' ends
Nipt with this breath, she out extends
Unto the sun, in great desire
To warm her digits at that fire:
Doth hold her temples in this state
Where pulse doth beat, and head doth ache:
Doth turn and stretch her body small,
Doth comb her velvet capital
As if her little brain-pan were
A volume of choice precepts clear:
As if her satin jacket hot
Contained apothecary's shop
Of Nature's receipts, that prevails
To remedy all her sad ails,
As if her velvet helmet high
Did turret rationality.
She fans her wing up to the wind
As if her petticoat were lined
With reason's fleece, and hoises sail
And humming flies in thankful gale
Unto her dun curled palace hall,
Her warm thanks offering for all.
    Lord, clear my misted sight that I
May hence view thy Divinity,
Some sparks whereof thou up dost hasp
Within this little downy wasp,
In whose small corporation we
A school and a schoolmaster see:
Where we may learn, and easily find
A nimble Spirit, bravely mind
Her work in every limb: and lace
It up neat with a vital grace,
Acting each part though ne'er so small,
Here of this fustian animal,
Till I enravished climb into
The Godhead on this ladder do:
Where all my pipes inspired upraise
An heavenly music, furred with praise.

                                    Edward Taylor

328   Upon a Spider Catching a Fly

Thou sorrow, venom elf:
  Is this thy play,
To spin a web out of thyself
  To catch a fly?
    For why?

I saw a pettish wasp
  Fall foul therein:
Whom yet thy whorl pins did
    not hasp
  Lest he should fling
    His sting.

But as afraid, remote
  Didst stand hereat,
And with thy little fingers
    stroke
  And gently tap
    His back.

Thus gently him didst treat
  Lest he should pet,
And in a froppish, aspish heat
  Should gently fret
    Thy net.

Whereas the silly fly,
  Caught by its leg,
Thou by the throat took'st
    hastily,
  And 'hind the head
    Bite dead.

This goes to pot, that not
  Nature doth call.
Strive not above what strength
    hath got,
  Lest in the brawle
    Thou fall.

This fray seems thus to us:
  Hell's spider gets
His entrails spun to whip
    cords thus
  And wove to nets,
    And sets.

To tangle Adam's race
  In's stratagems
To their destructions, spoil'd,
    made base
  By venom things,
    Damn'd sins.

But mighty, Gracious Lord,
  Communicate
Thy Grace to break the cord;
    afford
  Us glory's gate.
    And state.

We'll nightingale sing like,
  When perched on high
In glory's cage, thy glory,
    bright:
  Yea, thankfully,
    For joy.

Edward Taylor

329   Who Is at My Window?

Who is at my window? Who? Who?
  Go from my window! Go! Go!
Who calls there, like a strangèr,
  Go from my window! Go!

—Lord, I am here, a wretched mortàl,
That for thy mercy doth cry and call
Unto thee, my lord celestiàl,
See who is at thy window, who?—

Remember thy sin, remember thy smart,
And also for thee what was my part,
Remember the spear that pierced my heart,
And in at my door thou shalt go.

I ask no thing of thee therefore,
But love for love, to lay in store.
Give me thy heart; I ask no more,
And in at my door thou shalt go.

Who is at my window? Who?
Go from my window! Go!
Cry no more there, like a strangèr,
But in at my door thou go!

Anon.

330   News

News from a foreign country came
As if my treasure and my wealth lay there;
    So much it did my heart inflame,
'Twas wont to call my Soul into mine ear;
        Which thither went to meet
            The approaching sweet,
        And on the threshold stood
To entertain the unknown Good.
            It hover'd there
        As if 'twould leave mine ear,
    And was so eager to embrace
        The joyful tidings as they came,
'Twould almost leave its dwelling-place
        To entertain that same.

As if the tidings were the things,
My very joys themselves, my foreign treasure—
    Or else did bear them on their wings—
With so much joy they came, with so much pleasure.
        My Soul stood at that gate
            To recreate
        Itself with bliss, and to
Be pleased with speed. A fuller view

It fain would take,
Yet journeys back would make
Unto my heart; as if 'twould fain
Go out to meet, yet stay within
To fit a place to entertain
And bring the tidings in.

What sacred instinct did inspire
My soul in childhood with a hope so strong?
What secret force moved my desire
To expect my joys beyond the seas, so young?
Felicity I knew
Was out of view,
And being here alone,
I saw that happiness was gone
From me! For this
I thirsted absent bliss,
And thought that sure beyond the seas,
Or else in something near at hand—
I knew not yet—since naught did please
I knew—my Bliss did stand.

But little did the infant dream
That all the treasures of the world were by:
And that himself was so the cream
And crown of all which round about did lie.
Yet thus it was: the Gem,
The Diadem,
The ring enclosing all
That stood upon this earthly ball,
The Heavenly eye,
Much wider than the sky,
Wherein they all included were,
The glorious Soul, that was the King
Made to possess them, did appear
A small and little thing!

Thomas Traherne

331   **Batter My Heart**

Batter my heart, three personed God; for you
As yet but knock, breathe, shine, and seek to mend;
That I may rise and stand, o'erthrow me and bend
Your force to break, blow, burn and make me new.
I, like an usurped town, to another due,
Labour to admit you, but Oh, to no end;

Reason, your viceroy in me, me should defend,
But is captived and proves weak or untrue.
Yet dearly I love you and would be loved fain,
But am betrothed unto your enemy:
Divorce me, untie or break that knot again,
Take me to you, imprison me, for I
Except you enthrall me, never shall be free,
Nor ever chaste, except you ravish me.

John Donne

332   If Poisonous Minerals

If poisonous minerals, and if that tree
Whose fruit threw death on else immortal us,
If lecherous goats, if serpents envious
Cannot be damned, Alas! why should I be?
Why should intent or reason, born in me,
Make sins, else equal, in me more heinous?
And mercy being easy, and glorious
To God, in his stern wrath why threatens he?
But who am I, that dare dispute with thee,
O God? O! of thine only worthy blood,
And my tears, make a heavenly Lethean flood,
And drown in it my sin's black memory;
That thou remember them, some claim as debt,
I think it mercy, if thou wilt forget.

John Donne

333   A Nocturnal upon St. Lucy's Day

'Tis the year's midnight, and it is the day's,
Lucy's, who scarce seven hours herself unmasks;
   The sun is spent, and now his flasks
   Send forth light squibs, no constant rays;
      The world's whole sap is sunk;
The general balm th' hydroptic earth hath drunk,
Whither, as to the bed's feet, life is shrunk,
Dead and interred; yet all these seem to laugh,
Compared with me, who am their epitaph.

Study me then, you who shall lovers be
At the next world, that is, at the next spring;
   For I am every dead thing,
   In whom Love wrought new alchemy.
      For his art did express
A quintessence even from nothingness,

From dull privations, and lean emptiness;
He ruined me, and I am re-begot
Of absence, darkness, death—things which are not.

All others from all things draw all that's good,
Life, soul, form, spirit, whence they being have;
   I, by Love's limbec, am the grave
   Of all that's nothing. Oft a flood
     Have we two wept, and so
Drowned the whole world, us two; oft did we grow
To be two chaoses, when we did show
Care to aught else; and often absences
Withdrew our souls, and made us carcasses.

But I am by her death, which word wrongs her,
Of the first nothing the elixir grown;
   Were I a man, that I were one
   I needs must know; I should prefer,
     If I were any beast,
Some ends, some means; yea plants, yea stones detest
And love; all, all some properties invest;
If I am ordinary nothing were,
As shadow, a light and body must be here.

But I am none, nor will my sun renew.
You lovers, for whose sake the lesser sun
   At this time to the Goat is run
   To fetch new lust, and give it you,
     Enjoy your summer all;
Since she enjoys her long night's festival,
Let me prepare towards her, and let me call
This hour her vigil, and her eve, since this
Both the year's and the day's deep midnight is.

                          John Donne

334   **Jerusalem**

    And did those feet in ancient time
      Walk upon England's mountains green?
    And was the holy Lamb of God
      On England's pleasant pastures seen?

    And did the Countenance Divine
      Shine forth upon our clouded hills?
    And was Jerusalem builded here
      Among these dark Satanic Mills?

Bring me my bow of burning gold!
  Bring me my arrows of desire!
Bring me my spear! O clouds, unfold!
  Bring me my chariot of fire!

I will not cease from mental fight,
  Nor shall my sword sleep in my hand,
Till we have built Jerusalem
  In England's green and pleasant land.

William Blake

335   **The Tiger**

Tiger, tiger, burning bright
In the forests of the night,
What immortal hand or eye
Could frame thy fearful symmetry?

In what distant deeps or skies
Burnt the fire of thine eyes?
On what wings dare he aspire?
What the hand dare seize the fire?

And what shoulder and what art
Could twist the sinews of thy heart?
And, when thy heart began to beat,
What dread hand and what dread feet?

What the hammer? What the chain?
In what furnace was thy brain?
What the anvil? What dread grasp
Dare its deadly terrors clasp?

When the stars threw down their spears,
And water'd heaven with their tears,
Did He smile His work to see?
Did He who made the lamb make thee?

Tiger, tiger, burning bright
In the forests of the night,
What immortal hand or eye
Dare frame thy fearful symmetry?

William Blake

The Spacious Firmament

The spacious firmament on high,
With all the blue ethereal sky,
And spangled heavens, a shining frame,
Their great Original proclaim.
The unwearied sun from day to day
Does his Creator's power display,
And publishes to every land
The work of an Almighty hand.

Soon as the evening shades prevail,
The moon takes up the wondrous tale,
And nightly to the listening earth
Repeats the story of her birth;
Whilst all the stars that round her burn,
And all the planets in their turn,
Confirm the tidings as they roll,
And spread the truth from pole to pole.

What though in solemn silence, all
Move round this dark terrestrial ball?
What though nor real voice nor sound
Amidst their radiant orbs be found?
In Reason's ear they all rejoice,
And utter forth a glorious voice,
Forever singing as they shine:
'The hand that made us is divine!'

Joseph Addison

Hail, Holy Light . . .

Hail, holy Light, offspring of Heaven first-born,
Or of th' Eternal coeternal beam
May I express thee unblam'd? since God is light,
And never but in unapproached light
Dwelt from eternity, dwelt then in thee,
Bright effluence of bright essence increate.
Or hear'st thou rather pure ethereal stream,
Whose fountain who shall tell? Before the Sun,
Before the Heavens thou wert, and at the voice
Of God, as with a mantle didst invest
The rising world of waters dark and deep,
Won from the void and formless Infinite.
Thee I revisit now with bolder wing,
Escap'd the Stygian Pool, though long detain'd

In that obscure sojourn, while in my flight
Through utter and through middle darkness borne,
With other notes than to th' Orphean lyre
I sung of Chaos and eternal Night,
Taught by the heav'nly Muse to venture down
The dark descent, and up to reascend,
Though hard and rare: thee I revisit safe,
And feel thy sovran vital lamp; but thou
Revisit'st not these eyes, that roll in vain
To find thy piercing ray, and find no dawn;
So thick a drop serene hath quencht their orbs,
Or dim suffusion veil'd. Yet not the more
Cease I to wander where the Muses haunt
Clear spring, or shady grove, or sunny hill,
Smit with the love of sacred song; but chief
Thee Sion and the flowery brooks beneath,
That wash thy hallow'd feet, and warbling flow,
Nightly I visit: nor sometimes forget
Those other two enquall'd with me in fate,
So were I equall'd with them in renown,
Blind Thamyris and blind Maeonides,
And Tiresias and Phineus prophets old.
Then feed on thoughts, that voluntary move
Harmonious numbers; as the wakeful bird
Sings darkling, and in shadiest covert hid
Tunes her nocturnal note. Thus with the year
Seasons return, but not to me returns
Day, or the sweet approach of ev'n or morn,
Or sight of vernal bloom, or summer's rose,
Or flocks, or herds, or human face divine;
But cloud instead, and ever-during dark
Surrounds me, from the cheerful ways of men
Cut off, and for the book of knowledge fair
Presented with a universal blank
Of Nature's works to me expung'd and ras'd
And wisdom at one entrance quite shut out.
So much the rather thou Celestial Light
Shine inward, and the mind through all her powers
Irradiate, there plant eyes, all mist from thence
Purge and disperse, that I may see and tell
Of things invisible to mortal sight.

John Milton

338 Redemption

Having been tenant long to a rich lord,
Not thriving, I resolved to be bold,
And make a suit unto him, to afford
A new small-rented lease, and cancel the old.
In heaven at his manor I him sought:
They told me there, that he was lately gone
About some land, which he had dearly bought
Long since on earth to take possession,
I straight returned, and knowing his great birth,
Sought him accordingly in great resorts;
In cities, theatres, gardens, parks, and courts:
At length I heard a ragged noise and mirth
Of thieves and murderers: there I him espied,
Who straight, *Your suit is granted*, said, and died.

George Herbert

339 The Song of David

He sang of God, the mighty source
Of all things, the stupendous force
  On which all strength depends:
From Whose right arm, beneath Whose eyes,
All period, power, and enterprise
  Commences, reigns, and ends.

The world, the clustering spheres He made,
The glorious light, the soothing shade,
  Dale, champaign, grove and hill:
The multitudinous abyss,
Where secrecy remains in bliss,
  And wisdom hides her skill.

Tell them, I AM, Jehovah said
To Moses: while Earth heard in dread,
  And, smitten to the heart,
At once, above, beneath, around,
All Nature, without voice or sound,
  Replied, 'O Lord, THOU ART.'

Christopher Smart

340 The Man of Prayer

Strong is the horse upon his speed;
Strong in pursuit the rapid glede,
  Which makes at once his game:

Strong the tall ostrich on the ground;
Strong through the turbulent profound
　　Shoots Xiphias to his aim.

Strong is the lion—like a coal
His eyeball—like a bastion's mole
　　His chest against the foes:
Strong, the gier-eagle on his sail,
Strong against tide, th' enormous whale
　　Emerges as he goes.

But stronger still, in earth and air,
And in the sea, the man of prayer,
　　And far beneath the tide;
And in the seat to faith assigned,
Where ask is have, where seek is find,
　　Where knock is open wide.

　　　　　　　　　　　　　　Christopher Smart

341 　　　　　The Collar

I struck the board, and cried, 'No more;
　　I will abroad!
What, shall I ever sigh and pine?
My lines and life are free; free as the road,
　　Loose as the wind, as large as store.
　　　Shall I be still in suit?
　　Have I no harvest but a thorn
　　To let me blood, and not restore
What I have lost with cordial fruit?
　　　Sure there was wine
　　Before my sighs did dry it; there was corn
　　　Before my tears did drown it.
　　Is the year only lost to me?
　　　Have I no bays to crown it,
No flowers, no garlands gay? all blasted,
　　　All wasted?
　　Not so, my heart; but there is fruit,
　　　And thou hast hands.
　　Recover all thy sigh-blown age
On double pleasures; leave thy cold dispute
Of what is fit and not; forsake thy cage,
　　　Thy rope of sands
Which petty thoughts have made; and made to thee
　　Good cable, to enforce and draw,
　　　And be thy law,

While thou didst wink and wouldst not see.
    Away! take heed;
    I will abroad.
Call in thy death's head there, tip up thy fears:
    He that forbears
To suit and serve his need
    Deserves his load.'
But as I raved, and grew more fierce and wild
    At every word,
  Methought I heard one calling, 'Child';
    And I replied, 'My Lord.'

George Herber

342   **Housewifery**

Make me, O Lord, Thy spinning-wheel complete
    Thy hold Word my distaff make for me;
Make mine affections Thy swift flyers neat;
    And make my soul Thy holy spool to be;
    My conversation make to be Thy reel,
    And reel the yarn thereon spun of Thy wheel.

Make me Thy loom then; knit therein this twine;
    And make Thy Holy Spirit, Lord, wind quills.
Then weave the web Thyself. The yarn is fine.
    Thine ordinances make my fulling mills.
    Then dye the same in heavenly colors choice,
    All pinked with varnished flowers of paradise.

Then clothe therewith mine understanding will,
    Affections, judgment, conscience, memory,
My words and actions, that their shine may fill
    My ways with glory and Thee glorify.
    Then mine apparel shall display before Ye
    That I am clothed in holy robes for glory.

Edward Taylo

343   **The Tear**

What bright soft thing is this,
    Sweet Mary, thy fair eyes' expense?
A moist spark it is,
    A watery diamond; from whence
The very term, I think, was found,
The water of a diamond.

Oh! 'tis not a tear,
  'Tis a star about to drop
From thine eye, its sphere;
  The Sun will stoop and take it up.
Proud will his sister be to wear
This thine eye's jewel in her ear.

Oh! 'tis a tear,
  Too true a tear; for no sad eyne,
How sad soe'er,
  Rain so true a tear as thine;
Each drop, leaving a place so dear,
Weeps for itself, is its own tear.

Such a pearl as this is,
  (Slipped from Aurora's dewy breast)
The rose-bud's sweet lip kisses;
  And such the rose itself, when vexed
With ungentle flames, does shed,
Sweating in too warm a bed.

Such the maiden gem
  By wanton Spring put on,
Peeps from her parent stem,
  And blushes on the manly Sun:
This wat'ry blossom of thy eyne,
Ripe, will make the richer wine.

Fair drop, why quak'st thou so?
  'Cause thou straight must lay thy head
In the dust? Oh no;
  The dust shall never be thy bed:
A pillow for thee will I bring,
Stuffed with down of angel's wing.

Thus carried up on high,
  (For to heaven thou must go)
Sweetly shalt thou lie,
  And in soft slumbers bathe thy woe;
Till the singing orbs awake thee,
And one of their bright chorus make thee.

There thyself shalt be
  An eye, but not a weeping one;
Yet I doubt of thee,
  Wither th'hadst rather there have shown
An eye of Heaven; or still shine here
In th' Heaven of Mary's eye, a tear.

Richard Crashaw

On a Drop of Dew

See how the orient dew,
   Shed from the bosom of the morn
   Into the blowing roses,
Yet careless of its mansion new;
For the clear region where 'twas born
   Round in itself encloses:
And in its little globe's extent,
Frames as it can its native element.
   How it the purple flower does slight,
      Scarce touching where it lies,
      But gazing back upon the skies,
      Shines with a mournful light;
         Like its own tear,
Because so long divided from the sphere.
      Restless it rolls and unsecure,
         Trembling lest it grow impure:
      Till the warm sun pity its pain,
And to the skies exhale it back again.
      So the soul, that drop, that ray
Of the clear fountain of eternal day,
Could it within the human flower be seen,
      Rememb'ring still its former height,
      Shuns the sweet leaves and blossoms green;
      And, recollecting its own light,
Does, in its pure and circling thoughts, express
The greater heaven in a heaven less.
     In how coy a figure wound,
      Every way it turns away:
     So the world excluding round,
      Yet receiving in the day.
      Dark beneath, but bright above:
      Here disdaining, there in love.
   How loose and easy hence to go:
   How girt and ready to ascend.
   Moving but on a point below,
   It all about does upwards bend.
Such did the manna's sacred dew distill;
White, and entire, though congealed and chill.
Congealed on earth: but does, dissolving, run
Into the glories of the almighty sun.

Andrew Marve

345

I was angry with my friend:
I told my wrath, my wrath did end.
I was angry with my foe:
I told it not, my wrath did grow.

And I water'd it in fears,
Night and morning with my tears;
And I sunnèd it with smiles,
And with soft deceitful wiles.

And it grew both day and night,
Till it bore an apple bright;
And my foe beheld it shine,
And he knew that it was mine,

And into my garden stole
When the night had veil'd the pole:
In the morning glad I see
My foe outstretch'd beneath the tree.

William Blake

346

Against Hope

Hope, whose weak being ruined is
Alike if it succeed and if it miss;
Whom good or ill does equally confound,
And both the horns of fate's dilemma wound.
Vain shadow! which does vanish quite
Both at full noon and perfect night!
The stars have not a possibility
Of blessing thee;
If things then from their end we happy call,
'Tis hope is the most hopeless thing of all.

Hope, thou bold taster of delight,
Who whilst thou shouldst but taste devour'st it quite!
Thou bringst us an estate, yet leav'st us poor
By clogging it with legacies before!
The joys which we entire should wed
Come deflowered virgins to our bed;
Good fortunes without gain imported be,
Such mighty custom's paid to thee.
For joy, like wine, kept close does better taste;
If it take air before, its spirits waste.

Hope, fortune's cheating lottery!
Where for one prize an hundred blanks there be;
Fond archer, hope, who tak'st thy air so far,
That still or short or wide thine arrows are!
Thin empty cloud, which th'eye deceives
With shapes that our own fancy gives!
A cloud, which gilt and painted now appears,
But must drop presently in tears!
When thy false beams o'er reason's light prevail,
By *Ignes fatui* for north stars we sail.

Brother of fear, more gaily clad!
The merrier fool o' th' two, yet quite as mad:
Sire of repentance, child of fond desire!
That blow'st the alchemist's and lover's fire!
Leading them still insensibly on
By the strange witchcraft of anon!
By thee the one does changing nature through
Her endless labyrinths pursue,
And th'other chases woman, whilst she goes
More ways and turns than hunted nature knows.

Abraham Cowley

347   **For Hope**

Richard Crashaw's Answer

Dear hope! Earth's dowry and heaven's debt!
The entity of those that are not yet.
Subtlest, but surest being! Thou by whom
Our nothing has a definition!
Substantial shade! whose sweet allay
Blends both the noons of night and day.
Fates cannot find out a capacity
Of hurting thee.
From Thee their lean dilemma with blunt horn
Shrinks, as the sick moon from the wholesome morn.

Rich hope! Love's legacy under lock
Of faith! still spending and still growing stock!
Our crown-land lies above, yet each meal brings
A seemly portion for the sons of kings.
Nor will the virgin joys we wed
Come less unbroken to our bed
Because that from the bridal cheek of bliss
Thou steal'st us down a distant kiss.
Hope's chaste stealth harms no more joy's maidenhead
Than spousal rites prejudge the marriage bed.

Fair hope! Our earlier heaven, by thee
Young time is taster to eternity.
Thy generous wine with age grows strong, not sour.
Nor does it kill the fruit to smell the flower.
Thy golden, growing head never hangs down,
Till in the lap of love's full noon
It falls, and dies! O no, it melts away
As does the dawn into the day,
As lumps of sugar lose themselves and twine
Their supple essence with the soul of wine.

Fortune? Alas, above the world's low wars,
Hope walks, and kicks the curl'd heads of conspiring stars.
Her keel cuts not the waves where these winds stir;
Fortune's whole lottery is one blank to her.
Her shafts and she fly far above
And forage in the fields of light and love.
Sweet hope! Kind cheat! Fair fallacy! By thee
We are not Where nor What we be,
But What and Where we would be. Thus art thou
Our absent Presence and our future Now.

Faith's sister! Nurse of fair desire!
Fear's antidote! A wise and well-stay'd fire!
Temper 'twixt chill despair and torrid joy!
Queen Regent in young Love's minority!
Though the vext chymick vainly chases
His fugitive gold through all her faces,
Though Love's more fierce, more fugitive fires assay
One face more fugitive than all they,
True hope's a glorious hunter, and her chase
The God of Nature in the fields of grace.

Richard Crashaw

348   **The World**

I saw Eternity the other night,
Like a great ring of pure and endless light,
        All calm, as it was bright;
And round beneath it, Time in hours, days, years,
        Driven by the spheres
Like a vast shadow moved; in which the world
        And all her train were hurled.
The doting lover in his quaintest strain
        Did there complain;
Near him, his lute, his fancy, and his flights,

Wit's sour delights;
With gloves, and knots, the silly snares of pleasure,
    Yet his dear treasure,
All scattered lay, while he his eyes did pour
    Upon a flower.

The darksome statesman, hung with weights and woe
Like a thick midnight-fog, moved there so slow,
    He did not stay, nor go;
Condemning thoughts—like sad eclipses—scowl
    Upon his soul,
And clouds of crying witnesses without
    Pursued him with one shout.
Yet digged the mole, and lest his ways be found,
    Worked underground,
Where he did clutch his prey; but one did see
    That policy.
Churches and altars fed him; perjuries
    Were gnats and flies;
It rained about him blood and tears, but he
    Drank them as free.

The fearful miser on a heap of rust
Sat pining all his life there, did scarce trust
    His own hands with the dust,
Yet would not place one piece above, but lives
    In fear of thieves.
Thousands there were as frantic as himself,
    And hugged each one his pelf;
The downright epicure placed heav'n in sense,
    And scorned pretence;
While others, slipped into a wide excess,
    Said little less;
The weaker sort slight, trivial wares enslave,
    Who think them brave;
And poor, despisèd Truth sat counting by
    Their victory.

Yet some, who all this while did weep and sing,
And sing and weep, soared up into the ring;
    But most would use no wing.
Oh, fools—said I—thus to prefer dark night
    Before true light!
To live in grots and caves, and hate the day
    Because it shows the way;
The way, which from this dead and dark abode
    Leads up to God;

A way where you might tread the sun, and be
      More bright than he!
But as I did their madness so discuss,
      One whispered thus,
'This ring the Bridegroom did for none provide,
      But for His bride.'

Henry Vaughan

349   **What If This Present**

What if this present were the world's last night?
Mark in my heart, O Soul, where thou dost dwell,
The picture of Christ crucified, and tell
Whether that countenance can thee affright:
Tears in his eyes quench the amazing light,
Blood fills his frowns, which from his pierc'd head fell.
And can that tongue adjudge thee unto hell,
Which pray'd forgiveness for his foes' fierce spite?
No, no; but as in my idolatry
I said to all my profane mistresses,
Beauty, of pity, foulness only is
A sign of rigour: so I say to thee,
To wicked spirits are horrid shapes assign'd,
This beauteous form assures a piteous mind.

John Donne

350   **The Hour Glass**

Consider this small dust, here in the glass,
      By atoms moved:
Could you believe that this the body was
      Of one that loved;
And in his mistress' flame playing like a fly,
Was turned to cinders by her eye:
Yes; and in death, as life unblessed,
      To have it expressed,
Even ashes of lovers find no rest.

Ben Jonson

351   **O Western Wind**

O western wind, when wilt thou blow,
That the small rain down can rain?
Christ, if my love were in my arms
And I in my bed again!

Anon.

352
They Flee from Me

They flee from me that sometime did me seek,
With naked foot stalking in my chamber,
I have seen them gentle, tame, and meek,
That now are wild, and do not remember
That some time they put themselves in danger
To take bread at my hand; and now they range,
Busily seeking with a continual change.

Thanked be fortune, it hath been otherwise
Twenty times better; but once, in speciall,
In thin array, after a pleasant guise,
When her loose gown from her shoulders did fall,
And she me caught in her arms long and small,
Therewith all sweetly did me kiss,
And softly said, Dear heart, how like you this?

It was no dream; I lay broad awaking.
But all is turned now through my gentleness
Into a strange fashion of forsaking;
And I have leave to go of her goodness,
And she also to use newfangleness.
But since that I so kindly am served,
I fain would know what *she* hath deserved.

Sir Thomas Wyatt

353
O Sing Unto My Roundelay

O sing unto my roundelay,
O drop the briny tear with me;
Dance no more at holyday,
Like a running river be:
    My love is dead,
        Gone to his death-bed
All under the willow-tree.

Black his cryne as the winter night,
White his rode as the summer snow,
Red his face as the morning light,
Cold he lies in the grave below:
    My love is dead,
        Gone to his death-bed
All under the willow-tree.

Sweet his tongue as the throstle's note,
Quick in dance as thought can be,
Deft his tabor, cudgel stout;
O he lies by the willow-tree!
    My love is dead,
     Gone to his death-bed
All under the willow-tree.

Hark! the raven flaps his wing
In the brier'd dell below;
Hark! the death-owl loud doth sing
To the nightmares, as they go:
    My love is dead,
     Gone to his death-bed
All under the willow-tree.

See! the white moon shines on high;
Whiter is my true-love's shroud:
Whiter than the morning sky,
Whiter than the evening cloud:
    My love is dead,
     Gone to his death-bed
All under the willow-tree.

Here upon my true-love's grave
Shall the barren flowers be laid;
Not one holy saint to save
All the coldness of a maid:
    My love is dead,
     Gone to his death-bed
All under the willow-tree.

With my hands I'll dent the briers
Round his holy corse to gre:
Ouph and fairy, light your fires,
Here my body still shall be:
    My love is dead,
     Gone to his death-bed
All under the willow-tree.

Come, with acorn-cup and thorn,
Drain my heartès blood away;
Life and all its good I scorn,
Dance by night, or feast by day:
    My love is dead,
     Gone to his death-bed
All under the willow-tree.

Thomas Chatterton

354 **The Nightingale**

The nightingale, as soon as April bringeth
    Unto her rested sense a perfect waking,
While late bare earth, proud of new clothing, springeth,
    Sings out her woes, a thorn her song-book making,
      And mournfully bewailing,
Her throat in tunes expresseth
What grief her breast oppresseth
    For Tereus' force on her chaste will prevailing.
O Philomela fair, O take some gladness,
That here is juster cause of plaintful sadness:
Thine earth now springs, mine fadeth;
Thy thorn without, my thorn my heart invadeth.

Alas, she hath no other cause of anguish
    But Tereus' love, on her by strong hand wroken,
Wherein she suff'ring, all her spirits languish,
    Full womanlike complains her will was broken.
      But I, who, daily craving
Cannot have to content me,
Have more cause to lament me,
    Since wanting is more woe than too much having.
O Philomela fair, O take some gladness,
That here is juster cause of plaintful sadness:
Thine earth now springs, mine fadeth;
Thy thorn without, my thorn my heart invadeth.

                  Sir Philip Sidney

355 **To His Coy Mistress**

Had we but world enough, and time,
This coyness, lady, were no crime.
We would sit down, and think which way
To walk, and pass our long love's day.
Thou by the Indian Ganges' side
Should'st rubies find: I by the tide
Of Humber would complain. I would
Love you ten years before the Flood,
And you should, if you please, refuse
Till the conversion of the Jews.
My vegetable love should grow
Vaster than empires, and more slow.
An hundred years should go to praise
Thine eyes, and on thy forehead gaze:
Two hundred to adore each breast:
But thirty thousand to the rest,
An age at least to every part,

And the last age should show your heart.
For, lady, you deserve this state,
Nor would I love at lower rate.
  But at my back I always hear
Time's wingèd chariot hurrying near:
And yonder all before us lie
Deserts of vast eternity.
Thy beauty shall no more be found;
Nor, in thy marble vault, shall sound
My echoing song: then worms shall try
That long-preserved virginity,
And your quaint honour trun to dust,
And into ashes all my lust.
The grave's a fine and private place,
But none, I think, do there embrace.
  Now, therefore, while the youthful hue
Sits on thy skin like morning dew,
And while thy willing soul transpires
At every pore with instant fires,
Now let us sport us while we may;
And now, like amorous birds of prey,
Rather at once our Time devour,
Than languish in his slow-chapt power.
Let us roll all our strength and all
Our sweetness up into one ball,
And tear our pleasures with rough strife
Thorough the iron gates of life.
Thus, though we cannot make our sun
Stand still, yet we will make him run.

Andrew Marvell

356 Look in thy glass, and tell the face thou viewest
Now is the time that face should form another;
Whose fresh repair if now thou not renewest,
Thou dost beguile the world, unbless some mother.
For where is she so fair whose uneared womb
Disdains the tillage of thy husbandry?
Or who is he so fond will be the tomb
Of his self-love, to stop posterity?
Thou art thy mother's glass, and she in thee
Calls back the lovely April of her prime:
So thou through windows of thine age shalt see,
Despite of wrinkles, this thy golden time.
But if thou love, remembered not to be,
Die single, and thine image dies with thee.

William Shakespeare

357   **Chloris in the Snow**

I saw fair Chloris walk alone,
When feather'd rain came softly down,
As Jove descending from his Tower
To court her in a silver shower:
The wanton snow flew to her breast,
Like pretty birds into their nest,
But, overcome with whiteness there,
For grief it thaw'd into a tear:
Thence falling on her garments' hem,
To deck her, froze into a gem.   *William Strode*

358   **The Heavenly Rhetoric**

Did not the heavenly rhetoric of thine eye,
'Gainst whom the world cannot hold argument,
Persuade my heart to this false perjury?
Vows for thee broke deserve not punishment.
A woman I forswore; but I will prove,
Thou being a goddess, I forswore not thee:
My vow was earthly, thou a heavenly love;
Thy grace being gain'd cures all disgrace in me.
Vows are but breath, and breath a vapour is:
Then thou, fair sun, which on my earth doth shine,
Exhalest this vapour-vow; in thee it is:
If broken then, it is no fault of mine:
If by me broke, what fool is not so wise
To lose an oath to win a paradise?

                                     William Shakespeare

359   **What Is Your Substance**

What is your substance, whereof are you made,
That millions of strange shadows on you tend?
Since every one hath, every one, one shade,
And you, but one, can every shadow lend.
Describe Adonis, and the counterfeit
Is poorly imitated after you;
On Helen's cheek all art of beauty set,
And you in Grecian tires are painted new:
Speak of the spring and plenty of the year,
The one doth shadow of your beauty show,
The other as your bounty doth appear;
And you in every blessèd shape we know.
In all external grace you have some part,
But you like none, none you, for constant heart.

                                     William Shakespeare

360
The Highway

Highway, since you my chief Parnassus be,
And that my Muse, to some ears not unsweet,
Tempers her words to trampling horses' feet
More oft than to a chamber-melody,—
Now blessèd you bear onward blessèd me
To her, where I my heart, safe-left, shall meet;
My Muse and I must you of duty greet
With thanks and wishes, wishing thankfully;
Be you still fair, honour'd by public heed;
By no encroachment wrong'd, nor time forgot;
Nor blamed for blood, nor shamed for sinful deed;
And that you know I envy you no lot
Of highest wish, I wish you so much bliss,
Hundreds of years you Stella's feet may kiss!

Sir Philip Sidney

361
The Constant Lover

Out upon it, I have loved
  Three whole days together!
And am like to love three more,
  If it prove fair weather.

Time shall moult away his wings
  Ere he shall discover
In the whole wide world again
  Such a constant lover.

But the spite on't is, no praise
  Is due at all to me:
Love with me had made no stays,
  Had it any been but she.

Had it any been but she,
  And that very face,
There had been at least ere this
  A dozen dozen in her place.

Sir John Suckling

362
Go and catch a falling star,
  Get with child a mandrake root,
Tell me where all past years are,
  Or who cleft the devil's foot,

Teach me to hear mermaids' singing,
  Or to keep off envy's stinging,
      And find
      What wind
Serves to advance an honest mind.

If thou be'st born to strange sights,
  Things invisible go see,
Ride ten thousand days and nights,
  Till Age snow white hairs on thee;
Thou, when thou return'st, will tell me
All strange wonders that befell thee,
      And swear
      No where
Lives a woman true and fair.

If thou find'st one, let me know;
  Such a pilgrimage were sweet,
Yet do not; I would not go,
  Though at next door we might meet.
Though she were true when you met her,
And last till you write your letter,
      Yet she
      Will be
False, ere I come, to two or three.

                           John Donne

363   The Message

Send home my long-strayed eyes to me,
Which, oh! too long have dwelt on thee;
Yet since there they have learned such ill,
    Such forced fashions
    And false passions,
      That they be
      Made by thee
Fit for no good sight, keep them still.

Send home my harmless heart again,
Which no unworthy thought could stain;
But if it be taught by thine
    To make jestings
    Of protestings,
      And break both
      Word and oath,
Keep it, for then 'tis none of mine.

Yet send me back my heart and eyes,
That I may know and see thy lies,
And may laugh and joy, when thou
    Art in anguish
     And dost languish
      For some one
      That will none,
Or prove as false as thou art now.

John Donne

364   Still to Be Neat

Still to be neat, still to be drest
As you were going to a feast;
Still to be powder'd, still perfum'd:
Lady, it is to be presum'd,
Though art's hid causes are not found,
All is not sweet, all is not sound.

Give me a look, give me a face
That makes simplicity a grace;
Robes loosely flowing, hair as free:
Such sweet neglect more taketh me
Than all th' adulteries of art;
They strike mine eyes, but not my heart.

Ben Jonson

365   The Good Morrow

I wonder, by my troth, what thou and I
Did till we loved? were we not weaned till then,
But sucked on country pleasures, childishly?
Or snorted we in the Seven Sleepers' den?
'Twas so; but this, all pleasures fancies be.
If ever any beauty I did see
Which I desired, and got, 'twas but a dream of thee.

And now good morrow to our waking souls,
Which watch not one another out of fear;
For love all love of other sights controls,
And makes one little room an everywhere.
Let sea-discoverers to new worlds have gone;
Let maps to other, worlds on worlds have shown;
Let us possess one world; each hath one, and is one.

My face in thine eye, thine in mine appears,
And true, plain hearts do in the faces rest;
Where can we find two better hemispheres
Without sharp north, without declining west?
Whatever dies, was not mixed equally;
If our loves be one, or thou and I
Love so alike that none do slacken, none can die.

John Donne

366   **The Dream**

Dear love, for nothing less than thee
Would I have broke this happy dream;
   It was a theme
For reason, much too strong for fantasy.
Therefore thou waked'st me wisely; yet
My dream thou brok'st not, but continued'st it.
Thou art so true that thoughts of thee suffice
To make dreams truths and fables histories;
Enter these arms, for since thou thought'st it best
Not to dream all my dream, let's act the rest.

As lightning, or a taper's light,
Thine eyes, and not thy noise, waked me;
   Yet I thought thee—
For thou lov'st truth—an angel, at first sight;
But when I saw thou saw'st my heart,
And knew'st my thoughts beyond an angel's art,
When thou knew'st what I dreamt, when thou knew'st when
Excess of joy would wake me, and cam'st then,
I must confess it could not choose but be
Profane to think thee anything but thee.

Coming and staying show'd thee thee,
But rising makes me doubt that now
   Thou art not thou.
That Love is weak where Fear's as strong as he;
'Tis not all spirit pure and brave
If mixture it of Fear, Shame, Honour have.
Perchance as torches, which must ready be,
Men light and put out, so thou deal'st with me.
Thou cam'st to kindle, go'st to come; then I
Will dream that hope again, but else would die.

John Donne

367
Love's Growth

I scarce believe my love to be so pure
    As I had thought it was,
    Because it doth endure
Vicissitude, and season, as the grass;
Methinks I lied all winter, when I swore
My love was infinite, if spring make it more.

But if this medicine, love, which cures all sorrow
    With more, not only be no quintessence,
    But mix'd of all stuffs, vexing soul, or sense,
And of the sun his active vigour borrow,
Love's not so pure, and abstract, as they use
To say, which have no mistress but their Muse;
But as all else, being elemented too,
Love sometimes would contemplate, sometimes do.

And yet no greater, but more eminent,
    Love by the spring is grown;
    As in the firmament
Stars by the sun are not enlarged, but shown
Gentle love deeds, as blossoms on a bough,
From love's awaken'd root do bud out now.

If, as in water stirr'd more circles be
    Produced by one, love such additions take,
    Those like so many spheres but one heaven make,
For they are all concentric unto thee:
And though each spring do add to love new heat,
As princes do in times of action get
New taxes, and remit them not in peace,
No winter shall abate this spring's increase.

John Donne

368
The Canonization

For God sake hold your tongue, and let me love,
    Or chide my palsy, or my gout,
My five grey hairs, or ruined fortune flout,
    With wealth your state, your mind with arts improve,
        Take you a course, get you a place,
        Observe his honour, or his grace,
Or the king's real, or his stampèd face
    Contemplate, what you will approve,
    So you will let me love.

Alas, alas, who's injured by my love?
  What merchant's ships have my sighs drowned?
Who says my tears have overflowed his ground?
  When did my colds a forward spring remove?
    When did the heats which my veins fill
    Add one more to the plaguey bill?
Soldiers find wars, and lawyers find out still
  Litigious men, which quarrels move,
  Though she and I do love.

Call us what you will, we are made such by love;
  Call her one, me another fly,
We are tapers too, and at our own cost die,
  And we in us find the eagle and the dove.
    The phoenix riddle hath more wit
    By us, we two being one, are it.
So to one neutral thing both sexes fit,
  We die and rise the same, and prove
  Mysterious by this love.

We can die by it, if not live by love,
  And if unfit for tombs and hearse
Our legend be, it will be fit for verse;
  And if no piece of chronicle we prove,
    We'll build in sonnets pretty rooms;
    As well a well-wrought urn becomes
The greatest ashes, as half-acre tombs,
  And by these hymns, all shall approve
  Us *canonized* for love:

And thus invoke us; you whom reverend love
  Made one another's hermitage;
You, to whom love was peace, that now is rage;
  Who did the whole world's soul contract, and drove
    Into the glasses of your eyes
    (So made such mirrors, and such spies,
That they did all to you epitomize),
  Countries, towns, courts: beg from above
  A pattern of your love!

John Donne

369   **Lovers' Infiniteness**

If yet I have not all thy love,
  Dear, I shall never have it all,
I cannot breathe one other sigh, to move;

Nor can entreat one other tear to fall.
And all my treasure, which should purchase thee,
Sighs, tears, and oaths, and letters I have spent,
Yet no more can be due to me,
Than at the bargain made was meant,
If then thy gift of love were partial,
That some to me, some should to others fall,
   Dear, I shall never have thee all.

Or if then thou gavest me all,
All was but all, which thou hadst then,
But if in thy heart, since, there be or shall,
New love created be, by other men,
Which have their stocks entire, and can in tears,
In sighs, in oaths, and letters outbid me,
This new love may beget new fears,
For, this love was not vowed by thee.
And yet it was, thy gift being general,
The ground, thy heart is mine, what ever shall
   Grow there, dear, I should have it all.

Yet I would not have all yet,
He that hath all can have no more,
And since my love doth every day admit
New growth, thou shouldst have new rewards in store;
Thou canst not every day give me thy heart,
If thou canst give it, then thou never gavest it:
Love's riddles are, that though thy heart depart
It stays at home, and thou with losing savest it:
But we will have a way more liberal
Than changing hearts, to join them, so we shall
   Be one, and one another's all.

                         John Donne

370   How sweet I roam'd from field to field
        And tasted all the summer's pride,
        Till I the Prince of Love beheld,
        Who in the sunny beams did glide!

      He shew'd me lilies for my hair,
        And blushing roses for my brow;
        He led me through his gardens fair,
        Where all his golden pleasures grow.

      With sweet May dews my wings were wet,
        And Phoebus fired my vocal rage;

He caught me in his silken net,
And shut me in his golden cage.

He loves to sit and hear me sing;
Then, laughing, sports and plays with me;
Then stretches out my golden wing,
And mocks my loss of liberty.

William Blake

371 **To Chloe**

Who for his sake wished herself younger

There are two births; the one when light
   First strikes the new awaken'd sense;
The other when two souls unite,
   And we must count our life from thence:
When you loved me and I loved you
Then both of us were born anew.

Love then to us new souls did give
   And in those souls did plant new powers;
Since when another life we live,
   The breath we breathe is his, not ours:
Love makes those young whom age doth chill,
And whom he finds young keeps young still.

William Cartwright

372   I saw my Lady weep,
And Sorrow proud to be advancéd so
In those fair eyes where all perfections keep.
   Her face was full of woe,
But such a woe (believe me) as wins more hearts
Than Mirth can do with her enticing parts.

   Sorrow was there made fair,
And Passion, wise; Tears, a delightful thing;
Silence, beyond all speech, a wisdom rare:
   She made her sighs to sing,
And all things with so sweet a sadness move
As made my heart at once both grieve and love.

   O fairer than aught else
The world can show, leave off in time to grieve!
Enough, enough: your joyful look excels:
   Tears kill the heart, believe.
O strive not to be excellent in woe,
Which only breeds your beauty's overthrow.

Anon.

There Is a Lady Sweet and Kind

73

There is a Lady sweet and kind,
Was never face so pleased my mind;
I did but see her passing by,
And yet I love her till I die.

Her gesture, motion, and her smiles,
Her wit, her voice my heart beguiles,
Beguiles my heart, I know not why,
And yet I love her till I die.

Cupid is wingèd and doth range,
Her country so my love doth change:
But change she earth, or change the sky,
Yet will I love her till I die.

Anon.

374

I sighed and owned my love:
  Nor did the fair my passion disapprove.
    A soft engaging air,
    Not often apt to cause despair,
Declared she gave attention to my prayer.
    She seemed to pity my distress,
    And I expected nothing less
Than what her every look did then confess.

    But oh, her change destroys
The charming prospect of my promised joys:
    She's robbed of every grace
    That argued pity in her face,
And cold forbidding frowns supply their place.
    But, while she strives to chill desire,
    Her brighter eyes such warmth inspire,
She checks the flame, but cannot quench the fire.

Anon.

Helen

375

Was this the face that launched a thousand ships,
And burned the topless towers of Ilium?—
Sweet Helen, make me immortal with a kiss!—
Her lips suck forth my soul: see where it flees!—
Come, Helen, come, give me my soul again.
Here will I dwell, for heaven is in these lips,

And all is dross that is not Helena.
I will be Paris, and for love of thee,
Instead of Troy, shall Wittenberg be sacked,
And I will combat with weak Menelaus,
And wear thy colours on my plumèd crest;
Yes, I will wound Achilles in the heel,
And then return to Helen for a kiss.
Oh, thou art fairer than the evening air
Clad in the beauty of a thousand stars;
Brighter art thou than flaming Jupiter
When he appeared to hapless Semele;
More lovely than the monarch of the sky
In wanton Arethusa's azured arms;
And none but thou shalt be my paramour!

Christopher Marlowe

376 ### The Nymph's Reply to the Shepherd*

If all the world and love were young
And truth in every shepherd's tongue,
These pretty pleasures might me move
To live with thee and be thy love.

Time drives the flocks from field to fold
When rivers rage and rocks grow cold,
And Philomel becometh dumb;
The rest complain of cares to come.

The flowers do fade, and wanton fields
To wayward winter reckoning yields;
A honey tongue, a heart of gall,
Is fancy's spring, but sorrow's fall.

Thy gowns, thy shoes, thy beds of roses,
Thy cap, thy kirtle, and thy posies
Soon break, soon wither, soon forgotten,
In folly ripe, in reason rotten.

Thy belt of straw and ivy buds,
Thy coral clasps and amber studs,
All these in me no means can move
To come to thee and be thy love.

But could youth last and love still breed,
Had joys no date nor age no need,
Then these delights my mind might move
To live with thee and be thy love.

* See Poem No. 5.

Sir Walter Raleigh

377
Song

Ask me no more where Jove bestows,
When June is past, the fading rose;
For in your beauty's orient deep
These flowers, as in their causes, sleep.

Ask me no more whither do stray
The golden atoms of the day;
For, in pure love, heaven did prepare
Those powders to enrich your hair.

Ask me no more whither doth haste
The nightingale, when May is past;
For in your sweet dividing throat
She winters, and keeps warm her note.

Ask me no more where those stars light
That downwards fall in dead of night;
For in your eyes they sit, and there
Fixèd become, as in their sphere.

Ask me no more if east or west
The Phœnix builds her spicy nest;
For unto you at last she flies,
And in your fragrant bosom dies.

Thomas Carew

378
The Definition of Love

My love is of a birth as rare
As 'tis for object strange and high:
It was begotten by Despair
Upon Impossibility.

Magnanimous Despair alone
Could show me so divine a thing,
Where feeble Hope could ne'er have flown
But vainly flapt its tinsel wing.

And yet I quickly might arrive
Where my extended soul is fixt,
But Fate does iron wedges drive,
And always crowds itself betwixt.

For Fate with jealous eye does see
Two perfect loves, nor lets them close:

Their union would her ruin be,
And her tyrannic pow'r depose.

And therefore her decrees of steel
Us as the distant poles have plac'd,
(Though Love's whole world on us does wheel)
Not by themselves to be embrac'd

Unless the giddy heaven fall
And earth some new convulsion tear,
And, us to join, the world should all
Be cramp'd into a planisphere.

As lines so loves oblique may well
Themselves in every angle greet;
But ours so truly parallel,
Though infinite can never meet.

Therefore the love which doth us bind,
But Fate so enviously debars,
Is the conjunction of the mind,
And opposition of the stars.

Andrew Marvell

379   **No, No, Poor Suffering Heart**

No, no, poor suffering heart, no change endeavour;
Choose to sustain the smart rather than leave her;
My ravished eyes behold such charms about her,
I can die with her, but not live without her.
One tender sigh of hers to see me languish
Will more than pay the price of my past anguish;
Beware, O cruel fair, how you smile on me,
'Twas a kind look of yours that has undone me.

Love has in store for me one happy minute,
And she will end my pain who did begin it;
Then no day void of bliss or pleasure leaving
Ages shall slide away without perceiving:
Cupid shall guard the door the more to please us,
And keep out time and death when they would seize us;
Time and death shall depart and say in flying
Love has found out a way to live, by dying.

John Dryden

The Wish

Well then! I now do plainly see
This busy world and I shall ne'er agree.
The very honey of all earthly joy
Does of all meats the soonest cloy;
    And they, methinks, deserve my pity
Who for it can endure the stings,
The crowd, and buzz, and murmurings,
    Of this great hive, the city.

Ah, yet, ere I descend to the grave,
May I a small house and large garden have;
And a few friends, and many books, both true,
Both wise, and both delightful too!
    And since love ne'er will from me flee,
A Mistress moderately fair,
And good as guardian angels are,
    Only beloved and loving me.

O fountains! when in you shall I
Myself eased of unpeaceful thoughts espy?
O fields! O woods! when, when shall I be made
The happy tenant of your shade?
    Here's the spring-head of Pleasure's flood:
Here's wealthy Nature's treasury,
Where all the riches lie that she
    Has coin'd and stamp'd for good.

Pride and ambition here
Only in far-fetch'd metaphors appear;
Here nought but winds can hurtful murmurs scatter,
And nought but Echo flatter.
    The gods, when they descended, hither
From heaven did always choose their way:
And therefore we may boldly say
    That 'tis the way to thither.

How happy here should I
And one dear She live, and embracing die!
She who is all the world, and can exclude
In deserts solitude.
    I should have then this only fear:
Lest men, when they my pleasures see,
Should hither throng to live like me,
    And so make a city here.

Abraham Cowley

Myra

I, with those colours Myra dressed her head,
 I, that ware posies of her own hand-making,
I, that mine own name in the chimneys read
 By Myra finely wrought ere I was waking;
  Must I look on, in hope time coming may
  With change bring back my turn again to play?

I, that on Sunday at the church-stile found
 A garland sweet, with true-love knots in flowers,
Which I to wear about mine arm was bound,
 That each of us might know that all was ours;
  Must I now lead an idle life in wishes,
  And follow Cupid for his loaves and fishes?

I, that did wear the ring her mother left,
 I, for whose love she gloried to be blamed,
I, with whose eyes her eyes committed theft,
 I, who did make her blush when I was named;
  Must I lose ring, flowers, blush, theft, and go naked,
  Watching with sighs, till love be awakened?

I, that, when drowsy Argus fell asleep,
 Like jealousy o'erwatched with desire,
Was ever warned modesty to keep,
 While her breath, speaking, kindled Nature's fire;
  Must I look on a-cold, while other warm them?
  Do Vulcan's brothers in such fine nets arm them?

Was it for this that I might Myra see
 Washing the water, with her beauties, white?
Yet would she never write her love to me.
 Thinks wit of change, while thoughts are in delight?
  Mad girls must safely love, as they may leave;
  No man can print a kiss; lines may deceive.
   Fulke Greville, Lord Brooke

Ruth

She stood breast-high amid the corn,
Clasp'd by the golden light of morn,
Like the sweetheart of the sun,
Who many a glowing kiss had won.

On her cheek an autumn flush,
Deeply ripen'd;—such a blush

In the midst of brown was born,
Like red poppies grown with corn.

Round her eyes her tresses fell,
Which were blackest none could tell,
But long lashes veil'd a light,
That had else been all too bright.

And her hat, with shady brim,
Made her tressy forehead dim;
Thus she stood amid the stooks,
Praising God with sweetest looks:—

Sure, I said, Heav'n did not mean,
Where I reap thou shouldst but glean,
Lay thy sheaf adown and come,
Share my harvest and my home.

Thomas Hood

83 Believe me, if all those endearing young charms,
   Which I gaze on so fondly today,
Were to change by tomorrow, and fleet in my arms,
   Like fairy-gifts fading away,
Thou wouldst still be adored, as this moment thou art,
   Let thy loveliness fade as it will,
And around the dear ruin each wish of my heart
   Would entwine itself verdantly still.

It is not while beauty and youth are thine own,
   And thy cheeks unprofaned by a tear,
That the fervour and faith of a soul can be known,
   To which time will but make thee more dear;
No, the heart that has truly loved never forgets,
   But as truly loves on to the close,
As the sunflower turns on her god, when he sets,
   The same look which she turned when he rose.

Thomas Moore

84   Sweet Afton

Flow gently, sweet Afton! amang thy green braes,
Flow gently, I'll sing thee a song in thy praise;
My Mary's asleep by thy murmuring stream,
Flow gently, sweet Afton, disturb not her dream.

Thou stock dove whose echo resounds thro' the glen,
Ye wild whistling blackbirds, in yon thorny den,
Thou green crested lapwing thy screaming forbear,
I charge you, disturb not my slumbering fair.

How lofty, sweet Afton, thy neighbouring hills,
Far mark'd with the courses of clear, winding rills;
There daily I wander as noon rises high,
My flocks and my Mary's sweet cot in my eye.

How pleasant thy banks and green valleys below,
Where, wild in the woodlands, the primroses blow;
There oft, as mild evening weeps over the lea,
The sweet-scented birk shades my Mary and me.

Thy crystal stream, Afton, how lovely it glides,
And winds by the cot where my Mary resides;
How wanton thy waters her snowy feet lave,
As, gathering sweet flowerets, she stems thy clear wave.

Flow gently, sweet Afton, amang thy green braes,
Flow gently, sweet river, the theme of my lays;
My Mary's asleep by the murmuring stream,
Flow gently, sweet Afton, disturb not her dream.

Robert Burns

385 **Annie Laurie**

Maxwelton's braes are bonnie
Where early fa's the dew,
And it's there that Annie Laurie
Gie'd me her promise true;
Gie'd me her promise true;
Which ne'er forgot will be;
And for bonnie Annie Laurie
I'd lay me doun and dee.

Her brow is like the snaw drift;
Her throat is like the swan;
Her face it is the fairest
That e'er the sun shone on—
That e'er the sun shone on—
And dark blue is her ee;
And for bonnie Annie Laurie
I'd lay me doun and dee.

Like dew on the gowan lying
Is the fa' o' her fairy feet;
And like the winds in summer sighing,
Her voice is low and sweet—
Her voice is low and sweet—
And she's a' the world to me;
And for bonnie Annie Laurie
I'd lay me doun and dee.

William Douglas

386

Auld Lang Syne

Should auld acquaintance be forgot,
And never brought to mind?
Should auld acquaintance be forgot,
And auld lang syne?

Cho.—For auld lang syne, my dear,
For auld lang syne,
We'll tak a cup o' kindness yet
For auld lang syne!

And surely ye'll be your pint-stowp,
And surely I'll be mine,
And we'll tak a cup o' kindness yet
For auld lang syne!

We twa hae run about the braes
And pou'd the gowans fine,
But we've wandered monie a weary fit
Sin' auld lang syne.

We twa hae paidl'd in the burn
Frae morning sun till dine,
But seas between us braid hae roared
Sin' auld lang syne.

Robert Burns

387

To a Child of Quality

Five Years Old; The Author Forty

Lords, knights, and squires, the num'rous band,
That wear the fair Miss *Mary's* fetters,
Were summon'd, by her high command,
To show their passions by their letters.

My pen amongst the rest I took,
  Lest those bright eyes that cannot read
Shou'd dart their kindling fires, and look,
  The power they have to be obey'd.

Nor quality, nor reputation,
  Forbid me yet my flame to tell,
Dear five years old befriends my passion,
  And I may write till she can spell.

For while she makes her silk-worms beds
  With all the tender things I swear,
Whilst all the house my passion reads,
  In papers round her baby's hair,

She may receive and own my flame,
  For tho' the strictest prudes shou'd know it,
She'll pass for a most virtuous dame,
  And I for an unhappy poet.

Then too alas! when she shall tear
  The lines some younger rival sends,
She'll give me leave to write I fear,
  And we shall still continue friends;

For, as our diff'rent ages move,
  'Tis so ordain'd, wou'd fate but mend it,
That I shall be past making love
  When she begins to comprehend it.

                                        Matthew Prior

388   Not Marble, nor the Gilded Monuments

Not marble, nor the gilded monuments
Of princes, shall outlive this powerful rhyme;
But you shall shine more bright in these contents
Than unswept stone besmear'd with sluttish time.
When wasteful war shall statues overturn,
And broils root out the work of masonry,
Nor Mars his sword nor war's quick fire shall burn
The living record of your memory.
'Gainst death and all-oblivious enmity
Shall you pace forth; your praise shall still find room
Even in the eyes of all posterity
That wears this world out to the ending doom.
So, till the judgment that yourself arise,
You live in this, and dwell in lovers' eyes.

                                        William Shakespeare

389   Devouring Time, blunt thou the lion's paws,
     And make the earth devour her own sweet brood;
     Pluck the keen teeth from the fierce tiger's jaws,
     And burn the long-liv'd phœnix in her blood;
     Make glad the sorry seasons as thou fleet'st,
     And do whate'er thou wilt, swift-footed Time,
     To the wide world and all her fading sweets;
     But I forbid thee one most heinous crime:
     O! carve not with thy hours my love's fair brow,
     Nor draw no lines there with thine antique pen;
     Him in thy course untainted do allow
     For beauty's pattern to succeeding men.
     Yet, do thy worst, old Time: despite thy wrong,
     My love shall in my verse ever live young.

William Shakespeare

390   **Fair Is My Love**

  Fair is my Love and cruel as she's fair;
     Her brow-shades frown, although her eyes are sunny.
     Her smiles are lightning, though her pride despair,
     And her disdains are gall, her favours honey:
     A modest maid, deck'd with a blush of honour,
     Whose feet do tread green paths of youth and love;
     The wonder of all eyes that look upon her,
     Sacred on earth, design'd a Saint above.
     Chastity and Beauty, which were deadly foes,
     Live reconcilèd friends within her brow;
     And had she Pity to conjoin with those,
     Then who had heard the plaints I utter now?
     For had she not been fair, and thus unkind,
     My Muse had slept, and none had known my mind.

Samuel Daniel

391   **Loving in Truth**

Loving in truth, and fain in verse my love to show,
That she, dear she, might take some pleasure of my pain,
Pleasure might cause her read, reading might make her know,
Knowledge might pity win, and pity grace obtain,—
I sought fit words to paint the blackest face of woe;
Studying inventions fine, her wits to entertain,
Oft turning others' leaves to see if thence would flow
Some fresh and fruitful showers upon my sun-burned brain.
But words came halting forth, wanting invention's stay;
Invention, nature's child, fled step-dame Study's blows,

And others' feet still seemed but strangers in my way.
Thus, great with child to speak, and helpless in my throes,
Biting my truant pen, beating myself for spite,
Fool, said my muse to me, look in thy heart and write.

Sir Philip Sidney

392 ### To the Muses

Whether on Ida's shady brow
  Or in the chambers of the East,
The chambers of the Sun, that now
  From ancient melody have ceased;

Whether in heaven ye wander fair,
  Or the green corners of the earth,
Or the blue regions of the air
  Where the melodious winds have birth;

Whether on crystal rocks ye rove,
  Beneath the bosom of the sea,
Wandering in many a coral grove;
  Fair Nine, forsaking Poetry;

How have you left the ancient love
  That bards of old enjoy'd you!
The languid strings do scarcely move,
  The sound is forced, the notes are few.

William Blake

393 ### Imagination

Lovers and madmen have such seething brains,
Such shaping fantasies, that apprehend
More than cool reason ever comprehends.
The lunatic, the lover, and the poet
Are of imagination all compact:—
One sees more devils than vast hell can hold,—
That is the madman: the lover, all as frantic,
Sees Helen's beauty in a brow of Egypt:
The poet's eye, in a fine frenzy rolling,
Doth glance from heaven to earth, from earth to heaven;
And, as imagination bodies forth
The forms of things unknown, the poet's pen
Turns them to shapes, and gives to airy nothing
A local habitation and a name.
Such tricks hath strong imagination,

That, if it would but apprehend some joy,
It comprehends some bringer of that joy;
Or in the night, imagining some fear,
How easy is a bush supposed a bear!

William Shakespeare

894   Keen, fitful gusts are whisp'ring here and there
       Among the bushes half leafless, and dry;
       The stars look very cold about the sky,
       And I have many miles on foot to fare.
       Yet feel I little of the cool bleak air,
       Or of the dead leaves rustling drearily,
       Or of those silver lamps that burn on high,
       Or of the distance from home's pleasant lair:
       For I am brimfull of the friendliness
       That in a little cottage I have found;
       Of fair hair'd Milton's eloquent distress,
       And of his love for gentle Lycid drown'd;
       Of lovely Laura in her light green dress,
       And faithful Petrarch gloriously crown'd.

John Keats

895   **Reeds of Innocence**

       Piping down the valleys wild,
           Piping songs of pleasant glee,
       On a cloud I saw a child,
           And he laughing said to me:

       'Pipe a song about a Lamb!'
           So I piped with merry cheer.
       'Piper, pipe that song again;'
           So I piped: he wept to hear.

       'Drop thy pipe, thy happy pipe;
           Sing thy songs of happy cheer!'
       So I sung the same again,
           While he wept with joy to hear.

       'Piper, sit thee down and write
           In a book that all may read.'
       So he vanish'd from my sight;
           And I pluck'd a hollow reed,

       And I made a rural pen,
           And I stain'd the water clear,
       And I wrote my happy songs
           Every child may joy to hear.

William Blake

396 **On Shakespeare**

What needs my Shakespeare for his honored bones,
The labor of an age in piled stones?
Or that his hallowed reliques should be hid
Under a star-ypointing pyramid?
Dear son of memory, great heir of fame,
What need'st thou such weak witness of thy name?
Thou in our wonder and astonishment
Hast built thyself a livelong monument.
For whilst, to the shame of slow-endeavoring art,
Thy easy numbers flow, and that each heart
Hath from the leaves of thy unvalued book
Those Delphic lines with deep impression took;
Then thou, our fancy of itself bereaving,
Dost make us marble with too much conceiving,
And so sepulchred in such pomp dost lie
That kings for such a tomb would wish to die.

John Milton

397 **The Phoenix and the Turtle**

Let the bird of loudest lay
   On the sole Arabian tree,
   Herald sad and trumpet be,
To whose sound chaste wings obey.

But thou shrieking harbinger,
   Foul precurrer of the fiend,
   Augur of the fever's end,
To this troop come thou not near.

From the session interdict
   Every fowl of tyrant wing
   Save the eagle, feathered king.
Keep the obsequy so strict.

Let the priest in surplice white
   That defunctive music can,
   Be the death-divining swan,
Lest the requiem lack his right.

And thou, treble-dated crow,
   That thy sable gender mak'st
   With the breath thou giv'st and tak'st,
Mongst our mourners shalt thou go.

Here the anthem doth commence:—
  Love and constancy is dead;
  Phœnix and the turtle fled
In a mutual flame from hence.

So they loved, as love in twain
  Had the essence but in one;
  Two distincts, division none;
Number there in love was slain.

Hearts remote, yet not asunder;
  Distance, and no space was seen
  'Twixt the turtle and his queen:
But in them it were a wonder.

So between them love did shine,
  That the turtle saw his right
  Flaming in the phœnix' sight;
Either was the other's mine.

Property was thus appalled,
  That the self was not the same;
  Single nature's double name
Neither two nor one was called.

Reason, in itself confounded,
  Saw division grow together;
  To themselves yet either neither;
Simple were so well compounded,

That it cried: "How true a twain
  Seemeth this concordant one!
  Love hath reason, reason none
If what parts can so remain."

Whereupon it made this threne
  To the phœnix and the dove,
  Co-supremes and stars of love,
As chorus to their tragic scene.

THRENOS

Beauty, truth, and rarity,
Grace in all simplicity,
Here enclosed in cinders lie.

Death is now the phœnix' nest;
And the turtle's loyal breast
To eternity doth rest,

Leaving no posterity:
'Twas not their infirmity,
It was married chastity.

Truth may seem, but cannot be;
Beauty brag, but 'tis not she;
Truth and beauty buried be.

To this urn let those repair
That are either true or fair;
For these dead birds sigh a prayer.

William Shakespeare

398   **Our Revels Now Are Ended**

Our revels now are ended. These our actors,
As I foretold you, were all spirits, and
Are melted into air, into thin air;
And, like the baseless fabric of this vision,
The cloud-capped towers, the gorgeous palaces,
The solemn temples, the great globe itself,
Yea, all which it inherit, shall dissolve,
And, like this insubstantial pageant faded,
Leave not a rack behind. We are such stuff
As dreams are made on, and our little life
Is rounded with a sleep.

William Shakespeare

BOOK SIX

399

Pippa's Song

The year's at the spring,
And day's at the morn;
Morning's at seven;
The hill-side's dew-pearl'd;
The lark's on the wing;
The snail's on the thorn;
God's in His heaven—
All's right with the world!

Robert Browning

400

Reveille

Wake: the silver dusk returning
  Up the beach of darkness brims,
And the ship of sunrise burning
  Strands upon the eastern rims.

Wake: the vaulted shadow shatters,
  Trampled to the floor it spanned,
And the tent of night in tatters
  Straws the sky-pavilioned land.

Up, lad, up, 'tis late for lying:
  Hear the drums of morning play;
Hark, the empty highways crying
  'Who'll beyond the hills away?'

Towns and countries woo together,
  Forelands beacon, belfries call;
Never lad that trod on leather
  Lived to feast his heart with all.

Up, lad: thews that lie and cumber
  Sunlit pallets never thrive;
Morns abed and daylight slumber
  Were not meant for man alive.

Clay lies still, but blood's a rover;
   Breath's a ware that will not keep.
Up, lad: when the journey's over
   There'll be time enough to sleep.

A. E. Housman

401   Home-Thoughts from Abroad

Oh, to be in England
Now that April's there,
And whoever wakes in England
Sees, some morning, unaware,
That the lowest boughs and the brush-wood sheaf
Round the elm-tree bole are in tiny leaf,
While the chaffinch sings on the orchard bough
In England—now!

And after April, when May follows,
And the whitethroat builds, and all the swallows—
Hark! where my blossomed pear-tree in the hedge
Leans to the field and scatters on the clover
Blossoms and dewdrops—at the bent-spray's edge—
That's the wise thrush; he sings each song twice over,
Lest you should think he never could recapture
The first fine careless rapture!
And though the fields look rough with hoary dew,
All will be gay when noontide wakes anew
The buttercups, the little children's dower,
—Far brighter than this gaudy melon-flower!

Robert Browning

402   Inversnaid

This darksome burn, horseback brown,
His rollrock highroad roaring down,
In coop and in comb the fleece of his foam
Flutes and low to the lake falls home.

A windpuff-bonnet of fawn-froth
Turns and twindles over the broth
Of a pool so pitchblack, fell-frowning,
It rounds and rounds Despair to drowning.

Degged with dew, dappled with dew
Are the groins of the braes that the brook treads through,
Wiry heathpacks, flitches of fern,
And the beadbonny ash that sits over the burn.

What would the world be, once bereft
Of wet and of wildness? Let them be left,
O let them be left, wildness and wet;
Long live the weeds and the wilderness yet.

Gerard Manley Hopkins

403   Not only around our infancy
            Doth heaven with all its splendors lie;
            Daily, with souls that cringe and plot,
            We Sinais climb and know it not.

James Russell Lowell

404   **Prophecy**

For I dipt into the future, far as human eye could see,
Saw the Vision of the world, and all the wonder that would be;
Saw the heavens fill with commerce, argosies of magic sails,
Pilots of the purple twilight, dropping down with costly bales;
Heard the heavens fill with shouting, and there rain'd a ghastly
    dew
From the nations' air navies grappling in the central blue;
Far along the world-wide whisper of the south-wind rushing
    warm,
With the standards of the peoples plunging thro' the thunder
    storm;
Till the war-drum throbb'd no longer, and the battle flags were
    furl'd
In the Parliament of man, the Federation of the world.
There the common sense of most shall hold a fretful realm in
    awe,
And the kindly earth shall slumber, lapt in universal law.

Alfred, Lord Tennyson

405   **Kinship with the Stars**

            Cold as a mountain in its star-pitched tent,
            Stood high Philosophy, less friend than foe:
            Whom self-caged Passion, from its prison-bars,
            Is always watching with a wondering hate.
            Not till the fire is dying in the grate,
            Look we for any kinship with the stars.

George Meredith

406   Say not the struggle naught availeth,
               The labour and the wounds are vain,
           The enemy faints not, nor faileth,
               And as things have been they remain.

           If hopes were dupes, fears may be liars;
               It may be, in yon smoke conceal'd,
           Your comrades chase e'en now the fliers,
               And, but for you, possess the field.

           For while the tired waves, vainly breaking,
               Seem here no painful inch to gain,
           Far back, through creeks and inlets making,
               Comes silent, flooding in, the main.

           And not by eastern windows only,
               When daylight comes, comes in the light;
           In front the sun climbs slow, how slowly!
               But westward, look, the land is bright!
                                           Arthur Hugh Clough

407   **I Am a Parcel**

           I am a parcel of vain strivings tied
               By a chance bond together,
           Dangling this way and that, their links
               Were made so loose and wide,
                       Methinks,
                   For milder weather.

           A bunch of violets without their roots,
               And sorrel intermixed,
           Encircled by a wisp of straw
               Once coiled about their shoots,
                       The law
                   By which I'm fixed.

           A nosegay which Time clutched from out
               Those fair Elysian fields,
           With weeds and broken stems, in haste,
               Doth make the rabble rout
                       That waste
                   The day he yields.

           And here I bloom for a short hour unseen,
               Drinking my juices up,
           With no root in the land
               To keep my branches green,
                       But stand
                   In a bare cup.

Some tender buds were left upon my stem
    In mimicry of life,
  But ah, the children will not know,
    Till time has withered them,
      The woe
    With which they're rife.

But now I see I was not plucked for naught,
    And after in life's vase
  Of glass set while I might survive,
    But by a kind hand brought
      Alive
    To a strange place.

That stock thus thinned will soon redeem its hours,
    And by another year,
  Such as God knows, with freer air,
    More fruits and fairer flowers
      Will bear,
    While I droop here.

                Henry David Thoreau

Oh Yet We Trust

Oh yet we trust that somehow good
    Will be the final goal of ill,
    To pangs of nature, sins of will,
Defects of doubt, and taints of blood;

That nothing walks with aimless feet;
    That not one life shall be destroyed,
    Or cast as rubbish to the void,
When God hath made the pile complete;

That not a worm is cloven in vain;
    That not a moth with vain desire
    Is shrivelled in a fruitless fire,
Or but subserves another's gain.

Behold, we know not anything;
    I can but trust that good shall fall
    At last—far off—at last, to all,
And every winter change to spring.

So runs my dream: but what am I?
    An infant crying in the night:
    An infant crying for the light:
And with no language but a cry.

                Alfred, Lord Tennyson

The Rubáiyát of Omar Khayyám

409   I

The Moving Fingers writes, and, having writ,
Moves on: nor all your Piety nor Wit
        Shall lure it back to cancel half a Line,
Nor all your Tears wash out a Word of it.

And that inverted Bowl we call the Sky,
Whereunder crawling coop'd we live and die,
        Lift not your hands to *It* for help—for It
As impotently moves as You or I.

With Earth's first Clay They did the Last Man knead,
And then of the Last Harvest sow'd the Seed:
        And the first Morning of Creation wrote
What the Last Dawn of Reckoning shall read. . . .

And this I know; whether the one True Light
Kindle to Love, or Wrath-consume me quite,
        One Flash of It within the Tavern caught
Better than in the Temple lost outright.

O Thou who didst with Pitfall and with Gin
Beset the Road I was to wander in,
        Thou wilt not with Predestination round
Enmesh me, and impute my Fall to Sin? . . .

Nay, but, for terror of his wrathful Face,
I swear I will not call Injustice Grace.
        Not one Good Fellow of the Tavern but
Would kick so poor a Coward from the place.

Edward FitzGerald

410   II

A Book of Verses underneath the Bough,
A Jug of Wine, a Loaf of Bread, and Thou
        Beside me singing in the Wilderness—
Oh, Wilderness were Paradise enow!

Some for the Glories of This World, and some
Sigh for the Prophet's Paradise to come—
        Ah, take the Cash and let the Credit go,
Nor heed the rumble of a distant Drum!

Look to the blowing Rose about us. 'Lo,
Laughing,' she says, 'into the world I blow,
　　At once the silken tassel of my Purse
Tear, and its Treasure on the Garden throw.'

The Worldly Hope men set their Hearts upon
Turns Ashes, or it prospers; and anon,
　　Like Snow upon the Desert's dusty Face
Lighting a little hour or two, is gone.

Think, in this batter'd Caravanserai
Whose Portals are alternate Night and Day,
　　How Sultan after Sultan with his Pomp
Abode his destined Hour, and went his way.

They say the Lion and the Lizard keep
The Courts where Jamshyd gloried and drank deep:
　　And Bahram, that great Hunter—the Wild Ass
Stamps o'er his Head, but cannot break his Sleep.

　　　　　　　　　　　　　　Edward FitzGerald

III

Ah, with the Grape my fading Life provide,
And wash the Body whence the Life has died,
　　And lay me, shrouded in the living Leaf,
By some not unfrequented Garden-side.

That ev'n my buried Ashes such a snare
Of Perfume shall fling up into the Air
　　As not a True-believer passing by
But shall be overtaken unaware.

Indeed the Idols I have loved so long
Have done my credit in Men's Eye much wrong:
　　Have drown'd my Glory in a shallow Cup,
And sold my Reputation for a Song.

Indeed, indeed, Repentance oft before
I swore—but was I sober when I swore?
　　And then and then came Spring, and Rose-in-hand
My thread-bare Penitence apieces tore.

And much as Wine has play'd the Infidel,
And robb'd me of my Robe of Honour—well,
　　I wonder often what the Vintners buy
One half so precious as the goods they sell.

Alas, that Spring should vanish with the Rose!
That Youth's sweet-scented manuscript should close!
The Nigtingale that in the branches sang,
Ah whence, and whither flown again, who knows!

Ah Love! could thou and I with Fate conspire
To grasp this sorry Scheme of Things entire,
Would not we shatter it to bits—and then
Re-mould it nearer to the Heart's Desire!

Yon rising Moon that looks for us again—
How oft hereafter will she wax and wane;
How oft hereafter rising look for us
Through this same Garden—and for *one* in vain!

And when like her, oh Sákí, you shall pass
Among the Guests Star-scatter'd on the Grass,
And in your joyous errand reach the Spot
Where I made One—turn down an empty Glass!

TAMÁM SHUD

Edward FitzGerald

412   **Flower in the Crannied Wall**

Flower in the crannied wall,
I pluck you out of the crannies,
I hold you here, root and all, in my hand,
Little flower—but *if* I could understand
What you are, root and all, and all in all,
I should know what God and man is.

Alfred, Lord Tennyson

413   **Chorus**

Before the beginning of years
There came to the making of man
Time, with a gift of tears;
Grief, with a glass that ran;
Pleasure, with pain for leaven;
Summer, with flowers that fell;
Remembrance fallen from heaven,
And madness risen from hell;

Strength without hands to smite;
    Love that endures for a breath;
Night, the shadow of light,
    And life, the shadow of death.

And the high gods took in hand
    Fire, and the falling of tears,
And a measure of sliding sand
    From under the feet of the years;
And froth and drift of the sea;
    And dust of the labouring earth;
And bodies of things to be
    In the houses of death and of birth;
And wrought with weeping and laughter,
    And fashion'd with loathing and love,
With life before and after
    And death beneath and above,
For a day and a night and a morrow,
    That his strength might endure for a span
With travail and heavy sorrow,
    The holy spirit of man.

From the winds of the north and the south
    They gather'd as unto strife;
They breathed upon his mouth,
    They filled his body with life;
Eyesight and speech they wrought
    For the veils of the soul therein,
A time for labour and thought,
    A time to serve and to sin;
They gave him light in his ways,
    And love, and a space for delight,
And beauty and length of days,
    And night, and sleep in the night.
His speech is a burning fire;
    With his lips he travaileth;
In his heart is a blind desire,
    In his eyes foreknowledge of death;
He weaves, and is clothed with derision;
    Sows, and he shall not reap;
His life is a watch or a vision
    Between a sleep and a sleep.

Algernon Charles Swinburne

Grass

A child said *What is the grass?* fetching it to me with full
     hands;
How could I answer the child? I do not know what it is any
     more than he.

I guess it must be the flag of my disposition, out of hopeful
     green stuff woven.
Or I guess it is the handkerchief of the Lord,
A scented gift and remembrancer designedly dropt,
Bearing the owner's name some way in the corners, that we
     may see and remark, and say *Whose?*
Or I guess the grass is itself a child, the produced babe of the
     vegetation.
Or I guess it is a uniform hieroglyphic,
And it means, sprouting alike in broad zones and narrow zones,
Growing among black folks as among white,
Kanuck, Tuckahoe, Congressman, Cuff, I give them the same,
     I receive them the same.
And now it seems to me the beautiful uncut hair of graves.

Tenderly will I use you curling grass,
It may be you transpire from the breasts of young men,
It may be if I had known them I would have loved them,
It may be you are from old people, or from offspring taken
     soon out of their mothers' laps,
And here you are the mothers' laps.

This grass is very dark to be from the white heads of old
     mothers,
Darker than the colorless beards of old men,
Dark to come from under the faint red roofs of mouths.

O I perceive after all so many uttering tongues,
And I perceive they do not come from the roofs of mouths for
     nothing.
I wish I could translate the hints about the dead young men
     and women,
And the hints about old men and mothers, and the off-spring
     taken soon out of their laps.

What do you think has become of the young and old men?
And what do you think has become of the women and chil-
     dren?
They are alive and well somewhere,

The smallest sprout shows there is really no death,
And if ever there was it led forward life, and does not wait at
    the end to arrest it,
And ceas'd the moment life appear'd.
All goes onward and outward, nothing collapses,
And to die is different from what any one supposed, and
    luckier.

Walt Whitman

415   *Up the airy mountain,*
        Down the rushy glen,
    We daren't go a-hunting
        For fear of little men;
    Wee folk, good folk,
        Trooping all together;
    Green jacket, red cap,
        And white owl's feather.

They stole little Bridget
    For seven years long;
When she came down again
    Her friends were all gone.
They took her lightly back,
    Between the night and morrow;
They thought that she was fast asleep,
    But she was dead with sorrow. . . .

By the craggy hillside,
    Through the mosses bare,
They have planted thorn-trees
    For pleasure here and there.
Is any man so daring
    As dig one up in spite?
He shall find the sharpest thorn
    In his bed at night.

Up the airy mountain,
    Down the rushy glen,
We daren't go a-hunting
    For fear of little men;
We folk, good folk,
    Trooping all together;
Green jacket, red cap,
    And white owl's feather.

William Allingham

The Cutty Wren

O, where are you going, says Milder to Malder,
O, I cannot tell, says Festel to Fose,
We're going to the woods, says John the Red Nose,
We're going to the woods, says John the Red Nose.

O, what will you do there, says Milder to Malder,
O, I cannot tell, says Festel to Fose,
We'll shoot the Cutty Wren, says John the Red Nose,
We'll shoot the Cutty Wren, says John the Red Nose.

O, how will you shoot her, says Milder to Malder,
O, I cannot tell, says Festel to Fose,
With arrows and bows, says John the Red Nose,
With arrows and bows, says John the Red Nose.

O, that will not do, says Milder to Malder,
O, what will do then, says Festel to Fose,
Big guns and cannons, says John the Red Nose,
Big guns and cannons, says John the Red Nose.

O, how will you bring her home, says Milder to Malder,
O, I cannot tell, says Festel to Fose,
On four strong men's shoulders, says John the Red Nose,
On four strong men's shoulders, says John the Red Nose.

O, that will not do, says Milder to Malder,
O, what will do then, says Festel to Fose,
Big carts and waggons, says John the Red Nose,
Big carts and waggons, says John the Red Nose.

O, what will you cut her up with, says Milder to Malder,
O, I cannot tell, says Festel to Fose,
With knives and with forks, says John the Red Nose,
With knives and with forks, says John the Red Nose.

O, that will not do, says Milder to Malder,
O, I cannot tell, says Festel to Fose,
Hatchets and cleavers, says John the Red Nose,
Hatchets and cleavers, says John the Red Nose.

O, how will you boil her, says Milder to Malder,
O, I cannot tell, says Festel to Fose,
In pots and in kettles, says John the Red Nose,
In pots and in kettles, says John the Red Nose.

O, that will not do, says Milder to Malder,
O, what will do then, says Festel to Fose,
Brass pans and cauldrons, says John the Red Nose,
Brass pans and cauldrons, says John the Red Nose.

O, who'll have the spare ribs, says Milder to Malder,
O, I cannot tell, says Festel to Fose,
We'll give them to the poor, says John the Red Nose,
We'll give them to the poor, says John the Red Nose.

Anon.

17   Animals

think I could turn and live with animals, they are so placid
   and self-contained;
stand and look at them long and long.
They do not sweat and whine about their condition;
They do not lie awake in the dark and weep for their sins;
They do not make me sick discussing their duty to God;
Not one is dissatisfied—not one is demented with the mania
   of owning things;
Not one kneels to another, nor to his kind that lived thousands
   of years ago;
Not one is respectable or industrious over the whole earth.

Walt Whitman

18   Prospice

Fear death?—to feel the fog in my throat,
   The mist in my face,
When the snows begin, and the blasts denote
   I am nearing the place,
The power of the night, the press of the storm,
   The post of the foe;
Where he stands, the Arch Fear in a visible form,
   Yet the strong man must go:
For the journey is done and the summit attained,
   And the barriers fall,
Though a battle's to fight ere the guerdon be gained,
   The reward of it all.
I was ever a fighter, so—one fight more,
   The best and the last!
I would hate that death bandaged my eyes, and forbore,
   And bade me creep past.
No! let me taste the whole of it, fare like my peers
   The heroes of old,

Bear the brunt, in a minute pay glad life's arrears
 Of pain, darkness, and cold.
For sudden the worst turns the best to the brave,
 The black minute's at end,
And the element's rage, the fiend-voices that rave,
 Shall dwindle, shall blend,
Shall change, shall become first a peace out of pain,
 Then a light, then thy breast,
O thou soul of my soul! I shall clasp thee again,
 And with God be the rest!

Robert Browning

419   A Sight in Camp

A sight in camp in the daybreak gray and dim,
As from my tent I emerge so early sleepless,
As slow I walk in the cool fresh air the path near by the
 hospital tent,
Three forms I see on stretchers lying, brought out there un-
 tended lying,
Over each the blanket spread, ample brownish woolen blanket,
Gray and heavy blanket, folding, covering all.
Curious I halt and silent stand,
Then with light fingers I from the face of the nearest the first
 just lift the blanket;
Who are you elderly man so gaunt and grim, with well-gray'd
 hair, and flesh all sunken about the eyes?
Who are you my dear comrade?

Then to the second I step—and who are you my child and
 darling?
Who are you sweet boy with cheeks yet blooming?

Then to the third—a face nor child nor old, very calm, as of
 beautiful yellow-white ivory;
Young man I think I know you—I think this face is the face of
 the Christ himself,
Dead and divine and brother of all, and here again he lies.

Walt Whitman

420   Thanatopsis

To him who in the love of Nature holds
Communion with her visible forms, she speaks
A various language; for his gayer hours
She has a voice of gladness, and a smile

And eloquence of beauty, and she glides
Into his darker musings, with a mild
And healing sympathy, that steals away
Their sharpness, ere he is aware. When thoughts
Of the last bitter hour come like a blight
Over thy spirit, and sad images
Of the stern agony, and shroud, and pall,
And breathless darkness, and the narrow house,
Make thee to shudder, and grow sick at heart;—
Go forth, under the open sky, and list
To Nature's teachings, while from all around—
Earth and her waters, and the depths of air—
Comes a still voice—Yet a few days, and thee
The all-beholding sun shall see no more
In all his course; nor yet in the cold ground,
Where thy pale form was laid, with many tears,
Nor in the embrace of ocean, shall exist
Thy image. Earth, that nourished thee, shall claim
Thy growth, to be resolved to earth again,
And, lost each human trace, surrendering up
Thine individual being, shalt thou go
To mix for ever with the elements,
To be a brother to the insensible rock
And to the sluggish clod, which the rude swain
Turns with his share, and treads upon. The oak
Shall send his roots abroad, and pierce thy mould.

Yet not to thine eternal resting-place
Shalt thou retire alone, nor couldst thou wish
Couch more magnificent. Thou shalt lie down
With patriarchs of the infant world—with kings,
The powerful of the earth—the wise, the good,
Fair forms, and hoary seers of ages past,
All in one mighty sepulchre. The hills
Rock-ribbed and ancient as the sun,—the vales
Stretching in pensive quietness between;
The venerable woods—rivers that move
In majesty, and the complaining brooks
That make the meadows green; and, poured round all,
Old Ocean's gray and melancholy waste,—
Are but the solemn decorations all
Of the great tomb of man. The golden sun,
The planets, all the infinite host of heaven,
Are shining on the sad abodes of death,
Through the still lapse of ages. All that tread
The globe are but a handful to the tribes
That slumber in its bosom.—Take the wings

Of morning, pierce the Barcan wilderness,
Or lose thyself in the contiguous woods
Where rolls the Oregon, and hears no sound,
Save his own dashings—yet the dead are there:
And millions in those solitudes, since first
The flight of years began, have laid them down
In their last sleep—the dead reign there alone.
So shalt thou rest, and what if thou withdraw
In silence from the living, and no friend
Take note of thy departure? All that breathe
Will share thy destiny. The gay will laugh
When thou art gone, the solemn brood of care
Plod on, and each one as before will chase
His favorite phantom; yet all these shall leave
Their mirth and their employments, and shall come
And make their bed with thee. As the long train
Of ages glide away, the sons of men,
The youth in life's green spring, and he who goes
In the full strength of years, matron and maid,
The speechless babe, and the gray-headed man—
Shall one by one be gathered to thy side,
By those, who in their turn shall follow them.

So live, that when thy summons come to join
The innumerable caravan, which moves
To that mysterious realm, where each shall take
His chamber in the silent halls of death,
Thou go not, like the quarry-slave at night,
Scourged to his dungeon, but, sustained and soothed,
By an unfaltering trust, approach thy grave,
Like one who wraps the drapery of his couch
About him, and lies down to pleasant dreams.

William Cullen Bryan

421   O, May I Join the Choir Invisible!

O, may I join the choir invisible
Of those immortal dead who live again
In minds made better by their presence; live
In pulses stirred to generosity,
In deeds of daring rectitude, in scorn
Of miserable aims that end with self,
In thoughts sublime that pierce the night like stars,
And with their mild persistence urge men's minds
To vaster issues.

So to live is heaven:

To make undying music in the world,
Breathing a beauteous order, that controls
With growing sway the growing life of man.
So we inherit that sweet purity
For which we struggled, failed, and agonized
With widening retrospect that bred despair.
Rebellious flesh that would not be subdued,
A vicious parent shaming still its child,
Poor anxious penitence, is quick dissolved;
Its discords quenched by meeting harmonies,
Die in the large and charitable air.
And all our rarer, better, truer self,
That sobbed religiously in yearning song,
That watched to ease the burden of the world,
Laboriously tracing what must be,
And what may yet be better,—saw within
A worthier image for the sanctuary,
And shaped it forth before the multitude,
Divinely human, raising worship so
To higher reverence more mixed with love,
That better self shall live till human Time
Shall fold its eyelids, and the human sky
Be gathered like a scroll within the tomb,
Unread forever.   This is life to come,
Which martyred men have made more glorious
For us, who strive to follow.
                    May I reach
That purest heaven,—be to other souls
The cup of strength in some great agony,
Enkindle generous ardor, feed pure love,
Beget the smiles that have no cruelty,
Be the sweet presence of a good diffused,
And in diffusion ever more intense!
So shall I join the choir invisible,
Whose music is the gladness of the world.

George Eliot

22   **Monody**

To have known him, to have loved him
     After loneness long;
And then to be estranged in life,
     And neither in the wrong;
And now for death to set his seal—
     Ease me, a little ease, my song!

By wintry hills his hermit-mound
   The sheeted snow-drifts drape,
And houseless there the snow-bird flits
   Beneath the fir-trees' crape:
Glazed now with ice the cloistral vine
   That hid the shyest grape.

                Herman Melvil

423   **Annabel Lee**

It was many and many a year ago,
   In a kingdom by the sea,
That a maiden there lived whom you may know
   By the name of Annabel Lee;—
And this maiden she lived with no other thought
   Than to love and be loved by me.

I was a child and *she* was a child,
   In this kingdom by the sea,
But we loved with a love that was more than love—
   I and my Annabel Lee—
With a love that the wingèd seraphs in Heaven
   Coveted her and me.

And this was the reason that, long ago,
   In this kingdom by the sea,
A wind blew out of a cloud, chilling
   My beautiful Annabel Lee;
So that her high-born kinsmen came
   And bore her away from me,
To shut her up in a sepulcher
   In this kingdom by the sea.

The angels, not half so happy in Heaven,
   Went envying her and me:—
Yes!—that was the reason (as all men know,
   In this kingdom by the sea)
That the wind came out of the cloud, by night,
   Chilling and killing my Annabel Lee.

But our love it was stronger by far than the love
   Of those who were older than we—
   Of many far wiser than we—
And neither the angels in Heaven above,
   Nor the demons down under the sea,
Can ever dissever my soul from the soul
   Of the beautiful Annabel Lee:—

For the moon never beams without bringing me dreams
  Of the beautiful Annabel Lee;
And the stars never rise but I feel the bright eyes
  Of the beautiful Annabel Lee;
And so, all the night-tide, I lie down by the side
Of my darling,—my darling,—my life and my bride,
    In her sepulcher there by the sea—
    In her tomb by the sounding sea.

Edgar Allan Poe

424 **Rose Aylmer**

        Ah what avails the sceptred race,
          Ah what the form divine!
        What every virtue, every grace!
          Rose Aylmer, all were thine.

        Rose Aylmer, whom these wakeful eyes
          May weep, but never see,
        A night of memories and sighs
          I consecrate to thee.

Walter Savage Landor

425 **Remembrance**

Cold in the earth—and the deep snow piled above thee,
Far, far removed, cold in the dreary grave!
Have I forgot, my only love, to love thee,
Severed at last by Time's all-severing wave?

Now, when alone, do my thoughts no longer hover
Over the mountains, on that northern shore,
Resting their wings where heath and fern-leaves cover
The noble heart for ever, ever more?

Cold in the earth—and fifteen wild Decembers,
From those brown hills, have melted into spring:
Faithful, indeed, is the spirit that remembers
After such years of change and suffering!

Sweet Love of youth, forgive, if I forget thee,
While the world's tide is bearing me along;
Other desires and other hopes beset me,
Hopes which obscure, but cannot do thee wrong!

No later light has lightened up my heaven,
No second morn has ever shone for me;

All my life's bliss from thy dear life was given,
All my life's bliss is in the grave with thee.

But, when the days of golden dreams had perished,
And even Despair was powerless to destroy;
Then did I learn how existence could be cherished,
Strengthened and fed without the aid of joy.

Then did I check the tears of useless passion—
Weaned my young soul from yearning after thine;
Sternly denied its burning wish to hasten
Down to that tomb already more than mine.

And, even yet, I dare not let it languish,
Dare not indulge in memory's rapturous pain;
Once drinking deep of that divinest anguish,
How could I seek the empty world again?

Emily Brontë

426   **When I Am Dead, My Dearest**

When I am dead, my dearest,
    Sing no sad songs for me;
Plant thou no roses at my head,
    Nor shady cypress tree:
Be the green grass above me
    With showers and dewdrops wet;
And if thou wilt, remember,
    And if thou wilt, forget.

I shall not see the shadows,
    I shall not feel the rain;
I shall not hear the nightingale
    Sing on, as if in pain;
And dreaming through the twilight
    That doth not rise nor set,
Haply I may remember,
    And haply may forget.

Christina Rossetti

427   **Requiescat**

Strew on her roses, roses,
    And never a spray of yew.
In quiet she reposes:
    Ah! would that I did too.

Her mirth the world required:
    She bathed it in smiles of glee.
But her heart was tired, tired,
    And now they let her be.

Her life was turning, turning,
    In mazes of heat and sound.
But for peace her soul was yearning,
    And now peace laps her round.

Her cabin'd, ample Spirit,
    It flutter'd and fail'd for breath.
To-night it doth inherit
    The vasty hall of Death.

Matthew Arnold

428

Finis

I strove with none, for none was worth my strife.
Nature I loved and, next to Nature, Art:
I warm'd both hands before the fire of life;
It sinks, and I am ready to depart.

Walter Savage Landor

429

Break, Break, Break

Break, break, break,
    On thy cold grey stones, O Sea!
And I would that my tongue could utter
    The thoughts that arise in me.

O well for the fisherman's boy,
    That he shouts with his sister at play!
O well for the sailor lad,
    That he sings in his boat on the bay!

And the stately ships go on
    To their haven under the hill;
But O for the touch of a vanished hand,
    And the sound of a voice that is still!

Break, break, break,
    At the foot of thy crags, O Sea!
But the tender grace of a day that is dead
    Will never come back to me.

Alfred, Lord Tennyson

430   Into my heart an air that kills
                From yon far country blows:
        What are those blue remembered hills,
                What spires, what farms are those?

        That is the land of lost content,
                I see it shining plain,
        The happy highways where I went
                And cannot come again.

                                    A. E. Housman

431   **Tears, Idle Tears**

        Tears, idle tears, I know not what they mean,
        Tears from the depth of some divine despair
        Rise in the heart, and gather to the eyes,
        In looking on the happy autumn-fields,
        And thinking of the days that are no more.

        Fresh as the first beam glittering on a sail,
        That brings our friends up from the under-world,
        Sad as the last which reddens over one
        That sinks with all we love below the verge;
        So sad, so fresh, the days that are no more.

        Ah, sad and strange as in dark summer dawns
        The earliest pipe of half-awakened birds
        To dying ears, when unto dying eyes
        The casement slowly grows a glimmering square;
        So sad, so strange, the days that are no more.

        Dear as remembered kisses after death,
        And sweet as those by hopeless fancy feigned
        On lips that are for others; deep as love,
        Deep as first love, and wild with all regret;
        O Death in Life, the days that are no more!

                                    Alfred, Lord Tennyson

432   **The Happiest Day**

        The happiest day—the happiest hour
                My seared and blighted heart hath known,
        The highest hope of pride and power,
                I feel hath flown.

        Of power! said I? Yes! such I ween
                But they have vanished long, alas!

The visions of my youth have been—
    But let them pass.

And pride, what have I now with thee?
    Another brow may ev'n inherit
The venom thou hast poured on me—
    Be still my spirit!

The happiest day—the happiest hour
    Mine eyes shall see—have ever seen,
The brightest glance of pride and power
    I feel have been:

But were that hope of pride and power
    Now offered with the pain
Ev'n *then* I felt—the brightest hour
    I would not live again:

For on its wings was dark alloy
    And as it fluttered—fell
An essence—powerful to destroy
    A soul that knew it well.

Edgar Allan Poe

33   Blow, Bugle, Blow

The splendour falls on castle walls
    And snowy summits old in story:
The long light shakes across the lakes,
    And the wild cataract leaps in glory.
Blow, bugle, blow, set the wild echoes flying,
Blow, bugle; answer, echoes, dying, dying, dying.

    O hark, O hear! how thin and clear,
        And thinner, cleaner, farther going!
    O sweet and far from cliff and scar
        The horns of Elfland faintly blowing!
Blow, let us hear the purple glens replying:
Blow, bugle; answer, echoes, dying, dying, dying.

    O love, they die in yon rich sky,
        They faint on hill or field or river:
    Our echoes roll from soul to soul
        And grow for ever and for ever.
Blow, bugle, blow, set the wild echoes flying,
And answer, echoes, answer, dying, dying, dying.

Alfred, Lord Tennyson

My Lost Youth

Often I think of the beautiful town
   That is seated by the sea;
Often in thought go up and down
The pleasant streets of that dear old town,
    And my youth comes back to me.
      And a verse of a Lapland song
      Is haunting my memory still:
      'A boy's will is the wind's will,
And the thoughts of youth are long, long thoughts.'

I can see the shadowy lines of its trees,
   And catch, in sudden gleams,
The sheen of the far-surrounding seas,
And islands that were the Hesperides
    Of all my boyish dreams.
      And the burden of that old song,
      It murmurs and whispers still:
      'A boy's will is the wind's will,
And the thoughts of youth are long, long thoughts.'

I remember the black wharves and the slips,
   And the sea-tides tossing free;
And Spanish sailors with bearded lips,
And the beauty and mystery of the ships,
    And the magic of the sea.
      And the voice of the wayward song
      Is singing and saying still:
      'A boy's will is the wind's will,
And the thoughts of youth are long, long thoughts.'

I remember the bulwarks by the shore,
   And the fort upon the hill;
The sunrise gun, with its hollow roar,
The drum-beat repeated o'er and o'er,
    And the bugle wild and shrill.
      And the music of that old song
      Throbs in my memory still:
      'A boy's will is the wind's will,
And the thoughts of youth are long, long thoughts.'

I remember the sea-fight far away,
   How it thundered o'er the tide!
And the dead captains, as they lay
In their graves, o'erlooking the tranquil bay,
    Where they in battle died.

And the sound of that mournful song
Goes through me with a thrill:
'A boy's will is the wind's will,
And the thoughts of youth are long, long thoughts.'

I can see the breezy dome of groves,
The shadows of Deering's Woods;
And the friendship old and the early loves
Come back with a Sabbath sound, as of doves
In quiet neighborhoods.
And the verse of that sweet old song,
It flutters and murmurs still:
'A boy's will is the wind's will,
And the thoughts of youth are long, long thoughts.'

I remember the gleams and glooms that dart
Across the school-boy's brain;
The song and the silence in the heart,
That in part are prophecies, and in part
Are longings wild and vain.
And the voice of that fitful song
Sings on, and is never still:
'A boy's will is the wind's will,
And the thoughts of youth are long, long thoughts.'

There are things of which I may not speak;
There are dreams that cannot die;
There are thoughts that make the strong heart weak,
And bring a pallor into the cheek,
And a mist before the eye.
And the words of that fatal song
Come over me like a chill:
'A boy's will is the wind's will,
And the thoughts of youth are long, long thoughts.'

Strange to me now are the forms I meet
When I visit the dear old town;
But the native air is pure and sweet,
And the trees that o'ershadow each well-known street,
As they balance up and down,
Are singing the beautiful song,
Are sighing and whispering still:
'A boy's will is the wind's will,
And the thoughts of youth are long, long thoughts.'

And Deering's Woods are fresh and fair,
And with joy that is almost pain

My heart goes back to wander there,
And among the dreams of the days that were,
   I find my lost youth again.
     And the strange and beautiful song,
     The groves are repeating it still:
      'A boy's will is the wind's will,
And the thoughts of youth are long, long thoughts.'

                  Henry Wadsworth Longfellow

435   The Barefoot Boy

Blessings on thee, little man,
Barefoot boy, with cheek of tan!
With thy turned-up pantaloons,
And thy merry whistled tunes;
With thy red lip, redder still
Kissed by strawberries on the hill;
With the sunshine on thy face,
Through thy torn brim's jaunty grace;
From my heart I give thee joy,—
I was once a barefoot boy!

Prince thou art,—the grown-up man
Only is republican.
Let the million-dollared ride!
Barefoot, trudging at his side,
Thou hast more than he can buy
In the reach of ear and eye,—
Outward sunshine, inward joy:
Blessing on thee, barefoot boy!

Oh for boyhood's painless play,
Sleep that wakes in laughing day,
Health that mocks the doctor's rules,
Knowledge never learned of schools,
Of the wild bee's morning chase,
Of the wild-flower's time and place,
Flight of fowl and habitude
Of the tenants of the wood;
How the tortoise bears his shell,
How the woodchuck digs his cell,
And the ground-mole sings his well;
How the robin feeds her young,
How the oriole's nest is hung;
Where the whitest lilies blow,
Where the freshest berries grow,

Where the ground-nut trails its vine,
Where the wood-grape's clusters shine;
Of the black wasp's cunning way,
Mason of his walls of clay,
And the architectural plans
Of gray hornet artisans!
For, eschewing books and tasks,
Nature answers all he asks;
Hand in hand with her he walks,
Face to face with her he talks,
Part and parcel of her joy,—
Blessings on the barefoot boy!

Oh for boyhood's time of June,
Crowding years in one brief moon,
When all things I heard or saw,
Me, their master, waited for.
I was rich in flowers and trees,
Humming-birds and honey-bees;
For my sport the squirrel played,
Plied the snouted mole his spade;
For my taste the blackberry cone
Purpled over hedge and stone;
Laughed the brook for my delight
Through the day and through the night,
Whispering at the garden wall,
Talked with me from fall to fall;
Mine the sand-rimmed pickerel pond,
Mine the walnut slopes beyond,
Mine, on bending orchard trees,
Apples of Hesperides!
Still as my horizon grew,
Larger grew my riches too;
All the world I saw or knew
Seemed a complex Chinese toy,
Fashioned for a barefoot boy!

Oh for festal dainties spread,
Like my bowl of milk and bread;
Pewter spoon and bowl of wood,
On the door-stone, gray and rude!
O'er me, like a regal tent,
Cloudy-ribbed, the sunset bent,
Purple-curtained, fringed with gold,
Looped in many a wind-swung fold;
While for music came the play
Of the pied frog's orchestra;

And, to light the noisy choir,
Lit the fly his lamp of fire.
I was monarch: pomp and joy
Waited on the barefoot boy!

Cheerily, then, my little man,
Live and laugh, as boyhood can!
Though the flinty slopes be hard,
Stubble-speared the new-mown sward,
Every morn shall lead thee through
Fresh baptisms of the dew;
Every evening from thy feet
Shall the cool wind kiss the heat:
All too soon these feet must hide
In the prison cells of pride,
Lose the freedom of the sod,
Live like a colt's for work be shod,
Made to tread the mills of toil,
Up and down in ceaseless moil:
Happy if their track be found
Never on forbidden ground;
Happy if they sink not in
Quick and treacherous sands of sin.
Ah! that thou couldst know thy joy,
Ere it passes, barefoot boy!

John Greenleaf Whittier

436   The Chambered Nautilus

This is the ship of pearl, which, poets feign,
  Sails the unshadowed main,—
  The venturous bark that flings
On the sweet summer wind its purpled wings
In gulfs enchanted, where the Siren sings,
  And coral reefs lie bare,
Where the cold sea-maids rise to sun their streaming hair.

Its webs of living gauze no more unfurl;
  Wrecked is the ship of pearl!
  And every chambered cell,
Where its dim dreaming life was wont to dwell,
As the frail tenant shaped his growing shell,
  Before thee lies revealed,—
Its irised ceiling rent, its sunless crypt unsealed!

Year after year beheld the silent toil
   That spread his lustrous coil;
   Still, as the spiral grew,
He left the past year's dwelling for the new,
Stole with soft step its shining archway through,
   Built up its idle door,
Stretched in his last-found home, and knew the old no more.

Thanks for the heavenly message brought by thee,
   Child of the wandering sea,
   Cast from her lap, forlorn!
From thy dead lips a clearer note is born
Than ever Triton blew from wreathèd horn!
   While on mine ear it rings,
Through the deep caves of thought I hear a voice that sings:—

Build thee more stately mansions, O my soul,
   As the swift seasons roll!
   Leave thy low-vaulted past!
Let each new temple, nobler than the last,
Shut thee from heaven with a dome more vast,
   Till thou at length art free.
Leaving thine outgrown shell by life's unresting sea!
                   Oliver Wendell Holmes

437   Choric Song of the Lotos-Eaters

   There is sweet music here that softer falls
   Than petals from blown roses on the grass,
   Or night-dews on still water between walls
   Of shadowy granite, in a gleaming pass;
   Music that gentlier on the spirit lies,
   Than tired eyelids upon tired eyes;
   Music that brings sleep down from the blissful skies
   Here are cool mosses deep,
   And through the moss the ivies creep,
   And in the stream the long-leaved flowers weep,
   And from the craggy ledge the poppy hangs in sleep.
   Why are we weighed upon with heaviness,
   And utterly consumed with sharp distress,
   While all things else have rest from weariness?
   All things have rest; why should we toil alone,
   We only toil, who are the first of things,
   And make perpetual moan,
   Still from one sorrow to another thrown;
   Nor ever fold our wings,
   And cease from wanderings,

Nor steep our brows in slumber's holy balm;
Nor harken what the inner spirit sings,
"There is no joy but calm!"—
Why should we only toil, the roof and crown of things?

Lo! in the middle of the wood,
The folded leaf is wooed from out the bud
With winds upon the branch, and there
Grows green and broad, and takes no care,
Sun-steeped at noon, and in the moon
Nightly dew-fed; and turning yellow
Falls, and floats adown the air.
Lo! sweetened with the summer light,
The full-juiced apple, waxing over-mellow,
Drops in a silent autumn night.
All its allotted length of days
The flower ripens in its place,
Ripens and fades, and falls, and hath no toil,
Fast-rooted in the fruitful soil.

Hateful is the dark-blue sky,
Vaulted o'er the dark-blue sea.
Death is the end of life; ah, why
Should life all labour be?
Let us alone. Time driveth onward fast,
And in a little while our lips are dumb.
Let us alone. What is it that will last?
All things are taken from us, and become
Portions and parcels of the dreadful past.
Let us alone. What pleasure can we have
To war with evil? Is there any peace
In ever climbing up the climbing wave?
All things have rest, and ripen toward the grave
In silence—ripe, fall, and cease;
Give us long rest or death, dark death, or dreamful ease.

How sweet it were, hearing the downward stream
With half-shut eyes ever to seem
Falling asleep in a half-dream!
To dream and dream, like yonder amber light,
Which will not leave the myrrh-bush on the height;
To hear each other's whispered speech;
Eating the Lotos day by day,
To watch the crisping ripples on the beach,
And tender curving lines of creamy spray;
To lend our hearts and spirits wholly
To the influence of mild-minded melancholy;

To muse and brood and live again in memory,
With those old faces of our infancy
Heaped over with a mound of grass,
Two handfuls of white dust, shut in an urn of brass!

Dear is the memory of our wedded lives,
And dear the last embraces of our wives
And their warm tears; but all hath suffered change;
For surely now our household hearths are cold,
Our sons inherit us, our looks are strange,
And we should come like ghosts to trouble joy.
Or else the island princes over-bold
Have eat our substance, and the minstrel sings
Before them of the ten years' war in Troy,
And our great deeds, as half-forgotten things.
Is there confusion in the little isle?
Let what is broken so remain.
The gods are hard to reconcile;
'Tis hard to settle order once again.
There *is* confusion worse than death.
Trouble on trouble, pain on pain,
Long labour unto aged breath,
Sore task to hearts worn out by many wars
And eyes grown dim with gazing on the pilot-stars.

But, propped on beds of amaranth and moly,
How sweet—while warm airs lull us, blowing lowly—
With half-dropped eyelid still,
Beneath a heaven dark and holy,
To watch the long bright river drawing slowly
His waters from the purple hill—
To hear the dewy echoes calling
From cave to cave through the thick-twined vine—
To watch the emerald-coloured water falling
Through many a woven acanthus-wreath divine!
Only to hear and see the far-off sparkling brine,
Only to hear were sweet, stretched out beneath the pine.

The Lotos blooms below the barren peak,
The Lotos blows by every winding creek;
All day the wind breathes low with mellower tone;
Through every hollow cave and alley lone
Round and round the spicy downs the yellow Lotos-
    dust is blown.
We have had enough of action, and of motion we,
Rolled to starboard, rolled to larboard, when the surge
    was seething free,

Where the wallowing monster spouted his foam-fountains
    in the sea.
Let us swear an oath, and keep it with an equal mind,
In the hollow Lotos-land to live and lie reclined
On the hills like gods together, careless of mankind.
For they lie beside their nectar, and the bolts are hurled
Far below them in the valleys, and the clouds are lightly
    curled
Round their golden houses, girdled with the gleaming
    world;
Where they smile in secret, looking over wasted lands,
Blight and famine, plague and earthquake, roaring deeps
    and fiery sands,
Clanging fights, and flaming towns, and sinking ships,
    and praying hands.
But they smile, they find a music centered in a doleful
    song
Steaming up, a lamentation and an ancient tale of wrong,
Like a tale of little meaning though the words are strong;
Chanted from an ill-used race of men that cleave the
    soil,
Sow the seed, and reap the harvest with enduring toil,
Storing yearly little dues of wheat, and wine and oil;
Till they perish and they suffer—some, 'tis whispered
    —down in hell
Suffer endless anguish, others in Elysian valleys dwell,
Resting weary limbs at last on beds of asphodel,
Surely, surely, slumber is more sweet than toil, the shore
Than labour in the deep mid-ocean, wind and wave and
    oar;
O rest ye, brother mariners, we will not wander more.

Alfred, Lord Tennyson

438   **O Captain! My Captain!**

O Captain! my Captain! our fearful trip is done,
The ship has weather'd every rack, the prize we sought is
    won,
The port is near, the bells I hear, the people all exulting,
While follow eyes the steady keel, the vessel grim and daring;
          But O heart! heart! heart!
            O the bleeding drops of red,
              Where on the deck my Captain lies,
                Fallen cold and dead.

O Captain! my Captain! rise up and hear the bells;
Rise up—for you the flag is flung—for you the bugle trills,

or you bouquets and ribbon'd wreaths—for you the shores
        a-crowding,
'or you they call, the swaying mass, their eager faces turning;
      Here Captain! dear father!
        The arm beneath your head!
          It is some dream that on the deck,
            You've fallen cold and dead.

My Captain does not answer, his lips are pale and still,
My father does not feel my arm, he has no pulse nor will,
The ship is anchor'd safe and sound, its voyage closed and
        done,
'rom fearful trip the victor ship comes in with object won;
      Exult O shores, and ring O bells!
        But I with mournful tread,
          Walk the deck my Captain lies,
           Fallen cold and dead.

                    Walt Whitman

'39   The Lost Leader

ust for a handful of silver he left us,
    Just for a riband to stick in his coat—
'ound the one gift of which fortune bereft us,
    Lost all the others she lets us devote;
They, with the gold to give, doled him out silver,
    So much was theirs who so little allowed:
How all our copper had gone for his service!
    Rags—were they purple, his heart had been proud!
We that had loved him so, followed him, honoured him,
    Lived in his mild and magnificent eye,
Learned his great language, caught his clear accents,
    Made him our pattern to live and to die!
Shakespeare was of us, Milton was for us,
    Burns, Shelley, were with us,—they watch from their graves!
He alone breaks from the van and the freemen,
    —He alone sinks to the rear and the slaves!

We shall march prospering,—not thro' his presence;
    Songs may inspirit us,—not from his lyre;
Deeds will be done,—while he boasts his quiescence,
    Still bidding crouch whom the rest bade aspire:
Blot out his name, then, record one lost soul more,
    One task more declined, one more footpath untrod,
One more triumph for devils and sorrow for angels,
    One wrong more to man, one more insult to God!
Life's night begins: let him never come back to us!

There would be doubt, hesitation, and pain,
Forced praise on our part—the glimmer of twilight,
  Never glad confident morning again!
Best fight on well, for we taught him—strike gallantly,
  Menace our heart ere we master his own;
Then let him receive the new knowledge and wait us,
  Pardoned in Heaven, the first by the throne!

Robert Brownin

440   Concord Hymn

Sung at the Completion of the Concord Monument

By the rude bridge that arched the flood,
  Their flag to April's breeze unfurled,
Here once the embattled farmers stood,
  And fired the shot heard round the world.

The foe long since in silence slept;
  Alike the conqueror silent sleeps;
And Time the ruined bridge has swept
  Down the dark stream which seaward creeps.

On this green bank, by this soft stream,
  We set to-day a votive stone;
That memory may their deed redeem,
  When, like our sires, our sons are gone.

Spirit, that made those heroes dare
  To die, or leave their children free,
Bid Time and Nature gently spare
  The shaft we raise to them and thee.

Ralph Waldo Emerso

441   Days

Daughters of Time, the hypocritic Days.
Muffled and dumb like barefoot derivishes,
And marching single in an endless file,
Bring diadems and fagots in their hands.
To each they offer gifts after his will,
Bread, kingdoms, stars, and sky that holds them all.
I, in my pleached garden, watched the pomp,
Forgot my morning wishes, hastily
Took a few herbs and apples, the Day
Turned and departed silently. I, too late,
Under her solemn fillet saw the scorn.

Ralph Waldo Emerso

442

The Toys

My little Son, who look'd from thoughtful eyes
And moved and spoke in quiet grown-up wise,
Having my law the seventh time disobey'd,
I struck him, and dismiss'd
With hard words and unkiss'd,
—His Mother, who was patient, being dead.
Then, fearing lest his grief should hinder sleep,
I visited his bed,
But found him slumbering deep,
With darken'd eyelids, and their lashes yet
From his late sobbing wet.
And I, with moan,
Kissing away his tears, left others of my own;
For, on a table drawn beside his head,
He had put, within his reach,
A box of counters and a red-vein'd stone,
A piece of glass abraded by the beach
And six or seven shells,
A bottle with bluebells,
And two French copper coins, ranged there with careful art,
To comfort his sad heart.
So when that night I pray'd
To God, I wept, and said:
Ah, when at last we lie with trancèd breath,
Not vexing Thee in death,
And thou rememberest of what toys
We made our joys,
How weakly understood,
Thy great commanded good,
Then, fatherly not less
Than I whom thou hast moulded from the clay,
Thou'lt leave Thy wrath, and say,
"I will be sorry for their childishness."

Coventry Patmore

443   ## Rabbi Ben Ezra

Grow old along with me!
The best is yet to be,
The last of life, for which the
    first was made:
Our times are in His hand
Who saith 'A whole I planned,
Youth shows but half; trust
    God: see all, nor be afraid!'

Not that, amassing flowers,
Youth sighed 'Which rose
    make ours,
Which lily leave and then as
    best recall?'
Not that, admiring stars,
It yearned 'Nor Jove, nor
    Mars:

Mine be some figured flame
 which blends, transcends
 them all!'

Not for such hopes and fears
Annulling youth's brief years,
Do I remonstrate: folly wide
 the mark!
Rather I prize the doubt
Low kinds exist without,
Finished and finite clods, un-
 troubled by a spark.

Poor vaunt of life indeed,
Were man but formed to feed
On joy, to solely seek and find
 and feast:
Such feasting ended, then
As sure an end to men;
Irks care the crop-full bird?
 Frets doubt the maw-
 crammed beast?

Rejoice we are allied
To That which doth provide
And not partake, effect and
 not receive!
A spark disturbs our clod;
Nearer we hold of God
Who gives, than of His tribes
 that take, I must believe.

Then, welcome each rebuff
That turns earth's smoothness
 rough,
Each sting that bids nor sit
 nor stand but go!
Be our joys three-parts pain!
Strive, and hold cheap the
 strain;
Learn, nor account the pang;
 dare, never grudge the
 throe!

For thence,—a paradox
Which comforts while it
 mocks,—

Shall life succeed in that it
 seems to fail:
What I aspired to be,
And was not, comforts me:
A brute I might have been,
 but would not sink i' the
 scale.

What is he but a brute
Whose flesh hath soul to suit,
Whose spirit works lest arms
 and legs want play?
To man, propose this test—
Thy body at its best,
How far can that project thy
 soul on its lone way?

Yet gifts should prove their
 use:
I own the Past profuse
Of power each side, perfec-
 tion every turn:
Eyes, ears took in their dole,
Brain treasured up the whole;
Should not the heart beat
 once 'How good to live and
 learn'?

Not once beat 'Praise be
 Thine!
I see the whole design,
I, who saw power, see now
 Love perfect too:
Perfect I call Thy plan:
Thanks that I was a man!
Maker, remake, complete,—
 I trust what Thou shalt do!'

For pleasant is this flesh;
Our soul in its rose-mesh
Pulled ever to the earth, still
 yearns for rest:
Would we some prize might
 hold
To match those manifold
Possessions of the brute,—
 gain most, as we did best!

Let us not always say
'Spite of this flesh to-day
I strove, made head, gained
  ground upon the whole!'
As the bird wings and sings,
Let us cry 'All good things
Are ours, nor soul helps flesh
  more, now, than flesh helps
  soul!'

Therefore I summon age
To grant youth's heritage,
Life's struggle having so far
  reached its term:
Thence shall I pass, approved
A man, for ay removed
From the developed brute; a
  God though in the germ.

And I shall thereupon
Take rest, ere I be gone
Once more on my adventure
  brave and new:
Fearless and unperplexed,
When I wage battle next,
What weapons to select, what
  armour to indue.

Youth ended, I shall try
My gain or loss thereby;
Leave the fire ashes, what sur-
  vives is gold:
And I shall weigh the same,
Give life its praise or blame:
Young, all lay in dispute; I
  shall know, being old.

For note, when evening shuts,
A certain moment cuts
The deed off, calls the glory
  from the grey:
A whisper from the west
Shoots—'Add this to the rest,
Take it and try its worth: here
  dies another day.'

So, still within this life,

Though lifted o'er its strife,
Let me discern, compare, pro-
  nounce at last,
'This rage was right i' the
  main,
That acquiescence vain:
The Future I may face now I
  have proved the Past.'

For more is not reserved
To man, with soul just nerved
To act to-morrow what he
  learns to-day:
Here, work enough to watch
The Master work, and catch
Hints of the proper craft,
  tricks of the tool's true
  play.

As it was better, youth
Should strive, through acts
  uncouth,
Toward making, than repose
  on aught found made;
So, better, age, exempt
From strife, should know,
  than tempt
Further. Thou waitedst age;
  wait death nor be afraid!

Enough now, if the Right
And Good and Infinite
Be named here, as thou call-
  est thy hand thine own,
With knowledge absolute,
Subject to no dispute
From fools that crowded
  youth, nor let the feel
  alone.

Be there, for once and all,
Severed great minds from
  small,
Announced to each his station
  in the Past!
Was I, the world arraigned,
Were they, thy soul dis-
  dained,

Right? Let age speak the
    truth and give us peace at
    last!

Now, who shall arbitrate?
Ten men love what I hate,
Shun what I follow, slight
    what I receive;
Ten, who in ears and eyes
Match me: we all surmise,
They, this thing, and I, that:
    whom shall my soul be-
    lieve?

Not on the vulgar mass
Called 'work,' must sentence
    pass,
Things done, that took the
    eye and had the price;
O'er which, from level stand,
The low world laid its hand,
Found straightway to its
    mind, could value in a
    trice:

But all, the world's coarse
    thumb
And finger failed to plumb,
So passed in making up the
    main account;
All instincts immature,
All purposes unsure.
That weighed not as his work,
    yet swelled the man's
    amount:

Thoughts hardly to be packed
Into a narrow act,
Fancies that broke through
    language and escaped;
All I could never be,
All, men ignored in me.
This, I was worth to God,
    whose wheel the pitcher
    shaped.

Aye, note that Potter's wheel,
That metaphor! and feel

Why time spins fast, why pas-
    sive lies our clay,—
Thou, to whom fools pro-
    pound,
When the wine makes its
    round,
'Since life fleets, all is change;
    the Past gone, seize to-day!'

Fool! All that is, at all,
Lasts ever, past recall;
Earth changes, but thy soul
    and God stand sure:
What entered into thee,
That was, is, and shall be:
Time's wheel runs back or
    stops; Potter and clay en-
    dure.

He fixed thee mid this dance
Of plastic circumstance,
This Present, thou, forsooth,
    wouldst fain arrest:
Machinery just meant
To give thy soul its bent,
Try thee and turn thee forth,
    sufficiently impressed.

What though the earlier
    grooves
Which ran the laughing loves
Around thy base, no longer
    pause and press?
What though, about thy rim,
Skull-things in order grim
Grow out, in graver mood,
    obey the sterner stress?

Look not thou down but up!
To uses of a cup,
The festal board, lamp's flash
    and trumpet's peal,
The new wine's foaming flow,
The Master's lips aglow!
Thou, heaven's consummate
    cup, what needst thou with
    earth's wheel?

But I need, now as then,
Thee, God, who mouldest men;
And since, not even while the whirl was worst,
Did I,—to the wheel of life
With shapes and colours rife,
Bound dizzily,—mistake my end, to slake Thy thirst:

So, taken and use Thy work!
Amend what flaws may lurk,
What strain o' the stuff, what warpings past the aim!
My times be in Thy hand!
Perfect the cup as planned!
Let age approve of youth, and death complete the same!

Robert Browning

444

Strong Son of God, immortal Love,
    Whom we, that have not seen thy face,
    By faith, and faith alone, embrace,
Believing where we cannot prove;

Thine are these orbs of light and shade;
    Thou madest Life in man and brute;
    Thou madest Death; and lo, thy foot
Is on the skull which thou hast made.

Thou wilt not leave us in the dust:
    Thou madest man, he knows not why;
    He thinks he was not made to die;
And thou hast made him: thou art just.

Thou seemest human and divine,
    The highest, holiest manhood, thou:
    Our wills are ours, we know not how;
Our wills are ours, to make them thine.

Our little systems have their day;
    They have their day and cease to be:
    They are but broken lights of thee,
And thou, O Lord, art more than they.

We have but faith: we cannot know;
    For knowledge is of things we see;
    And yet we trust it comes from thee,
A beam in darkness: let it grow.

Let knowledge grow from more to more,
    But more of reverence in us dwell;
    That mind and soul, according well,
May make one music as before,

But vaster. We are fools and slight;
    We mock thee when we do not fear:
    But help thy foolish ones to bear;
Help thy vain worlds to bear thy light.

Forgive what seemed my sin in me;
    What seemed my worth since I began;
    For merit lives from man to man,
And not from man, O Lord, to thee.

Forgive my grief for one removed,
    Thy creature, whom I found so fair.
    I trust he lives in thee, and there
I find him worthier to be loved.

Forgive these wild and wandering cries,
    Confusions of a wasted youth;
    Forgive them where they fail in truth,
And in thy wisdom make me wise.

Alfred, Lord Tennyson

445   I never saw a moor,
             I never saw the sea;
             Yet know I how the heather looks,
             And what a wave must be.

             I never spoke with God,
             Nor visited in heaven;
             Yet certain am I of the spot
             As if the chart were given.

Emily Dickinson

446   Invictus

Out of the night that covers me,
    Black as the Pit from pole to pole,
I thank whatever gods may be
    For my unconquerable soul.

In the fell clutch of circumstance
    I have not winced nor cried aloud.
Under the bludgeonings of chance
    My head is bloody, but unbowed.

Beyond this place of wrath and tears
  Looms but the horror of the shade,
And yet the menace of the years
  Finds, and shall find me, unafraid.

It matters not how strait the gate,
  How charged with punishments the scroll,
I am the master of my fate:
  I am the captain of my soul.

William Ernest Henley

447   Crossing the Bar

Sunset and evening star,
  And one clear call for me!
And may there be no moaning of the bar,
  When I put out to sea.

But such a tide as moving seems asleep,
  Too full for sound and foam,
When that which drew from out the boundless deep
  Turns again home.

Twilight and evening bell,
  And after that the dark!
And may there be no sadness of farewell,
  When I embark;

For tho' from out our bourne of Time and Place
  The flood may bear me far,
I hope to see my Pilot face to face
  When I have crost the bar.

Alfred, Lord Tennyson

448   No Coward Soul Is Mine

No coward soul is mine,
No trembler in the world's storm-troubled sphere:
  I see Heaven's glories shine,
And Faith shines equal, arming me from Fear.

O God within my breast,
Almighty, ever-present Deity!
  Life, that in me hast rest
As I, undying Life, have power in Thee!

Vain are the thousand creeds
That move men's hearts; unutterably vain;
   Worthless as withered weeds,
Or idlest froth amid the boundless main,

   To waken doubt in one
Holding so fast by Thy infinity,
   So surely anchored on
The steadfast rock of Immortality.

   With wide embracing love
Thy Spirit animates eternal years,
   Pervades and broods above,
Changes, sustains, dissolves, creates, and rears.

   Though earth and moon were gone,
And suns and universes cease to be,
   And Thou wert left alone,
Every existence would exist in Thee.

   There is not room for Death,
Nor atom that his might could render void:
   Since Thou are Being and Breath
And what Thou art may never be destroyed.

                                   Emily Brontë

449   **I Wake and Feel the Fell of Dark**

I wake and feel the fell of dark, not day.
What hours, O what black hoürs we have spent
This night! what sights you, heart, saw; ways you went!
And more must, in yet longer light's delay.
With witness I speak this. But where I say
Hours I mean years, mean life. And my lament
Is cries countless, cries like dead letters sent
To dearest him that lives alas! away.

I am gall, I am heartburn. God's most deep decree
Bitter would have me taste; my taste was me;
Bones built in me, flesh filled, blood brimmed the curse.
Selfyeast of spirit a dull dough sours. I see
The lost are like this, and their scourge to be
As I am mine, their sweating selves; but worse.

                              Gerard Manley Hopkins

450
A Ballad of Trees and the Master

Into the woods my Master went,
Clean forspent, forspent.
Into the woods my Master came,
Forspent with love and shame.
But the olives they were not blind to Him,
The little gray leaves were kind to Him:
The thorn-tree had a mind to Him
When into the woods He came.

Out of the woods my Master went,
And He was well content.
Out of the woods my Master came,
Content with death and shame.
When Death and Shame would woo Him last,
From under the trees they drew Him last:
'Twas on a tree they slew Him—last
When out of the woods He came.

Sidney Lanier

451
The Dark Angel

Dark Angel, with thine aching lust
To rid the world of penitence:
Malicious Angel, who still dost
My soul such subtle violence!

Because of thee, no thought, no thing
Abides for me undesecrate:
Dark Angel, ever on the wing,
Who never reachest me too late!

When music sounds, then changest thou
Its silvery to a sultry fire:
Nor will thine envious heart allow
Delight untortured by desire.

Through thee, the gracious Muses turn
To Furies, O mine Enemy!
And all the things of beauty burn
With flames of evil ecstasy.

Because of thee, the land of dreams
Becomes a gathering-place of fears:
Until tormented slumber seems
One vehemence of useless tears.

When sunlight glows upon the flowers,
Or ripples down the dancing sea:
Thou, with thy troop of passionate powers,
Beleaguerest, bewilderest me.

Within the breath of autumn woods,
Within the winter silences:
Thy venomous spirit stirs and broods,
O master of impieties!

The ardour of red flame is thine,
And thin the steely soul of ice:
Thou poisonest the fair design
Of nature, with unfair device.

Apples of ashes, golden bright;
Waters of bitterness, how sweet!
O banquet of a foul delight,
Prepared by thee, dark Paraclete.

Thou art the whisper in the gloom,
The hinting tone, the haunting laugh:
Thou art the adorner of my tomb,
The minstrel of mine epitaph.

I fight thee, in the Holy Name!
Yet, what thou dost, is what God saith:
Tempter! should I escape thy flame,
Thou wilt have helped my soul from Death:

The second Death, that never dies,
That cannot die, when time is dead:
Live Death, wherein the lost soul cries,
Eternally uncomforted.

Dark Angel, with thine aching lust!
Of two defeats, of two despairs:
Less dread, a change to drifting dust,
Than thine eternity of cares.

Do what thou wilt, thou shalt not so,
Dark Angel! triumph over me:
Lonely, unto the Lone I go;
Divine, to the Divinity.

Lionel Johnson

The Hound of Heaven

fled Him, down the nights and down the days;
 I fled Him, down the arches of the years;
fled Him, down the labyrinthine ways
 Of my own mind; and in the mist of tears
hid from Him, and under running laughter.
            Up vistaed hopes, I sped;
            And shot, precipitated,
  down Titanic glooms of chasmèd fears,
 From those strong Feet that followed, followed after.
            But with unhurrying chase,
            And unperturbèd pace,
  Deliberate speed, majestic instancy,
            They beat—and a Voice beat
            More instant than the Feet—
 'All things betray thee, who betrayest Me.'

            I pleaded, outlaw-wise,
 y many a hearted casement, curtained red,
  Trellised with intertwining charities;
 For, though I knew His love Who followèd,
            Yet was I sore adread
 est, having Him, I must have naught beside.)
 ut, if one little casement parted wide,
  The gust of His approach would clash it to.
  Fear wist not to evade as Love wist to pursue.
 cross the margent of the world I fled,
  And troubled the gold gateways of the stars,
  Smiting for shelter on their clangèd bars;
            Fretted to dulcet jars
 nd silvern chatter the pale ports o' the moon.
  said to dawn: Be sudden; to eve: Be soon—
  With thy young skyey blossoms heap me over
            From this tremendous Lover!
 loat thy vague veil about me, lest He see!
  I tempted all His servitors, but to find
 y own betrayal in their constancy,
  n faith to Him their fickleness to me,
  Their traitorous trueness, and their loyal deceit.
 o all swift things for swiftness did I sue;
  Clung to the whistling mane of every wind.
            But whether they swept, smoothly fleet,
  The long savannahs of the blue;
            Or whether, Thunder-driven,
  They clanged His chariot 'thwart a heaven,

Plashy with flying lightnings round the spurn o' their feet:—
  Fear wist not to evade as Love wist to pursue.
      Still with unhurrying chase,
      And unperturbèd pace,
  Deliberate speed, majestic instancy,
      Came on the following Feet,
      And a Voice above their beat—
  'Naught shelters thee, who wilt not shelter Me.'

I sought no more that after which I strayed
      In face of man or maid;
But still within the little children's eyes
      Seems something, something that replies,
They at least are for me, surely for me!
I turned me to them very wistfully;
But just as their young eyes grew sudden fair
      With dawning answers there,
Their angel plucked them from me by the hair.
'Come then, ye other children, Nature's—share
With me' (said I) 'your delicate fellowship;
      Let me greet you lip to lip,
      Let me twine with you caresses,
          Wantoning
      With our Lady-Mother's vagrant tresses,
          Banqueting
      With her in her wind-walled palace,
      Underneath her azured daïs,
      Quaffing, as your taintless way is,
          From a chalice
Lucent-weeping out of the dayspring.'
      So it was done:
I in their delicate fellowship was one—
Drew the bolt of Nature's secrecies.
      I knew all the swift importings
      On the wilful face of skies;
      I knew how the clouds arise,
      Spumèd of the wild sea-snortings;
          All that's born or dies
Rose and drooped with; made them shapers
Of mine own moods, or wailful or divine—
      With them joyed and was bereaven.
      I was heavy with the even,
When she lit her glimmering tapers
      Round the day's dead sanctities.
      I laughed in the morning's eyes.

I triumphed and I saddened with all weather,
    Heaven and I wept together,
And its sweet tears were salt with mortal mine;
Against the red throb of its sunset-heart
      I laid my own to beat,
      And share commingling heat;
But not by that, by that, was eased my human smart.
In vain my tears were wet on Heaven's gray cheek.
For ah! we know not what each other says,
    These things and I; in sound *I* speak—
Their sound is but their stir, they speak by silences.
Nature, poor stepdame, cannot slake my drouth;
    Let her, if she would owe me,
Drop yon blue bosom-veil of sky, and show me
    The breasts o' her tenderness:
Never did any milk of hers once bless
      My thirsting mouth.
     Nigh and nigh draws the chase,
      With unperturbèd pace,
  Deliberate speed, majestic instancy,
     And past those noisèd Feet
     A Voice comes yet more fleet—
    'Lo! naught contents thee, who content'st not Me.'

Naked I wait Thy love's uplifted stroke!
My harness piece by piece Thou hast hewn from me,
     And smitten me to my knee;
     I am defenseless utterly.
     I slept, methinks, and woke,
And, slowly gazing, find me stripped in sleep.
In the rash lustihead of my young powers,
    I shook the pillaring hours
And pulled my life upon me; grimed with smears,
I stand amid the dust o' the mounded years—
My mangled youth lies dead beneath the heap.
My days have crackled and gone up in smoke,
Have puffed and burst as sun-starts on a stream.
     Yea, faileth now even dream
The dreamer, and the lute the lutanist;
Even the linkèd fantasies, in whose blossomy twist
I swung the earth a trinket at my wrist,
Are yielding; cords of all too weak account
For earth, with heavy griefs so overplussed,
     Ah! is Thy love indeed
A weed, albeit an amaranthine weed,

Suffering no flowers except its own to mount?
      Ah! must—
      Designer infinite!—
Ah! must Thou char the wood ere Thou canst limn with it?
My freshness spent its wavering shower i' the dust;
And now my heart is as a broken fount,
Wherein tear-drippings stagnate, spilt down ever
      From the dank thoughts that shiver
Upon the sighful branches of my mind.
      Such is; what is to be?
The pulp so bitter, how shall taste the rind?
I dimly guess what Time in mists confounds;
Yet ever and anon a trumpet sounds
From the hid battlements of Eternity:
Those shaken mists a space unsettle, then
Round the half-glimpsèd turrets slowly wash again;
      But not ere him who summoneth
      I first have seen, enwound
With glooming robes purpureal, cypress-crowned;
His name I know, and what his trumpet saith.
Whether man's heart or life it be which yields
      Thee harvest, must Thy harvest fields
      Be dunged with rotten death?

      Now of that long pursuit
      Comes on at hand the bruit;
That Voice is round me like a bursting sea:
      "And is thy earth so marred,
      Shattered in shard on shard?
  Lo, all things fly thee, for thou fliest Me!
      Strange, piteous, futile thing!
Wherefore should any set thee love apart?
Seeing none but I makes much of naught'
      (He said),
'And human love needs human meriting:
      How hast thou merited—
Of all man's clotted clay the dingiest clot?
      Alack, thou knowest not
How little worthy of any love thou art!
Whom wilt thou find to love ignoble thee,
      Save Me, save only Me?
All which I took from thee I did but take,
      Not for thy harms,
But just that thou might'st seek it in My arms,
  All which thy child's mistake

ncies as lost, I have stored for thee at home:
Rise, clasp My hand, and come!'
    Halts by me that footfall:
    Is my gloom, after all,
ade of His hand, outstretched caressingly?
    'Ah, fondest, blindest, weakest,
    I am He Whom thou seekest!
ou dravest love from thee, who dravest Me.'

Francis Thompson

3   Passing Away

Passing away, saith the World, passing away:
Chances, beauty and youth sapped day by day:
Thy life never continueth in one stay.
Is the eye waxen dim, is the dark hair changing to grey
That hath won neither laurel nor bay?
I shall clothe myself in Spring and bud in May:
Thou, root-stricken, shalt not rebuild thy decay
On my bosom for aye.
Then I answered: Yea.

Passing away, saith my Soul, passing away:
With its burden of fear and hope, of labour and play,
Hearken what the past doth witness and say:
Rust in thy gold, a moth is in thine array,
A canker is in thy bud, thy leaf must decay.
At midnight, at cockcrow, at morning, one certain day
Lo, the Bridegroom shall come and shall not delay:
Watch thou and pray.
Then I answered: Yea.

Passing away, saith my God, passing away:
Winter passeth after the long delay:
New grapes on the vine, new figs on the tender spray
Turtle calleth turtle in Heaven's May.
Though I tarry, wait for Me, trust Me, watch and pray.
Arise, come away, night is past and lo it is day,
My love, My sister, My spouse, thou shalt hear Me say—
Then I answered: Yea.

Christina Rossetti

454 **A Noiseless Patient Spider**

A noiseless patient spider,
I mark'd where on a little promontory it stood isolated,
Mark'd how to explore the vacant vast surrounding,
It launch'd forth filament, filament, filament, out of itself.
Ever unreeling them, ever tirelessly speeding them.

And you O my soul where you stand,
Surrounded, detached, in measureless oceans of space,
Ceaselessly musing, venturing, throwing, seeking the spher
  to connect them,
Till the bridge you will need be form'd, till the ductile anch
  hold,
Till the gossamer thread you fling catch somewhere, O my so
          Walt Whitm

455 **Earth's Night**

  Earth's night is where she rolls
   In her own shade;
  And even thus the Soul's
   Dark hours are made.

        William Allingha

456 **Brahma**

  If the red slayer think he slays,
   Or if the slain think he is slain,
  They know not well the subtle ways
   I keep, and pass, and turn again.

  Far or forgot to me is near;
   Shadow and sunlight are the same;
  The vanished gods to me appear;
   And one to me are shame and fame.

  They reckon ill who leave me out;
   When me they fly, I am the wings;
  I am the doubter and the doubt,
   And I the hymn the Brahmin sings.

  The strong gods pine for my abode,
   And pine in vain the sacred Seven;
  But thou, meek lover of the good!
   Find me, and turn thy back on heaven.

        Ralph Waldo Emers

357

St. Agnes' Eve

Deep on the convent-roof the snows
    Are sparkling to the moon:
My breath to heaven like vapour goes:
    May my soul follow soon!
The shadows of the convent-towers
    Slant down the snowy sward,
Still creeping with the creeping hours
    That lead me to my Lord:
Make Thou my spirit pure and clear
    As are the frosty skies,
Or this first snowdrop of the year
    That in my bosom lies.

As these white robes are soil'd and dark,
    To yonder shining ground;
As this pale taper's earthly spark,
    To yonder argent round;
So shows my soul before the Lamb,
    My spirit before Thee;
So in mine earthly house I am,
    To that I hope to be.
Break up the heavens, O Lord! and far,
    Thro' all yon starlight keen,
Draw me, thy bride, a glittering star,
    In raiment white and clean.

He lifts me to the golden doors;
    The flashes come and go;
All heaven bursts her starry floors,
    And strows her lights below,
And deepens on and up! the gates
    Roll back, and far within
For me the Heavenly Bridegroom waits,
    To make me pure of sin.
The sabbaths of Eternity,
    One sabbath deep and wide—
A light upon the shining sea—
    The Bridegroom with his bride!

                      Alfred, Lord Tennyson

358

Ring Out, Wild Bells

Ring out, wild bells, to the wild sky,
    The flying cloud, the frosty light:
    The year is dying in the night;
Ring out, wild bells, and let him die.

Ring out the old, ring in the new,
 Ring, happy bells, across the snow;
 The year is going, let him go;
Ring out the false, ring in the true.

Ring out the grief that saps the mind,
 For those that here we see no more;
 Ring out the feud of rich and poor,
Ring in redress to all mankind.

Ring out a slowly dying cause,
 And ancient forms of party strife;
 Ring in the nobler modes of life,
With sweeter manners, purer laws.

Ring out the want, the care, the sin,
 The faithless coldness of the times;
 Ring out, ring out my mournful rhymes,
But ring the fuller minstrel in.

Ring out false pride in place and blood,
 The civic slander and the spite;
 Ring in the love of truth and right,
Ring in the common love of good.

Ring out old shapes of foul disease,
 Ring out the narrowing lust of gold;
 Ring out the thousand wars of old,
Ring in the thousand years of peace.

Ring in the valiant man and free,
 The larger heart, the kindlier hand;
 Ring out the darkness of the land,
Ring in the Christ that is to be.

     Alfred, Lord Tennyson

459   London Snow

When men were all asleep the snow came flying,
 In large white flakes falling on the city brown,
Stealthily and perpetually settling and loosely lying,
 Hushing the latest traffic of the drowsy town;
Deadening, muffling, stifling its murmurs failing;
Lazily and incessantly floating down and down:
 Silently sifting and veiling road, roof and railing;
Hiding difference, making unevenness even,

to angles and crevices softly drifting and sailing.
All night it fell, and when full inches seven
lay in the depth of its uncompacted lightness,
the clouds blew off from a high and frosty heaven;
And all woke earlier for the unaccustomed brightness
of the winter dawning, the strange unheavenly glare:
the eye marvelled—marvelled at the dazzling whiteness;
The ear hearkened to the stillness of the solemn air;
no sound of wheel rumbling nor of foot falling,
and the busy morning cries came thin and spare.
Then boys I heard, as they went to school, calling,
They gathered up the crystal manna to freeze
their tongues with tasting, their hands with snowballing;
Or rioted in a drift, plunging up to the knees;
: peering up from under the white-mossed wonder,
look at the trees!' they cried, 'O look at the trees!'
With lessened load a few carts creak and blunder,
ollowing along the white deserted way,
country company long dispersed asunder:
When now already the sun, in pale display
anding by Paul's high dome, spread forth below
is sparkling beams, and awoke the stir of the day.
For now doors open, and war is waged with the snow;
and trains of somber men, past tale of number,
tread long brown paths, as toward their toil they go:
But even for them awhile no cares encumber
their minds diverted; the daily word is unspoken,
the daily thoughts of labor and sorrow slumber
at the sight of the beauty that greets them, for the charm they
      have broken.

Robert Bridges

The Snow-Storm

Announced by all the trumpets of the sky,
Arrives the snow, and, driving o'er the fields,
Seems nowhere to alight: the whited air
Hides hills and woods, the river, and the heaven,
And veils the farm-house at the garden's end.
The sled and traveller stopped, the courier's feet
Delayed, all friends shut out, the housemates sit
Around the radiant fireplace, enclosed
In a tumultuous privacy of storm.

Come see the north wind's masonry.
Out of an unseen quarry evermore

Furnished with tile, the fierce artificer
Curves his white bastions with projected roof
Round every windward stake, or tree, or door.
Speeding, the myriad-handed, his wild work
So fanciful, so savage, nought cares he
For number or proportion. Mockingly,
On coop or kennel he hangs Parian wreaths;
A swan-like form invests the hidden thorn;
Fills up the farmer's lane from wall to wall,
Maugre the farmer's sighs; and at the gate
A tapering turret overtops the work.
And when his hours are numbered, and the world
Is all his own, retiring, as he were not,
Leaves, when the sun appears, astonished Art
To mimic in slow structures, stone by stone,
Built in an age, the mad wind's nightwork,
The frolic architecture of the snow.

Ralph Waldo Emerso

461   Auspex

My heart, I cannot still it,
Nest that had song-birds in it;
And when the last shall go,
The dreary days to fill it,
Instead of lark or linnet,
Shall whirl dead leaves and
   snow.

Had they been swallows only,
Without the passion stronger,
That skyward longs and sings

Woe's me, I shall be lonely
When I can feel no longer
The impatience of their wing

A moment, sweet delusion,
Like birds the brown leav
   hover;
But it will not be long
Before their wild confusion
Fall wavering down to cov
The poet and his song.

James Russell Low

462   The Solitary Lyre

Wherefore, unlaurell'd Boy,
  Whom the contemptuous Muse will not inspire,
With a sad kind of joy
  Still sing'st thou to thy solitary lyre?

The melancholy winds
  Pour through unnumber'd reeds their idle woes,
And every Naiad finds
  A stream to weep her sorrow as it flows.

Her sighs unto the air
   The Wood-maid's native oak doth broadly tell,
And Echo's fond despair
   Intelligible rocks re-syllable.

Wherefore then should not I,
   Albeit no haughty Muse my heart inspire,
Fated of grief to die,
   Impart it to my solitary lyre?   *George Darley*

463   A Sonnet is a moment's monument,—
     Memorial from the Soul's eternity
     To one dead deathless hour. Look that it be,
Whether for lustral rite or dire portent,
Of its own arduous fullness reverent:
     Carve it in ivory or in ebony,
     As Night or Day may rule; and let Time see
Its flowering crest impearled and orient.
A Sonnet is a coin: its face reveals
     The soul,—its converse, to what Power 'tis due:—
Whether for tribute to the august appeals
     Of Life, or dower in Love's high retinue,
It serve; or, mid the dark wharf's cavernous breath,
In Charon's palm it pay the toll to Death.
                      Dante Gabriel Rossetti

464   **Memorabilia**

Ah, did you once see Shelley plain,
   And did he stop and speak to you,
And did you speak to him again?
   How strange it seems and new!

But you were living before that,
   And also you are living after;
And the memory I started at—
   My starting moves your laughter!

I crossed a moor, with a name of its own
   And a certain use in the world no doubt,
Yet a hand's-breadth of it shines alone
   'Mid the blank miles round about:

For there I picked up on the heather
   And there I put inside my breast
A molted feather, an eagle-feather!
   Well, I forget the rest.   *Robert Browning*

THE GOLDEN TREASURY

An Apology

Of Heaven or Hell I have no power to sing;
I cannot ease the burden of your fears,
Or make quick-coming death a little thing,
Or bring again the pleasure of past years,
Nor for my words shall ye forget your tears,
Or hope again for aught that I can say,—
The idle singer of an empty day.

But rather when, aweary of your mirth,
From full hearts still unsatisfied ye sigh,
And, feeling kindly unto all the earth,
Grudge every minute as it passes by,
Made the more mindful that the sweet days die:
Remember me a little then, I pray,—
The idle singer of an empty day.

The heavy trouble, the bewildering care
That weighs us down who live and earn our bread,
These idle verses have no power to bear;
So let me sing of names rememberèd,
Because they, living not, can ne'er be dead,
Or long time take their memory quite away
From us poor singers of an empty day.

Dreamer of dreams, born out of my due time,
Why should I strive to set the crooked straight?
Let it suffice me that my murmuring rhyme
Beats with light wing against the ivory gate,—
Telling a tale not too importunate
To those who in the sleepy region stay,
Lulled by the singer of an empty day.

Folk say, a wizard to a northern king
At Christmas-tide such wondrous things did show,
That through one window men beheld the spring,
And through another saw the summer glow,
And through a third the fruited vines a-row,—
While still, unheard, but on its wonted way,
Piped the drear wind of that December day.

So with this Earthly Paradise it is,
If ye will read aright, and pardon me,
Who strive to build a shadowy isle of bliss
Midmost the beating of the steely sea,
Where tossed about all hearts of men must be;
Whose ravening monsters mighty men shall slay—
Not the poor singer of an empty day.

William Morris

466

We are the music-makers.
  And we are the dreamers of dreams,
Wandering by lone sea-breakers,
  And sitting by desolate streams;
World-losers and world-forsakers,
  On whom the pale moon gleams:
Yet we are the movers and shakers
  Of the world forever, it seems.

With wonderful deathless ditties
We build up the world's great cities,
  And out of a fabulous story
  We fashion an empire's glory:
One man with a dream, at pleasure,
  Shall go forth and conquer a crown;
And three with a new song's measure
  Can trample a kingdom down.

We, in the ages lying
  In the buried past of the earth,
Built Nineveh with our sighing,
  And Babel itself in our mirth;
And o'erthrew them with prophesying
  To the old of the new world's worth;
For each age is a dream that is dying,
  Or one that is coming to birth.

                    A. W. E. O'Shaughnessy

467   Ask Me No More

Ask me no more: the moon may draw the sea;
  The cloud may stoop from heaven and take shape,
  With fold to fold, of mountain or of cape;
But O too fond, when have I answer'd thee?
        Ask me no more.
Ask me no more: what answer should I give?
  I love not hollow cheek or faded eye:
  Yet O my friend, I will not have thee die!
Ask me no more, lest I should bid thee live;
        Ask me no more.
Ask me no more: thy fate and mine are seal'd:
  I strove against the stream and all in vain:
  Let the great river take me to the main:
No more, dear love, for at a touch I yield;
        Ask me no more.

                    Alfred, Lord Tennyson

468   **Parting**

My life closed twice before its close;
  It yet remains to see
If Immortality unveil
  A third event to me,

So huge, so hopeless to conceive,
  As these that twice befell.
Parting is all we know of heaven,
  And all we need of hell.

                                            Emily Dickinson

469   **To Helen**

Helen, thy beauty is to me
  Like those Nicæan barks of yore,
That gently, o'er a perfumed sea,
  The weary, wayworn wanderer bore
    To his own native shore.

On desperate seas long wont to roam,
  Thy hyacinth hair, thy classic face,
Thy Naiad airs have brought me home
  To the glory that was Greece
    And the grandeur that was Rome.

Lo! in yon brilliant window-niche
  How statue-like I see thee stand,
The agate lamp within thy hand!
  Ah, Psyche, from the regions which
    Are Holy Land!

                                            Edgar Allan Poe

470 **Non Sum Qualis Eram Bonae sub Regno Cynarae**

Last night, ah, yesternight, betwixt her lips and mine
There fell thy shadow, Cynara! thy breath was shed
Upon my soul between the kisses and the wine;
And I was desolate and sick of an old passion,
  Yeh, I was desolate and bowed my head:
I have been faithful to thee, Cynara! in my fashion.

All night upon mine heart I felt her warm heart beat,
Night-long within mine arms in love and sleep she lay;
Surely the kisses of her bought red mouth were sweet;

But I was desolate and sick of an old passion,
　When I awoke and found the dawn was gray:
I have been faithful to thee, Cynara! in my fashion.

I have forgot much, Cynara! gone with the wind,
Flung roses, roses riotously with the throng,
Dancing, to put thy pale, lost lilies out of mind;
But I was desolate and sick of an old passion,
　Yea, all the time, because the dance was long:
I have been faithful to thee, Cynara! in my fashion.

I cried for madder music and for stronger wine,
But when the feast is finished and the lamps expire,
Then falls thy shadow, Cynara! the night is thine;
And I am desolate and sick of an old passion,
　Yea hungry for the lips of my desire:
I have been faithful to thee, Cynara! in my fashion.

Ernest Dowson

471   **Song**

　　Nay, but you, who do not love her,
　　　Is she not pure gold, my mistress?
　　Holds earth aught—speak truth—above her?
　　　Aught like this tress, see, and this tress,
　　And this last fairest tress of all,
　　So fair, see, ere I let it fall?

　　Because, you spend your lives in praising;
　　　To praise, you search the wide world over;
　　Then, why not witness, calmly gazing,
　　　If earth holds aught—speak truth—above her?
　　Above this tress, and this I touch
　　But cannot praise, I love so much!

Robert Browning

472   **Love in the Valley**

Under yonder beech-tree single on the green-sward,
　Couch'd with her arms behind her golden head,
Knees and tresses folded to slip and ripple idly,
　Lies my young love sleeping in the shade.
Had I the heart to slide an arm beneath her,
　Press her parting lips as her waist I gather slow,
Waking in amazement she could not but embrace me:
　Then would she hold me and never let me go?

Shy as the squirrel and wayward as the swallow,
   Swift as the swallow along the river's light
Circleting the surface to meet his mirror'd winglets,
   Fleeter she seems in her stay than in her flight.
Shy as the squirrel that leaps among the pine-tops,
   Wayward as the swallow overhead at set of sun,
She whom I love is hard to catch and conquer,
   Hard, but O the glory of the winning were she won!

George Meredith

473   Maud

   Come into the garden, Maud,
      For the black bat, Night, has flown,
   Come into the garden, Maud,
      I am here at the gate alone;
   And the woodbine spices are wafted abroad,
      And the musk of the roses blown.

   For a breeze of morning moves,
      And the planet of Love is on high,
   Beginning to faint in the light that she loves
      On a bed of daffodil sky,
   To faint in the light of the sun she loves,
      To faint in his light, and to die.

   All night have the roses heard
      The flute, violin, bassoon;
   All night has the casement jessamine stirr'd
      To the dancers dancing in tune;
   Till a silence fell with the waking bird,
      And a hush with the setting moon.

   I said to the lily, 'There is but one
      With whom she has heart to be gay.
   When will the dancers leave her alone?
      She is weary of dance and play.'
   Now half to the setting moon are gone,
      And half to the rising day;
   Low on the sand and loud on the stone
      The last wheel echoes away.

   I said to the rose, 'The brief night goes
      In babble and revel and wine.
   O young lord-lover, what sighs are those
      For one that will never be thine?

But mine, but mine,' so I sware to the rose,
  'For ever and ever, mine.'

And the soul of the rose went into my blood,
  As the music clash'd in the hall;
And long by the garden lake I stood,
  For I heard your rivulet fall
From the lake to the meadow and on to the wood,
  Our wood, that is dearer than all;

From the meadow your walks have left so sweet
  That whenever a March-wind sighs
He sets the jewel-print of your feet
  In violets blue as your eyes,
To the woody hollows in which we meet
  And the valleys of Paradise.

The slender acacia would not shake
  One long milk-bloom on the tree;
The white lake-blossom fell into the lake,
  As the pimpernel dozed on the lea;
But the rose was awake all night for your sake,
  Knowing your promise to me;
The lilies and roses were all awake,
  They sigh'd for the dawn and thee.

Queen rose of the rosebud garden of girls,
  Come hither, the dances are done,
In gloss of satin and glimmer of pearls,
  Queen lily and rose in one;
Shine out, little head, sunning over with curls,
  To the flowers, and be their sun.

There has fallen a splendid tear
  From the passion-flower at the gate,
She is coming, my dove, my dear;
  She is coming, my life, my fate;
The red rose cries, 'She is near, she is near;'
  And the white rose weeps, 'She is late;'
The larkspur listens, 'I hear, I hear;'
  And the lily whispers, 'I wait.'

She is coming, my own, my sweet;
  Were it ever so airy a tread,
My heart would hear her and beat,
  Were it earth in an earthy bed;

My dust would hear her and beat,
 Had I lain for a century dead;
Would start and tremble under her feet,
 And blossom in purple and red.

Alfred, Lord Tennyson

474 How do I love thee? Let me count the ways.
I love thee to the depth and breadth and height
My soul can reach, when feeling out of sight
For the ends of Being and ideal Grace.
I love thee to the level of everyday's
Most quiet need, by sun and candle-light.
I love thee freely, as men strive for Right;
I love thee purely, as they turn from Praise.
I love thee with the passion put to use
In my old griefs, and with my childhood's faith.
I love thee with a love I seemed to lose
With my lost saints,—I love thee with the breath,
Smiles, tears, of all my life!—and, if God choose,
I shall but love thee better after death.

Elizabeth Barrett Browning

475   **I Heard a Linnet Courting**

I heard a linnet courting
 His lady in the spring:
His mates were idly sporting,
 Nor stayed to hear him sing
  His song of love.—
I fear my speech distorting
  His tender love.

The phrases of his pleading
 Were full of young delight;
And she that gave him heeding
 Interpreted aright
  His gay, sweet notes,—
So sadly marred in the reading,—
  His tender notes.

And when he ceased, the hearer
 Awaited the refrain,
Till swiftly perching nearer
 He sang his song again,

His pretty song:—
Would that my verse spake clearer
His tender song!

Ye happy, airy creatures!
That in the merry spring
Think not of what misfeatures
Or cares the year may bring;
But unto love
Resign your simple natures
To tender love.

Robert Bridges

476   **All in All**

In Love, if Love be Love, if Love be ours,
Faith and unfaith can ne'er be equal powers:
Unfaith in aught is want of faith in all.

It is the little rift within the lute,
That by and by will make the music mute,
And ever widening slowly silence all.

The little rift within the lover's lute,
Or little pitted speck in garner'd fruit,
That rotting inward slowly moulders all.

It is not worth the keeping: let it go:
But shall it? answer, darling, answer, no.
And trust me not at all or all in all.

Alfred, Lord Tennyson

477 If thou must love me, let it be for naught
Except for love's sake only. Do not say,
'I love her for her smile—her look—her way
Of speaking gently,—for a trick of thought
That falls in well with mine, and certes brought
A sense of pleasant ease on such a day'—
For these things in themselves, Belovéd, may
Be changed, or change for thee,—and love, so wrought,
May be unwrought so. Neither love me for
Thine own dear pity's wiping my cheeks dry,—
A creature might forget to weep, who bore
Thy comfort long, and lose thy love thereby!
But love me for love's sake, that evermore
Thou mayst love on, through love's eternity.

Elizabeth Barrett Browning

478

A Match

If love were what the rose is,
　　And I were like the leaf,
Our lives would grow together
In sad or singing weather,
Blown fields or flowerful closes,
　　Green pleasure or gray grief;
If love were what the rose is,
　　And I were like the leaf.

If I were what the words are,
　　And love were like the tune,
With double sound and single
Delight our lips would mingle,
With kisses glad as birds are
　　That get sweet rain at noon;
If I were what the words are,
　　And love were like the tune. . . .

If you were April's lady,
　　And I were lord in May,
We'd throw with leaves for hours,
And draw for days with flowers,
Till day like night were shady,
　　And night were bright like day;
If you were April's lady,
　　And I were lord in May.

If you were queen of pleasure,
　　And I were king of pain,
We'd hunt down love together,
Pluck out his flying-feather,
And teach his feet a measure,
　　And find his mouth a rein;
If you were queen of pleasure,
　　And I were king of pain.

Algernon Charles Swinburne

479　　Jenny kissed me when we met,
　　　　Jumping from the chair she sat in;
　　Time, you thief, who love to get
　　　　Sweets into your list, put that in!
　　Say I'm weary, say I'm sad,
　　　　Say that health and wealth have missed me,
　　Say I'm growing old, but add,
　　　　Jenny kissed me.

Leigh Hun

Without Her

What of her glass without her? The blank grey
   There where the pool is blind of the moon's face.
   Her dress without her? The tossed empty space
Of cloud-rack whence the moon has passed away.
Her paths without her? Day's appointed sway
   Usurped by desolate night. Her pillowed place
   Without her? Tears, ah me! for love's good grace,
And cold forgetfulness of night or day.
What of the heart without her? Nay, poor heart,
   Of thee what word remains ere speech be still?
   A wayfarer by barren ways and chill,
Steep ways and weary, without her thou art,
Where the long cloud, the long wood's counterpart,
   Sheds doubled darkness up the labouring hill.

Dante Gabriel Rossetti

   It is the miller's daughter,
   And she is grown so dear, so dear,
   That I would be the jewel
   That trembles at her ear:
   For hid in ringlets day and night,
   I'd touch her neck so warm and white.

   And I would be the girdle
   About her dainty dainty waist,
   And her heart would beat against me,
   In sorrow and in rest:
   And I should know if it beat right,
   I'd clasp it round so close and tight.

   And I would be the necklace,
   And all day long to fall and rise
   Upon her balmy bosom,
   With her laughter or her sighs,
   And I would lie so light, so light,
   I scarce would be unclasp'd at night.

Alfred, Lord Tennyson

Meeting at Night

   The grey sea and the long black land;
   And the yellow half-moon large and low;
   And the startled little waves that leap
   In fiery ringlets from their sleep,
   As I gain the cove with pushing prow,
   And quench its speed i' the slushy sand.

Then a mile of warm sea-scented beach;
Three fields to cross till a farm appears;
A tap at the pane, the quick sharp scratch
And blue spurt of a lighted match,
And a voice less loud, thro' its joys and fears,
Than the two hearts beating each to each!

Robert Browning

483 As we rush, as we rush in the Train,
  The trees and the houses go wheeling back,
But the starry heavens above the plain
  Come flying on our track.

All the beautiful stars of the sky,
  The silver doves of the forest of Night,
Over the dull earth swarm and fly,
  Companions of our flight.

We will rush ever on without fear;
  Let the goal be far, the flight be fleet!
For we carry the Heavens with us, dear,
  While the earth slips from our feet!

James Thomson

484   **When I Peruse the Conquer'd Fame**

When I peruse the conquer'd fame of heroes and the victories
  of mighty generals, I do not envy the generals,
Nor the President in his Presidency, nor the rich in his great
  house,
But when I hear of the brotherhood of lovers, how it was with
  them,
How together through life, through dangers, odium, unchanging, long and long,
Through youth and through middle and old age, how unfaltering, how affectionate and faithful they were,
Then I am pensive—I hastily walk away fill'd with the bitterest
  envy.

Walt Whitman

485   **As Thro' the Land at Eve We Went**

As thro' the land at eve we went,
  And pluck'd the ripen'd ears,
We fell out, my wife and I,
O we fell out I know not why,

And kiss'd again with tears!
And blessings on the falling out
  That all the more endears,
When we fall out with those we love
  And kiss again with tears!
For when we came where lies the child
  We lost in other years,
There above the little grave,
O there above the little grave,
  We kiss'd again with tears.

Alfred, Lord Tennyson

86   **Young and Old**

When all the world is young, lad,
  And all the trees are green;
And every goose a swan, lad,
  And every lass a queen;
Then hey for boot and horse, lad,
  And round the world away;
Young blood must have its course, lad,
  And every dog his day.

When all the world is old, lad,
  And all the trees are brown;
And all the sport is stale, lad,
  And all the wheels run down;
Creep home, and take your place there,
  The spent and maimed among:
God grant you find one face there,
  You loved when all was young.

Charles Kingsley

87   **A Letter from a Girl to Her Own Old Age**

Listen, and when my hand this paper presses,
O time-worn woman, think of her who blesses
What thy thin fingers touch, with her caresses.
O mother, for the weight of years that break thee!
O daughter, for slow time must yet awake thee!
And from the changes of my heart must make thee.
O fainting traveller, morn is grey in heaven.
Dost thou remember how the clouds were driven?
And are they calm about the fall of even?
Pause near the ending of thy long migration,
For this one sudden hour of desolation
Appeals to one hour of thy meditation.

Suffer, O silent one, that I remind thee
Of the great hills that stormed the sky behind thee,
Of the wild winds of power that have resigned thee.
Know that the mournful plain where thou must wander
Is but a grey and silent world, but ponder
The misty mountains of the morning yonder.
Listen:—the mountain winds with rain were fretting,
And sudden gleams the mountain-tops besetting.
I cannot let thee fade to death, forgetting.
What part of this wild heart of mine I know not
Will follow with thee where the great winds blow not,
And where the young flowers of the mountain grow not.
Yet let my letter with thy lost thoughts in it
Tell what the way was when thou didst begin it,
And win with thee the goal when thou shall win it.
Oh, in some hour of thine my thoughts shall guide thee,
Suddenly, though time, darkness, silence hide thee,
This wind from thy lost country flits beside thee,—
Telling thee: all thy memories moved the maiden,
With thy regrets was morning over-shaden,
With sorrow thou hast left, her life was laden.
But whither shall my thoughts turn to pursue thee?
Life changes, and the years and days renew thee.
Oh, Nature brings my straying heart unto thee.
Her winds will join us, with their constant kisses
Upon the evening as the morning tresses,
Her summers breathe the same unchanging blisses.
And we, so altered in our shifting phases,
Track one another 'mid the many mazes
By the eternal child-breath of the daisies.
I have not writ this letter of divining
To make a glory of thy silent pining,
A triumph of thy mute and strange declining.
Only one youth, and the bright life was shrouded.
Only one morning, and the day was clouded.
And one old age with all regrets is crowded.
Oh, hush; oh, hush! Thy tears my words are steeping.
Oh, hush, hush, hush! So full, the fount of weeping?
Poor eyes, so quickly moved, so near to sleeping?
Pardon the girl, such strange desires beset her.
Poor woman, lay aside the mournful letter
That breaks thy heart; the one who wrote, forget her.
The one who now thy faded features guesses,
With filial fingers thy grey hair caresses,
With morning tears thy mournful twilight blesses.

Alice Meynel

Dover Beach

The sea is calm to-night.
The tide is full, the moon lies fair
Upon the straits;—on the French coast the light
Gleams and is gone; the cliffs of England stand
Glimmering and vast, out in the tranquil bay.

Come to the window, sweet is the night-air!
Only, from the long line of spray
Where the sea meets the moon-blanch'd land,
Listen! you hear the grating roar
Of pebbles which the waves draw back, and fling,
At their return, up the high strand,
Begin, and cease, and then again begin,
With tremulous cadence slow, and bring
The eternal note of sadness in.

Sophocles long ago
Heard it on the Ægean, and it brought
Into his mind the turbid ebb and flow,
Of human misery; we
Find also in the sound a thought,
Hearing it by this distant northern sea.

The Sea of Faith
Was once, too, at the full, and round earth's shore
Lay like the folds of a bright girdle furl'd.
But now I only hear
Its melancholy, long, withdrawing roar,
Retreating, to the breath
Of the night-wind, down the vast edges drear
And naked shingles of the world.

Ah, love, let us be true
To one another! for the world, which seems
To lie before us like a land of dreams,
So various, so beautiful, so new,
Hath really neither joy, nor love, nor light,
Nor certitude, nor peace, nor help for pain;
And we are here as on a darkling plain
Swept with confused alarms of struggle and flight,
Where ignorant armies clash by night.

Matthew Arnold

BOOK SEVEN

489 **The Darkling Thrush**

I leant upon a coppice gate
    When Frost was spectre-gray,
And Winter's dregs made desolate
    The weakening eye of day.
The tangled bine-stems scored the sky
    Like strings of broken lyres,
And all mankind that haunted nigh
    Had sought their household fires.

The land's sharp features seem'd to be
    The Century's corpse outleant,
His crypt the cloudy canopy,
    The wind his death-lament.
The ancient pulse of germ and birth
    Was shrunken hard and dry,
And every spirit upon earth
    Seem'd fervourless as I.

At once a voice arose among
    The bleak twigs overhead
In a full-hearted evensong
    Of joy illimited;
An aged thrush, frail, gaunt, and small,
    In blast-beruffled plume,
Had chosen thus to fling his soul
    Upon the growing gloom.

So little cause for carollings
    Of such ecstatic sound
Was written on terrestrial things
    Afar or nigh around,
That I could think there trembled through
    His happy good-night air
Some blessèd Hope, whereof he knew
    And I was unaware.

Thomas Hardy

Loveliest of Trees

90

Loveliest of trees, the cherry now
Is hung with bloom along the bough,
And stands about the woodland ride
Wearing white for Eastertide.

Now, of my threescore years and ten,
Twenty will not come again,
And take from seventy springs a score,
It only leaves me fifty more.

And since to look at things in bloom
Fifty springs are little room,
About the woodlands I will go
To see the cherry hung with snow.

A. E. Housman

91

Spring is like a perhaps hand
(which comes carefully
out of Nowhere) arranging
a window, into which people look (while
people stare
arranging and changing placing
carefully there a strange
thing and a known thing here) and

changing everything carefully

spring is like a perhaps
Hand in a window
(carefully to
and fro moving New and
Old things, while
people stare carefully
moving a perhaps
fraction of flower here placing
an inch of air there) and

without breaking anything.

E. E. Cummings

492　　　　　　　**God's Grandeur**

The world is charged with the grandeur of God.
It will flame out, like shining from shook foil;
It gathers to a greatness, like the ooze of oil
Crushed. Why do men then now not reck his rod?
Generations have trod, have trod, have trod;
And all is seared with trade; bleared, smeared with toil;
And wears man's smudge and shares man's smell: the soil
Is bare now, nor can foot feel, being shod.
And for all this, nature is never spent;
There lives the dearest freshness deep down things;
And though the last lights off the black West went
Oh, morning, at the brown brink eastward, springs—
Because the Holy Ghost over the bent
World broods with warm breast and with ah! bright wings.

Gerard Manley Hopkins

493　　　　　　　**Petition**

Sir, no man's enemy, forgiving all
But will his negative inversion, be prodigal:
Send to us power and light, a sovereign touch
Curing the intolerable neural itch,
The exhaustion of weaning, the liar's quinsy,
And the distortions of ingrown virginity.
Prohibit sharply the rehearsed response
And gradually correct the coward's stance;
Cover in time with beams those in retreat
That, spotted, they turn though the reverse were great;
Publish each healer that in city lives
Or country house at the end of drives;
Harrow the house of the dead; look shining at
New styles of architecture, a change of heart.

W. H. Auden

494　　　　**In the Naked Bed, in Plato's Cave**

In the naked bed, in Plato's cave,
Reflected headlights slowly slid the wall,
Carpenters hammered under the shaded window,
Wind troubled the window curtains all night long,
A fleet of trucks strained uphill, grinding,
Their freights covered, as usual.
The ceiling lightened again, the slanting diagram
Slid slowly forth.

　　　　　　Hearing the milkman's chop,

His striving up the stair, the bottle's chink,
I rose from bed, lit a cigarette,
And walked to the window. The stony street
Displayed the stillness in which buildings stand,
The street-lamp's vigil and the horse's patience.
The winter sky's pure capital
Turned me back to bed with exhausted eyes.

Strangeness grew in the motionless air. The loose
Film grayed. Shaking wagons, hooves' waterfalls,
Sounded far off, increasing, louder and nearer.
A car coughed, starting. Morning, softly
Melting the air, lifted the half-covered chair
From underseas, kindled the looking-glass,
Distinguished the dresses and the white wall.
The bird called tentatively, whistled, called,
Bubbled and whistled, so! Perplexed, still wet
With sleep, affectionate, hungry and cold. So, so,
O son of man, the ignorant night, the travail
Of early morning, the mystery of beginning
Again and again,

> while History is unforgiven.
>
> *Delmore Schwartz*

95   Pied Beauty

Glory be to God for dappled things—
  For skies of couple-colour as a brinded cow;
    For rose-moles all in stipple upon trout that swim;
Fresh-firecoal chestnut-falls; finches' wings;
  Landscape plotted and pieced—fold, fallow, and plough;
    And áll trádes, their gear and tackle and trim.

All things counter, original, spare, strange;
  Whatever is fickle, freckled (who knows how?)
    With swift, slow; sweet, sour; adazzle, dim;
He fathers-forth whose beauty is past change:
> Praise him.
>
> *Gerard Manley Hopkins*

96   I Think Continually of Those

I think continually of those who were truly great.
Who, from the womb, remembered the soul's history
Through corridors of light where the hours are suns,
Endless and singing. Whose lovely ambition
Was that their lips, still touched with fire,

Should tell of the spirit clothed from head to foot in son,
And who hoarded from the spring branches
The desires falling across their bodies like blossoms.

What is precious is never to forget
The delight of the blood drawn from ageless springs
Breaking through rocks in worlds before our earth;
Never to deny its pleasure in the simple morning light,
Nor its grave evening demand for love;
Never to allow gradually the traffic to smother
With noise and fog the flowering of the spirit.

Near the snow, near the sun, in the highest fields
See how those names are fêted by the waving grass,
And by the streamers of white cloud,
And whispers of wind in the listening sky;
The names of those who in their lives fought for life,
Who wore at their hearts the fire's centre.
Born of the sun they traveled a short while towards the sur
And left the vivid air signed with their honour.

Stephen Spend

497   The First Born

The world is born ahead of me. O mine own twin!
I put a bud forth beneath a bower full of things,
Branches, all elbows, but gestures ending in fruit;
Shadows of clouds tilting with shadows of leaves;
The whole world got here before me, a crowd.

I spend a lifetime panting, who have lost
In a fearful race with the swift hand of God;
My eyes fly through the storm in my head;
Small are the shadows cast by feathers of sight;
The clouds, one dimension images brush the ground.

I cannot travel fast enough to catch the world
Successfully born first; the meadows run off with grass;
I close my eyes, the sun leaps beneath my thought
A fireball on the string of an idea, the fruit above
Swings, blossoms rain, the rain blossoms aloud.

It was a head-on collision of the atom with
The planet, a birth in the face of everything dying!
O garden, clasping a bud to your miles of bosom,
You are caught in the act celebrating my coming:
A welcome so big, it can never be worn out!

Oscar Willian

Poem in October

It was my thirtieth year to heaven
Woke to my hearing from harbour and neighbour wood
    And the mussel pooled and the heron
           Priested shore
        The morning beckon
With water praying and call of seagull and rook
And the knock of sailing boats on the net-webbed wall
        Myself to set foot
           That second
In the still sleeping town and set forth.

My birthday began with the water—
Birds and the birds of the winged trees flying my name
    Above the farms and the white horses
        And I rose
        In rainy autumn
And walked abroad in a shower of all my days.
High tide and the heron dived when I took the road
        Over the border
           And the gates
Of the town closed as the town awoke.

A springful of larks in a rolling
Cloud and the roadside bushes brimming with whistling
    Blackbirds and the sun of October
           Summery
        On the hill's shoulder,
Here were fond climates and sweet singers suddenly
Come in the morning where I wandered and listened
        To the rain wringing
          Wind blow cold
In the wood faraway under me.

Pale rain over the dwindling harbour
And ever the sea-wet church the size of a snail
    With its horns through mist and the castle
        Brown as owls,
        But all the gardens
Of spring and summer were blooming in the tall tales
Beyond the border and under the lark-full cloud.
        There could I marvel
           My birthday
Away but the weather turned around.

It turned away from the blithe country,
And down the other air and the blue altered sky
        Streamed again a wonder of summer
                    With apples
                Pears and red currants,
And I saw in the turning so clearly a child's
Forgotten mornings when he walked with his mother
                Through the parables
                    Of sunlight
        And the legends of the green chapels.

        And the twice told fields of infancy
That his tears burned my cheeks and his heart moved in mine
These were the woods the river and sea
                Where a boy
                In the listening
Summertime of the dead whispered the truth of his joy
To the trees and the stones and the fish in the tide.
                And the mystery
                    Sang alive
    Still in the water and singing birds.

        And there could I marvel my birthday
Away but the weather turned around. And the true
        Joy of the long-dead child sang burning
                    In the sun.
            It was my thirtieth
Year to heaven stood there then in the summer noon
Though the town below lay leaved with October blood.
        O may my heart's truth
                Still be sung
    On this high hill in a year's turning.

                                Dylan Thomas

499   **The Voyage**

        That sea was greater than we knew.
        Week after week the empty round
        Went with us; the Unchanging grew,
        And we were headed for that bound.

        How we came there we could not tell.
        Seven storms had piled us in that peace,
        Put us in check and barred us well
        With seven walls of seven seas.

As one may vanish in a day
In some untravelled fold of space
And there pursue his patient way
Yet never come to any place

Though following still by star and sun,
For every chart is raised and furled,
And he out of this world has run
And wanders now another world,

So we by line and compass steered
And conned the book of sun and star,
Yet where it should no sign appeared
To tell us. You are there or there.

Familiar landfall, slender mast:
We on the ocean were alone.
The busy lanes where fleets had passed
Showed us no sail except our own.

Still south we steered day after day
And only water lay around
As if the land had stolen away
Or sprawled upon the ocean ground.

The sun by day, the stars by night
Had only us to look upon,
Bent on us their collected light,
And followed on as we went on.

Some times in utter wonder lost
That loneliness like this could be
We stood and stared until almost
We saw no longer sky or sea,

But only the frame of time and space,
An empty floor, a vacant wall,
And on that blank no line to trace
Movement, if we moved at all.

What thoughts came then! Sometimes it seemed
We long had passed the living by
On other seas and only dreamed
This sea, this journey and this sky,

Or traced a ghostly parallel
That limned the land but could not merge,

And haven and home and harbour bell
Were just behind the horizon verge,

Or the world itself had ended so
Without a cry, and we should sail
To and fro, to and fro,
Long past the lightning and the gale.

O then what crowding fantasies,
Poured in from empty sea and sky!
At night we heard the whispering quays,
Line after line, slide softly by.

Delusions in the silent noon;
Fields in the hollows of the waves;
Or spread beneath the yellow moon,
A land of harvest and of graves.

The soft sea-sounds beguiled our ear.
We thought we walked by mountain rills
Or listened half a night to hear
The spring wind hunting on the hills.

And faces, faces, faces came
Across the salt sea-desert air,
And rooms in which a candle flame
Made everything renowned and rare.

The words we knew like our right hand,
Mountain and valley, meadow and grove,
Composed a legendary land
Rich with the broken tombs of love.

Delusion or truth? We were content
Thenceforth to sail the harmless seas
Safe past the Fate and the Accident,
And called a blessing on that peace.

And blessing, we ourselves were blest,
Lauded the loss that brought our gain,
Sang the tumultuous world to rest,
And wishless called it back again.

For loss was then our only joy,
Privation of all, fulfilled desire,
The world our treasure and our toy
In destitution clean as fear.

Our days were then—I cannot tell
How we were then fulfilled and crowned
With life as in a parable,
And sweetly as gods together bound.

Delusion and dream! Our captain knew
Compass and clock had never yet
Failed him; the sun and stars were true.
The mark was there that we should hit.

And it rose up, a sullen stain
Flawing the crystal firmament.
A wound! We felt the familiar pain
And knew the place to which we were sent.

The crowd drew near, the toppling towers;
In hope and dread we drove to birth;
The dream and a truth we clutched as ours,
And gladly, blindly stepped on earth.

Edwin Muir

Credo

00

I cannot find my way: there is no star
In all the shrouded heavens anywhere;
And there is not a whisper in the air
Of any living voice but one so far
That I can hear it only as a bar
Of lost, imperial music, played when fair
And angel fingers wove, and unware,
Dead leaves to garlands where no roses are.
No, there is not a glimmer, nor a call,
For one that welcomes, welcomes when he fears,
The black and awful chaos of the night;
For through it all—above, beyond it all—
I know the far-sent message of the years,
I feel the coming glory of the Light.

Edwin Arlington Robinson

01

If ever against this easy blue and silver
Hazed-over countryside of thoughtfulness
Far behind in the mind and above,
Boots from before and below approach tramping,
Watch how their premonition will display

A forward countryside, low in the distance,
A picture-postcard square of June grass,
Will warm a summer season, trim the hedges,
Cast the river about on either flank,
Start the late cuckoo emptily calling,
Invent a rambling tale of moles and voles,
Furnish a path with stiles.
Watch how the field will broaden, the feet nearing
Sprout with great dandelions and buttercups,
Widen and heighten. The blue and silver
Fogs at the border of this all-grass.
Interruption looms gigantified,
Lurches against, treads thundering through,
Blots the landscape, scatters all,
Roars and rumbles like a dark tunnel,
Is gone.

The picture-postcard grass and trees
Swim back to central: it is a large patch,
It is a modest, failing patch of green,
The postage-stamp of its departure,
Clouded with blue and silver, closing in now
To a plain countryside of less and less,
Unpeopled and unfeathered blue and silver,
Before, behind, above.

Robert Grav

502   **Neither Here Nor There**

In that land all Is and nothing's Ought;
No owners or notices, only birds;
No walls anywhere, only lean wire of words
Worming brokenly out from eaten thought;
No oats growing, only ankle-lace grass
Easing and not resenting the feet that pass;
No enormous beasts, only names of them;
No bones made, bans laid, or boons expected,
No contracts, entails, hereditaments,
Anything at all that might tie or hem.

In that land all's lackadaisical;
No lakes of coddled spawn, and no locked ponds
Of settled purpose, no netted fishes;
But only inkling streams and running fronds,
Fritillaried with dreams, weedy with wishes;

Nor arrogant talk is heard, haggling phrase,
But undertones, and hesitance, and haze;
On clear days mountains of meaning are seen
Humped high on the horizon; no one goes
To con their meaning, no one cares or knows.

In that land all's flat, indifferent; there
Is neither springing house nor hanging tent,
No aims are entertained, and nothing is meant,
For there are no ends and no trends, no roads,
Only follow your nose to anywhere.
No one is born there, no one stays or dies,
For it is a timeless land, it lies
Between the act and the attrition, it
Marks off bound from rebound, make from break, tit
From tat, also to-day from to-morrow.
No Cause there comes to term, but each departs
Elsewhere to whelp its deeds, expel its darts;
There are no homecomings, of course, no good-byes
In that land, neither yearning nor scorning,
Though at night there is the smell of morning.

W. R. Rodgers

503 Supple and turbulent, a ring of men
Shall chant in orgy on a summer morn
Their boisterous devotion to the sun,
Not as a god, but as a god might be,
Naked among them, like a savage source.

Their chant shall be a chant of paradise,
Out of their blood, returning to the sky;
And in their chant shall enter, voice by voice,
The windy lake wherein their lord delights,
The trees, like serafim, and echoing hills,
That choir among themselves long afterward.

They shall know well the heavenly fellowship
Of men that perish and of summer morn.

And whence they came and whither they shall go
The dew upon their feet shall manifest.

Wallace Stevens

504   **With Rue My Heart Is Laden**

With rue my heart is laden
   For golden friends I had,
For many a rose-lipt maiden
   And many a lightfoot lad.

By brooks too broad for leaping
   The lightfoot boys are laid;
The rose-lipt girls are sleeping
   In fields where roses fade.

A. E. Housman

505   **What Lips My Lips Have Kissed**

What lips my lips have kissed, and where, and why,
I have forgotten, and what arms have lain
Under my head till morning; but the rain
Is full of ghosts tonight, that tap and sigh
Upon the glass and listen for reply;
And in my heart there stirs a quiet pain
For unremembered lads that not again
Will turn to me at midnight with a cry.
Thus in the winter stands the lonely tree,
Nor knows what birds have vanished one by one,
Yet knows its boughs more silent than before:
I cannot say what loves have come and gone;
I only know that summer sang in me
A little while, that in me sings no more.

Edna St. Vincent Millay

506   **A Love for Patsy**

See the little maunderer
Stretch out on the grass!
His heart is burst asunder
The pieces cry Alas.

Upright, fat pink pieces
Of fluffy cloud float overhead.
The little facets of his eyes
Split by salty tears, so tired

Of seeing pieces of the world.
Close, and rustling grass,

Caws of an old unpleasant
   bird
Are sounds that say Alas;

They float like notes in the
   funny paper,
Round notes with sharp little
   tails.
Oh I'm blue, the supine
   moper
Says, I'm trapped in the toils

Of Patsy's black black hair.
Her hair is like the cool dry
night
That waves through the win-
dow-bar
Where a moody jailbird sits
apart

Shuffling his broken heart.
I'm sad
As I can be. Her black
Black hair can never be com-
pared
To dull dichotomic

Trees or prickly grass, in-
flated

Clouds, even a great
One draped on the sun. Over-
rated
Senseless things to stare at.

One here one there they're
strewn,
Impinging pieces left out of
The world. Her eyes are
green!
Oh oh, he says, I die of love.

See the weeping little wretch
He rolls in a frenzy!
In all the world no two things
match
But the green eyes of Patsy.

John Thompson, Jr.

407   The love-grip, first excited by the eye,
Fastens its pleasing mortar; then the thigh
Moves like a tractor rocketing to fate.
The head reclines, the mind will gladly wait;
But pearly blood and sockets made of gum,
Less than immobile, seek the pleasing hum
Of fall and exaltation. Eyebrows made
Of ships and shaped like islands cannot shade
The walnut hull of eyes, the husk of brown
Under whose cover lies the kernel-down,
The certainty of love. Each jointed knee
Strolls in the wake of new fraternity,
And wishes elbows well; itself does grace
To flesh and bone, extracting from its place
All that made Solomon declare of myrrh,
Frankincense, flowers, upon touching her.

Ruth Hershberger

508   **The Thieves**

Lovers in the act dispense
With such meum-teum sense
As might warningly reveal
What they must not pick or steal,

And their nostrum is to say:
I and you are both away.

After, when they disentwine
You from me and yours from mine,
Neither can be certain who
Was that I whose mine was you.
To the act again they go
More completely not to know.

Theft is theft and raid is raid
Though reciprocally made.
Lovers, the conclusion is
Doubled sighs and jealousies
In a single heart that grieves
For lost honour among thieves.

Robert Grave

509 And you as well must die, belovèd dust,
And all your beauty stand you in no stead;
This flawless, vital hand, this perfect head,
This body of flame and steel, before the gust
Of Death, or under his autumnal frost,
Shall be as any leaf, be no less dead
Than the first leaf that fell,—this wonder fled.
Altered, estranged, disintegrated, lost.

Nor shall my love avail you in your hour.
In spite of all my love, you will arise
Upon that day and wander down the air
Obscurely as the unattended flower,
It mattering not how beautiful you were,
Or how belovèd above all else that dies.

Edna St. Vincent Milla

510

somewhere i have never travelled, gladly beyond
any experience, your eyes have their silence:
in your most frail gesture are things which enclose me,
or which i cannot touch because they are too near

your slightest look easily will unclose me
though i have closed myself as fingers,

ou open always petal by petal myself as Spring opens
touching skilfully, mysteriously) her first rose

r if your wish be to close me, i and
ny life will shut very beautifully, suddenly,
s when the heart of this flower imagines
he snow carefully everywhere descending;

othing which we are to perceive in this world equals
he power of your intense fragility: whose texture
ompels me with the colour of its countries,
endering death and forever with each breathing

i do not know what it is about you that closes
nd opens; only something in me understands
he voice of your eyes is deeper than all roses)
obody, not even the rain, has such small hands

E. E. Cummings

11   **By Fiat of Adoration**

This is what we really want
Who drink the kingdom of the heart
A toast to the imagination

She is flowering in a doorway
Eyes cheeks haze of hair
Stepping out of time into here

This is what we really have
Who see the one we adore becoming
The two that she is in the light

Ah God bounces all the waters
From hand to jubilant hand
He cannot contain Himself

But comes over into being
With benediction of painted cloud
The being whom to look at is to become

By fiat of adoration do we reach
The very muscle of miracle
The ease with which beauty is beauty

Oscar Williams

512   For Anne Gregory

'Never shall a young man,
Thrown into despair
By those great honey-colored
Ramparts at your ear,
Love you for yourself alone
And not your yellow hair.'

'But I can get a hair-dye
And set such color there,
Brown, or black, or carrot
That young men in despair
May love me for myself alone
And not my yellow hair.'

'I heard an old religious man
But yesternight declare
That he had found a text to prove
That only God, my dear,
Could love you for yourself alone
And not your yellow hair.'

William Butler Yeats

513   Music I Heard

Music I heard with you was more than music,
And bread I broke with you was more than bread;
Now that I am without you, all is desolate;
All that was once so beautiful is dead.

Your hands once touched this table and this silver,
And I have seen your fingers hold this glass.
These things do not remember you, beloved,
And yet your touch upon them will not pass.

For it was in my heart you moved among them,
And blessed them with your hands and with your eyes;
And in my heart they will remember always,—
They knew you once, O beautiful and wise.

Conrad Aiken

Spring Air

In blows the loitering air of spring,
Scarcely a-blow, a-blow, a lively gas.
It makes the secret life-cells ring
And quicken, while the blood-waves pass.
Floss nothingness, we feel it cling,
Resile,—silent as space, unseen as glass
Unlustred, softer than the weakest thing.
Such air can enter nostrils, sudden as light
The eye, fair words the ear, or flight
The nerve-knot, or your unexpected love
My startled heart. Down from above,
Or from the south, or flowered west,
Or from the oceaned east, or here
Blown first by spring, this air possessed
By spring is Ah! so lithe this year.
The curtain flies before this wonder.
Talk fast. Speak swift before the heart's asunder.

And for this guile . . . no cold-ice gates?
Nothing to hold it quietly down, a-down,
The while the senses sleep? Full spates
Of air enter this room in town.
Such air draws creatures to their mates
And, wild, peels off the winter's brown
From tree; ruffles the bird and motivates
The northern winging to the utmost nest;
Breaks out the bud's first scent and, lest
Two living things escape and keep hearts steady,
Beguiles us at this window; heady
And rich, murmurs; touches like flesh
Of loving fingers, timorous but sure.
Intoxicant in this mild, fresh
Warm breath of spring, all mad and pure.
Is this my hand in yours? Am I
So close? Wait till the insinuant wind's gone by . . .

Gene Derwood

Mendacity

Truth is love and love is truth,
Either neither in good sooth:
Truth is truth and love is love,
Give us grace to taste thereof.

But if truth offend my sweet
Then I will have none of it,
And if love offend the other,
Farewell truth, I will not bother.

Happy truth when truth accords
With love in lovers' words!
Harm not truth in any part,
But keep its shadow from love's heart.
Men must love, though lovers' lies
Outpoll the stars in florid skies,
And none may keep, and few can merit,
The fond joy that they inherit.

Who with love at his command
Dare give truth a welcome hand?
Believe it, or believe it not,
'Tis a lore most vainly got.
Truth requites no penny-fee,
Niggard's honey feeds no bee,
Ere this trick of truth undo me
Little love, my love, come to me.

A. E. Coppard

516   When I Was One-and-Twenty

When I was one-and-twenty
    I heard a wise man say,
'Give crowns and pounds and guineas
    But not your heart away;
Give pearls away and rubies
    But keep your fancy free.'
But I was one-and-twenty,
    No use to talk to me.

When I was one-and-twenty
    I heard him say again,
'The heart out of the bosom
    Was never given in vain;
'Tis paid with sighs a plenty
    And sold for endless rue.'
And I am two-and-twenty,
    And oh, 'tis true, 'tis true.

A. E. Housman

7   Elegy Before Death

There will be rose and rhododendron
    When you are dead and under ground;
Still will be heard from white syringas
    Heavy with bees, a sunny sound.

Still will the tamaracks be raining
    After the rain has ceased, and still
Will there be robins in the stubble,
    Brown sheep upon the warm green hill.

Spring will not ail nor autumn falter;
    Nothing will know that you are gone,
Saving alone some sullen plough-land
    None but yourself set foot upon;

Saving the may-weed and the pig-weed
    Nothing will know that you are dead,—
These, and perhaps a useless wagon
    Standing beside some tumbled shed.

Oh, there will pass with your great passing
    Little of beauty not your own,—
Only the light from common water,
    Only the grace from simple stone.

                              Edna St. Vincent Millay

8   Fife Tune

(6/8) for Sixth Platoon, 308th I. T. C.

ne morning in spring
'e marched from Devizes
ll shapes and all sizes
ike beads on a string,
ut yet with a swing
'e trod the bluemetal
nd full of high fettle
'e started to sing.

he ran down the stair
 twelve-year-old darling
nd laughing and calling
he tossed her bright hair;

Then silent to stare
At the men flowing past her—
There were all she could
    master
Adoring her there.

It's seldom I'll see
A sweeter or prettier;
I doubt we'll forget her
In two years or three.
And lucky he'll be
She takes for a lover
While we are far over
The treacherous sea.

                              John Manifold

519   **In Time of 'The Breaking of Nations'**

Only a man harrowing clods
    In a slow silent walk
With an old horse that stumbles and nods
    Half asleep as they stalk.

Only thin smoke without flame
    From the heaps of couch-grass;
Yet this will go onward the same
    Though Dynasties pass.

Yonder a maid and her wight
    Come whispering by:
War's annals will cloud into night
    Ere their story die.

                                    Thomas Har[dy]

520   **Greater Love**

Red lips are not so red
    As the stained stones kissed by the English dead.
Kindness of wooed and wooer
Seems shame to their love pure.
O Love, your eyes lose lure
    When I behold eyes blinded in my stead!

Your slender attitude
Trembles not exquisite like limbs knife-skewed,
Rolling and rolling there
Where God seems not to care;
Till the fierce Love they bear
    Cramps them in death's extreme decrepitude.

Your voice sings not so soft,—
    Though even as wind murmuring through raftered loft,—
Your dear voice is not dear,
Gentle, and evening clear,
As theirs whom none now hear,
    Now earth has stopped their piteous mouths that coughe[d].

Heart, you were never hot,
    Nor large, nor full like hearts made great with shot;
And though your hand be pale,
Paler are all which trail
Your cross through flame and hail:
    Weep, you may weep, for you may touch them not.

                                    Wilfred Ow[en]

521

The Man He Killed

'Had he and I but met
    By some old ancient inn,
We should have sat us down to wet
    Right many a nipperkin!

'But ranged as infantry,
    And staring face to face,
I shot at him as he at me,
    And killed him in his place.

'I shot him dead because—
    Because he was my foe,
Just so: my foe of course he was;
    That's clear enough; although

'He thought he'd 'list, perhaps,
    Off-hand like—just as I;
Was out of work, had sold his traps—
    No other reason why.

'Yes; quaint and curious war is!
    You shoot a fellow down
You'd treat if met where any bar is,
    Or help to half-a-crown.'

Thomas Hardy

522

Arms and the Boy

Let the boy try along this bayonet-blade
How cold steel is, and keen with hunger of blood;
Blue with all malice, like a madman's flash;
And thinly drawn with famishing for flesh.

Lend him to stroke these blind, blunt bullet-heads
Which long to nuzzle in the hearts of lads,
Or give him cartridges of fine zinc teeth,
Sharp with the sharpness of grief and death.

For his teeth seem for laughing round an apple.
There lurk no claws behind his fingers supple;
And God will grow no talons at his heels,
Nor antlers through the thickness of his curls.

Wilfred Owen

523   **A Refusal to Mourn the Death, by Fire,**
                        of a Child in London

Never until the mankind making
Bird beast and flower
Fathering and all humbling darkness
Tells with silence the last light breaking
And the still hour
Is come of the sea tumbling in harness

And I must enter again the round
Zion of the water bead
And the synagogue of the ear of corn
Shall I let pray the shadow of a sound
Or sow my salt seed
In the least valley of sackcloth to mourn

The majesty and burning of the child's death.
I shall not murder
The mankind of her going with a grave truth
Nor blaspheme down the stations of the breath
With any further
Elegy of innocence and youth

Deep with the first dead lies London's daughter,
Robed in the long friends,
The grains beyond age, the dark veins of her mother
Secret by the unmourning water
Of the riding Thames.
After the first death, there is no other.

                                        Dylan Thoma

524   **Strange Meeting**

It seemed that out of the battle I escaped
Down some profound dull tunnel, long since scooped
Through granites which Titanic wars had groined.
Yet also there encumbered sleepers groaned,
Too fast in thought or death to be bestirred.
Then, as I probed them, one sprang up, and stared
With piteous recognition in fixed eyes,
Lifting distressful hands as if to bless.
And by his smile, I knew that sullen hall;
By his dead smile I knew we stood in Hell.
With a thousand pains that vision's face was grained;
Yet no blood reached there from the upper ground,

And no guns thumped, or down the flues made moan.
"Strange, friend," I said, "here is no cause to mourn."
"None," said the other, "save the undone years,
The hopelessness. Whatever hope is yours,
Was my life also; I went hunting wild
After the wildest beauty in the world,
Which lies not calm in eyes, or braided hair,
But mocks the steady running of the hour,
And if it grieves, grieves richlier than here.
For by my glee might many men have laughed,
And of my weeping something has been left,
Which must die now. I mean the truth untold,
The pity of war, the pity war distilled.
Now men will go content with what we spoiled,
Or, discontent, boil bloody, and be spilled.
They will be swift with swiftness of the tigress,
None will break ranks, though nations trek from progress.
Courage was mine, and I had mystery,
Wisdom was mine, and I had mastery;
To miss the march of this retreating world
Into vain citadels that are not walled.
Then when much blood had clogged their chariot-wheels
I would go up and wash them from sweet wells,
Even with truths that lie too deep for taint.
I would have poured my spirit without stint
But not through wounds; not on the cess of war.
Foreheads of men have bled where no wounds were.
I am the enemy you killed, my friend.
I knew you in this dark; for so you frowned
Yesterday through me as you jabbed and killed.
I parried; but my hands were loath and cold.
Let us sleep now. . . ."

Wilfred Owen

Insensibility

I   Happy are men who yet before they are killed
     Can let their veins run cold.
     Whom no compassion fleers
     Or makes their feet
     Sore on the alleys cobbled with their brothers.
     The front line withers,
     But they are troops who fade, not flowers,
     For poets' tearful fooling:
     Men, gaps for filling:
     Losses who might have fought
     Longer; but no one bothers.

II And some cease feeling
Even themselves or for themselves.
Dullness best solves
The tease and doubt of shelling,
And Chance's strange arithmetic
Comes simpler than the reckoning of their shilling.
They keep no check on armies' decimation.

III Happy are these who lose imagination:
They have enough to carry with ammunition.
Their spirit drags no pack,
Their old wounds save with cold can not more ache.
Having seen all things red,
Their eyes are rid
Of the hurt of the colour of blood for ever.
And terror's first constriction over,
Their hearts remain small-drawn.
Their senses in some scorching cautery of battle
Now long since ironed,
Can laugh among the dying, unconcerned.

IV Happy the soldier home, with not a notion
How somewhere, every dawn, some men attack,
And many sighs are drained.
Happy the lad whose mind was never trained:
His days are worth forgetting more than not.
He sings along the march
Which we march taciturn, because of dusk,
The long, forlorn, relentless trend
From larger day to huger night.

V We wise, who with a thought besmirch
Blood over all our soul,
How should we see our task
But through his blunt and lashless eyes?
Alive, he is not vital overmuch;
Dying, not mortal overmuch;
Nor sad, nor proud,
Nor curious at all.
He cannot tell
Old men's placidity from his.

VI But cursed are dullards whom no cannon stuns,
That they should be as stones;
Wretched are they, and mean
With paucity that never was simplicity.
By choice they made themselves immune
To pity and whatever moans in man
Before the last sea and the hapless stars;

Whatever mourns when many leave these shores;
Whatever shares
The eternal reciprocity of tears.

Wilfred Owen

Elegy

On Gordon Barber, Lamentably Drowned in His Eighteenth Year.

When in the mirror of a permanent tear
Over the iris of your mother's eye
I beheld the dark tremor of your face, austere
With space of death, spun too benign for youth,
Icicle of the past to pierce her living sigh—
I saw you wish the last kiss of mother's mouth,
Who took the salted waters rather in the suck
Of seas, sighing yourself to fill and drench
With water the plum-rich glory of your breast
Where beat the heart escaping from war's luck.

Gordon, I mourn your wrist, your running foot,
Your curious brows, your thigh, your unborn daughters,
Yet mourn more deep the drought-caught war dry boy
Who goes, a killer, to join you in your sleep
And envy you what made you blench
Taking your purple back to drought-less waters.
What choke of terror filled you in the wet
What fierce surprise caught you when play turned fate
And all the rains you loved became your net,
Formlessly yielding, yet stronger than your breath?
Then did you dream of mother or hopes hatched
When the cold cramp held you from nape to foot
And time dissolved, promise dissolved, in Death?
Did you cry 'cruel' to all the hands that stretched
Not near, but played afar, when you sank down
Your sponge of lungs hurt to the quick
Till you had left the quick to join the dead,
Whom, now, your mother mourns grief-sick.
You were too young to drown.

Never will you take bride to happy bed,
Who lay awash in water yet no laving
Needed, so pure so young for sudden leaving.

Gone, gone is Gordon, tall and brilliant lad
Whose mind was science. Now hollow his skull

A noble sculpture, is but sunken bone,
His cells from water come by water laid
Grave-deep, to water gone.
Lost, lost the hope he had
Washed to a cipher his splendour and his skill.

But Gordon's gone, it's other boys who live afraid.

Two years, and lads have grown to hold a gun.
In dust must splendid lads go down and choke,
Red dry their hands and dry their one day's sun
From which they earthward fall to fiery tomb
Bomb-weighted, from bloodying children's hair.

Never a boy but takes as cross Cain's crime
And goes to death by making death, to pass
Death's gate distorted with the dried brown grime—
Better the watery death than death by air
Or death by sand
Where fall hard fish of fear
Loud in unwetted dust.

Spun on a lucky wave, O early boy!
Now ocean's fish you are
As heretofore.
Perhaps you had sweet mercy's tenderness
To win so soon largesse of choice
That you, by grace, went gayly to the wave
And all our mourning should be to rejoice.

Gene Derwood

527   **Anthem for Doomed Youth**

What passing-bells for these who die as cattle?
Only the monstrous anger of the guns.
Only the stuttering rifles' rapid rattle
Can patter out their hasty orisons.
No mockeries for them; no prayers nor bells,
Nor any voice of mourning save the choirs,—
The shrill, demented choirs of wailing shells;
And bugles calling for them from sad shires.
What candles may be held to speed them all?
Not in the hands of boys, but in their eyes
Shall shine the holy glimmers of good-byes.
The pallor of girls' brows shall be their pall;
Their flowers the tenderness of patient minds,
And each slow dusk a drawing-down of blinds.

Wilfred Owen

528

The Soldier

If I should die, think only this of me:
That there's some corner of a foreign field
That is for ever England. There shall be
In that rich earth a richer dust concealed;
A dust whom England bore, shaped, made aware,
Gave, once, her flowers to love, her ways to roam,
A body of England's, breathing English air,
Washed by the rivers, blest by suns of home.
And think, this heart, all evil shed away,
A pulse in the eternal mind, no less
Gives somewhere back the thoughts by England given;
Her sights and sounds; dreams happy as her day;
And laughter, learnt of friends; and gentleness,
In hearts at peace, under an English heaven.

Rupert Brooke

529

The Dark Hills

Dark hills at evening in the west,
Where sunset hovers like a sound
Of golden horns that sang to rest
Old bones of warriors under ground,
Far now from all the bannered ways
Where flash the legions of the sun,
You fade—as if the last of days
Were fading, and all wars were done.

Edwin Arlington Robinson

530

Fire and Ice

Some say the world will end in fire;
Some say in ice.
From what I've tasted of desire
I hold with those who favor fire.
But if it had to perish twice,
I think I know enough of hate
To know that for destruction ice
Is also great
And would suffice.

Robert Frost

The Rider Victory

The rider victory reins his horse
Midway across the empty bridge
As if head-tall he had met a wall.
Yet there was nothing there at all,
No bodiless barrier, ghostly ridge
To check the charger in his course
So suddenly, you'd think he'd fall.

Suspended, steed and rider stare,
Leaping on air and legendary.
In front the waiting kingdom lies,
The bridge and all the roads are free.
But halted in implacable air
Rider and horse with stony eyes
Uprear their motionless statuary.

                                        Edwin Muir

532   Garlic and sapphires in the mud
                   Clot the bedded axle-tree.
                   The trilling wire in the blood
                   Sings below inveterate scars
                   And reconciles forgotten wars.
                   The dance along the artery
                   The circulation of the lymph
                   Are figured in the drift of stars
                   Ascend to summer in the tree
                   We move above the moving tree
                   In light upon the figured leaf
                   And hear upon the sodden floor
                   Below, the boarhound and the boar
                   Pursue their pattern as before
                   But reconciled among the stars.

                                        T. S. Eliot

533   **The Eye**

The Atlantic is a stormy moat, and the Mediterranean,
The blue pool in the old garden,
More than five thousand years has drunk sacrifice
Of ships and blood and shines in the sun; but here the Pacific:
The ships, planes, wars are perfectly irrelevant.

Neither our present blood-feud with the brave dwarfs
Nor any future world-quarrel of westering
And eastering man, the bloody migrations, greed of power,
    battle-falcons,
Are a mote of dust in the great scale-pan.
Here from this mountain shore, headland beyond stormy head-
    land plunging like dolphins through the gray sea-smoke
Into pale sea, look west at the hill of water: it is half the
    planet: this dome, this half-globe, this bulging
Eyeball of water, arched over to Asia,
Australia and white Antarctica: those are the eyelids that never
    close; this is the staring unsleeping
Eye of the earth, and what it watches is not our wars.

Robinson Jeffers

34   What if a Much of a Which of a Wind

what if a much of a which of a wind
gives the truth to summer's lie;
bloodies with dizzying leaves the sun
and yanks immortal stars awry?
Blow king to beggar and queen to seem
(blow friend to fiend: blow space to time)
—when skies are hanged and oceans drowned,
the single secret will still be man

what if a keen of a lean wind flays
screaming hills with sleet and snow:
strangles valleys by ropes of thing
and stifles forests in white ago?
Blow hope to terror; blow seeing to blind
(blow pity to envy and soul to mind)
—whose hearts are mountains, roots are trees,
it's they shall cry hello to the spring

what if a dawn of a doom of a dream
bites this universe in two,
peels forever out of his grave
and sprinkles nowhere with me and you?
Blow soon to never and never to twice
(blow life to isn't: blow death to was)
—all nothing's only our hugest home;
the most who die, the more we live

E. E. Cummings

535

Sailing to Byzantium

That is no country for old men. The young
In one another's arms, birds in the trees
—Those dying generations—at their song,
The salmon-falls, the mackerel-crowded seas,
Fish, flesh, or fowl, commend all summer long
Whatever is begotten, born, and dies.
Caught in that sensual music all neglect
Monuments of unaging intellect.

An aged man is but a paltry thing,
A tattered coat upon a stick, unless
Soul clap its hands and sing, and louder sing
For every tatter in its mortal dress,
Nor is there singing school but studying
Monuments of its own magnificence;
And therefore I have sailed the seas and come
To the holy city of Byzantium.

O sages standing in God's holy fire
As in the gold mosaic of a wall,
Come from the holy fire, perne in a gyre,
And be the singing-masters of my soul.
Consume my heart away; sick with desire
And fastened to a dying animal
It knows not what it is; and gather me
Into the artifice of eternity.

Once out of nature I shall never take
My bodily form from any natural thing,
But such a form as Grecian goldsmiths make
Of hammered gold and gold enameling
To keep a drowsy Emperor awake;
Or set upon a golden bough to sing
To lords and ladies of Byzantium
Of what is past, or passing, or to come.

William Butler Yeats

536

Spring and Fall: To a Young Child

Márgarét, are you gríeving
Over Goldengrove unleaving?
Leáves, like the things of man, you
With your fresh thoughts care for, can you?

Ah! ás the heart grows older
It will come to such sights colder
By and by, nor spare a sigh
Though worlds of wanwood leafmeal lie;
And yet you wíll weep and know why.
Now no matter, child, the name:
Sórrow's spríngs áre the same.
Nor mouth had, no nor mind, expressed
What heart heard of, ghost guessed:
It ís the blight man was born for,
It is Margaret you mourn for.

Gerard Manley Hopkins

37   **The Leaden Echo and the Golden Echo**
(*Maidens' Song from St. Winefred's Well*)

THE LEADEN ECHO

Íow to kéep—is there any any, is there none such, nowhere
    known some, bow or brooch or braid or brace, láce, latch
    or catch or key to keep
Back beauty, keep it, beauty, beauty, beauty, . . . from vanish-
    ing away?
O is there no frowning of these wrinkles, rankèd wrinkles deep,
Dówn? no waving off of these most mournful messengers, still
    messengers, sad and stealing messengers of grey?
No there's none, there's none, O no there's none,
Nor can you long be, what you now are, called fair,
Do what you may do, what, do what you may,
And wisdom is early to despair:
Be beginning; since, no, nothing can be done to keep at bay
Age and age's evils, hoar hair,
Ruck and wrinkle, drooping, dying, death's worst, winding
    sheets, tombs and worms and tumbling to decay;
So be beginning, be beginning to despair.
O there's none; no no no there's none:
Be beginning to despair, to despair,
Despair, despair, despair, despair.

THE GOLDEN ECHO

    Spare!
There ís one, yes I have one (Hush there!);
Only not within seeing of the sun,
Not within the singeing of the strong sun,
Tall sun's tingeing, or treacherous the tainting of the earth's air,

Somewhere elsewhere there is ah well where! one,
One. Yes I can tell such a key, I do know such a place,
Where whatever's prized and passes of us, everything that's
    fresh and fast flying of us, seems to us sweet of us and
    swiftly away with, done away with, undone,
Undone, done with, soon done with, and yet dearly and dan
    gerously sweet
Of us, the wimpled-water-dimpled, not-by-morning-matchèd
    face
The flower of beauty, fleece of beauty, too too apt to, ah! to
    fleet,
Never fleets móre, fastened with the tenderest truth
To its own best being and its loveliness of youth: it is an ever
    lastingness of, O it is an all youth!
Come then, your ways and airs and looks, locks, maiden gear,
    gallantry and gaiety and grace,
Winning ways, airs innocent, maiden manners, sweet looks,
    loose locks, long locks, lovelocks, gaygear, going gallant,
    girlgrace—
Resign them, sign them, seal them, send them, motion them
    with breath,
And with sighs soaring, soaring síghs deliver
Them; beauty-in-the-ghost, deliver it, early now, long before
    death
Give beauty back, beauty, beauty, beauty, back to God,
    beauty's self and beauty's giver.
See; not a hair is, not an eyelash, not the least lash lost; every
    hair
Is, hair of the head, numbered.
Nay, what we had lighthanded left in surly the mere mould
Will have waked and have waxed and have walked with the
    wind whatwhile we slept,
This side, that side hurling a heavyheaded hundredfold
Whatwhile we, while we slumbered.
O then, weary then why should we tread? O why are we so
    haggard at the heart, so care-coiled, care-killed, so fagged,
    so fashed, so cogged, so cumbered,
When the thing we freely fórfeit is kept with fonder a care,
Fonder a care kept than we could have kept it, kept
Far with fonder a care (and we, we should have lost it) finer,
    fonder
A care kept.—Where kept? Do but tell us where kept, where.—
Yonder.—What high as that! We follow, now we follow.
    —Yonder, yes yonder, yonder.
Yonder.

Gerard Manley Hopkins

Geronion

*Thou hast nor youth nor age
But as it were an after dinner sleep
Dreaming of both.*

Here I am, an old man in a dry month,
Being read to by a boy, waiting for rain.
I was neither at the hot gates
Nor fought in the warm rain
Nor knee deep in the salt marsh, heaving a cutlass,
Bitten by flies, fought.
My house is a decayed house,
And the Jew squats on the window sill, the owner,
Spawned in some estaminet of Antwerp,
Blistered in Brussels, patched and peeled in London.
The goat coughs at night in the field overhead;
Rocks, moss, stonecrop, iron, merds.
The woman keeps the kitchen, makes tea,
Sneezes at evening, poking the peevish gutter.
                                    I an old man,
A dull head among windy spaces.

Signs are taken for wonders. 'We would see a sign!'
The word within a word, unable to speak a word,
Swaddled with darkness. In the juvescence of the year
Came Christ the tiger

In depraved May, dogwood and chestnut, flowering judas,
To be eaten, to be divided, to be drunk
Among whispers; by Mr. Silvero
With caressing hands, at Limoges
Who walked all night in the next room;
By Hakagawa, bowing among the Titians;
By Madame de Tornquist, in the dark room
Shifting the candles; Fraülein von Kulp
Who turned in the hall, one hand on the door. Vacant shuttles
Weave the wind. I have no ghosts,
An old man in a draughty house
Under a windy knob.

After such knowledge, what forgiveness? Think now
History has many cunning passages, contrived corridors
And issues, deceives with whispering ambitions,
Guides us by vanities. Think now.
She gives when our attention is distracted

And what she gives, gives with such supple confusions
That the giving famishes the craving. Gives too late
What's not believed in, or if still believed,
In memory only, reconsidered passion. Gives too soon
Into weak hands, what's thought can be dispensed with
Till the refusal propagates a fear. Think
Neither fear nor courage saves us. Unnatural vices
Are fathered by our heroism. Virtues
Are forced upon us by our impudent crimes.
These tears are shaken from the wrath-bearing tree.

The tiger springs in the new year. Us he devours. Think at last
We have not reached conclusion, when I
Stiffen in a rented house. Think at last
I have not made this show purposelessly
And it is not by any concitation
Of the backward devils.
I would meet you upon this honestly.
I that was near your heart was removed therefrom
To lose beauty in terror, terror in inquisition.
I have lost my passion: why should I need to keep it
Since what is kept must be adulterated?
I have lost my sight, smell, hearing, taste and touch:
How should I use them for your closer contact?

These with a thousand small deliberations
Protract the profit of their chilled delirium,
Excite the membrane, when the sense has cooled,
With pungent sauces, multiply variety
In a wilderness of mirrors. What will the spider do,
Suspend its operations, will the weevil
Delay? De Bailhache, Fresca, Mrs. Cammel, whirled
Beyond the circuit of the shuddering Bear
In fractured atoms. Gull against the wind, in the windy straits
Of Belle Isle, or running on the Horn,
White feathers in the snow, the Gulf claims,
And an old man driven by the Trades
To a sleepy corner.

                                    Tenants of the house,
Thoughts of a dry brain in a dry season.

                                                T. S. Eliot

39
Should Lanterns Shine

Should lanterns shine, the holy face,
Caught in an octagon of unaccustomed light,
Would wither up, and any boy of love
Look twice before he fell from grace.
The features in their private dark
Are formed of flesh, but let the false day come
And from her lips the faded pigments fall,
The mummy cloths expose an ancient breast.

I have been told to reason by the heart,
But heart, like head, leads helplessly;
I have been told to reason by the pulse,
And, when it quickens, alter the actions' pace
Till field and roof lie level and the same
So fast I move defying time, the quiet gentleman
Whose beard wags in Egyptian wind.

I have heard many years of telling,
And many years should see some change.

The ball I threw while playing in the park
Has not yet reached the ground.

Dylan Thomas

40
Captain Carpenter

Captain Carpenter rose up in his prime
Put on his pistols and went riding out
But had got wellnigh nowhere at that time
Till he fell in with ladies in a rout.

It was a pretty lady and all her train
That played with him so sweetly but before
An hour she'd taken a sword with all her main
And twined him of his nose for evermore.

Captain Carpenter mounted up one day
And rode straightway into a stranger rogue
That looked unchristian but be that as may
The Captain did not wait upon prologue.

But drew upon him out of his great heart
The other swing against him with a club
And cracked his two legs at the shinny part
And let him roll and stick like any tub.

Captain Carpenter rode many a time
From male and female took he sundry harms
He met the wife of Satan crying "I'm
The she-wolf bids you shall bear no more arms."

Their strokes and counters whistled in the wind
I wish he had delivered half his blows
But where she could have made off like a hind
The bitch bit off his arms at the elbows.

And Captain Carpenter parted with his ears
To a black devil that used him in this wise
O Jesus ere his threescore and ten years
Another had plucked out his sweet blue eyes.

Captain Carpenter got up on his roan
And sallied from the gate in hell's despite
I heard him asking in the grimmest tone
If any enemy yet there was to fight?

"To any adversary it is fame
If he risk to be wounded by my tongue
Or burnt in two beneath my red heart's flame
Such are the perils he is cast among.

"But if he can he has a pretty choice
From an anatomy with little to lose
Whether he cut my tongue and take my voice
Or whether it be my round red heart he choose."

It was the neatest knave that ever was seen
Stepping in perfume from his lady's bower
Who at this word put in his merry mien
And fell on Captain Carpenter like a tower.

I would not knock old fellows in the dust
But there lay Captain Carpenter on his back
His weapons were the old heart in his bust
And a blade shook between rotten teeth alack.

The rogue in scarlet and grey soon knew his mind
He wished to get his trophy and depart
With gentle apology and touch refined
He pierced him and produced the Captain's heart.

God's mercy rest on Captain Carpenter now
I thought him Sirs an honest gentleman
Citizen husband soldier and scholar enow
Let jangling kites eat of him if they can.

But God's deep curses follow after those
That shore him of his goodly nose and ears
His legs and strong arms at the two elbows
And eyes that had not watered seventy years.

The curse of hell upon the sleek upstart
Who got the Captain finally on his back
And took the red red vitals of his heart
And made the kites to whet their beaks clack clack.

John Crowe Ransom

1   After Long Silence

Speech after long silence; it is right,
All other lovers being estranged or dead,
Unfriendly lamplight hid under its shade,
The curtains drawn upon unfriendly night,
That we descant and yet again descant
Upon the supreme theme of Art and Song:
Bodily decrepitude is wisdom; young
We loved each other and were ignorant.

William Butler Yeats

2   This Side of the Truth

for Llewelyn

This side of the truth
you may not see, my son,
King of your blue eyes
In the blinding country of
    youth,
That all is undone,
Under the unminding skies,
Of innocence and guilt
Before you move to make
One gesture of the heart or
    head,
Is gathered and split
Into the winding dark
Like the dust of the dead.

Good and bad, two ways
Of moving about your death
By the grinding sea,
King of your heart in the
    blind days,

Blow away like breath,
Go crying through you
    and me
And the souls of all men
Into the innocent
Dark, and the guilty dark,
    and good
Death, and bad death, and
    then
In the last element
Fly like the stars' blood,

Like the sun's tears
Like the moon's seed, rubbish
And fire, the flying rant
Of the sky, king of your
    six years.
And the wicked wish,
Down the beginning
    of plants.

And animals and birds,
Water and light, the earth
    and sky,
Is cast before you move,

And all your deeds and wor
Each truth, each lie,
Die in unjudging love.

Dylan Thomas

543   A Prayer for My Daughter

Once more the storm is howling, and half hid
Under this cradle-hood and coverlid
My child sleeps on. There is no obstacle
But Gregory's wood and one bare hill
Whereby the haystack- and roof-levelling wind,
Bred on the Atlantic, can be stayed;
And for an hour I have walked and prayed
Because of the great gloom that is in my mind.

I have walked and prayed for this young child an hour
And heard the sea-wind scream upon the tower,
Ander under the arches of the bridge, and scream
In the elms above the flooded stream;
Imagining in excited reverie
That the future years had come,
Dancing to a frenzied drum,
Out of the murderous innocence of the sea.

May she be granted beauty and yet not
Beauty to make a stranger's eye distraught,
Or hers before a looking-glass, for such,
Being made beautiful overmuch,
Consider beauty a sufficient end,
Lose natural kindness and maybe
The heart-revealing intimacy
That chooses right, and never find a friend.

Helen being chosen found life flat and dull
And later had much trouble from a fool,
While the great Queen, that rose out of the spray,
Being fatherless could have her way
Yet chose a bandy-leggèd smith for man.
It's certain that fine women eat
A crazy salad with their meat
Whereby the Horn of Plenty is undone.

In courtesy I'd have her chiefly learned;
Hearts are not had as a gift but hearts are earned

By those that are not entirely beautiful;
Yet many, that have played the fool
For beauty's very self, has charm made wise,
And many a poor man that has roved,
Loved and thought himself beloved,
From a glad kindness cannot take his eyes.

May she become a flourishing hidden tree
That all her thoughts may like the linnet be,
And have no business but dispensing round
Their magnanimities of sound,
Nor but in merriment begin a chase,
Nor but in merriment a quarrel.
O may she live like some green laurel
Rooted in one dear perpetual place.

My mind, because the minds that I have loved,
The sort of beauty that I have approved,
Prosper but little, has dried up of late,
Yet knows that to be choked with hate
May well be of all evil chances chief.
If there's no hatred in a mind
Assault and battery of the wind
Can never tear the linnet from the leaf.

An intellectual hatred is the worst,
So let her think opinions are accursed.
Have I not seen the loveliest woman born
Out of the mouth of Plenty's horn,
Because of her opinionated mind
Barter that horn and every good
By quiet natures understood
For an old bellows full of angry wind?

Considering that, all hatred driven hence,
The soul recovers radical innocence
And learns at last that it is self-delighting,
Self-appeasing, self-affrighting,
And that its own sweet will is Heaven's will;
She can, though every face should scowl
And every windy quarter howl
Or every bellows burst, be happy still.

And may her bridegroom bring her to a house
Where all's accustomed, ceremonious;
For arrogance and hatred are the wares
Peddled in the thoroughfares.

How but in custom and in ceremony
Are innocence and beauty born?
Ceremony's a name for the rich horn,
And custom for the spreading laurel tree.

William Butler Ye

544   **Sonnet to My Mother**

Most near, most dear, most loved and most far,
Under the window where I often found her
Sitting as huge as Asia, seismic with laughter,
Gin and chicken helpless in her Irish hand,
Irresistible as Rabelais but most tender for
The lame dogs and hurt birds that surround her,—
She is a procession no one can follow after
But be like a little dog following a brass band.
She will not glance up at the bomber nor condescend
To drop her gin and scuttle to a cellar,
But lean on the mahogany table like a mountain
Whom only faith can move, and so I send
O all my faith and all my love to tell her
That she will move from mourning into morning.

George Bark

545   **The Return**

Earth does not understand her child,
    Who from the loud gregarious town
Returns, depleted and defiled,
    To the still woods, to fling him down.

Earth cannot count the sons she bore:
    The wounded lynx, the wounded man
Come trailing blood unto her door;
    She shelters both as best she can.

But she is early up and out,
    To trim the year or strip its bones;
She has no time to stand about
    Talking of him in undertones

Who has no aim but to forget,
    Be left in peace, be lying thus
For days, for years, for centuries yet,
    Unshaven and anonymous;

Who, marked for failure, dulled by grief,
   Has traded in his wife and friend
For this warm ledge, this alder leaf:
   Comfort that does not comprehend.

Edna St. Vincent Millay

Richard Cory

Whenever Richard Cory went down town,
   We people on the pavement looked at him:
He was a gentleman from sole to crown,
   Clean favored, and imperially slim.

And he was always quietly arrayed,
   And he was always human when he talked;
But still he fluttered pulses when he said,
   "Good-morning," and he glittered when he walked.

And he was rich—yes, richer than a king,
   And admirably schooled in every grace:
In fine, we thought that he was everything
   To make us wish that we were in his place.

So on we worked, and waited for the light,
   And went without the meat, and cursed the bread;
And Richard Cory, one calm summer night,
   Went home and put a bullet through his head.

Edwin Arlington Robinson

For a Dead Lady

No more with overflowing light
   Shall fill the eyes that now are faded,
Nor shall another's fringe with night
   Their woman-hidden world as they did.
No more shall quiver down the days
The flowing wonder of her ways,
Whereof no language may requite
   The shifting and the many-shaded.

The grace, divine, definitive,
   Clings only as a faint forestalling;
The laugh that love could not forgive
   Is hushed, and answers to no calling;
The forehead and the little ears
   Have gone where Saturn keeps the years;

The breast where roses could not live
Has done with rising and with falling.

The beauty, shattered by the laws
That have creation in their keeping,
No longer trembles at applause,
Or over children that are sleeping;
And we who delve in beauty's lore
Know all that we have known before
Of what inexorable cause
Makes Time so vicious in his reaping.

Edwin Arlington Robinson

548   **A Certain Slant of Light**

There's a certain slant of light,
On winter afternoons,
That oppresses, like the weight
Of cathedral tunes.

Heavenly hurt it gives us;
We can find no scar,
But internal difference
Where the meanings are.

None may teach it anything
'Tis the seal, despair,—
An imperial affliction
Sent us of the air.

When it comes, the landscape listens,
Shadows hold their breath;
When it goes, 'tis like the distance
On the look of death.

Emily Dickinson

549   **I Heard a Fly Buzz When I Died**

I heard a fly buzz when I died;
    The stillness round my form
Was like the stillness in the air
    Between the heaves of storm.

The eyes beside had wrung them dry,
    And breaths were gathering sure
For that last onset, when the king
    Be witnessed in his power.

I willed my keepsakes, signed away
    What portion of me I
Could make assignable,—and then
    There interposed a fly,

With blue, uncertain, stumbling buzz,
    Between the light and me;
And then the windows failed, and then
    I could not see to see.

Emily Dickinson

Ash on an Old Man's Sleeve

    Ash on an old man's sleeve
Is all the ash the burnt roses leave.
Dust in the air suspended
Marks the place where a story ended.
Dust inbreathed was a house—
The wall, the wainscot and the mouse.
The death of hope and despair,
    This is the death of air.

    There are flood and drouth
Over the eyes and in the mouth,
Dead water and dead sand
Contending for the upper hand.
The parched eviscerate soil
Gapes at the vanity of toil,
Laughs without mirth.
    This is the death of earth.

    Water and fire succeed
The town, the pasture and the weed.
Water and fire deride
The sacrifice that we denied.
Water and fire shall rot
The marred foundations we forgot,
Of sanctuary and choir.
    This is the death of water and fire.

T. S. Eliot

The Groundhog

In June, amid the golden fields,
I saw a groundhog lying dead.
Dead lay he; my senses shook,
And mind outshot our naked frailty.

There lowly in the vigorous summer
His form began its senseless change,
And made my senses waver dim
Seeing nature ferocious in him.
Inspecting close his maggots' might
And seething cauldron of his being,
Half with loathing, half with a strange love,
I poked him with an angry stick.
The fever arose, became a flame
And Vigour circumscribed the skies,
Immense energy in the sun,
And through my frame a sunless trembling.
My stick had done nor good nor harm.
Then stood I silent in the day
Watching the object, as before;
And kept my reverence for knowledge
Trying for control, to be still,
To quell the passion of the blood;
Until I had bent down on my knees
Praying for joy in the sight of decay.
And so I left; and I returned
In Autumn strict of eye, to see
The sap gone out of the groundhog,
But the bony sodden hulk remained.
But the year had lost its meaning,
And in intellectual chains
I lost both love and loathing,
Mured up in the wall of wisdom.
Another summer took the fields again
Massive and burning, full of life,
But when I chanced upon the spot
There was only a little hair left,
And bones bleaching in the sunlight
Beautiful as architecture;
I watched them like a geometer,
And cut a walking stick from a birch.
It has been three years, now.
There is no sign of the groundhog.
I stood there in the whirling summer,
My hand capped a withered heart,
And thought of China and of Greece,
Of Alexander in his tent;
Of Montaigne in his tower,
Of Saint Theresa in her wild lament.

Richard Eberhart

52

Because I Could Not Stop fo rDeath

Because I could not stop for Death,
He kindly stopped for me;
The carriage held but just ourselves
And Immortality.

We slowly drove, he knew no haste,
And I had put away
My labor, and my leisure too,
For his civility.

We passed the school where children played
At wrestling in a ring;
We passed the fields of gazing grain,
We passed the setting sun.

We paused before a house that seemed
A swelling of the ground;
The roof was scarcely visible,
The cornice but a mound.

Since then 'tis centuries; but each
Feels shorter than the day
I first surmised the horses' heads
Were toward eternity.

Emily Dickinson

53

The Dead

These hearts were woven of human joys and cares,
    Washed marvellously with sorrow, swift to mirth.
The years had given them kindness. Dawn was theirs,
    And sunset, and the colors of the earth.
These had seen movement, and heard music; known
    Slumber and waking; loved; gone proudly friended;
Felt the quick stir of wonder; sat alone;
    Touched flowers and furs and cheeks. All this is ended.
There are waters blown by changing winds to laughter
And lit by the rich skies, all day. And after,
    Frost, with a gesture, stays the waves that dance
And wandering loveliness. He leaves a white
    Unbroken glory, a gathered radiance,
A width, a shining peace, under the night.

Rupert Brooke

If I could have
Two things in one:
The peace of the grave,
And the light of the sun;

My hands across
My thin breast-bone,
But aware of the moss
Invading the stone,

Aware of the flight
Of the golden flicker
With his wing to the light;
To hear him nicker

And drum with his bill
On the rotted window;
Snug and still
On a gray pillow

Deep in the clay
Where digging is hard,
One of the way,—
The blue shard

Of a broken platter—
If I might be
Insensate matter
With sensate me

Sitting within,
Harking and prying,
I might begin
To dicker with dying.

For the body at best
Is a bundle of aches,
Longing for rest;
It cries when it wakes

"Alas, 'tis light!"
At set of sun
"Alas, 'tis night,
And nothing done!"

Death, however,
Is a spongy wall,
Is a sticky river,
Is nothing at all.

Summon the weeper,
Wail and sing;
Call him Reaper,
Angel, King;

Call him Evil
Drunk to the lees,
Monster, Devil—
He is less than these.

Call him Thief,
The Maggot in the Cheese,
The Canker in the Leaf—
He is less than these.

Dusk without sound,
Where the spirit by pain
Uncoiled, is wound
To spring again;

The mind enmeshed
Laid straight in repose,
And the body refreshed
By feeding the rose—

These are but visions;
These would be
The grave's derisions,
Could the grave see.

Here is the wish
Of one that died
Like a beached fish
On the ebb of the tide:

That he might wait
Till the tide came back,
To see if a crate,
Or a bottle, or a black

Boot, or an oar,
Or an orange peel
Be washed ashore. . . .
About his heel

The sand slips;
The last he hears
From the world's lips
Is the sand in his ears.

What thing is little?—
The aphis hid
In a house of spittle?
The hinge of the lid

Of the spider's eye
At the spider's birth?
"Greater am I
By the earth's girth

"Than Mighty Death!"
All creatures cry
That can summon breath—
And speak no lie.

For he is nothing;
He is less
Than Echo answering
"Nothingness!"—

Less than the heat
Of the furthest star
To the ripening wheat;
Less by far,

When all the lipping
Is said and sung,
Than the sweat dripping
From a dog's tongue.

This being so,
And I being such,
I would liever go
On a cripple's crutch,

Lopped and felled;
Liever be dependent

On a chair propelled
By a surly attendant

With a foul breath,
And be spooned my food,
Than go with Death
Where nothing good,

Not even the thrust
Of the summer gnat,
Consoles the dust
For being that.

Needy, lonely,
Stitched by pain,
Left with only
The drip of the rain

Out of all I had;
The books of the wise,
Badly read
By other eyes,

Lewdly bawled
At my closing ear;
Hated, called
A lingerer here—

Withstanding Death
Till Life be gone,
I shall treasure my breath,
I shall linger on.

I shall bolt my door
With a bolt and a cable;
I shall lock my door
With a bureau and a table;

With all my might
My door shall be barred.
I shall put up a fight,
I shall take it hard.

With his hand on my mouth
He shall drag me forth,
Shrieking to the south
And clutching at the north.

Edna St. Vincent Millay

555   ## To an Athlete Dying Young

The time you won your town the race
We chaired you through the market-place;
Man and boy stood cheering by,
And home we brought you shoulder-high.

To-day, the road all runners come,
Shoulder-high we bring you home,
And set you at your threshold down,
Townsman of a stiller town.

Smart lad, to slip betimes away
From fields where glory does not stay
And early though the laurel grows
It withers quicker than the rose.

Eyes the shady night has shut
Cannot see the record cut,
And silence sounds no worse than cheers
After earth has stopped the ears:

Now you will not swell the rout
Of lads that wore their honours out,
Runners whom renown outran
And the name died before the man.

So set, before its echoes fade,
The fleet foot on the sill of shade,
And hold to the low lintel up
The still-defended challenge-cup.

And round that early-laurelled head
Will flock to gaze the strengthless dead,
And find unwithered on its curls
The garland briefer than a girl's.

A. E. Housman

556   ## Elegy for Jane

(My student, thrown by a horse)

I remember the neckcurls, limp and damp as tendrils;
And her quick look, a sidelong pickerel smile;
And how, once startled into talk, the light syllables leaped
   for her,
And she balanced in the delight of her thought,

A wren, happy, tail into the wind,
Her song trembling the twigs and small branches.
The shade sang with her;
The leaves, their whispers turned to kissing,
And the mould sang in the bleached valleys under the rose.

Oh, when she was sad, she cast herself down into such a
   pure depth,
Even a father could not find her:
Scraping her cheek against straw,
Stirring the clearest water.

My sparrow, you are not here,
Waiting like a fern, making a spiney shadow.
The sides of wet stones cannot console me,
Nor the moss, wound with the last light.

If only I could nudge you from this sleep,
My maimed darling, my skittery pigeon.
Over the damp grave I speak the words of my love:
I, with no rights in this matter,
Neither father nor lover.

                                        Theodore Roethke

557   **Felix Randal**

Felix Randal the farrier, O he is dead then? my duty all ended,
Who have watched his mould of man, big-boned and hardy-
   handsome
Pining, pining, till time when reason rambled in it and some
Fatal four disorders, fleshed there, all contended?
Sickness broke him. Impatient he cursed at first, but mended
Being anointed and all; though a heavenlier heart began some
Months earlier, since I had our sweet reprieve and ransom
Tendered to him. Ah well, God rest him all road ever he
   offended!
This seeing the sick endears them to us, us too it endears.
My tongue had taught thee comfort, touch had quenched thy
   tears,
Thy tears that touched my heart, child, Felix, poor Felix
   Randal;
How far from then forethought of, all thy more boisterous
   years,
When thou at the random grim forge, powerful amidst peers,
Didst fettle for the great grey drayhorse his bright and batter-
   ing sandal!

                                 Gerard Manley Hopkins

Dirge without Music

I am not resigned to the shutting away of loving hearts in the
    hard ground.
So it is, and so it will be, for so it has been, time out of mind:
Into the darkness they go, the wise and the lovely. Crowned
With lilies and with laurel they go; but I am not resigned.

Lovers and thinkers, into the earth with you.
Be one with the dull, the indiscriminate dust.
A fragment of what you felt, of what you knew,
A formula, a phrase remains,—but the best is lost.

The answers quick & keen, the honest look, the laughter, the
    love,
They are gone. They have gone to feed the roses. Elegant and
    curled
Is the blossom. Fragrant is the blossom. I know. But I do not
    approve.
More precious was the light in your eyes than all the roses in
    the world.

Down, down, down into the darkness of the grave
Gently they go, the beautiful, the tender, the kind;
Quietly they go, the intelligent, the witty, the brave.
I know. But I do not approve. And I am not resigned.
                                    Edna St. Vincent Millay

After the Funeral

In Memory of Ann Jones

After the funeral, mule praises, brays,
Windshake of sailshaped ears, muffle-toed tap
Tap happily of one peg in the thick
Grave's foot, blinds down the lids, the teeth in black,
The spittled eyes, the salt ponds in the sleeves,
Morning smack of the spade that wakes up sleep,
Shakes a desolate boy who slits his throat
In the dark of the coffin and sheds dry leaves
That breaks one bone to light with a judgment clout,
After the feast of tear-stuffed time and thistles
In a room with a stuffed fox and a stale fern,
I stand, for this memorial's sake, alone
In the snivelling hours with dead, humped Ann
Whose hooded, fountain heart once fell in puddles
Round the parched worlds of Wales & drowned each sun
(Though this for her is a monstrous image blindly
Magnified out of praise; her death was a still drop;

e would not have me sinking in the holy
ood of her heart's fame; she would lie dumb and deep
d need no druid of her broken body).
t I, Ann's bard on a raised hearth, call all
e seas to service that her wood-tongued virtue
bble like a bellbuoy over the hymning heads,
w down the walls of the ferned and foxy woods
at her love sing and swing through a brown chapel,
ss her bent spirit with four, crossing birds.
r flesh was meek as milk, but this skyward statue
ith the wild breast and blessed and giant skull
carved from her in a room with a wet window
a fiercely mourning house in a crooked year.
know her scrubbed and sour humble hands
e with religion in their cramp, her threadbare
hisper in a damp word, her wits drilled hollow,
r fist of a face died clenched on a round pain;
d sculptured Ann is seventy years of stone.
ese cloud-sopped, marble hands, this monumental
gument of the hewn voice, gesture and psalm
rm me forever over her grave until
e stuffed lung of the fox twitch and cry Love
d the strutting fern lay seeds on the black sill.

Dylan Thomas

Tywater

Death of Sir Nihil, book the *nth*,
Upon the charred and clotted sward,
Lacking the lily of our Lord,
Alases of the hyacinth.

Could flicker from behind his ear
A whistling silver throwing knife
And with a holler punch the life
Out of a swallow in the air.

Behind the lariat's butterfly
Shuttled his white and gritted grin,
And cuts of sky would roll within
The noose-hole, when he spun it high.

The violent, neat and practiced skill
Was all he loved and all he learned;
When he was hit, his body turned
To clumsy dirt before it fell.

And what to say of him, God knows.
Such violence. And such repose.

Richard Wilbur

561　　　　　　The Eagle and the Mole

Avoid the reeking herd,
Shun the polluted flock,
Live like that stoic bird,
The eagle of the rock.

The huddled warmth of
　　crowds
Begets and fosters hate;
He keeps, above the clouds,
His cliff inviolate.

When flocks are folded warm
And herds to shelter run,
He sails above the storm,
He stares into the sun.

If in the eagle's track
Your sinews cannot leap,
Avoid the lathered pack,
Turn from the steami
　　sheep.

If you would keep your sc
From spotted sight or sour
Live like the velvet mole;
Go burrow underground.

And there hold intercours
With roots of trees and ston
With rivers at their source
And disembodied bones.
　　　　　　　　　Elinor Wylie

562　　　　　　I Died for Beauty

I died for beauty, but was scarce
　　Adjusted in the tomb,
When one who died for truth was lain
　　In an adjoining room.

He questioned softly why I failed?
　　"For beauty," I replied.
　"And I for truth,—the two are one;
　　We brethren are," he said.

And so, as kinsmen met a night,
　　We talked between the rooms,
Until the moss had reached our lips,
　　And covered up our names.
　　　　　　　　　Emily Dickinse

563　　　　　　Promise of Peace

The heads of strong old age are beautiful
Beyond all grace of youth. They have strange quiet,
Integrity, health, soundness, to the full
They've dealt with life and been attempered by it.
A young man must not sleep; his years are war,
Civil and foreign but the former's worse;
But the old can breathe in safety now that they are

Forgetting what youth meant, the being perverse,
Running the fool's gauntlet and being cut
By the whips of the five senses. As for me,
If I should wish to live long it were but
To trade those fevers for tranquillity,
Thinking though that's entire and sweet in the grave
How shall the dead taste the deep treasure they have?

Robinson Jeffers

4 ### The Too-Late Born

We too, we too, descending once again
The hills of our own land, we too have heard
Far off—Ah, que ce cor a longue haleine—
The horn of Roland in the passages of Spain,
The first, the second blast, the failing third,
And with the third turned back and climbed once more
The steep road southward, and heard faint the sound
Of swords, of horses, the disastrous war,
And crossed the dark defile at last, and found
At Roncevaux upon the darkening plain
The dead against the dead and on the silent ground
The silent slain—

Archibald MacLeish

5 ### The Hand That Signed the Paper Felled a City

The hand that signed the paper felled a city;
Five sovereign fingers taxed the breath,
Doubled the globe of dead and halved a country;
These five kings did a king to death.

The mighty hand leads to a sloping shoulder,
The finger joints are cramped with chalk;
A goose's quill has put an end to murder
That put an end to talk.

The hand that signed the treaty bred a fever,
And famine grew, and locusts came;
Great is the hand that holds dominion over
Man by a scribbled name.

The five kings count the dead but do not soften
The crusted wound nor pat the brow;
A hand rules pity as a hand rules heaven;
Hands have no tears to flow.

Dylan Thomas

White Christmas

Punctually at Christmas the soft plush
Of sentiment snows down, embosoms all
The sharp and pointed shapes of venom, shawls
The hills and hides the shocking holes of this
Uneven world of want and wealth, cushions
With cosy wish like cotton-wool the cool
Arm's-length interstices of caste and class,
And into obese folds subfracts from sight
All truculent acts, bleeding the world white.

Punctually that glib pair, Peace and Goodwill,
Emerges royally to take the air,
Collect the bows, assimilate the smiles,
Of waiting men. It is a genial time;
Angels like stalactites descend from heaven;
Bishops distribute their own weight in words,
Congratulate the poor on Christlike lack;
And the member for the constituency
Feeds the five thousand, and has plenty back.

Punctually, to-night, in old stone circles
Of set reunion, families stiffly sit
And listen: this is the night and this the happy time
When the tinned milk of human kindness is
Upheld and holed by radio-appeal:
Hushed are hurrying heels on hard roads,
And every parlour's pink pond of light
To the cold and travelling man going by
In the dark, without a bark or a bite.

But punctually to-morrow you will see
All this silent and dissembling world
Of stilted sentiment suddenly melt
Into mush and watery welter of words
Beneath the warm and moving traffic of
Feet and actual fact. Over the stark plain
The stilted mill-chimneys once again spread
Their sackcloth and ashes, a flowing mane
Of repentance for the false day that's fled.

                                        W. R. Rodgers

Original Sin: A Short Story

Nodding, its great head rattling like a gourd,
And locks like seaweed strung on the stinking stone,
The nightmare stumbles past, and you have heard
It fumble your door before it whimpers and is gone:
It acts like the old hound that used to snuffle your door and
        moan.

You thought you had lost it when you left Omaha,
For it seemed connected then with your grandpa, who
Had a wen on his forehead and sat on the veranda
To finger the precious protuberance, as was his habit to do,
Which glinted in sun like rough garnet or the rich old brain
        bulging through.

But you met it in Harvard Yard as the historic steeple
Was confirming the midnight with its hideous racket,
And you wondered how it had come, for it stood so imbecile,
With empty hands, humble, and surely nothing in pocket:
Riding the rods, perhaps—or grandpa's will paid the ticket.

You were almost kindly then, in your first homesickness,
As it tortured its stiff face to speak, but scarcely mewed;
Since then you have outlived all your homesickness,
But have met it in many another distempered latitude:
Oh, nothing is lost, ever lost! at last you understood.

But it never came in the quantum glare of sun
To shame you before your friends, and had nothing to do
With your public experience or private reformation:
But it thought no bed too narrow—it stood with lips askew
And shook its great head sadly like the abstract Jew.

Never met you in the lyric arsenical meadow
When children call and your heart goes stone in the bosom;
At the orchard anguish never, nor ovoid horror,
Which is furred like a peach or avid like the delicious plum.
It takes no part in your classic prudence or fondled axiom.

Not there when you exclaimed: "Hope is betrayed by
Disastrous glory of sea-capes, sun-torment of whitecaps
—There must be a new innocence for us to be stayed by."
But there it stood, after all the timetables, all the maps,
In the crepuscular clutter of *always, always,* or *perhaps.*

You have moved often and rarely left an address,
And hear of the deaths of friends with a sly pleasure,

A sense of cleansing and hope, which blooms from distress;
But it has not died, it comes, its hand childish, unsure,
Clutching the bribe of chocolate or a toy you used to treasure

It tries the lock; you hear, but simply drowse:
There is nothing remarkable in that sound at the door.
Later you hear it wander the dark house
Like a mother who rises at night to seek a childhood picture
Or it goes to the backyard and stands like an old horse cold i
the pasture.

Robert Penn Warren

568 The Master

*(Lincoln. Supposed to have been written
not long after the Civil War)*

A flying word from there and there
Had sown the name at which we sneered,
But soon the name was everywhere,
To be reviled and then revered:
A presence to be loved and feared,
We cannot hide it, or deny
That we, the gentlemen who jeered,
May be forgotten by and by.

He came when days were perilous
And hearts of men were sore beguiled;
And having made his note of us,
He pondered and was reconciled.
Was ever master yet so mild
As he, and so untamable?
We doubted, even when he smiled,
Not knowing what he knew so well.

He knew that undeceiving fate
Would shame us whom he served unsought;
He knew that he must wince and wait—
The jest of those for whom he fought;
He knew devoutly what he thought
Of us and of our ridicule;
He knew that we must all be taught
Like little children in a school.

We gave a glamour to the task
That he encountered and saw through,
But little of us did he ask,
And little did we ever do.

And what appears if we review
The season when we railed and chaffed?
It is the face of one who knew
That we were learning while we laughed.

The face that in our vision feels
Again the venom that we flung,
Transfigured to the world reveals
The vigilance to which we clung,
Shrewd, hallowed, harassed, and among
The mysteries that are untold,
The face we see was never young,
Nor could it ever have been old.

For he, to whom we had applied
Our shopman's test of age and worth,
Was elemental when he died,
As he was ancient at his birth:
The saddest among kings of earth,
Bowed with a galling crown, this man
Met rancor with a cryptic mirth,
Laconic—and Olympian.

The love, the grandeur, and the fame
Are bounded by the world alone;
The calm, the smoldering, and the flame
Of awful patience were his own:
With him they are forever flown
Past all our fond self-shadowings,
Wherewith we cumber the Unknown
As with inept Icarian wings.

For we were not as other men:
'Twas ours to soar and his to see.
But we are coming down again,
And we shall come down pleasantly;
Nor shall we longer disagree
On what it is to be sublime,
But flourish in our perigee
And have one Titan at a time.

Edwin Arlington Robinson

The Stars Go Over the Lonely Ocean

Unhappy about some far off things
That are not my affair, wandering
Along the coast and up the lean ridges,
I saw in the evening

The stars go over the lonely ocean,
And a black-maned wild boar
Plowing with his snout on Mal Paso Mountain.

The old monster snuffled, "Here are sweet roots,
Fat grubs, slick beetles and sprouted acorns.
The best nation in Europe has fallen,
And that is Finland,
But the stars go over the lonely ocean,"
The old black-bristled boar,
Tearing the sod on Mal Paso Mountain.

"The world's in a bad way, my man,
And bound to be worse before it mends;
Better lie up in the mountain here
Four or five centuries,
While the stars go over the lonely ocean,"
Said the old father of wild pigs,
Plowing the fallow on Mal Paso Mountain.

"Keep clear of the dupes that talk democracy
And the dogs that bark revolution,
Drunk with talk, liars and believers,
I believe in my tusks.
Long live freedom and damn the ideologies,"
Said the gamey black-maned wild boar
Tusking the turf on Mal Paso Mountain.

Robinson Jeffe

570   **On Shooting Particles Beyond the World**

*"White Sands, N. M., Dec. 18 (UP). 'We first throw a little
something into the skies,' Zwicky said. 'Then a little more,
then a shipload of instruments—then ourselves.' "*

On this day man's disgust is known
Incipient before but now full blown
With minor wars of major consequence,
Duly building empirical delusions.

Now this little creature in a rage
Like new-born infant screaming compleat angler
Objects to the whole globe itself
And with a vicious lunge he throws

Metal particles beyond the orbit of mankind.
Beethoven shaking his fist at death,
A giant dignity in human terms,
Is nothing to this imbecile metal fury.

The world is too much for him. The green
Of earth is not enough, love's deities.

Peaceful intercourse, happiness of nations,
The wild animal dazzled on the desert.

If the maniac would only realize
The comforts of his padded cell
He would have penetrated the
Impenetrability of the spiritual.

It is not intelligent to go too far.
How he frets that he can't go too!
But his particles would maim a star,
His free-floating bombards rock the moon.

Good Boy! We pat the baby to eructate,
We pat him then for eructation.
Good Boy Man! Your innards are put out,
From now all space will be your vomitorium.

The atom bomb accepted this world,
Its hatred of man blew death in his face.
But not content, he'll send slugs beyond,
His particles of intellect will spit on the sun.

Not God he'll catch, in the mystery of space.
He flaunts his own out-cast state
As he throws his imperfections outward bound
And his shout that gives a hissing sound.

Richard Eberhart

571   **In the Proscenium**

The night, too long illumined, comes a stranger
Driving to roof this audience hard-weathered
Through the play of rage and bitter luck of danger.
Born to these uniform seats, they claim
No hunter's pleasure, the historic name.

Long foundered is our prow that feathered
The warm archaic wave.

The limelight warns, the need to worship waits
A serious humour, the laud-lifted clown.
The lights are fluorescent,
Pale, pale and cold, ice flickering incessant
As at Asgärd's fall, were north gods' twilight
Ceaselessly from no star.
The nerveless curtain, like dead water, parts.
Increasing thousands raise their long slow stare
To the pacified shroud, our silver screen of fêtes.

No choral song arises, no drama starts.
This pantomime, like beauty, only lies
In the entrancèd eyes.
Our mask of shadow comes, there pantaloon
How massive stands, anabasis of stone
Toward the prickling cells: the final form of Gilles.
Quick with electric chill
All profiles right and left unending freeze
Not as at death's pole or Gordon's locks,
But tight to one grounded wire, in paralysis.

Nothing will happen but fear's thrill on the nerve
Which makes the heart a nave.

If this were but enchantment or a dream
Even of solstice sacrifice, a rite
Of Druids moving with dark seasonal pace
Barefoot beneath Stonehenge's antique weight,
Endurance might ennoble the trancèd face
Or quell emotion with a natural light.

But here projection worse than mirror's spell
Our clown's oiled paradox
Drips from his skull and sockets' peacock pride.
The last cry for justice dies.
The sterile form of megalomaniac woe
Is malice; violence at recurrent speed
Is death's boredom motionless, thus is hell
Gone vacant, and so mocks.
The fawn has horned the doe.

The old, below their naked eyeballs' trance,
Recall Pierrot, the dance,
The silken lips, the fluttering love whose lease
Was years, fountains of smiles, the tears' duet
Before the risk was hate, the vines' empurpled lace.
The young lack memory. They fiercely throw
From the blank iris gun-glances for Gilles,
At Gilles, whose mask has the strength they make grow.

Innocent are their eyes, as pure as cruel,
Innocent of compassion, innocent as rue.
For the tuberose scent of love
Takes time and time to breathe;
This is amusement, to see the skull heave
Hard on the plastic ruff of hardened milk.

ven the young remember Punch. They're tough.
unch had these heavy hands, but not this bat-winged hulk.
hey have two hands for sticks, and hands enough.
yros of flowers and veterans of flight,
orn without firmament
the planetary prison with a ceiling for skies,
ne hour for love, short days,
hey may not wing like bees through hearts of flowers
ut wing like ants in regiments
apturing aphides.

he undecipherable fate of Cain,
is mark, may saturate us with clown's pain.

illes sates our hunger and bloats hypnotized
the proscenium. But he'll burst
the easy rain of bombs, our uranium sin.
he ascending dust will sift the son of Cain,
his generation dust, or lost, or dazed.

animals were equal at the first.
e studied hunch of bison claw of cat
or duels. In the deep caves of the bat
ur risk was beautiful.
ow, at the slaughter pen, moans the young bull.

hrist's love! Who dreed our weird? Nobility
roubles the heart in unexpected moments,
eart's ease.
                    New Human creatures tranquilly
ew seasons will inhabit, safe as the wren,
ike the lion the chicken the hyena,
atural as the veronica and the verbena,
agricultural health.

Gene Derwood

72   **Preludes**

(1)   The winter evening settles down
       With smell of steaks in passageways.
       Six o'clock.
       The burnt-out ends of smoky days.
       And now a gusty shower wraps
       The grimy scraps
       Of withered leaves about your feet
       And newspapers from vacant lots;
       The showers beat

On broken blinds and chimney-pots,
And at the corner of the street
A lonely cab-horse steams and stamps.
And then the lighting of the lamps.

(II) The morning comes to consciousness
Of faint stale smells of beer
From the sawdust-trampled street
With all its muddy feet that press
To early coffee-stands.
With the other masquerades
That time resumes,
One thinks of all the hands
That are raising dingy shades
In a thousand furnished rooms.

(III) You tossed a blanket from the bed,
You lay upon your back, and waited;
You dozed, and watched the night revealing
The thousand sordid images
Of which your soul was constituted;
They flickered against the ceiling.
And when all the world came back
And the light crept up between the shutters,
And you heard the sparrows in the gutters,
You had such a vision of the street
As the street hardly understands;
Sitting along the bed's edge, where
You curled the papers from your hair,
Or clasped the yellow soles of feet
In the palms of both soiled hands.

(IV) His soul stretched tight across the skies
That fade behind a city block,
Or trampled by insistent feet
At four and five and six o'clock;
And short square fingers stuffing pipes,
And evening newspapers, and eyes
Assured of certain certainties,
The conscience of a blackened street
Impatient to assume the world.
I am moved by fancies that are curled
Around these images, and cling:
The notion of some infinitely gentle
Infinitely suffering thing.
Wipe your hand across your mouth, and laugh;
The worlds revolve like ancient women
Gathering fuel in vacant lots.

T. S. Elio

573

The Congo

(A Study of the Negro Race)

I—THEIR BASIC SAVAGERY

A deep rolling bass

Fat black bucks in a wine-barrel room,
Barrel-house kings, with feet unstable,
Sagged and reeled and pounded on the table,
Pounded on the table,
Beat an empty barrel with the handle of a broom,
Hard as they were able,
Boom, boom, BOOM,
With a silk umbrella and the handle of a broom,

More deliberate. Solemnly chanted

Boomlay, boomlay, boomlay, BOOM.
THEN I had religion, THEN I had a vision.
I could not turn from their revel in derision.
THEN I SAW THE CONGO, CREEPING THROUGH THE
      BLACK,
CUTTING THROUGH THE JUNGLE WITH A GOLDEN
      TRACK.
Then along that riverbank
A thousand miles
Tattooed cannibals danced in files;
Then I heard the boom of the blood-lust son
And a thigh-bone beating on a tin-pan gong.
And "BLOOD!" screamed the whistles and the fifes
      of the warriors,

A rapidly boiling climax of speed and racket

"BLOOD!" screamed the skull-faced, lean witch-
      doctors;
"Whirl ye the deadly voo-doo rattle,
Harry the uplands,
Steal all the cattle,
Rattle-rattle, rattle-rattle, Bing!

With a philosophic pause

Boomlay, boomlay, boomlay, BOOM!"
A roaring, epic, rag-time tune
From the mouth of the Congo
To the Mountains of the Moon.
Death is an Elephant,

Shrilly and with a heavily accented metre

Torch-eyed and horrible,
Foam-flanked and terrible,
BOOM, steal the pygmies,
BOOM, kill the Arabs,
BOOM, kill the white men,
Hoo, Hoo, Hoo.

Like the wind in the chimney

Listen to the yell of Leopold's ghost
Burning in Hell for his hand-maimed host.

Hear how the demons chuckle and yell
Cutting his hands off down in Hell.
Listen to the creepy proclamation,
Blown through the lairs of the forest-nation,
Blown past the white-ants' hill of clay,
Blown past the marsh where the butterflies play:—

All the O sounds very golden. Heavy accents very heavy. Light accents very light. Last line whispered

"Be careful what you do,
Or Mumbo-Jumbo, god of the Congo,
And all of the other
Gods of the Congo,
Mumbo-Jumbo will hoo-doo you,
Mumbo-Jumbo will hoo-doo you,
Mumbo-Jumbo will hoo-doo you."

II—THEIR IRREPRESSIBLE HIGH SPIRITS

Rather shrill and high

Wild crap-shooters with a whoop and a call
Danced the juba in their gambling-hall,
And laughed fit to kill, and shook the town,
And guyed the policemen and laughed them down
With a boomlay, boomlay, boomlay, Boom.
THEN I SAW THE CONGO, CREEPING THROUGH THE
    BLACK,
CUTTING THROUGH THE JUNGLE WITH A GOLDEN
    TRACK.

Read exactly as in first section. Lay emphasis on the delicate ideas. Keep as light-footed as possible

A negro fairyland swung into view,
A minstrel river
Where dreams come true.
The ebony palace soared on high
Through the blossoming trees to the evening sky
The inlaid porches and casements shone
With gold and ivory and elephant-bone.
And the black crowd laughed till their sides were
    sore
At the baboon butler in the agate door,
And the well-known tunes of the parrot band
That trilled on the bushes of that magic land.
A troupe of skull-faced witch-men came

With pomposity

Through the agate doorway in suits of flame—
Yea, long-tailed coats with a gold-leaf crust
And hats that were covered with diamond dust.
And the crowd in the court gave a whoop and a call
And danced the juba from wall to wall.

With a great deliberation and ghostliness

But the witch-men suddenly stilled the throng
With a stern cold glare, and a stern old song:
"Mumbo-Jumbo will hoo-doo you." . . .

*With over-
whelming
assurance,
good cheer,
and pomp*

Just then from the doorway, as fat as shotes
Came the cake-walk princes in their long red coats,
Canes with a brilliant lacquer shine,
And tall silk hats that were red as wine.

*With grow-
ing speed
and sharply
marked
dance-
rhythm*

And they pranced with their butterfly partners
   there,
Coal-black maidens with pearls in their hair,
Knee-skirts trimmed with the jassamine sweet,
And bells on their ankles and little black feet.
And the couples railed at the chant and the frown
Of the witch-men lean, and laughed them down.
(Oh, rare was the revel, and well worth while
That made those glowering witch-men smile.)
The cake-walk royalty then began

*With a touch
of Negro dia-
lect, and as
rapidly as
possible to-
ward the end*

To walk for a cake that was tall as a man
To the tune of "Boomlay, boomlay, BOOM,"
While the witch-men laughed, with a sinister air,
And sang with the scalawags prancing there:
"Walk with care, walk with care,
Or Mumbo-Jumbo, god of the Congo,
And all of the other
Gods of the Congo,
Mumbo-Jumbo will hoo-doo you.
Beware, beware, walk with care,
Boomlay, boomlay, boomlay, boom,
Boomlay, boomlay, boomlay, boom,
Boomlay, boomlay, boomlay, boom,
Boomlay, boomlay, boomlay,
BOOM."

*Slow philo-
sophic calm*

Oh, rare was the revel, and well worth while
That made those glowering witch-men smile.

III—THE HOPE OF THEIR RELIGION

*Heavy bass.
With a literal
imitation of
camp-meet-
ing racket
and trance*

A good old Negro in the slums of the town
Preached at a sister for her velvet gown.
Howled at a brother for his low-down ways,
His prowling, guzzling, sneak-thief days.
Beat on the Bible till he wore it out
Starting the jubilee revival shout.
And some had visions, as they stood on chairs,
And sang of Jacob, and the golden stairs.
And they all repented, a thousand strong,
From their stupor and savagery and sin and wrong,
And slammed with their hymn-books till they
   shook the room

With "Glory, glory, glory."
And "Boom, boom, BOOM."
THEN I SAW THE CONGO, CREEPING THROUGH THE
 BLACK,
CUTTING THROUGH THE JUNGLE WITH A GOLDEN
 TRACK.

*Exactly as in
the first sec-
tion. Begin
with terror
and power,
end with joy*

And the gray sky opened like a new-rent veil
And showed the apostles with their coats of mail.
In bright white steel they were seated round,
And their fire-eyes watched where the Congo
 wound.

*Sung to the
tune of
"Hark, ten
thousand
harps and
voices"*

And the twelve Apostles, from their thrones on
 high,
Thrilled all the forest with their heavenly cry:
"Mumbo-Jumbo will die in the jungle;
Never again will he hoo-doo you,
Never again will he hoo-doo you."

*With grow-
ing delibera-
tion and joy*

Then along that river, a thousand miles,
The vine-snared trees fell down in files.
Pioneer angels cleared the way
For a Congo paradise, for babes at play,
For sacred capitals, for temples clean.
Gone were the skull-faced witch-men lean;

*In a rather
high key—as
delicately as
possible*

There, where the wild ghost-gods had wailed,
A million boats of the angels sailed
With oars of silver, and prows of blue,
And silken pennants that the sun shone through
'Twas a land transfigured, 'twas a new creation.
Oh, a singing wind swept the Negro nation,
And on through the backwoods clearing flew:—

*To the tune
of "Hark,
ten thousand
harps and
voices"*

"Mumbo-Jumbo is dead in the jungle.
Never again will he hoo-doo you,
Never again will he hoo-doo you."

Redeemed were the forests, the beasts and the
 men,
And only the vulture dared again

*Dying down
into a pene-
trating,
terrified
whisper*

By the far lone mountains of the moon
To cry, in the silence, the Congo tune:
"Mumbo-Jumbo will hoo-doo you,
Mumbo-Jumbo will hoo-doo you.
Mumbo . . . Jumbo . . . will . . . hoo-doo . . . you."
                              Vachel Lindsay

The Leaden-Eyed

Let not young souls be smothered out before
They do quaint deeds and fully flaunt their pride.
It is the world's one crime its babes grow dull,
Its poor are ox-like, limp and leaden-eyed.
Not that they starve, but starve so dreamlessly;
Not that they sow, but that they seldom reap;
Not that they serve, but have no gods to serve;
Not that they die, but that they die like sheep.

Vachel Lindsay

Exodus

Uranium cumulus mushrooms bursting sores
Upon empyrean lawns impressed Them there,
Beneath the wondrous tree; the poison spores
Of radiocirrus fungi spread fresh fare
For theoretic thought in triplicate.

In unison with single voice They spoke:
"Since Adam's day the sacrificial smoke
Has grown too lushy rank to tolerate;
Our primal verdict favoring industry
Took no account of this polluted air.

"That notion of expanding space may be
The stretch of time to save Our triune neck;
Let's pick a spot of universe to spare,
Perhaps between the Great and Lesser Bear,
And out of here right quickly get the heck!"

Roy Basler

To Brooklyn Bridge

How many dawns, chill from his rippling rest
The seagull's wings shall dip and pivot him,
Shedding white rings of tumult, building high
Over the chained bay waters Liberty—

Then, with inviolate curve, forsake our eyes
As apparitional as sails that cross
Some page of figures to be filed away;
—Till elevators drop us from our day . . .

I think of cinemas, panoramic sleights
With multitudes bent toward some flashing scene
Never disclosed, but hastened to again,
Foretold to other eyes on the same screen;

And Thee, across the harbor, silver-paced
As though the sun took step of thee, yet left
Some motion ever unspent in thy stride,—
Implicitly thy freedom staying thee!

Out of some subway scuttle, cell or loft
A bedlamite speeds to thy parapets,
Tilting there momently, shrill shirt ballooning,
A jest falls from the speechless caravan.

Down Wall, from girder into street noon leaks,
A rip-tooth of the sky's acetylene;
All afternoon the cloud-flown derricks turn . . .
Thy cables breathe the North Atlantic still.

And obscure as that heaven of the Jews,
Thy guerdon . . . Accolade thou dost bestow
Of anonymity time cannot raise:
Vibrant reprieve and pardon thou dost show.

O harp and altar, of the fury fused,
(How could mere toil align thy choiring strings!)
Terrific threshold of the prophet's pledge,
Prayer of pariah, and the lover's cry,—

Again the traffic lights that skim thy swift
Unfractioned idiom, immaculate sigh of stars,
Beading thy path—condense eternity:
And we have seen night lifted in thine arms.

Under thy shadow by the piers I waited;
Only in darkness is thy shadow clear.
The City's fiery parcels all undone,
Already snow submerges an iron year . . .

O Sleepless as the river under thee,
Vaulting the sea, the prairies' dreaming sod,
Unto us lowliest sometime sweep, descend
And of the curveship lend a myth to God.

Hart Crane

The Man with the Hoe

God made man in His own image
In the image of God He made him.—GENESIS

Bowed by the weight of centuries he leans
Upon his hoe and gazes on the ground,
The emptiness of ages in his face,
And on his back the burden of the world.
Who made him dead to rapture and despair,
A thing that grieves not and that never hopes,
Stolid and stunned, a brother to the ox?
Who loosened and let down this brutal jaw?
Whose was the hand that slanted back this brow?
Whose breath blew out the light within this brain?

Is this the Thing the Lord God made and gave
To have dominion over sea and land;
To trace the stars and search the heavens for power;
To feel the passion of Eternity?
Is this the dream He dreamed who shaped the suns
And markt their ways upon the ancient deep?
Down all the caverns of Hell to their last gulf
There is no shape more terrible than this—
More tongued with censure of the world's blind greed—
More filled with signs and portents for the soul—
More packt with danger to the universe.

What gulfs between him and the seraphim!
Slave of the wheel of labor, what to him
Are Plato and the swing of Pleiades?
What the long reaches of the peaks of song,
The rift of dawn, the reddening of the rose?
Through this dread shape the suffering ages look;
Time's tragedy is in that aching stoop;
Through this dread shape humanity betrayed,
Plundered, profaned and disinherited,
Cries protest to the Powers that made the world,
A protest that is also prophecy.

O masters, lords and rulers in all lands,
Is this the handiwork you give to God,
This monstrous thing distorted and soul-quencht?
How will you ever straighten up this shape;
Touch it again with immortality;
Give back the upward looking and the light;

Rebuild in it the music and the dream;
Make right the immemorial infamies,
Perfidious wrongs, immedicable woes?

O masters, lords and rulers in all lands,
How will the future reckon with this Man?
How answer his brute question in that hour
When whirlwinds of rebellion shake all shores?
How will it be with kingdoms and with kings—
With those who shaped him to the thing he is—
When this dumb Terror shall rise to judge the world,
After the silence of the centuries?

Edwin Markham

578   **Recessional**

God of our fathers, known of old—
Lord of our far-flung battle-line—
Beneath whose awful Hand we hold
    Dominion over palm and pine—
Lord God of Hosts, be with us yet,
Lest we forget, lest we forget!

The tumult and the shouting dies—
    The captains and the kings depart—
Still stands Thine ancient sacrifice,
    An humble and a contrite heart.
Lord God of Hosts, be with us yet,
Lest we forget, lest we forget!

Far-call'd our navies melt away—
    On dune and headland sinks the fire—
Lo, all our pomp of yesterday
    Is one with Nineveh and Tyre!
Judge of the Nations, spare us yet,
Lest we forget, lest we forget!

If, drunk with sight of power, we loose
    Wild tongues that have not Thee in awe—
Such boasting as the Gentiles use
    Or lesser breeds without the Law—
Lord God of Hosts, be with us yet,
Lest we forget, lest we forget!

For heathen heart that puts her trust
    In reeking tube and iron shard—

All valiant dust that builds on dust,
  And guarding calls not Thee to guard—
For frantic boast and foolish word,
Thy Mercy on Thy People, Lord!

Rudyard Kipling

The Second Coming

rning and turning in the widening gyre
e falcon cannot hear the falconer;
ings fall apart; the centre cannot hold;
ere anarchy is loosed upon the world,
e blood-dimmed tide is loosed, and everywhere
e ceremony of innocence is drowned;
e best lack all conviction, while the worst
e full of passionate intensity.

rely some revelation is at hand;
rely the Second Coming is at hand.
e Second Coming! Hardly are those words out
hen a vast image out of *Spiritus Mundi*
oubles my sight: somewhere in sands of the desert
shape with lion body and the head of a man,
gaze blank and pitiless as the sun,
moving its slow thighs, while all about it
el shadows of the indignant desert birds.
e darkness drops again; but now I know
at twenty centuries of stony sleep
ere vexed to nightmare by a rocking cradle,
d what rough beast, its hour come round at last,
ouches towards Bethlehem to be born?

William Butler Yeats

Journey of the Magi

cold coming we had of it,
st the worst time of the year
r a journey, and such a long journey:
e ways deep and the weather sharp,
e very dead of winter."
d the camels galled, sore-footed, refractory,
ing down in the melting snow.
ere were times we regretted
e summer palaces on slopes, the terraces,
d the silken girls bringing sherbet.
en the camel men cursing and grumbling

And running away, and wanting their liquor and women,
And the night-fires going out, and the lack of shelters,
And the cities hostile and the towns unfriendly
And the villages dirty and charging high prices:
A hard time we had of it.
At the end we preferred to travel all night,
Sleeping in snatches,
With the voices singing in our ears, saying
That this was all folly.

Then at dawn we came down to a temperate valley,
Wet, below the snow line, smelling of vegetation;
With a running stream and a water-mill beating the darkness
And three trees on the low sky,
And an old white horse galloped away in the meadow.
Then we came to a tavern with vine-leaves over the lintel,
Six hands at an open door dicing for pieces of silver,
And feet kicking the empty wine-skins.
But there was no information, and so we continued
And arrived at evening, not a moment too soon
Finding the place; it was (you may say) satisfactory.
All this was a long time ago, I remember,
And I would do it again, but set down
This set down
This: were we led all that way for
Birth or Death? There was a birth, certainly,
We had evidence and no doubt. I had seen birth and death
But had thought they were different; this Birth was
Hard and bitter agony for us, like Death, our death.
We returned to our places, these Kingdoms,
But no longer at ease here, in the old dispensation,
With an alien people clutching their gods.
I should be glad of another death.

T. S. Eliot

581   **The Last Supper**

I

Apostles of the hidden sun
Are come unto the room of breath
Hung with the banging blinds of death,
The body twelve, the spirit one,
Far as the eye, in earth arrayed,
The night shining, the supper laid.

II

The wine shone on the table that evening of history
Like an enormous ruby in the bauble and mystery.

In the glowing walls of the flickering decanter
There moved His face as at the world's center.

The hands of Judas showed up red and hurried
And the light hit them so, like a cross carried.

The faces of the others were there and moving
In the crystal of the dome, swiftly hovering.

The saints, under a lens, shrunken to pigmies,
Gesticulated in birds or in colored enigmas.

Outside there was a storm, the sound of temblors,
The blood bubbled and sprang into the tumblers.

When the morning came like a white wall of stone.
The day lay in the glass and the blood was gone.

Oscar Williams

Sonnets at Christmas

I

This is the day His hour of life draws near,
Let me get ready from head to foot for it
Most handily with eyes to pick the year
For small feed to reward a feathered wit.
Some men would see it an epiphany
At ease, at food and drink, others at chase
Yet I, stung lassitude, with ecstasy
Unspent argue the season's difficult case
So: Man, dull critter of enormous head,
What would he look at in the coiling sky?
But I must kneel again unto the Dead
While Christmas bells of paper white and red,
Figured with boys and girls spilt from a sled,
Ring out the silence I am nourished by.

Allen Tate

583   II

Ah, Christ, I love you rings to the wild sky
And I must think a little of the past:
When I was ten I told a stinking lie
That got a black boy whipped; but now at last
The going years, caught in an accurate glow,
Reverse like balls englished upon green baize—
Let them return, let the round trumpets blow
The ancient crackle of the Christ's deep gaze.
Deafened and blind, with senses yet unfound,
Am I, untutored to the after-wit
Of knowledge, knowing a nightmare has no sound;
Therefore with idle hands and head I sit
In late December before the fire's daze
Punished by crimes of which I would be quit.

                                                  Allen Ta

584   **Thou Art Indeed Just, Lord**

Justus quidem tu es, Domine, si disputem tecum: verumtam
justa loquar ad te: Quare vie impiorum prosperatur? etc.

Thou art indeed just, Lord, if I contend
With thee; but, sir, so what I plead is just.
Why do sinners' ways prosper? and why must
Disappointment all I endeavour end?
Wert thou my enemy, O thou my friend,
How wouldst thou worse, I wonder, than thou dost
Defeat, thwart me? Oh, the sots and thralls of lust
Do in spare hours more thrive than I that spend,
Sir, life upon thy cause. See, banks and brakes
Now, leavèd how thick! lacèd they are again
With fretty chervil, look, and fresh wind shakes
Them; birds build—but not I build; no, but strain,
Time's eunuch, and not breed one work that wakes.
Mine, O thou lord of life, send my roots rain.

                                           Gerard Manley Hopk

585   **The Oxen**

Christmas Eve, and twelve of the clock,
    "Now they are all on their knees,"
An elder said as we sat in a flock
    By the embers in hearthside ease.

We pictured the meek mild creatures where
    They dwelt in their strawy pen,
Nor did it occur to one of us there
    To doubt they were kneeling then.

So fair a fancy few would weave
    In these years! Yet, I feel,
If someone said on Christmas Eve,
    "Come; see the oxen kneel

"In the lonely barton by yonder coomb
    Our childhood used to know,"
I should go with him in the gloom,
    Hoping it might be so.

Thomas Hardy

586   Now stamp the Lord's Prayer on a grain of rice,
A Bible-leaved of all the written woods
Strip to this tree: a rocking alphabet,
Genesis in the root, the scarecrow word,
And one light's language in the book of trees;
Doom on deniers at the wind-turned statement.
Time's tune my ladies with the teats of music,
The scaled sea-sawers, fix in a naked sponge
Who sucks the bell-voiced Adam out of magic,
Time, milk, and magic, from the world beginning.
Time is the tune my ladies lend their heartbreak,
From bald pavilions and the house of bread
Time tracks the sound of shape on man and cloud,
On rose and icicle the ringing handprint.

Dylan Thomas

587   **As a Plane Tree by the Water**

Darkness has called to darkness, and disgrace
Elbows about our windows in this planned
Babel of Boston where our money talks
And multiplies the darkness of a land
Of preparation where the Virgin walks
And roses spiral her enamelled face
Or fall to splinters on unwatered streets.
Our Lady of Babylon, go by, go by,
I was once the apple of your eye;
Flies, flies are on the plane tree, on the streets.

The flies, the flies, the flies of Babylon
Buzz in my ear-drums while the devil's long
Dirge of the people detonates the hour
For floating cities where his golden tongue
Enchants the masons of the Babel Tower
To raise tomorrow's city to the sun
That never sets upon these hell-fire streets
Of Boston, where the sunlight is a sword
Striking at the withholder of the Lord:
Flies, flies are on the plane tree, on the streets.

Flies strike the miraculous waters of the iced
Atlantic and the eyes of Bernadette
Who saw Our Lady standing in the cave
At Massabielle, saw her so squarely that
Her vision put out reason's eyes. The grave
Is open-mouthed and swallowed up in Christ.
O walls of Jericho! And all the streets
To our Atlantic wall are singing: "Sing,
Sing for the resurrection of the King."
Flies, flies are on the plane tree, on the streets.

Robert Lowell

588   **Elegy: Separation of Man from God**

I   These errors loved no less than the saint loves arrows
Repeat, Love has left the world. He is not here.
O God, like Love revealing yourself in absence
So that, though farther than stars, like Love that sorrows
In separation, the desire in the heart of hearts
To come home to you makes you most manifest.
The booming zero spins as his halo where
Ashes of pride on all the tongues of sense
Crown us with negatives. O deal us in our deserts
The crumb of falling vanity. It is eucharist.

II Everyone walking everywhere goes in a glow
Of geometrical progression, all meteors, in praise:
Hosannas on the tongues of the dumb shall raise
Roads for the gangs in chains to return to
God. They go hugging the traumas like halleluias
To the bodies that earn this beatitude. The Seven
Seas they crowd like the great sailing Clippers,
Those homing migrants that, with their swallow-like
    sails set,
Swayed forward along the loneliness that opposed,
For nothing more than a meeting in heaven.

II Therefore all things, in all three tenses,
Alone like the statue in an alcove of love,
Moving in obedient machinery, sleeping
Happy in impossible achievements, keeping
Close to each other because the night is dark;
The great man dreaming on the stones of circumstances,
The small wringing hands because rocks will not move:
The beast in its red kingdom, the star in its arc:
O all things, therefore, in shapes or in senses,
Know that they exist in the kiss of his Love.

V Incubus. Anæsthetist with glory in a bag,
Foreman with a sweatbox and a whip. Asphyxiator
Of the ecstatic. Sergeant with a grudge
Against the lost lovers in the park of creation,
Fiend behind the fiend behind the fiend behind the
Friend. Mastodon with mastery, monster with an ache
At the tooth of the ego, the dead drunk judge:
Wheresoever Thou art our agony will find Thee
Enthroned on the darkest altar of our heartbreak
Perfect. Beast, brute, bastard. O dog my God!

George Barker

The Broken Tower

The bell-rope that gathers God at dawn
Dispatches me as though I dropped down the knell
Of a spent day—to wander the cathedral lawn
From pit to crucifix, feet chill on steps from hell.

Have you not heard, have you not seen that corps
Of shadows in the tower, whose shoulders sway
Antiphonal carillons launched before
The stars are caught and hived in the sun's ray?

The bells, I say, the bells break down their tower;
And swing I know not where. Their tongues engrave
Membrane through marrow, my long-scattered score
Of broken intervals. . . . And I, their sexton slave!

Oval encyclicals in canyons heaping
The impasse high with choir. Banked voices slain!
Pagodas, campaniles with reveilles outleaping—
O terraced echoes prostrate on the plain! . . .

And so it was I entered the broken world
To trace the visionary company of love, its voice

An instant in the wind (I know not whither hurled)
But not for long to hold each desperate choice.

My word I poured. But was it cognate, scored
Of that tribunal monarch of the air
Whose thigh embronzes earth, strikes crystal Word
In wounds pledged once to hope—cleft to despair?

The steep encroachments of my blood left me
No answer (could blood hold such a lofty tower
As flings the question true?)—or is it she
Whose sweet mortality stirs latent power?—

And through whose pulse I hear, counting the strokes
My veins recall and add, revived and sure
The angelus of wars my chest evokes:
What I hold healed, original now, and pure . . .

And builds, within, a tower that is not stone
(Not stone can jacket heaven)—but slip
Of pebbles—visible wings of silence sown
In azure circles, widening as they dip

The matrix of the heart, lift down the eye
That shrines the quiet lake and swells a tower . . .
The commodious, tall decorum of that sky
Unseals her earth, and lifts love in its shower.

Hart Crane

590   **Star'ight Night**

Look at the stars! look, look up at the skies!
    O look at all the fire-folk sitting in the air!
    The bright boroughs, the circle-citadels there!
Down in dim woods the diamond delves! the elves'-eyes!
The gray lawns cold where gold, where quickgold lies!
    Wind-beat whitebeam! airy abeles set on a flare!
    Flake-doves sent floating forth at a farmyard scare!
Ah, well! it is all a purchase, all is a prize.
Buy then! bid then!—What?—Prayer, patience, alms, vows
Look, look: a May-mess, like on orchard boughs!
    Look! March-bloom, like on mealed-with-yellow sallows
These are indeed the barn; withindoors house
The shocks. This piece-bright paling shuts the spouse
    Christ home, Christ and his mother and all his hallows.

Gerard Manley Hopkin

Once by the Pacific

The shattered water made a misty din.
Great waves looked over others coming in,
And thought of doing something to the shore
That water never did to land before.
The clouds were low and hairy in the skies,
Like locks blown forward in the gleam of eyes.
You could not tell, and yet it looked as if
The shore was lucky in being backed by cliff,
The cliff in being backed by continent;
It looked as if a night of dark intent
Was coming, and not only a night, an age.
Someone had better be prepared for rage.
There would be more than ocean-water broken
Before God's last *Put out the Light* was spoken.

Robert Frost

The Soul Selects Her Own Society

The soul selects her own society
Then shuts the door;
On her divine majority
Obtrude no more.

Unmoved, she notes the chariot's pausing
At her low gate;
Unmoved, an emperor is kneeling
Upon her mat.

I've known her from an ample nation
Choose one;
Then close the valves of her attention
Like stone.

Emily Dickinson

The Candle Indoors

Some candle clear burns somewhere I come by.
I muse at how its being puts blissful back
With yellowy moisture mild night's blear-all black,
Or to-fro tender trambeams truckle at the eye.
By that window what task what fingers ply,
I plod wondering, a-wanting, just for lack
Of answer the eagerer a-wanting Jessy or Jack
There, God to aggrándize, God to glorify.—

Come you indoors, come home; your fading fire
Mend first and vital candle in close heart's vault:
You there are master, do your own desire;
What hinders? Are you beam-blind, yet to a fault
In a neighbour deft-handed? Are you that liar
And, cast by conscience out, spendsavour salt?

Gerard Manley Hopkins

594   I could not sleep for thinking of the sky,
The unending sky, with all its million suns
Which turn their planets everlastingly
In nothing, where the fire-haired comet runs.
If I could sail that nothing, I should cross
Silence and emptiness with dark stars passing,
Then, in the darkness, see a point of gloss
Burn to a glow, and glare, and keep amassing,
And rage into a sun with wandering planets
And drop behind, and then, as I proceed,
See his last light upon his last moon's granites
Die to a dark that would be night indeed.
Night where my soul might sail a million years
In nothing, not even Death, not even tears.

John Masefield

595   **Byzantium**

The unpurged images of day recede;
The Emperor's drunken soldiery are abed;
Night resonance recedes, night-walkers' song
After great cathedral gong;
A starlit or a moonlit dome disdains
All that man is,
All mere complexities,
The fury and the mire of human veins.

Before me floats an image, man or shade,
Shade more than man, more image than a shade;
For Hades' bobbin bound in mummy-cloth
May unwind the winding path;
A mouth that has no moisture and no breath
Breathless mouths may summon;
I hail the superhuman;
I call it death-in-life and life-in-death.

Miracle, bird or golden handiwork,
More miracle than bird or handiwork,

Planted on the star-lit golden bough,
Can like the cocks of Hades crow,
Or, by the moon embittered, scorn aloud
In glory of changeless metal
Common bird or petal
And all complexities of mire or blood.

At midnight on the Emperor's pavement flit
Flames that no faggot feeds, nor steel has lit,
Nor storm disturbs, flames begotten of flame,
Where blood-begotten spirits come
And all complexities of fury leave,
Dying into a dance,
An agony of trance,
An agony of flame that cannot singe a sleeve.

Astraddle on the dolphin's mire and blood,
Spirit after spirit! The smithies break the flood,
The golden smithies of the Emperor!
Marbles of the dancing floor
Break bitter furies of complexity,
Those images that yet
Fresh images beget,
That dolphin-torn, that gong-tormented sea.

William Butler Yeats

Night on the Downland

Night is on the downland, on the lonely moorland,
On the hills where the wind goes over sheep-bitten turf,
Where the bent grass beats upon the unplowed poorland
And the pine-woods roar like the surf.

Here the Roman lived on the wind-barren lonely,
Dark now and haunted by the moorland fowl;
None comes here now but the peewit only,
And moth-like death in the owl.

Beauty was here on this beetle-droning downland;
The thought of a Caesar in the purple came
From the palace by the Tiber in the Roman townland
To this wind-swept hill with no name.

Lonely Beauty came here and was here in sadness,
Brave as a thought on the frontier of the mind,
In the camp of the wild upon the march of madness,
The bright-eyed Queen of the Blind.

Now where Beauty was are the wind-withered gorses,
Moaning like old men in the hill-wind's blast;
The flying sky is dark with running horses,
And the night is full of the past.

John Masefield

597   And yet this great wink of eternity,
        Of rimless floods, unfettered leewardings,
        Samite sheeted and processioned where
        Her undinal vast belly moonward bends,
        Laughing the wrapt inflections of our love;

        Take this Sea, whose diapason knells
        On scrolls of silver snowy sentences,
        The sceptred terror of whose sessions rends
        As her demeanors motion well or ill,
        All but the pieties of lovers' hands.

        And onward, as bells off San Salvador
        Salute the crocus lustres of the stars,
        In these poinsettia meadows of her tides,—
        Adagios of islands, O my Prodigal,
        Complete the dark confessions her veins spell.

        Mark how her turning shoulders wind the hours,
        And hasten while her penniles rich palms
        Pass superscription of bent foam and wave,—
        Hasten, while they are true,—sleep, death, desire,
        Close round one instant in one floating flower.

        Bind us in time, O Seasons clear, and awe.
        O minstrel galleons of Carib fire,
        Bequeath us to no earthly shore until
        Is answered in the vortex of our grave
        The seal's wide spindrift gaze toward paradise.

Hart Crane

598   **Perseus**

Borrowed wings on his ankles
Carrying a stone death
The hero entered the hall,
All in the hall looked up
Their breath frozen on them
And there was no more shuffle or clatter in the hall at all.

So a friend of a man comes in
And leaves a book he is lending or flowers

And goes again, alive but as good as dead,
And you are left alive, no better than dead,
And you dare not turn the leaden pages of the book or touch
    the flowers, the hooded and arrested hours.

Close your eyes,
There are suns beneath your lids
Or look in the looking-glass in the end room
You will find it full of eyes
The ancient smiles of men cut out with scissors and kept in
    mirrors.

Ever to meet me comes, in sun or dull,
The gay hero swinging the Gorgon's head
And I am left, with the dull drumming of the sun suspended
    and dead
Or the dumb grey-brown of the day is a leper's cloth
And one feels the earth going round and round the globe of
    the blackening mantle, a mad moth.

Louis MacNeice

599   An Extract
from Addresses to the Academy of Fine Ideas

On an early Sunday in April, a feeble day,
He felt curious about the winter hills
And wondered about the water in the lake.
It had been cold since December. Snow fell, first,
At New Year and, from then until April, lay
On everything. Now it had melted, leaving
The gray grass like a pallet, closely pressed;
And dirt. The wind blew in the empty place.
The winter wind blew in an empty place—
There was that difference between the and an,
The difference between himself and no man,
No man that heard a wind in an empty place.
It was time to be himself again, to see
If the place, in spite of its witheredness, was still
Within the difference. He felt curious
Whether the water was black and lashed about
Or whether the ice still covered the lake. There was still
Snow under the trees and on the northern rocks,
The dead rocks, not the green rocks, the live rocks. If,
When he looked, the water ran up the air or grew white
Against the edge of the ice, the abstraction would
Be broken and winter would be broken and done,
And being would be being himself again,
Being, becoming seeing and feeling and self,
Black water breaking into reality.

Wallace Stevens

The Labyrinth

Anthropos apteros for days
Walked whistling round and round the Maze,
Relying happily upon
His temperament for getting on.

The hundredth time he sighted, though,
A bush he left an hour ago,
He halted where four alleys crossed,
And recognised that he was lost.

"Where am I? Metaphysics says
No question can be asked unless
It has an answer, so I can
Assume this maze has got a plan.

If theologians are correct,
A Plan implies an Architect:
A God-built maze would be, I'm sure,
The Universe in miniature.

Are data from the world of Sense,
In that case, valid evidence?
What in the universe I know
Can give directions how to go?

All Mathematics would suggest
A steady straight line as the best,
But left and right alternately
Is consonant with History.

Aesthetics, though, believes all Art
Intends to gratify the Heart:
Rejecting disciplines like these,
Must I, then, go which way I please?

Such reasoning is only true
If we accept the classic view,
Which we have no right to assert,
According to the Introvert.

His absolute pre-supposition
Is—Man creates his own condition:
This maze was not divinely built,
But is secreted by my guilt.

The centre that I cannot find
Is known to my Unconscious Mind;
I have no reason to despair
Because I am already there.

My problem is how *not* to will;
They move most quickly who stand still;
I'm only lost until I see
I'm lost because I want to be.

If this should fail, perhaps I should,
As certain educators would,
Content myself with the conclusion;
In theory there is no solution.

All statements about what I feel,
Like I-am-lost, are quite unreal:
My knowledge ends where it began;
A hedge is taller than a man."

*Anthropos apteros, perplexed
To know which turning to take next,
Looked up and wished he were the bird
To whom such doubts must seem absurd.*

W. H. Auden

The Road Not Taken

Two roads diverged in a yellow wood,
And sorry I could not travel both
And be one traveller, long I stood
And looked down one as far as I could
To where it bent in the undergrowth;

Then took the other, as just as fair,
And having perhaps the better claim,
Because it was grassy and wanted wear;
Though as for that the passing there
Had worn them really about the same,

And both that morning equally lay
In leaves no step had trodden black.
Oh, I kept the first for another day!
Yet knowing how way leads on to way,
I doubted if I should ever come back.

I shall be telling this with a sigh
Somewhere ages and ages hence:
Two roads diverged in a wood, and I—
I took the one less travelled by,
And that has made all the difference.

Robert Frost

602 **The Atoll in the Mind**

Out of what calms and pools the cool shell grows
dumb teeth under clear waters, where no currents
fracture the coral's porous horn

Grows up the mind's stone tree, the honeycomb,
the plump brain coral breaking the pool's mirror,
the ebony antler, the cold sugared fan.

All these strange trees stand upward through the water,
the mind's grey candied points tend to the surface,
the greater part is out of sight below.

But when on the island's whaleback spring green blades
new land over water wavers, birds bring seeds
and tides plant slender trunks by the lagoon

I find the image of the mind's two trees, cast downward,
one tilting leaves to catch the sun's bright pennies,
one dark as water, rooted among the bones.

Alex Comfort

603 **Spenser's Ireland**

Has not altered;—
    the kindest place I've never been,
    the greenest place I've never seen.
Every name is a tune.
Denunciations do not affect
        the culprit;   nor blows, but it
is torture to him to not be spoken to.
They're natural,—
            the coat, like Venus'
mantle lined with stars,
buttoned close at the neck,—the
        sleeves new from disuse.

If in Ireland
    they play the harp backward at need,
    and gather at midday the seed
of the fern, eluding

their "giants all covered with iron," might
    there be fern   seed for unlearn-
ing obduracy and for reinstating
the enchantment?
        Hindered characters
seldom have mothers—
in Irish stories—
    but they all have grandmothers.

It was Irish;
   a match not a marriage was made
    when my great great grandmother'd said
with native genius for
disunion, "although your suitor be
    perfection,   one objection
is enough; he is not
Irish." Outwitting
    the fairies, befriending the furies,
whoever again
and again says, "I'll never
    give in," never sees

that you're not free
   until you've been made captive by
    supreme belief,—credulity
you say? When large dainty
fingers tremblingly divide the wings
    of the fly   for mid-July
with a needle and wrap it with peacock-tail,
or tie wool and
    buzzard's wing, their pride,
like the enchanter's
is in care, not madness. Con-
    curring hands divide

flax for damask
   that when bleached by Irish weather
    has the silvered chamois-leather
water-tightness of a
skin. Twisted torcs and gold new-moon-shaped
    lunulae   aren't jewelry
like the purple-coral fuchsia-tree's. If Eire—
"the guillemot
    so neat" and the hen
of the heath and "the
linnet spinet-sweet"—bespeak
    relentlessness, then

they are to me
   like enchanted Earl Gerald who
   changed himself into a stag, to
a great green-eyed cat of
the mountain. Discommodity makes
     them invis   ible; they've dis-
appeared. The Irish say "Your trouble is their
trouble and your
      joy their joy?" I wish
I could believe it;
I am troubled, I'm dissat-
    isfied, I'm Irish.

Marianne Moore

604   **Moonrise**

And who has seen the moon, who has not seen
Her rise from out the chamber of the deep,
Flushed and grand and naked, as from the chamber
Of finished bridegroom, seen her rise and throw
Confession of delight upon the wave,
Littering the waves with her own superscription
Of bliss, till all her lambent beauty shakes toward us
Spread out and known at last, and we are sure
That beauty is a thing beyond the grave,
That perfect, bright experience never falls
To nothingness, and time will dim the moon
Sooner than our full consummation here
In this odd life will tarnish or pass away.

D. H. Lawrence

605   **Success Is Counted Sweetest**

Success is counted sweetest
By those who ne'er succeed.
To comprehend a nectar
Requires sorest need.

Not one of all the purple host
Who took the flag to-day
Can tell the definition,
So clear, of victory,

As he, defeated, dying,
On whose forbidden ear
The distant strains of triumph
Break, agonized and clear.

Emily Dickinson

306

Anecdote of the Jar

I placed a jar in Tennessee,
And round it was, upon a hill.
It made the slovenly wilderness
Surround that hill.

The wilderness rose up to it,
And sprawled around, no longer wild.
The jar was round upon the ground
And tall and of a port in air.

It took dominion everywhere.
The jar was gray and bare.
It did not give of bird or bush,
Like nothing else in Tennessee.

Wallace Stevens

307

A Passer-By

Whither, O splendid ship, thy white sails crowding,
    Leaning across the bosom of the urgent West
That fearest nor sea rising, nor sky clouding,
    Whither away, fair rover, and what thy quest?
    Ah! soon, when Winter has all our vales opprest,
When skies are cold and misty, and hail is hurling,
    Wilt thou glide on the Blue Pacific, or rest
In a summer haven asleep, thy white sails furling.

I there before thee, in the country that well thou knowest,
    Already arrived am inhaling the odorous air:
I watch thee enter unerringly where thou goest,
    And anchor queen of the strange shipping there,
    Thy sails for awnings spread, thy masts bare;
Nor is aught from the foaming reef to the snow-capped,
        grandest
    Peak, that is over the feathery palms more fair
Than thou, so upright, so stately, and still thou standest.

And yet, O splendid ship, unhailed and nameless,
    I know not if, aiming a fancy, I rightly divine
That thou hast a purpose joyful, a courage blameless,
    Thy port assured in a happier land than mine.
    But for all I have given thee, beauty enough is thine,
As thou, aslant with trim tackle and shrouding,
    From the proud nostril curve of a prow's line
In the offing scatterest foam, thy white sails crowding.

Robert Bridges

608   To a Friend Whose Work Has Come to Nothing

Now all the truth is out,
Be secret and take defeat
From any brazen throat,
For how can you compete,
Being honor bred, with one
Who, were it proved he lies,
Were neither shamed in his own
Nor in his neighbors' eyes?
Bred to a harder thing
Than Triumph, turn away
And like a laughing string
Whereon mad fingers play
Amid a place of stone,
Be secret and exult,
Because of all things known
That is most difficult.

William Butler Yea

609   The Double Shame

You must live through the time when everything hurts
When the space of the ripe, loaded afternoon
Expands to a landscape of white heat frozen
And trees are weighed down with hearts of stone
And green stares back where you stare alone,
And the walking eyes throw flinty comments
And the words which carry most knives are the blind
Phrases searching to be kind.

Solid and usual objects are ghosts
The furniture carries great cargoes of memory,
The staircase has corners which remember
As fire blows most red in gusty embers,
And each empty dress cuts out an image
In fur and evening and summer and gold
Of her who was different in each.

Pull down the blind and lie on the bed
And clasp the hour in the glass of one room
Against your mouth like a crystal of doom
Take up the book and look at the letters
Hieroglyphs on sand and as meaningless—
Here birds crossed once and cries were uttered
In a mist where sight and sound are blurred.

For the story of those who made mistakes
Of one whose happiness pierced like a star
Eludes and evades between sentences
And the letters break into eyes which read
What the blood is now writing in your head
As though the characters sought for some clue
To their being so perfectly living and dead
In your story, worse than theirs, but true.

Set in the mind of their poet, they compare
Their tragic bliss with your trivial despair
And they have fingers which accuse
You of the double way of shame.
At first you did not love enough
And afterwards you loved too much
And you lacked the confidence to choose
And you have only yourself to blame.

Stephen Spender

610   **Mending Wall**

Something there is that doesn't love a wall,
That sends the frozen-ground-swell under it,
And spills the upper boulders in the sun;
And makes gaps even two can pass abreast.
The work of hunters is another thing:
I have come after them and made repair
Where they have left not one stone on a stone,
But they would have the rabbit out of hiding,
To please the yelping dogs. The gaps I mean,
No one has seen them made or heard them made,
But at spring mending-time we find them there.
I let my neighbor know beyond the hill;
And on a day we meet to walk the line
And set the wall between us once again.
We keep the wall between us as we go.
To each the boulders that have fallen to each.
And some are loaves and some so nearly balls
We have to use a spell to make them balance:
"Stay where you are until our backs are turned!"
We wear our fingers rough with handling them.
Oh, just another kind of out-door game,
One on a side. It comes to little more:
There where it is we do not need the wall:
He is all pine and I am apple orchard.
My apple trees will never get across
And eat the cones under his pines, I tell him.

He only says, "Good fences make good neighbors."
Spring is the mischief in me, and I wonder
If I could put a notion in his head:
"*Why* do they make good neighbors? Isn't it
Where there are cows? But here there are no cows.
Before I built a wall I'd ask to know
What I was walling in or walling out,
And to whom I was like to give offence.
Something there is that doesn't love a wall,
That wants it down." I could say "Elves" to him,
But it's not elves exactly, and I'd rather
He said it for himself. I see him there
Bringing a stone grasped firmly by the top
In each hand, like an old-stone savage armed.
He moves in darkness as it seems to me,
Not of woods only and the shade of trees.
He will not go behind his father's saying,
And he likes having thought of it so well
He says again, "Good fences make good neighbors."

Robert Frost

611   **Nearing Again the Legendary Isle**

Nearing again the legendary isle
Where sirens sang and mariners were skinned,
We wonder now what was there to beguile
That such stout fellows left their bones behind.
Those chorus-girls are surely past their prime,
Voices grow shrill and paint is wearing thin,
Lips that sealed up the sense from gnawing time
Now beg the favour with a graveyard grin.
We have no flesh to spare and they can't bite,
Hunger and sweat have stripped us to the bone;
A skeleton crew we toil upon the tide
And mock the theme-song meant to lure us on:
No need to stop the ears, avert the eyes
From purple rhetoric of evening skies.

C. Day Lewis

612   **Procne**

So she became a bird and bird-like danced
On a long sloe-bough, treading the silver blossom
With a bird's lovely feet,
And shaken blososms fell into the hands
Of sunlight, and he held them for a moment

And let them drop.
And in the autumn Procne came again
And leapt upon the crooked sloe-bough singing
And the dark berries winked like earth-dimmed beads,
As the branch swung beneath her dancing feet.

Peter Quennell

13   **The Listeners**

'Is there anybody there?' said the Traveller,
   Knocking on the moonlit door;
And his horse in the silence champ'd the grasses
   Of the forest's ferny floor:
And a bird flew up out of the turret,
   Above the Traveller's head:
And he smote upon the door again a second time;
   'Is there anybody there?' he said.
But no one descended to the Traveller;
   No head from the leaf-fringed sill
Lean'd over and look'd into his grey eyes,
   Where he stood perplex'd and still.
But only a host of phantom listeners
   That dwelt in the lone house then
Stood listening in the quiet of the moonlight
   To that voice from the world of men:
Stood thronging the faint moonbeams on the dark stair,
   That goes down to the empty hall,
Hearkening in an air stirr'd and shaken
   By the lonely Traveller's call.
And he felt in his heart their strangeness,
   Their stillness answering his cry,
While his horse moved, cropping the dark turf,
   'Neath the starr'd and leafy sky;
For he suddenly smote on the door, even
   Louder, and lifted his head:—
'Tell them I came, and no one answer'd,
   That I kept my word,' he said.
Never the least stir made the listeners,
   Though every word he spake
Fell echoing through the shadowiness of the still house
   From the one man left awake:
Ay, they heard his foot upon the stirrup,
   And the sound of iron on stone,
And how the silence surged softly backward,
   When the plunging hoofs were gone.

Walter De La Mare

614   **Warning to Children**

Children, if you dare to think
Of the greatness, rareness, muchness,
Fewness of this precious only
Endless world in which you say
You live, you think of things like this:
Blocks of slate enclosing dappled
Red and green, enclosing tawny
Yellow nets, enclosing white
And black acres of dominoes,
Where a neat brown paper parcel
Tempts you to untie the string,
In the parcel a small island,
On the island a large tree,
On the tree a husky fruit.
Strip the husk and cut the rind off:
In the centre you will see
Blocks of slate enclosed by dappled
Red and green, enclosed by tawny
Yellow nets, enclosed by white
And black acres of dominoes,
Where the same brown paper parcel—
Children, leave the string untied!
For who dares undo the parcel
Finds himself at once inside it,
On the island, in the fruit,
Blocks of slate about his head,
Finds himself enclosed by dappled
Green and red, enclosed by yellow
Tawny nets, enclosed by black
And white acres of dominoes,
But the same brown paper parcel
Still untied upon his knee.
And, if he then should dare to think
Of the fewness, muchness, rareness,
Greatness of this endless only
Precious world in which he says
He lives—he then unties the string.

                                        Robert Graves

615   **The Bells of Heaven**

'Twould ring the bells of Heaven
The wildest peal for years,
If Parson lost his senses
And people came to theirs,

And he and they together
Knelt down with angry prayers
For tamed and shabby tigers
And dancing dogs and bears,
And wretched, blind pit ponies,
And little hunted hares.

Ralph Hodgson

Heaven

Fish (fly-replete, in depth of June,
Dawdling away their wat'ry noon)
Ponder deep wisdom, dark or clear,
Each secret fishy hope or fear.
Fish say, they have their Stream and Pond;
But is there anything Beyond?
This life cannot be All, they swear,
For how unpleasant, if it were!
One may not doubt that, somehow, Good
Shall come of Water and of Mud;
And, sure, the reverent eye must see
A purpose in Liquidity.
We darkly know, by Faith we cry,
The future is not Wholly Dry.
Mud unto mud!—Death eddies near—
Not here the appointed End, not here!
But somewhere, beyond Space and Time,
Is wetter water, slimier slime!
And there (they trust) there swimmeth One
Who swam ere rivers were begun,
Immense, of fishy form and mind,
Squamous, omnipotent, and kind;
And under that Almighty Fin,
The littlest fish may enter in.
Oh! never fly conceals a hook,
Fish say, in the Eternal Brook,
But more than mundane weeds are there,
And mud, celestially fair;
Fat caterpillars drift around,
And Paradisal grubs are found;
Unfading moths, immortal flies,
And the worm that never dies.
And in that Heaven of all their wish,
There shall be no more land, say fish.

Rupert Brooke

Aladdin and the Jinn

"Bring me soft song," said Aladdin.
"This tailor-shop sings not at all.
Chant me a word of the twilight,
Of roses that mourn in the fall.
Bring me a song like hashish
That will comfort the stale and the sad,
For I would be mending my spirit,
Forgetting these days that are bad,
Forgetting companions too shallow,
Their quarrels and arguments thin,
Forgetting the shouting Muezzin:"—
"I AM YOUR SLAVE," said the Jinn.

"Bring me old wines," said Aladdin.
"I have been a starved pauper too long.
Serve them in vessels of jade and of shell,
Serve them with fruit and with song:—
Wines of pre-Adamite Sultans
Digged from beneath the black seas:—
New-gathered dew from the heavens
Dripped down from Heaven's sweet trees,
Cups from the angels' pale tables
That will make me both handsome and wise,
For I have beheld her, the princess,
Firelight and starlight her eyes.
Pauper I am, I would woo her.
And—let me drink wine, to begin,
Though the Koran expressly forbids it."
"I AM YOUR SLAVE," said the Jinn.

"Plan me a dome," said Aladdin,
"That is drawn like the dawn of the MOON,
When the sphere seems to rest on the mountains,
Half-hidden, yet full-risen soon.
Build me a dome," said Aladdin,
"That shall cause all young lovers to sigh,
The fullness of life and of beauty,
Peace beyond peace to the eye—
A palace of foam and of opal,
Pure moonlight without and within,
Where I may enthrone my sweet lady."
"I AM YOUR SLAVE," said the Jinn.

Vachel Lindsa

618

Stopping by Woods on a Snowy Evening

Whose woods these are I think I know.
His house is in the village though;
He will not see me stopping here
To watch his woods fill up with snow.

My little horse must think it queer
To stop without a farmhouse near
Between the woods and frozen lake
The darkest evening of the year.

He gives his harness bells a shake
To ask if there is some mistake.
The only other sound's the sweep
Of easy wind and downy flake.

The woods are lovely, dark and deep.
But I have promises to keep,
And miles to go before I sleep,
And miles to go before I sleep.

Robert Frost

619

The Fire in the Snow

White lambs leap. Through miles of snow
Across the muffled fields you go,
Frost-furled and gazing deep,
Lost in a world where white lambs leap.

Into a million eyes of light
You look, beneath that mask of white
Where lambs, wrinkled, without sound,
Bound in the air and print the ground.

You find through crystals white and wet
The buried breath of the violet,
And lost nearsunken cairns of stone
Drone-suckled flowers that breed alone.

Your shadow, black on the white snow-field,
Covers the blades your mind revealed.
You linger where gray rocks are still
Covered by a drifted hill.

Your eyes, I know, now read the tract
Beneath snow, where the grain lies packed,
Nor can the Winter sun deceive:
Black shuttles give you their leaves to weave.

Crisp, where you touch the secret loom,
Snow, from the fire-blue sky and from
A black root where all leaves begin,
Flames with a white light on your skin.

Come in. The brilliant, beautiful
Sun has dropped, and the noon-cracked pool
Freezes back. Come, seek from night
Gloom's fire, where the unlit room is white.

I wait, intent, by the firelit stones
Strewn with chopped wood and fallen cones.
Come in, and watch with me in dark
The red spark eating the black bark.

Bright, from fields where the snow lies thick,
From sunk fields to the latch's click
You come; and your eyes, most watchful, glow,
Seeing in the firelight the brightness of snow.

Vernon Watkins

620   **Milk at the Bottom of the Sea**

In the bowl of buildings *alias* the back yard
The milk of snow endlessly pours, but the bowl never
Fills. The century's live inhabitant caught behind
The window pane watches the single rakish tree
Blaze forth in ponderously immaculate italics.
The snowflakes pour everywhere in a panic, dizzyingly,
Or whirl to re-organize in the mid-air and float
Undecided; the sky tilts its ominous mountain, insuring
Another waterfall of snowflakes with all feathery speed.
Such activity should be noisy, a school's-out! of sounds,
But the silence is reverberating on the window glass
Exploring the deep-sea life of waywardness.

I am the traveller in the middle of the winter
In a wood-and-glass ship on the deeps of the age.
From peril's hold I watch the white germs from heaven
And blithe nothingness, the delicate roe of purity
Splurging to fill the air with their multipleness,
Making not even the sound of rain against rock.
I am an eye, I know, frozen in an undersea façade,
And have lost my hearing in such fantastic depths
Where the pressures cave in the senses, but still
My eye kindles to all this whiteness bearing down
In a dance of spiritual blindspots on our town.

In the end the wandering snowflakes are driven
Together, foam fat in the bottom of time, and I
Assuage through the mouth of the mind my entity;
The army of my veins, blood-drops, pores, thoughts,
Crowds to my bones in one supreme act of gravity,
Closer than earth to a hill, than leaves to a tree,
Till I am the very body of oneness and cannot go
Pure, cold, diffuse and wayward like the snow.

Oscar Williams

1 Snow

he room was suddenly rich and the great bay-window was
awning snow and pink roses against it
undlessly collateral and incompatible:
orld is suddener than we fancy it.

orld is crazier and more of it than we think,
corrigibly plural. I peel and portion
tangerine and spit the pips and feel
he drunkenness of things being various.

nd the fire flames with a bubbling sound for world
more spiteful and gay than one supposes—
n the tongue on the eyes on the ears in the palms of your
hands—
here is more than glass between the snow and the huge roses.

Louis MacNeice

2 The Lake Isle of Innisfree

will arise and go now, and go to Innisfree,
nd a small cabin build there, of clay and wattles made;
ine bean rows will I have there, a hive for the honey bee,
And live alone in the bee-loud glade.

nd I shall have some peace there, for peace comes dropping
slow,
ropping from the veils of the morning to where the cricket
sings;
here midnight's all a-glimmer, and noon a purple glow,
And evening full of the linnet's wings.

will arise and go now, for always night and day
hear lake water lapping with low sounds by the shore;
hile I stand on the roadway, or on the pavements gray,
I hear it in the deep heart's core.

William Butler Yeats

623   I shall go back again to the bleak shore
And build a little shanty on the sand
In such a way that the extremest band
Of brittle seaweed will escape my door
But by a yard or two, and nevermore
Shall I return to take you by the hand;
I shall be gone to what I understand
And happier than I ever was before.

The love that stood a moment in your eyes,
The words that lay a moment on your tongue,
Are one with all that in a moment dies,
A little under-said and over-sung;
But I shall find the sullen rocks and skies
Unchanged from what they were when I was young.

Edna St. Vincent Millay

624   **The West Wind**

It's a warm wind, the west wind, full of birds' cries;
I never hear the west wind but tears are in my eyes.
For it comes from the west lands, the old brown hills,
And April's in the west wind, and daffodils.

It's a fine land, the west land, for hearts as tired as mine,
Apple orchards blossom there, and the air's like wine.
There is cool green grass there, where men may lie at rest,
And the thrushes are in song there, fluting from the nest.

"Will ye not come home, brother? ye have been long away
It's April, and blossom time, and white is the may:
And bright is the sun, brother, and warm is the rain,—
Will ye not come home, brother, home to us again?

"The young corn is green, brother, where the rabbits run,
It's blue sky, and white clouds, and warm rain and sun.
It's song to a man's soul, brother, fire to a man's brain,
To hear the wild bees and see the merry spring again.

"Larks are singing in the west, brother, above the green wheat,
So will ye not come home, brother, and rest your tired feet,
I've a balm for bruised hearts, brother, sleep for aching eyes,
Says the warm wind, the west wind, full of birds' cries.

It's the white road westwards is the road I must tread
To the green grass, the cool grass, and rest for heart and head,
To the violets and the warm hearts and the thrushes' song,
In the fine land, the west land, the land where I belong.

John Masefield

25
First Warm Days

April, up on a twig a leaftuft stands
And heaven lifts a hundred miles mildly
Comes and fondles our faces, playing friends—
Such a one day often concludes coldly—
Then in dark coats in the bare afternoon view
Idle people—we few who that day are—
Stroll in the park aimless and stroll by twos
Easy in the weather of our home star.
And human faces—hardly changed after
Millennia—the separate single face
Placid, it turns toward friendly laughing
Or makes an iridescence, being at peace.
We all are pleased by an air like of loving
Going home quiet in the subway-shoving.

Edwin Denby

26
Shopping for Meat in Winter

What lewd, naked and revolting shape is this?
A frozen oxtail in the butcher's shop
Long and lifeless upon the huge block of wood
On which the ogre's axe begins *chop chop*.

The sun like incense fumes on the smoky glass,
The street frets with people, the winter wind
Throws knives, prices dangle from shoppers' mouths
While the grim vegetables, on parade, bring to mind

The great countryside bathed in golden sleep,
The trees, the bees, the soft peace everywhere—
I think of the cow's tail, how all summer long
It beat the shapes of harps into the air.

Oscar Williams

27
Adlestrop

Yes, I remember Adlestrop—
The name—because one afternoon
Of heat the express-train drew up there
Unwontedly. It was late June.

The steam hissed. Someone cleared his throat.
No one left and no one came
On the bare platform. What I saw
Was Adlestrop—only the name—

And willows, willow-herb, and grass,
And meadowsweet, and haycocks dry;
No whit less still and lonely fair
Than the high cloudlets in the sky.

And for that minute a blackbird sang
Close by, and round him, mistier,
Farther and farther, all the birds
Of Oxfordshire and Gloucestershire.

Edward Thomas

628   **Come In**

As I came to the edge of the woods,
Thrush music—hark!
Now if it was dusk outside,
Inside it was dark.

The dark in the woods for a bird
By sleight of wing
To better its perch for the night,
Though it still could sing.

The last of the light of the sun
That had died in the west
Still lived for one song more
In a thrush's breast.

Far in the pillared dark
Thrush music went—
Almost like a call to come in
To the dark and lament.

But no, I was out for stars:
I would not come in.
I meant not even if asked;
And I hadn't been.

Robert Frost

629   **Mirage**

The wind was in another country, and
the day had gathered to its heart of noon
the sum of silence, heat, and stricken time.
Not a ripple spread. The sea mirrored
perfectly all the nothing in the sky.
We had to walk about to keep our eyes

from seeing nothing, and our hearts from stopping
at nothing. Then most suddenly we saw
horizon on horizon lifting up
out of the sea's edge a shining mountain
sun-yellow and sea-green; against it surf
flung spray and spume into the miles of sky.
Somebody said mirage, and it was gone,
but there I have been living ever since.

R. P. Blackmur

30   On Hearing a Symphony of Beethoven

Sweet sounds, oh, beautiful music, do not cease!
Reject me not into the world again.
With you alone is excellence and peace,
Mankind made plausible, his purpose plain.
Enchanted in your air benign and shrewd,
With limbs a-sprawl and empty faces pale,
The spiteful and the stingy and the rude
Sleep like the scullions in the fairy-tale.
This moment is the best the world can give:
The tranquil blossom on the tortured stem.
Reject me not, sweet sounds; oh, let me live,
Till Doom espy my towers and scatter them,
A city spell-bound under the aging sun.
Music my rampart, and my only one.

Edna St. Vincent Millay

31   Lapis Lazuli

I have heard that hysterical women say
They are sick of the palette and fiddle-bow,
Of poets that are always gay,
For everybody knows or else should know
That if nothing drastic is done
Aeroplane and Zeppelin will come out,
Pitch like King Billy bomb-balls in
Until the town lie beaten flat.

All perform their tragic play,
There struts Hamlet, there is Lear,
That's Ophelia, that Cordelia;
Yet they, should the last scene be there,
The great stage curtain about to drop,
If worthy their prominent part in the play,
Do not break up their lines to weep.

They know that Hamlet and Lear are gay;
Gaiety transfiguring all that dread.
All men have aimed at, found and lost;
Black out; Heaven blazing into the head:
Tragedy wrought to its uttermost.
Though Hamlet rambles and Lear rages,
And all the drop-scenes drop at once
Upon a hundred thousand stages,
It cannot grow by an inch or an ounce.

On their own feet they came, or on shipboard,
Camel-back, horse-back, ass-back, mule-back,
Old civilizations put to the sword.
Then they and their wisdom went to rack:
No handiwork of Callimachus,
Who handled marble as if it were bronze,
Made draperies that seemed to rise
When sea-winds swept the corner, stands;
His long lamp-chimney shaped like the stem
Of a slender palm, stood but a day;
All things fall and are built again,
And those that build them again are gay.

Two Chinamen, behind them a third,
Are carved in lapis lazuli,
Over them flies a long-legged bird,
A symbol of longevity;
The third, doubtless a serving-man,
Carries a musical instrument.

Every discoloration of the stone,
Every accidental crack or dent,
Seems a water-course or an avalanche,
Or lofty slope where it still snows
Though doubtless plum or cherry-branch
Sweetens the little half-way house
Those Chinamen climb towards, and I
Delight to imagine them seated there;
There, on the mountain and the sky,
On all the tragic scene they stare.
One asks for mournful melodies;
Accomplished fingers begin to play.
Their eyes mid many wrinkles, their eyes,
Their ancient, glittering eyes, are gay.

                              William Butler Yeat

Voltaire at Ferney

erfectly happy now, he looked at his estate.
An exile making watches glanced up as he passed
And went on working; where a hospital was rising fast,
A joiner touched his cap; an agent came to tell
ome of the trees he'd planted were progressing well.
The white alps glittered. It was summer. He was very great.

Far off in Paris where his enemies
Whispered that he was wicked, in an upright chair
A blind old woman longed for death and letters. He would
    write,
"Nothing is better than life." But was it? Yes, the fight
Against the false and the unfair
Was always worth it. So was gardening. Civilize.

Cajoling, scolding, screaming, cleverest of them all,
He'd had the other children in a holy war
Against the infamous grown-ups; and, like a child, been sly
And humble, when there was occasion for
The two-faced answer or the plain protective lie,
But, patient like a peasant, waited for their fall.

And never doubted, like D'Alembert, he would win:
Only Pascal was a great enemy, the rest
Were rats already poisoned; there was much, though, to be
    done,
And only himself to count upon.
Dear Diderot was dull but did his best;
Rousseau, he'd always known, would blubber and give in.

Night fell and made him think of women: Lust
Was one of the great teachers; Pascal was a fool.
How Emilie had loved astronomy and bed;
Pimpette had loved him too, like scandal; he was glad.
He'd done his share of weeping for Jerusalem: As a rule,
It was the pleasure-haters who became unjust.

Yet, like a sentinel, he could not sleep. The night was full of
    wrong,
Earthquakes and executions: Soon he would be dead,
And still all over Europe stood the horrible nurses
Itching to boil their children. Only his verses
Perhaps could stop them: He must go on working: Overhead,
The uncomplaining stars composed their lucid song.

                                        W. H. Auden

Herman Melville

Towards the end he sailed into an extraordinary mildnes
And anchored in his home and reached his wife
And rode within the harbour of her hand,
And went across each morning to an office
As though his occupation were another island.

Goodness existed: that was the new knowledge.
His terror had to blow itself quite out
To let him see it; but it was the gale had blown him
Past the Cape Horn of sensible success
Which cries: "This rock is Eden. Shipwreck here."

But deafened him with thunder and confused with lightning
—The maniac hero hunting like a jewel
The rare ambiguous monster that had maimed his sex,
Hatred for hatred ending in a scream,
The unexplained survivor breaking off the nightmare—
All that was intricate and false; the truth was simple.

Evil is unspectacular and always human,
And shares our bed and eats at our own table,
And we are introduced to Goodness every day,
Even in drawing-rooms among a crowd of faults;
He has a name like Billy and is almost perfect
But wears a stammer like a decoration:
And every time they meet the same thing has to happen;
It is the Evil that is helpless like a lover
And has to pick a quarrel and succeeds,
And both are openly destroyed before our eyes.

For now he was awake and knew
No one is ever spared except in dreams;
But there was something else the nightmare had distorted—
Even the punishment was human and a form of love:
The howling storm had been his father's presence
And all the time he had been carried on his father's breast

Who now had set him gently down and left him.
He stood upon the narrow balcony and listened:
And all the stars above him sang as in his childhood
"All, all is vanity," but it was not the same;
For now the words descended like the calm of mountains
—Nathaniel had been shy because his love was selfish—
But now he cried in exultation and surrender
"The Godhead is broken like bread. We are the pieces."

And sat down at his desk and wrote a story.

                                        W. H. Aude

n Memory of W. B. Yeats

(d. Jan. 1939)

I

Ie disappeared in the dead of winter:
The brooks were frozen, the air-ports almost deserted,
And snow disfigured the public statues;
The mercury sank in the mouth of the dying day.
O all the instruments agree
The day of his death was a dark cold day.

Far from his illness
The wolves ran on through the evergreen forests,
The peasant river was untempted by the fashionable quays;
By mourning tongues
The death of the poet was kept from his poems.

But for him it was his last afternoon as himself,
An afternoon of nurses and rumours;
The provinces of his body revolted,
The squares of his mind were empty,
Silence invaded the suburbs,
The current of his feeling failed: he became his admirers.

Now he is scattered among a hundred cities
And wholly given over to unfamiliar affections;
To find his happiness in another kind of wood
And be punished under a foreign code of conscience.
The words of a dead man
Are modified in the guts of the living.

But in the importance and noise of to-morrow
When the brokers are roaring like beasts on the floor of the
    Bourse,
And the poor have the sufferings to which they are fairly
    accustomed,
And each in the cell of himself is almost convinced of his
    freedom;
A few thousand will think of this day
As one thinks of a day when one did something slightly un-
    usual.

O all the instruments agree
The day of his death was a dark cold day.

II

You were silly like us: your gift survived it all;
The parish of rich women, physical decay,
Yourself; mad Ireland hurt you into poetry.
Now Ireland has her madness and her weather still,
For poetry makes nothing happen: it survives
In the valley of its saying where executives
Would never want to tamper; it flows south
From ranches of isolation and the busy griefs,
Raw towns that we believe and die in; it survives,
A way of happening, a mouth.

III

Earth, receive an honoured guest;
William Yeats is laid to rest:
Let the Irish vessel lie
Emptied of its poetry.

Time that is intolerant
Of the brave and innocent,
And indifferent in a week
To a beautiful physique,

Worships language and forgives
Everyone by whom it lives;
Pardons cowardice, conceit,
Lays its honours at their feet.

Time that with this strange excuse
Pardoned Kipling and his views,
And will pardon Paul Claudel,
Pardons him for writing well.

In the nightmare of the dark
All the dogs of Europe bark,

And the living nations wait,
Each sequestered in its hate;

Intellectual disgrace
Stares from every human face,
And the seas of pity lie
Locked and frozen in each eye.

Follow, poet, follow right
To the bottom of the night,
With your unconstraining voice
Still persuade us to rejoice;

With the farming of a verse
Make a vineyard of the curse
Sing of human unsuccess
In a rapture of distress;

In the deserts of the heart
Let the healing fountain start
In the prison of his days
Teach the free man how to praise.

W. H. Auden

In Love for Long

335

I've been in love for long
With what I cannot tell
And will contrive a song
For the intangible
That has no mould or shape,
From which there's no
  escape.

It is not even a name,
Yet is all constancy;
Tried or untried, the same,
It cannot part from me;
A breath, yet as still
As the established hill.

It is not any thing,
And yet all being is;
Being, being, being,
Its burden and its bliss.
How can I ever prove
What it is I love?

This happy happy love
I sieged with crying sorrows,
Crushed beneath and above
Between to-days and mor-
  rows;
A little paradise
Held in the world's vice.

And there it is content
And careless as a child,
And in imprisonment
Flourishes sweet and wild;
In wrong, beyond wrong,
All the world's day long.

This love a moment known
For what I do not know
And in a moment gone
Is like the happy doe
That keeps its perfect laws
Between the tiger's paws
And vindicates its cause.

Edwin Muir

In My Craft or Sullen Art

336

In my craft or sullen art
Exercised in the still night
When only the moon rages
And the lovers lie abed
With all their griefs in their
  arms,
I labour by singing light
Not for ambition or bread
Or the strut and trade of
  charms
On the ivory stages
But for the common wages
Of their most secret heart.

Not for the proud man apart
From the raging moon I write
On these spindrift pages
Not for the towering dead
With their nightingales and
  psalms
But for the lovers, their arms
Round the griefs of the ages,
Who pay no praise or wages
Nor heed my craft or art.

Dylan Thomas

The Bards

337

Their cheeks are blotched for shame, their running verse
Stumbles, with marrow-bones the drunken diners
Pelt them as they delay:
It is a something fearful in the song

Plagues them, an unknown grief that like a churl
Goes commonplace in cowskin
And bursts unheralded, crowing and coughing,
An unpilled holly-club twirled in his hand,
Into their many-shielded, samite-curtained
Jewel-bright hall where twelve kings sit at chess
Over the white-bronze pieces and the gold,
And by a gross enchantment
Flails down the rafters and leads off the queens—
The wild-swan-breasted, the rose-ruddy-cheeked
Raven-haired daughters of their admiration—
To stir his black pots and to bed on straw.

Robert Graves

638   **You, Andrew Marvell**

And here face down beneath the sun
And here upon earth's noonward height
To feel the always coming on
The always rising of the night

To feel creep up the curving east
The earthy chill of dusk and slow
Upon those under lands the vast
And ever climbing shadow grow

And strange at Ecbatan the trees
Take leaf by leaf the evening strange
The flooding dark about their knees
The mountains over Persia change

And now at Kermanshah the gate
Dark empty and the withered grass
And through the twilight now the late
Few travelers in the westward pass

And Baghdad darken and the bridge
Across the silent river gone
And through Arabia the edge
Of evening widen and steal on

And deepen on Palmyra's street
The wheel rut in the ruined stone
And Lebanon fade out and Crete
High through the clouds and overblown

And over Sicily the air
Still flashing with the landward gulls
And loom and slowly disappear
The sails above the shadowy hulls

And Spain go under and the shore
Of Africa the gilded sand
And evening vanish and no more
The low pale light across that land

Nor now the long light on the sea

And here face downward in the sun
To feel how swift how secretly
The shadow of the night comes on . . .

Archibald MacLeish

39. A Coat

made my song a coat
Covered with embroideries
Out of old mythologies
From heel to throat;
But the fools caught it,

Wore it in the world's eyes
As though they'd wrought it.
Song, let them take it,
For there's more enterprise
In walking naked.

William Butler Yeats

40. Envoi

Go, dumb-born book,
Tell her that sang me once that song of Lawes:
Hadst thou but song
As thou hast subjects known,
Then were there cause in thee that should condone
Even my faults that heavy upon me lie,
And build her glories their longevity.

Tell her that sheds
Such treasure in the air,
Recking naught else but that her graces give
Life to the moment,
I would bid them live
As roses might, in magic amber laid,
Red overwrought with orange and all made
One substance and one colour
Braving time.

Tell her that goes
With song upon her lips
But sings not out the song, nor knows
The maker of it, some other mouth,
May be as fair as hers,
Might, in new ages, gain her worshippers,
When our two dusts with Waller's shall be laid,
Siftings on siftings in oblivion,
Till change hath broken down
All things save Beauty alone.

Ezra Pound

Poetry

I, too, dislike it: there are things that are important beyond
      all this fiddle.
    Reading it, however, with a perfect contempt for it, one
      discovers in
it after all, a place for the genuine.
      Hands that can grasp, eyes
        that can dilate, hair that can rise
          if it must, these things are important not because a

high-sounding interpretation can be put upon them but because
      they are
    useful. When they become so derivative as to become
      unintelligible,
the same thing may be said for all of us, that we
      do not admire what
      we cannot understand: the bat
        holding on upside down or in quest of something to

eat, elephants pushing, a wild horse taking a roll, a tireless
      wolf under
    a tree, the immovable critic twitching his skin like a horse
      that feels a flea, the base-
ball fan, the statistician—
      nor is it valid
      to discriminate against "business documents and

school-books"; all these phenomena are important. One must
      make a distinction
    however: when dragged into prominence by half poets, the
      result is not poetry,
nor till the poets among us can be
      "literalists of
      the imagination"—above
        insolence and triviality and can present

for inspection, "imaginary gardens with real toads in them," *
      shall we have
    it. In the meantime, if you demand on the one hand,
      the raw material of poetry in
    all its rawness and
    that which is on the other hand
      genuine, then you are interested in poetry.

                        Marianne Moore

* *A quotation from W. B. Yeats' "Ideas of Good and Evil."*

Ars Poetica

A poem should be palpable and mute
As a globed fruit

Dumb
As old medallions to the thumb

Silent as the sleeve-worn stone
Of casement ledges where the moss has grown—

A poem should be wordless
As the flight of birds

A poem should be motionless in time
As the moon climbs

Leaving, as the moon releases
Twig by twig the night-entangled trees,

Leaving, as the moon behind the winter leaves,
Memory by memory the mind—

A poem should be motionless in time
As the moon climbs

A poem should be equal to:
Not true

For all the history of grief
An empty doorway and a maple leaf

For love
The leaning grasses and two lights above the sea—

A poem should not mean
But be.

Archibald MacLeish

A Pact

I make a pact with you, Walt Whitman—
I have detested you long enough.
I come to you as a grown child
Who has had a pig-headed father;
I am old enough now to make friends.
It was you that broke the new wood,
Now is a time for carving.
We have one sap and one root—
Let there be commerce between us.

Ezra Pound

This day winding down now
At God speeded summer's
end
In the torrent salmon sun,
In my seashaken house
On a breakneck of rocks
Tangled with chirrup and
fruit,
Froth, flute, fin and quill
At a wood's dancing hoof,
By scummed, starfish sands
With their fishwife cross
Gulls, pipers, cockles, and
sails,
Out there, crow black, men
Tackled with clouds, who
kneel
To the sunset nets,
Geese nearly in heaven, boys
Stabbing, and herons, and
shells
That speak seven seas,
Eternal waters away
From the cities of nine
Days' night whose towers will
catch
In the religious wind
Like stalks of tall, dry straw,
At poor peace I sing
To you strangers (though
song
Is a burning and crested act,
The fire of birds in
The world's turning wood,
For my sawn, splay sounds),
Out of these seathumbed
leaves
That will fly and fall
Like leaves of trees and as
soon
Crumble and undie
Into the dogdayed night.
Seaward the salmon, sucked
sun slips,

And the dumb swans drub
blue
My dabbed bay's dusk, as I
hack
This rumpus of shapes
For you to know
How I, a spinning man,
Glory also this star, bird
Roared, sea born, man torn,
blood blest.
Hark: I trumpet the place,
From fish to jumping hill!
Look:
I build my bellowing ark
To the best of my love
As the flood begins,
Out of the fountainhead
Of fear, rage red, manalive,
Molten and mountainous to
stream
Over the wound asleep
Sheep white hollow farms

To Wales in my arms,
Hoo, there, in castle keep,
You king singsong owls, who
moonbeam
The flickering runs and dive
The dingle furred deer dead!
Huloo, on plumbed bryns,
O my ruffled ring dove
In the hooting, nearly dark
With Welsh and reverent
rook,
Coo rooing the woods' praise,
Who moons her blue notes
from her nest
Down to the curlew herd!
Ho, hullaballoing clan
Agape with woe
In your beaks, on the gabbing
capes!
Heigh, on horseback hill, jack
Whisking hare! who

Hears, there, this fox light,
   my flood ship's
Clangour as I hew and smite
A clash of anvils for my
Hubbub and fiddle, this tune
(On a tongued puffball)
But animals thick as thieves
On God's rough tumbling
   grounds
Hail to His beasthood!).
Beasts who sleep good and
   thin,
Hist, in hogsback woods!
   The haystacked
Hollow farms in a throng
Of waters cluck and cling,
And barnroofs cockcrow war!
O kingdom of neighbours,
   finned
Felled and quilled, flash to
   my patch
Work ark and the moonshine
Drinking Noah of the bay,
With pelt, and scale, and
   fleece:

Only the drowned deep bells
Of sheep and churches noise
Poor peace as the sun sets
And dark shoals every holy
   field.
We will ride out alone, and
   then,
Under the stars of Wales,
Cry, Multitudes of arks!
   Across
The water lidded lands,
Manned with their loves
   they'll move,
Like wooden islands, hill to
   hill.
Huloo, my prowed dove with
   a flute!
Ahoy, old, sea-legged fox,
Tom tit and Dai mouse!
My ark sings in the sun
At God speeded summer's
   end
And the flood flowers now.

Dylan Thomas

545   The Thought-Fox

I imagine this midnight moment's forest:
Something else is alive
Beside the clock's loneliness
And this blank page where my fingers move.

Through the window I see no star:
Something more near
Though deeper within darkness
Is entering the loneliness:

Cold, delicately as the dark snow,
A fox's nose touches twig, leaf;
Two eyes serve a movement, that now
And again now, and now, and now

Sets neat prints into the snow
Between trees, and warily a lame
Shadow lags by stump and in hollow
Of a body that is bold to come

Across clearings, an eye,
A widening deepening greenness,
Brilliantly, concentratedly,
Coming about its own business

Till, with a sudden sharp hot stink of fox
It enters the dark hole of the head.
The window is starless still; the clock ticks,
The page is printed.

Ted Hughes

646   Musée des Beaux Arts

About suffering they were never wrong,
The Old Masters: how well they understood
Its human position; how it takes place
While someone else is eating or opening a window or just
    walking dully along;
How, when the aged are reverently, passionately waiting
For the miraculous birth, there always must be
Children who did not specially want it to happen, skating
On a pond at the edge of the wood:
They never forgot
That even the dreadful martyrdom must run its course
Anyhow in a corner, some untidy spot
Where the dogs go on with their doggy life and the torturer's horse
Scratches its innocent behind on a tree.

In Brueghel's *Icarus*, for instance: how everything turns away
Quite leisurely from the disaster; the ploughman may
Have heard the splash, the forsaken cry,
But for him it was not an important failure; the sun shone
As it had to on the white legs disappearing into the green
Water; and the expensive delicate ship that must have seen
Something amazing, a boy falling out of the sky,
Had somewhere to get to and sailed calmly on.

W. H. Auden

Missing Dates

Slowly the poison the whole blood stream fills.
It is not the effort nor the failure tires.
The waste remains, the waste remains and kills.

It is not your system or clear sight that mills
Down small to the consequence a life requires;
Slowly the poison the whole blood stream fills.

They bled an old dog dry yet the exchange rills
Of young dog blood gave but a month's desires;
The waste remains, the waste remains and kills.

It is the Chinese tombs and the slag hills
Usurp the soil, and not the soil retires.
Slowly the poison the whole blood stream fills.

Not to have fire is to be a skin that shrills.
The complete fire is death. From partial fires
The waste remains, the waste remains and kills.

It is the poems you have lost, the ills
From missing dates, at which the heart expires.
Slowly the poison the whole blood stream fills.
The waste remains, the waste remains and kills.

William Empson

A Ball of Gold

A man saw a ball of gold in the sky;
He climbed for it,
And eventually he achieved it—
It was clay.

Now this is the strange part:
When the man went to the earth
And looked again,
Lo, there was the ball of gold.
Now this is the strange part:
It was a ball of gold.
Ay, by the heavens, it was a ball of gold.

Stephen Crane

649

The Mount

"No, I have tempered haste,"
The joyous traveler said,
"The steed has passed me now
Whose hurrying hooves I fled.
My specter rides thereon,
I learned what mount he has,
Upon what summers fed;
And wept to know again,
Beneath the saddle swung,
Treasure for whose great theft
This breast was wrung.
His bridle bells sang out,
I could not tell their chime,
So brilliantly he rings,
But called his name as Time.
His bin was morning light,
Those straws which gild his bed
Are of the fallen West.
Although green lands consume
Beneath their burning tread,
In everlasting bright
His hooves have rest."

Léonie Adams

650   **To a Hostess Saying Good Night**

Shake out the ruffle, turn and go,
Over the trellis blow the kiss.
Some of the guests will never know
Another night to shadow this.
Some of the birds awake in vines
Will never see another face
So frail, so lovely anyplace
Between the birdbath and the bines.

O dark come never down to you.
I look away and look away:
Over the moon the shadows go,
Over your shoulder, nebulae.
Some of the vast, the vacant stars
Will never see your face at all,
Your frail, your lovely eyelids fall
Between Andromeda and Mars.

James Wright

651   **The Sense of the Sleight-of-Hand Man**

One's grand flights, one's Sunday baths,
One's tootings at the weddings of the soul
Occur as they occur. So bluish clouds
Occurred above the empty house and the leaves
Of the rhododendrons rattled their gold,
As if someone lived there. Such floods of white
Came bursting from the clouds. So the wind
Threw its contorted strength around the sky.

Could you have said the bluejay suddenly
Would swoop to earth? It is a wheel, the rays
Around the sun. The wheel survives the myths.
The fire eye in the clouds survives the gods.
To think of a dove with an eye of grenadine
And pines that are cornets, so it occurs,

And a little island full of geese and stars:
It may be that the ignorant man, alone,
Has any chance to mate his life with life
That is the sensual, pearly spouse, the life
That is fluent in even the wintriest bronze.

Wallace Stevens

652   **The Imaginary Iceberg**

We'd rather have the iceberg than the ship,
Although it meant the end of travel.
Although it stood stock still like cloudy rock
And all the sea were moving marble.
We'd rather have the iceberg than the ship;
We'd rather own this breathing plain of snow
Though the ship's sails were laid upon the sea
As the snow lies undissolved upon the water.
O solemn, floating field,
Are you aware an iceberg takes repose
With you, and when it wakes may pasture on your snows?

This is a scene a sailor'd give his eyes for.
The ship's ignored. The iceberg rises
And sinks again; its glassy pinnacles
Correct elliptics in the sky.
This is a scene where he who treads the boards
Is artlessly rhetorical. The curtain
Is light enough to rise on finest ropes

That airy twists of snow provide.
The wits of these white peaks
Spar with the sun. Its weight the iceberg dares
Upon a shifting stage and stands and stares.

This iceberg cuts its facets from within.
Like jewelry from a grave
It saves itself perpetually and adorns
Only itself, perhaps the snows
Which so surprise us lying on the sea.
Goodbye, we say, goodbye, the ship steers off
Where waves give in to one another's waves
And clouds run in a warmer sky.
Icebergs behoove the soul
(Both being self-made from elements least visible)
To see them so: fleshed, fair, erected indivisible.

Elizabeth Bishop

653   Anne Rutledge*

Out of me unworthy and unknown
The vibrations of deathless music;
'With malice toward none, with charity for all.'
Out of me the forgiveness of millions toward millions,
And the beneficent face of a nation
Shining with justice and truth.
I am Anne Rutledge who sleep beneath these weeds,
Beloved in life of Abraham Lincoln,
Wedded to him, not through union,
But through separation.
Bloom forever, O Republic,
From the dust of my bosom!

Edgar Lee Masters

654   An Epitaph

HERE lies a most beautiful lady:
Light of step and heart was she;
I think she was the most beautiful lady
That ever was in the West Country.
But beauty vanishes; beauty passes;
However rare—rare it be;
And when I crumble, who will remember
This lady of the West Country?

Walter de la Mare

* See "The Master," page 458, and "O Captain! My Captain!", page 364.

655

Do Not Go Gentle into That Good Night

Do not go gentle into that good night,
Old age should burn and rave at close of day;
Rage, rage against the dying of the light.

Though wise men at their end know dark is right,
Because their words had forked no lightning they
Do not go gentle into that good night.

Good men, the last wave by, crying how bright
Their frail deeds might have danced in a green bay,
Rage, rage against the dying of the light.

Wild men who caught and sang the sun in flight,
And learn, too late, they grieved it on its way,
Do not go gentle into that good night.

Grave men, near death, who see with blinding sight
Blind eyes could blaze like meteors and be gay,
Rage, rage against the dying of the light.

And you, my father, there on the sad height,
Curse, bless, me now with your fierce tears, I pray.
Do not go gentle into that good night.
Rage, rage against the dying of the light.

Dylan Thomas

656

Death

Nor dread nor hope attend
A dying animal;
A man awaits his end
Dreading and hoping all;
Many times he died,
Many times rose again.
A great man in his pride
Confronting murderous men
Casts derision upon
Supersession of breath;
He knows death to the bone—
Man has created death.

William Butler Yeats

The Heavy Bear

"the withness of the body"—WHITEHEAD

The heavy bear who goes with me,
A manifold honey to smear his face,
Clumsy and lumbering here and there,
The central ton of every place,
The hungry beating brutish one
In love with candy, anger, and sleep,
Crazy factotum, dishevelling all,
Climbs the building, kicks the football,
Boxes his brother in the hate-ridden city.

Breathing at my side, that heavy animal,
That heavy bear who sleeps with me,
Howls in his sleep for a world of sugar,
A sweetness intimate as the water's clasp,
Howls in his sleep because the tight-rope
Trembles and shows the darkness beneath.
—The strutting show-off is terrified,
Dressed in his dress-suit, bulging his pants,
Trembles to think that his quivering meat
Must finally wince to nothing at all.

That inescapable animal walks with me,
Has followed me since the black womb held,
Moves where I move, distorting my gesture,
A caricature, a swollen shadow,
A stupid clown of the spirit's motive,
Perplexes and affronts with his own darkness,
The secret life of belly and bone,
Opaque, too near, my private, yet unknown,
Stretches to embrace the very dear
With whom I would walk without him near,
Touches her grossly, although a word
Would bare my heart and make me clear,
Stumbles, flounders, and strives to be fed
Dragging me with him in his mouthing care,
Amid the hundred million of his kind,
The scrimmage of appetite everywhere.

Delmore Schwartz

Fern Hill

Now as I was young and easy under the apple boughs
About the lilting house and happy as the grass was green,
 The night above the dingle starry,
  Time let me hail and climb
 Golden in the heydays of his eyes,
And honoured among wagons I was prince of the apple towns
And once below a time I lordly had the trees and leaves
  Trail with daisies and barley
 Down the rivers of the windfall light.

And as I was green and carefree, famous among the barns
About the happy yard and singing as the farm was home,
 In the sun that is young once only,
  Time let me play and be
 Golden in the mercy of his means,
And green and golden I was huntsman and herdsman, the calves
Sang to my horn, the foxes on the hills barked clear and cold,
  And the sabbath rang slowly
 In the pebbles of the holy streams.

All the sun long it was running, it was lovely, the hay-
Fields high as the house, the tunes from the chimneys, it was air
 And playing, lovely and watery
  And fire green as grass
 And nightly under the simple stars
As I rode to sleep the owls were bearing the farm away,
All the moon long I heard, blessed among stables, the nightjars
 Flying with the ricks, and the horses
  Flashing into the dark.

And then to awake, and the farm, like a wanderer white
With the dew, come back, the cock on his shoulder: it was all
 Shining, it was Adam and maiden,
  The sky gathered again
 And the sun grew round that very day.
So it must have been after the birth of the simple light
In the first, spinning place, the spellbound horses walking warm
 Out of the whinnying green stable
  On to the fields of praise.

And honoured among foxes and pheasants by the gay house
Under the new made clouds and happy as the heart was long,
 In the sun born over and over,
  I ran my heedless ways,

My wishes raced through the house-high hay
And nothing I cared, at my sky blue trades, that time allows
In all his tuneful turning so few and such morning songs
Before the children green and golden
Follow him out of grace,

Nothing I cared, in the lamb white days, that time would take me
Up to the swallow thronged loft by the shadow of my hand,
In the moon that is always rising,
Nor that riding to sleep
I should hear him fly with the high fields
And wake to the farm forever fled from the childless land.
Oh as I was young and easy in the mercy of his means,
Time held me green and dying
Though I sang in my chains like the sea.

Dylan Thomas

659	**Love Is Not All**

Love is not all: it is not meat nor drink
Nor slumber nor a roof against the rain;
Nor yet a floating spar to men that sink
And rise and sink and rise and sink again;
Love can not fill the thickened lung with breath,
Nor clean the blood, nor set the fractured bone;
Yet many a man is making friends with death
Even as I speak, for lack of love alone.
It well may be that in a difficult hour,
Pinned down by pain and moaning for release,
Or nagged by want past resolution's power,
I might be driven to sell your love for peace,
Or trade the memory of this night for food.
It well may be. I do not think I would.

Edna St. Vincent Millay

660	**I Knew a Woman, Lovely in Her Bones**

I knew a woman, lovely in her bones,
When small birds sighed, she would sigh back at them;
Ah, when she moved, she moved more ways than one:
The shapes a bright container can contain!
Of her choice virtues only gods should speak,
Or English poets who grew up on Greek

(I'd have them sing in chorus, cheek to cheek.)

How well her wishes went! She stroked my chin,
She taught me Turn, and Counter-turn, and Stand;
She taught me Touch, that undulant white skin:
I nibbled meekly from her proffered hand;
She was the sickle; I, poor I, the rake,
Coming behind her for her pretty sake
(But what prodigious mowing we did make.)

Love likes a gander, and adores a goose:
Her full lips pursed, the errant note to seize;
She played it quick, she played it light and loose;
My eyes, they dazzled at her flowing knees;
Her several parts could keep a pure repose,
Or one hip quiver with a mobile nose
(She moved in circles, and those circles moved.)

Let seed be grass, and grass turn into hay:
I'm martyr to a motion not my own;
What's freedom for? To know eternity.
I swear she cast a shadow white as stone.
But who would count eternity in days?
These old bones live to learn her wanton ways:
(I measure time by how a body sways.)

Theodore Roethke

661   Recuerdo

We were very tired, we were very merry—
We had gone back and forth all night on the ferry.
It was bare and bright, and smelled like a stable—
But we looked into a fire, we leaned across a table,
We lay on a hill-top underneath the moon;
And the whistles kept blowing, and the dawn came soon.

We were very tired, we were very merry—
We had gone back and forth all night on the ferry;
And you ate an apple, and I ate a pear,
From a dozen of each we had bought somewhere;
And the sky went wan, and the wind came cold,
And the sun rose dripping, a bucketful of gold.

We were very tired, we were very merry,
We had gone back and forth all night on the ferry.
We hailed, "Good-morrow, mother!" to a shawl-covered head,
And bought a morning paper, which neither of us read;
And she wept, "God bless you!" for the apples and pears,
And we gave her all our money but our subway fares.

Edna St. Vincent Millay

662 **Song**

I can't be talkin' of love, dear,
I can't be talkin' of love.
If there be one thing I can't talk of
That one thing do be love.

But that's not sayin' that I'm not lovin'——
Still water, you know, runs deep,
An' I do be lovin' so deep, dear,
I be lovin' you in my sleep.

But I can't be talkin' of love, dear,
I can't be talkin' of love,
If there be one thing I can't talk of
That one thing do be love.

Esther Mathews

663 **When You Are Old**

When you are old and grey and full of sleep,
And nodding by the fire, take down this book,
And slowly read, and dream of the soft look
Your eyes had once, and of their shadows deep;

How many loved your moments of glad grace,
And loved your beauty with love false or true,
But one man loved the pilgrim soul in you,
And loved the sorrows of your changing face;

And bending down beside the glowing bars,
Murmur, a little sadly, how Love fled
And paced upon the mountains overhead
And hid his face amid a crowd of stars.

William Butler Yeats

664 **Politics**

"In our time the destiny of man presents its meaning in political terms."
—THOMAS MANN

How can I, that girl standing there,
My attention fix
On Roman or on Russian
Or on Spanish politics?
Yet here's a travelled man that knows
What he talks about,

And there's a politician
That has read and thought,
And maybe what they say is true
Of war and war's alarms,
But O that I were young again
And held her in my arms!

William Butler Yeats

665 **Never May the Fruit Be Plucked**

Never, never may the fruit be plucked from the bough
And gathered into barrels.
He that would eat of love must eat it where it hangs.
Though the branches bend like reeds,
Though the ripe fruit splash in the grass or wrinkle on the tree,
He that would eat of love may bear away with him
Only what his belly can hold,
Nothing in the apron,
Nothing in the pockets.
Never, never may the fruit be gathered from the bough
And harvested in barrels.
The winter of love is a cellar of empty bins,
In an orchard soft with rot.

Edna St. Vincent Millay

666 **An Immorality**

Sing we for love and idleness,
Naught else is worth the having.

Though I have been in many a land,
There is naught else in living.

And I would rather have my sweet,
Though rose-leaves die of grieving,

Than do high deeds in Hungary
To pass all men's believing.

Ezra Pound

667 **Song for the Clatter-Bones**

God rest that wicked woman,
Queen Jezebel, the bitch
Who peeled the clothes from her shoulder-bones
Down to her spent teats
As she stretched out of the window
Among the geraniums, where
She chaffed and laughed like one half daft
Titivating her painted hair—

King Jehu he drove to her,
She tipped him a fancy beck;
But he from his knacky side-car spoke,
"Who'll break that dewlapped neck?"
And so she was thrown from the window;
Like Lucifer she fell
Beneath the feet of the horses and they beat
The light out of Jezebel.

That corpse wasn't planted in clover;
Ah, nothing of her was found
Save those grey bones that Hare-foot Mike
Gave me for their lovely sound;
And as once her dancing body
Made star-lit princes sweat,
So I'll just clack: though her ghost lacks a back
There's music in the old bones yet.

F. R. Higgins

668   Discoveries

The poles are flying where the two eyes set:
America has not found Columbus yet.

Ptolemy's planets, playing fast and loose,
Foretell the wisdom of Copernicus.

Dante calls Primum Mobile, the First Cause:
Love that moves the world and the other stars.

Great Galileo, twisted by the rack,
Groans the bright sun from heaven, then breathes it back.

Blake, on the world alighting, holds the skies,
And all the stars shine down through human eyes.

Donne sees those stars, yet will not let them lie:
'We're tapers, too, and at our own cost die.'

The shroud-lamp catches. Lips are smiling there.
'Les flammes—déjà?'—The world dies, or Voltaire.

Swift, a cold mourner at his burial-rite,
Burns to the world's heart like a meteorite.

Beethoven deaf, in deafness hearing all,
Unwinds all music from sound's funeral.

Three prophets fall, the litter of one night,
Blind Milton gazes in fixed deeps of light.

Beggar of those Minute Particulars,
Yeats lights again the turmoil of the stars.

Motionless motion! Come, Tiresias,
The eternal flies, what's passing cannot pass.

'Solace in flight,' old Heraclitus cries;
Light changing to Von Hügel's butterflies.

Rilke bears all, thinks like a tree, believes,
Sinks in the hand that bears the falling leaves.

The stars! The signs! Great Angelo hurls them back.
His whirling ceiling draws the zodiac.

The pulse of Keats testing the axiom;
The second music when the sound is dumb.

The Christian Paradox, bringing its great reward
By loss; the moment known to Kierkegaard.

Vernon Watkins

669   **Ballad of the Goodly Fere**

Simon Zelotes speaketh it somewhile after the Crucifixion

    Ha' we lost the goodliest fere o' all
    For the priests and the gallows tree?
    Aye lover he was of brawny men,
    O' ships and the open sea.

    When they came wi' a host to take Our Man
    His smile was good to see,
    "First let these go!" quo' our Goodly Fere,
    "Or I'll see ye damned," says he.

    Aye he sent us out through the crossed high spears
    And the scorn of his laugh rang free,
    "Why took ye not me when I walked about
    Alone in the town?" says he.

    Oh we drunk his "Hale" in the good red wine
    When we last made company,
    No capon priest was the Goodly Fere
    But a man o' men was he.

I ha' seen him drive a hundred men
Wi' a bundle o' cords swung free,
That they took the high and holy house
For their pawn and treasury.

They'll no' get him a' in a book I think
Though they write it cunningly;
No mouse of the scrolls was the Goodly Fere
But aye loved the open sea.

If they think they ha' snared our Goodly Fere
They are fools to the last degree.
"I'll go to the feast," quo' our Goodly Fere,
"Though I go to the gallows tree."

"Ye ha' seen me heal the lame and blind,
And wake the dead," says he,
"Ye shall see one thing to master all:
'Tis how a brave man dies on the tree."

A son of God was the Goodly Fere
That bade us his brothers be.
I ha' seen him cow a thousand men.
I have seen him upon the tree.

He cried no cry when they drave the nails
And the blood gushed hot and free,
The hounds of the crimson sky gave tongue
But never a cry cried he.

I ha' seen him cow a thousand men
On the hills o' Galilee,
They whined as he walked out calm between,
Wi' his eyes like the grey o' the sea,

Like the sea that brooks no voyaging
With the winds unleashed and free,
Like the sea that he cowed at Genseret
Wi' twey words spoke' suddenly.

A master of men was the Goodly Fere,
A mate of the wind and sea,
If they think they ha' slain our Goodly Fere
They are fools eternally.

I ha' seen him eat o' the honey-comb
Sin' they nailed him to the tree.

Ezra Pound

570

After Reading St. John the Divine

Moon's glow by seven fold multiplied, turned red,
Burned fierce by the coronal limbs at last
Out-leaping insulating space, a-blast
The searing heat sheeting round earth ahead
Of the scorched geoid's course; and I a-bed
Watching that increased flame and holding fast
To pulse and pillow. Worse! No shadow cast
By chair or cat. All people waking dead . . .
Earth lurches spacial waste; my room is hot;
That moon waxes her monstrous, brimstone disk;
Thick fear stretches before the febrile light;
Green fires pierce at my clenching eye's blind spot . . .
My buried soul, rising to face the risk,
With one pure deed restores the natural night.

Gene Derwood

571

The Drunken Fisherman

Wallowing in this bloody sty,
I cast for fish that pleased my eye
(Truly Jehovah's bow suspends
No pots of gold to weight its ends);
Only the blood-mouthed rainbow trout
Rose to my bait. They flopped about
My canvas creel until the moth
Corrupted its unstable cloth.

A calendar to tell the day;
A handkerchief to wave away
The gnats; a couch unstuffed with storm
Pouching a bottle in one arm;
A whiskey bottle full of worms;
And bedroom slacks: are these fit terms
To mete the worm whose molten rage
Boils in the belly of old age?

Once fishing was a rabbit's foot—
O wind blow cold, O wind blow hot,
Let suns stay in or suns step out:
Life danced a jig on the sperm-whale's spout—
The fisher's fluent and obscene
Catches kept his conscience clean.
Children, the raging memory drools
Over the glory of past pools.

Now the hot river, ebbing hauls
Its bloody water into holes;
A grain of sand inside my shoe
Mimics the moon that might undo
Man and Creation too; remorse
Stinking, has puddled up its source;
Here tantrums thrash to a whale's rage.
This is the pot-hole of old age.

Is there no way to cast my hook
Out of this dynamited brook?
The Fisher's sons must cast about
When shallow waters peter out.
I will catch Christ with a greased worm,
And when the Prince of Darkness stalks
My bloodstream to its Stygian term . . .
On water the Man-Fisher walks.

Robert Lowell

672   **Memorial for Two Young Seamen**

(Lost overboard in a storm in Mid-Pacific, January 1940)

I

The seagull, spreadeagled, splayed on the wind,
Span backwards shrieking, belly facing upward,
Fled backwards with a gimlet in its heart
To see the two youths swimming hand in hand
Through green eternity. O swept overboard
Not could the thirty-foot jaws them part,
On the flouncing skirts that swept them over
Separate what death pronounced was love.
I saw them, the hand flapping like a flag,
And another like a dolphin with a child
Supporting him. Was I the shape of Jesus
When to me hopeward their eyeballs swivelled,
Saw I was standing in the posture of vague
Horror, oh paralyzed with mere pity's peace?

II

From thorax of storms the voices of verbs
Shall call to me without sound, like the vowel
Round which cyclones rage, to nurse my nerve,
My shaken, my broken, my oh I shall grovel

Heart. I taste the sea swilling in my bowels,
As now I sit shivering in the swing of waves
Like a face in a bubble. As the hull heaves
I and my mind go walking over hell.
The greedy bitch with sailors in her guts,
Green as a dream and formidable as God,
Spitting at stars, gnawing at shores, mad, randy,
Riots with us on her abdomen and puts
Eternity in our cabins, pitches our pod
To the mouth of the death for which no one is ready.

III

At midday they looked up and saw their death
Standing up overhead as loud as thunder
As white as angels and formidable as God:
Then, then the shock, the last gasp of breath,
As grazing the bulwarks they swept over and under,
All the green arms around them that load
Their eyes, their ears, their stomachs with eternals,
Whirled away in a white pool to the stern.
But the most possible of all miracles
Is that the useful tear that did not fall
From the corner of their eyes, was the prize,
The flowers, the gifts, the crystal sepulcher,
The funeral contribution and memorial,
The perfect and non-existent obsequies.

George Barker

73

With God Conversing

Red paths that wander through the gray, and cells
Of strangeness, rutted mouldings in the brain,
Untempered fevers heated by old kills,
By the pampered word, by the pat printed rune,
Unbalanced coil under glaucous blooms of thought,
A turning mind, unmitigated thinking that
Feeds human hunger and eats us alive
While cringing to the death, expecting love,—
Such make the self we are. And do you make it?
And practice on us? For we cannot take it.

Listen. Grow mild before the flicking lash
Seems welded to your hand, self-wounder.
What are we, cry we, while our pain leaps lush,

Too jungle thick: the jungle where we wander,
No seeded faith before, nor after, miracle,
Of bidden faith in things unseen, no particle.
For we think only through our troubled selves;
We note the worm that in the apple delves,
See gibbous moons and spots upon the sun,
Speak gibberish, and keep the poor in sin.

Plus birth and death must war-lash winnow
While every pod-burst leaf of May sucks life?
Because we think shall we be less than minnow,
Cat, carrot, rat, bat and such from sense aloof?
What doorless maze is this we wander through
With fuming souls parched of our morning dew?
Reason confounds as it presents to NAUGHT:
Earth worn, man moving into self-made night.
Reason-begotten science sets war's pace
And, civil-mouthed, makes civilization pass.

Created in your image, made up of words,
Till words reduce you to a zero-O,
We, then, reflecting you, are less than birds,
Bugs, or empty dugs, still less than minus no.
There must be something wrong with being wise—
Talking we go, wondering and wandering with woes,
Big thoughts have got us, hence we organize,
Govern our heroes with unmeant yeas and nays,
And breathe in dungeons of our nervous mesh
An air too blank to snare meandering flesh.

Night melting dawn shall turn the renewed sky,
Aurora Borealis and Australis
Fanfaring leap the poles, the moon fall by;
But if our science does not quickly fail us
How long for us will space blue light the dun
Of populaces, while wonderers eye the sun?
The gloomy silhouettes of wings we forged
With reason reasonless, are now enlarged,
The falsified subconscious, beast a-woken?
We-you? Post-suicides, shall we awaken?

                                        Gene Derwood

574

The Flight into Egypt

Within Heaven's circle I had not guessed at this,
I had not guessed at pleasure such as this,
So sharp a pleasure,
That, like a lamp burning in foggy night,
Makes its own orb and sphere of flowing gold
And tents itself in light.

Going before you, now how many days,
Thoughts, all turned back like birds against the wind,
Wheeled sullenly towards my Father's house,
Considered his blind presence and the gathered, bustling pæan,
The affluence of his sweetness, his grace and unageing might.

My flesh glowed then in the shadow of a loose cloak
And my brightness troubled the ground with every pulse of
    the blood,
My wings lax on the air, my eyes open and grave,
With the vacant pride of hardly less than a god.

We passed thickets that quaked with hidden deer,
And wide shallows dividing before my feet,
Empty plains threaded, and between stiff aloes
I took the ass's bridle to climb into mountain pathways.

When cold bit you, through your peasant's mantle,
And my Father filled the air with meaningless stars,
I brought dung and dead white grass for fuel,
Blowing a fire with the breath of the holy word.

Your drudge, Joseph, slept; you would sit unmoving,
In marble quiet, or by the unbroken voice of a river,
Would sometimes bare your maiden breast to his mouth,
The suckling, to the conscious God balanced upon your knees.

Apart I considered the melodious names of my brothers,
As again in my Father's house, and the even spheres
Slowly, nightlong recalled the splendour of numbers;
I heard again the voluptuous measure of praise.

Sometimes pacing beneath clarity immeasurable
I saw my mind lie open and desert,
The wavering streams frozen up and each coppice quieted,
A whole valley in starlight with leaves and waters.

Coming at last to these farthest Syrian hills,
Attis or Adon, some ambushed lust looked out;
My skin grows pale and smooth, shrunken as silk,
Without the rough effulgence of a God.

And here no voice has spoken;
There is no shrine of any godhead here
No grove or hallowed fires,
And godhead seems asleep.

Only the vine has woven
Strange houses and blind rooms and palaces,
Into each hollow and crevice continually
Dropped yearlong irrecoverable flowers.

The sprawling vine has built us a close room
Obedient Hymen fills the air with mist;
And to make dumb our theft
The white and moving sand that will not bear a print.

                                        Peter Quennell

675   The Horse Chestnut Tree

Boys in sporadic but tenacious droves
Come with sticks, as certainly as Autumn,
To assault the great horse chestnut tree.

There is a law governs their lawlessness,
Desire is in them for a shining amulet
And the best are those that are highest up.

They will not pick them easily from the ground.
With shrill arms they fling to the higher branches,
To hurry the work of nature for their pleasure.

I have seen them trooping down the street
Their pockets stuffed with chestnuts shucked, unshucked.
It is only evening keeps them from their wish.

Sometimes I run out in a kind of rage
To chase the boys away; I catch an arm,
Maybe, and laugh to think of being the lawgiver.

I was once such a young sprout myself
And fingered in my pocket the prize and trophy.
But still I moralize upon the day

And see that we, outlaws on God's property,
Fling out imagination beyond the skies
Wishing a tangible good from the unknown.

And likewise death will drive us from the scene
With the great flowering world unbroken yet,
Which we held in idea, a little handful.

Richard Eberhart

576

Shelter

While people hunt for what can satisfy their wants,
There is a watching and a sharp recording.
Both seekers and the watchers are the palpitants,
And much is said with no deep, ferny wording.

Under the various shelters sits the soul
Not necessarily in misty, devious hiding;
The body housed, the body's firm, pale bole
Clothed, the body's self a blank abiding.

There sometimes goes a woman, fur on neck,
A man with hands immersed in pockets,
An insect crouched behind a built-up speck,
Or memories enclosed in fastened lockets.

But cease! The peering sleight-of-sight
Probing behind such partial enclosures
Is more befooled, because the definite might
Is open, like water seen through osiers.

Walking or languid, through the night or day,
Something familiar for a hiding wall
We carry, as a glove, or stare, or play
Of lips and brows. That's just a stall

That balks no frankness of the essence,
The too lightning truth of what we are—
No man can hide the presence or the absence,
We've come too quickly and too far.

Gene Derwood

Meeting a monster of mourning wherever I go
Who crosses me at morning and evening also,
For whom are you miserable I ask and he murmurs
I am miserable for innumerable man: for him
Who wanders through Woolworth's gazing at tin stars;
I mourn the maternal future tense, Time's mother,
Who has him in her lap, and I mourn also her,
Time whose dial face flashes with scars.

I gave the ghost my money and he smiled and said,
Keep it for the eyeballs of the dead instead.
Why here, I asked, why is it here you come
Breaking into the evening line going to another,
Edging your axe between my pencil fingers,
Twisting my word from a comedy to a crime?
I am the face once seen never forgotten,
Whose human look your dirty page will smother.

I know what it was, he said, that you were beginning;
The rigmarole of private life's belongings.
Birth, boyhood, and the adolescent baloney. So I say
Good go ahead, and see what happens then.
I promise you horror shall stand in your shoes,
And when your register of youth is through
What will it be but about the horror of man?
Try telling about birth and observe the issue.

Epping Forest where the deer and girls
Mope like lost ones looking for Love's gaols—
Among the dilapidated glades my mother wandered
With me as a kid, and sadly we saw
The deer in the rain near the trees, the leaf-hidden dirt,
The Sunday papers, and the foliage's falling world;
I not knowing nothing was our possession,
Not knowing Poverty my position.

Epping Forest glutted with the green tree
Grew up again like a sea wood inside me.
I had the deer browsing on my heart,
This was my mother; and I had the dirt.
Inside was well with the green well of love,
Outside privation, poverty, all dearth.
Thus like the pearl I came from hurt,
Like the prize pig I came from love.

Now I know what was wanting in my youth,
It was not water or a loving mouth.
It was what makes the apple-tree grow big,
The mountain fall, and the minnow die.
It was hard cash I needed at my root.
I now know that how I grew was due
To echoing guts and the empty bag—
My song was out of tune for a few notes.

Oh, my ghost cried, the charming chimes of coincidence!
I was born also there, where distress collects the rents.
Guttersnipe gutless, I was planted in your guts there,
The tear of time my sperm. I rose from
The woe-womb of the want-raped mind,
Empty hunger cracked with stomach's thunder.
Remember the rags that flattered your frame
Froze hard and formed this flesh my rind.

So close over the chapter of my birth,
Blessed by distress, baptized by dearth.
How I swung myself from the tree's bough
Demonstrating death in my gay play:
How the germ of the sperm of this ghost like a worm
I caught from the cold comfort of never enough.
How by being miserable for myself I began,
And now am miserable for the mass of man.

George Barker

78   Two Tramps in Mud Time

Out of the mud two strangers came
And caught me splitting wood in the yard.
And one of them put me off my aim
By hailing cheerily "Hit them hard!"
I knew pretty well why he dropped behind
And let the other go on a way.
I knew pretty well what he had in mind:
He wanted to take my job for pay.

Good blocks of beech it was I split,
As large around as the chopping block;
And every piece I squarely hit
Fell splinterless as a cloven rock.
The blows that a life of self-control
Spares to strike for the common good
That day, giving a loose to my soul,
I spent on the unimportant wood.

The sun was warm but the wind was chill.
You know how it is with an April day
When the sun is out and the wind is still,
You're one month on in the middle of May.
But if you so much as dare to speak,
A cloud comes over the sunlit arch,
A wind comes off a frozen peak,
And you're two months back in the middle of March.

A bluebird comes tenderly up to alight
And fronts the wind to unruffle a plume
His song so pitched as not to excite
A single flower as yet to bloom.
It is snowing a flake: and he half knew
Winter was only playing possum.
Except in color he isn't blue,
But he wouldn't advise a thing to blossom.

The water for which we may have to look
In summertime with a witching-wand,
In every wheelrut's now a brook,
In every print of a hoof a pond.
Be glad of water, but don't forget
The lurking frost in the earth beneath
That will steal forth after the sun is set
And show on the water its crystal teeth.

The time when most I loved my task
These two must make me love it more
By coming with what they came to ask.
You'd think I never had felt before
The weight of an ax-head poised aloft,
The grip on earth of outspread feet,
The life of muscles rocking soft
And smooth and moist in vernal heat.

Out of the woods two hulking tramps
(From sleeping God knows where last night,
But not long since in the lumber camps).
They thought all chopping was theirs of right.
Men of the woods and lumberjacks,
They judged me by their appropriate tool.
Except as a fellow handled an ax,
They had no way of knowing a fool.

Nothing on either side was said.
They knew they had but to stay their stay
And all their logic would fill my head:
As that I had no right to play
With what was another man's work for gain.
My right might be love but theirs was need.
And where the two exist in twain
Theirs was the better right—agreed.

But yield who will to their separation,
My object in living is to unite
My avocation and my vocation
As my two eyes make one in sight.
Only where love and need are one,
And the work is play for mortal stakes,
Is the deed ever really done
For Heaven and the future's sakes.

Robert Frost

79   **The Slaughter-House**

Under the big 500-watted lamps, in the huge sawdusted
          government inspected slaughter-house,
head down from hooks and clamps, run on trolleys over
          troughs,
the animals die.
Whatever terror their dull intelligences feel
          or what agony distorts their most protruding eyes
the incommunicable narrow skulls conceal.
          Across the sawdusted floor,
ignorant as children, they see the butcher's slow
          methodical approach
in the bloodied apron, leather cap above, thick square
          shoes below,
struggling to comprehend this unique vision upside down,
and then approximate a human scream
          as from the throat slit like a letter
the blood empties, and the windpipe, like a blown valve,
          spurts steam.

But I, sickened equally with the ox and lamb,
          misread my fate,
mistake the butcher's love
          who kills me for the meat I am

to feed a hungry multitude beyond the sliding doors.
      I, too, misjudge the real
purpose of this huge shed I'm herded in: not for my love
      or lovely wool am I here,
but to make some world a meal.
      See, how on the unsubstantial air
I kick, bleating my private woe,
      as upside down my rolling sight
somesaults, and frantically I try to set my world upright;
      too late learning why I'm hung here,
whose nostrils bleed, whose life runs out from eye and ear.

Alfred Haye

680   **The Yachts**

contend in a sea which the land partly encloses
shielding them from the too heavy blows
of an ungoverned ocean which when it chooses

tortures the biggest hulls, the best man knows
to pit against its beatings, and sinks them pitilessly.
Mothlike in mists, scintillant in the minute

brilliance of cloudless days, with broad bellying sails
they glide to the wind tossing green water
from their sharp prows while over them the crew crawls

ant like, solicitously grooming them, releasing,
making fast as they turn, lean far over and having
caught the wind again, side by side, head for the mark.

In a well guarded arena of open water surrounded by
lesser and greater craft which, sycophant, lumbering
and flittering follow them, they appear youthful, rare

as the light of a happy eye, live with the grace
of all that in the mind is feckless, free and
naturally to be desired. Now the sea which holds them

is moody, lapping their glossy sides, as if feeling
for some slightest flaw but fails completely.
Today no race. Then the wind comes again. The yachts

move, jockeying for a start, the signal is set and they
are off. Now the waves strike at them but they are too
well made, they slip through, though they take in canvas.

rms with hands grasping seek to clutch at the prows.
odies thrown recklessly in the way are cut aside.
t is a sea of faces about them in agony, in despair

ntil the horror of the race dawns staggering the mind,
he whole sea become an entanglement of watery bodies
ost to the world bearing what they cannot hold. Broken,

eaten, desolate, reaching from the dead to be taken up
hey cry out, failing, failing! their cries rising
n waves still as the skillful yachts pass over.

William Carlos Williams

Thirty Bob a Week

ouldn't touch a step and turn a screw,
nd set the blooming world a-work for me,
e such as cut their teeth—I hope, like you—
n the handle of a skeleton gold key;
t mine on a leek, which I eat it every week:
m a clerk at thirty bob as you can see.

I don't allow it's luck and all a toss;
here's no such thing as being starred and crossed;
just the power of some to be a boss,
nd the bally power of others to be bossed:
ce the music, sir; you bet I ain't a cur;
trike me lucky if I don't believe I'm lost!

like a mole I journey in the dark,
-travelling along the underground
m my Pillar'd Halls and broad Suburban Park,
o come the daily dull official round;
home again at night with my pipe all alight,
-scheming how to count ten bob a pound.

it's often very cold and very wet,
nd my missis stitches towels for a hunks;
the Pillar'd Halls is half of it to let—
hree rooms about the size of travelling trunks.
we cough, my wife and I, to dislocate a sigh,
hen the noisy little kids are in their bunks.

you never hear her do a growl or whine,
or she's made of flint and roses, very odd;
I've got to cut my meaning rather fine,

Or I'd blubber, for I'm made of greens and sod:
So p'r'aps we are in Hell for all that I can tell,
  And lost and damn'd and served up hot to God.

I ain't blaspheming, Mr. Silver-tongue;
  I'm saying things a bit beyond your art:
Of all the rummy starts you ever sprung,
  Thirty bob a week's the rummiest start!
With your science and your books and your the'ries about
      spooks,
  Did you ever hear of looking in your heart?

I didn't mean your pocket, Mr., no:
  I mean that having children and a wife,
With thirty bob on which to come and go,
  Isn't dancing to the tabor and the fife:
When it doesn't make you drink, by Heaven! it makes you
      think,
  And notice curious items about life.

I step into my heart and there I meet
  A god-almighty devil singing small,
Who would like to shout and whistle in the street,
  And squelch the passers flat against the wall;
If the whole world was a cake he had the power to take,
  He would take it, ask for more, and eat it all.

And I meet a sort of simpleton beside,
  The kind that life is always giving beans;
With thirty bob a week to keep a bride
  He fell in love and married in his teens:
At thirty bob he stuck; but he knows it isn't luck:
  He knows the seas are deeper than tureens.

And the god-almighty devil and the fool
  That meet me in the High Street on the strike,
When I walk about my heart a-gathering wool,
  Are my good and evil angels if you like.
And both of them together in every kind of weather
  Ride me like a double-seated bike.

That's rough a bit and needs its meaning curled.
  But I have a high old hot un in my mind—
A most engrugious notion of the world,
  That leaves your lightning 'rithmetic behind:
I give it at a glance when I say "There ain't no chance,
  Nor nothing of the lucky-lottery kind."

And it's this way I make it out to be:
  No fathers, mothers, countries, climates—none;

ot Adam was responsible for me,
Nor society, nor systems, nary one:
little sleeping seed, I woke—I did, indeed—
A million years before the blooming sun.

woke because I thought the time had come;
Beyond my will there was no other cause;
nd every where I found myself at home,
Because I chose to be the thing I was;
nd in what ever shape of mollusc or of ape
I always went according to the laws.

was the love that chose my mother out;
I joined two lives and from the union burst;
Iy weakness and my strength without a doubt
Are mine alone for ever from the first:
's just the very same with a difference in the name
As "Thy will be done." You say it if you durst!

hey say it daily up and down the land
As easy as you take a drink, it's true;
ut the difficultest go to understand,
And the difficultest job a man can do,
to come it brave and meek with thirty bob a week,
And feel that that's the proper thing for you.

's a naked child against a hungry wolf;
It's playing bowls upon a splitting wreck;
's walking on a string across the gulf
With millstones fore-and-aft about your neck;
ut the thing is daily done by many and many a one;
nd we fall, face forward, fighting, on the deck.

John Davidson

In Common

ere am I, this carrot eating—
range but hard common;
ut the window sun is treat-
ing,
aying still its gold on;
he color still is yellow,
ed now, but a late hello.

oes this, living feel, and
starting,
y when out of earth it's
sucked?
there tear in every parting,

Even from loose earth when
plucked?
The last day shall we be very
Terrorized or merry?

Health itself is bled from this
Wandering dynamic in my
veins;
What can be the vegetable
bliss
Compensatory for the pains?
Here's sweet carrot, here am
I,
Souls immortal we decry.

Gene Derwood

683   **Carl Hamblin**

The press of the Spoon River *Clarion* was wrecked,
And I was tarred and feathered,
For publishing this on the day the Anarchists were hanged
      in Chicago:
"I saw a beautiful woman with bandaged eyes
Standing on the steps of a marble temple.
Great multitudes passed in front of her,
Lifting their faces to her imploringly.
In her left hand she held a sword.
She was brandishing the sword,
Sometimes striking a child, again a laborer,
Again a slinking woman, again a lunatic.
In her right hand she held a scale;
Into the scale pieces of gold were tossed
By those who dodged the strokes of the sword.
A man in a black gown read from a manuscript:
'She is no respecter of persons.'
Then a youth wearing a red cap
Leaped to her side and snatched away the bandage.
And lo, the lashes had been eaten away
From the oozy eye-lids;
The eye-balls were seared with a milky mucus;
The madness of a dying soul
Was written on her face—
But the multitude saw why she wore the bandage."

                              Edgar Lee Masters

684   Consider These, for We Have Condemned Them

Consider these, for we have condemned them;
Leaders to no sure land, guides their bearings lost
Or in league with robbers have reversed the signposts,
Disrespectful to ancestors, irresponsible to heirs.
Born barren, a freak growth, root in rubble,
Fruitlessly blossoming, whose foliage suffocates,
Their sap is sluggish, they reject the sun.

The man with his tongue in his cheek, the woman
With her heart in the wrong place, unhandsome, unwholesome;
Have exposed the new-born to worse than weather,
Exiled the honest and sacked the seer.
These drowned the farms to form a pleasure-lake,
In time of drought they drain the reservoir
Through private pipes for baths and sprinklers.

Getters not begetters; gainers not beginners;
Whiners, no winners; no triers, betrayers;
Who steer by no star, whose moon means nothing.
Daily denying, unable to dig:
At bay in villas from blood relations,
Counters of spoons and content with cushions
They pray for peace, they hand down disaster.

They that take the bribe shall perish by the bribe,
Dying of dry rot, ending in asylums,
A curse to children, a charge on the state.
But still their fears and frenzies infect us;
Drug nor isolation will cure this cancer:
It is now or never, the hour of the knife,
The break with the past, the major operation.

C. Day-Lewis

685   September 1, 1939

I sit in one of the dives
On Fifty-second Street
Uncertain and afraid
As the clever hopes expire
Of a low dishonest decade:
Waves of anger and fear
Circulate over the bright
And darkened lands of the
    earth,
Obsessing our private lives;
The unmentionable odour
    of death
Offends the September
    night.

Exiled Thucydides knew
All that a speech can say
About Democracy,
And what dictators do,
The elderly rubbish they
    talk
To an apathetic grave;
Analysed all in his book,
The enlightenment driven
    away,
The habit-forming pain,
Mismanagement and grief:
We must suffer them all
    again.

Accurate scholarship can
Unearth the whole offence
From Luther until now
That has driven a culture
    mad,
Find what occurred at Linz,
What huge image made
A psychopathic god:
I and the public know
What all schoolchildren
    learn,
Those to whom evil is done
Do evil in return.

Into this neutral air
Where blind skyscrapers
    use
Their full height to proclaim
The strength of Collective
    Man,
Each language pours its vain
Competitive excuse:
But who can live for long
In an euphoric dream;
Out of the mirror they stare,
Imperialism's face
And the international wrong.

Faces along the bar
Cling to their average day:
The lights must never go out,
The music must always play,
All the conventions conspire
To make this fort assume
The furniture of home;
Lest we should see where
    we are,
Lost in a haunted wood,
Children afraid of the night
Who have never been happy
    or good.

The windiest militant trash
Important Persons shout
Is not so crude as our wish:
What mad Nijinsky wrote
About Diaghilev
Is true of the normal heart;
For the error bred in the
    bone
Of each woman and each
    man
Craves what it cannot have,
Not universal love
But to be loved alone.

From the conservative dark
Into the ethical life
The dense commuters come,
Repeating their morning vow;
"I *will* be true to the wife,
I'll concentrate more on my
    work,"

And helpless governors wake
To resume their compulsory
    game:
Who can release them now,
Who can reach the deaf,
Who can speak for the dumb?

All I have is a voice
To undo the folded lie,
The romantic lie in the brain
Of the sensual man-in-the-
    street
And the lie of Authority
Whose buildings grope the
    sky:
There is no such thing as the
    State
And no one exists alone;
Hunger allows no choice
To the citizen or the police;
We must love one another
    or die.

Defenceless under the night
Our world in stupor lies;
Yet, dotted everywhere,
Ironic points of light
Flash out wherever the Just
Exchange their messages:
May I, composed like them
Of Eros and of dust,
Beleaguered by the same
Negation and despair,
Show an affirming flame.

                              W. H. Auden

686   **Naming of Parts**

Today we have naming of parts. Yesterday,
We had daily cleaning. And tomorrow morning,
We shall have what to do after firing. But today,
Today we have naming of parts. Japonica
Glistens like coral in all of the neighboring gardens,
    And today we have naming of parts.

This is the lower sling swivel. And this
Is the upper sling swivel, whose use you will see,

When you are given your slings. And this is the piling swivel,
Which in your case you have not got. The branches
Hold in the gardens their silent, eloquent gestures,
    Which in our case we have not got.

This is the safety catch, which is always released
With an easy flick of the thumb. And please do not let me
See anyone using his finger. You can do it quite easy
If you have any strength in your thumb. The blossoms
Are fragile and motionless, never letting anyone see
    Any of them using their fingers.

And this you can see is the bolt. The purpose of this
Is to open the breech, as you see. We can slide it
Rapidly backwards and forwards: we call this
Easing the spring. And rapidly backwards and forwards
The early bees are assaulting and fumbling the flowers:
    They call it easing the Spring.

They call it easing the Spring: it is perfectly easy
If you have any strength in your thumb: like the bolt,
And the breech, and the cocking-piece, and the point of
    balance,
Which in our case we have not got; and the almond blossom
Silent in all of the gardens and the bees going backwards and
    forwards,
    For today we have naming of parts.

Henry Reed

687   Soldiers Bathing

The sea at evening moves across the sand,
And under a sunset sky I watch the freedom of a band
Of soldiers who belong to me: stripped bare
For bathing in the sea, they shout and run in the warm air.
Their flesh, worn by the trade of war, revives
And watching them, my mind towards the meaning of it strives.

All's pathos now. The body that was gross,
Rank, ravening, disgusting in the act and in repose,
All fever, filth and sweat, all bestial strength
And bestial decay, by pain and labour grows at length
Fragile and luminous. 'Poor bare forked animal,'
Conscious of his desires and needs and flesh that rise and fall,
Stands in the soft air, tasting after toil
The sweetness of his nakedness: letting the sea-waves coil
Their frothy tongues about his feet, forgets

His hatred of the war, its terrible pressure that begets
A machinery of death and slavery,
Each being a slave and making slaves of others: finds that he
Remembers his old freedom in a game
Mocking himself, and comically mimics fear and shame.

He plays with death and animality,
And reading in the shadows of his pallid flesh, I see
The idea of Michelangelo's cartoon
Of soldiers bathing, breaking off before they were half done
At some sortie of the enemy, an episode
Of the Pisan wars with Florence. I remember how he showed
Their muscular limbs that clamber from the water
And heads that turn across the shoulder, eager for the slaughter,
Forgetful of their bodies that are bare,
And hot to buckle on and use the weapons lying there.
And I think too of the theme another found
When, shadowing lean bodies on a sinister red ground—
Was it Antonio Pollaiuolo?—
Painted a naked battle: warriors straddled, hacked the foe,
Dug their bare toes into the soil and slew
The brother-naked man who lay between their feet and drew
His lips back from his teeth in a grimace.

They were Italians who knew war's sorrow and disgrace
And showed the thing suspended, stripped, a theme
Born out of experience of war's horrible extreme
Beneath a sky where even the air flows
With *Lachrimæ Christi;* and that rage, that bitterness, those
That hatred of the slain, what could it be   [blows,
But indirectly or brutally a commentary
On the Crucifixion? for the picture burns
With indignation and pity and despair and love by turns
Because it is the obverse of the scene
Where Christ hangs murdered, stripped, upon the Cross: I
That is the explanation of its rage.   [mean,

And we too have our bitterness and pity that engage
Thought, horror in this war. But night begins,
Night of the mind: who nowadays is conscious of our sins?
Though every human deed concerns our blood,
And even we must know what no one yet has understood,
That some great love is over what we do,
And that is what has driven us to this fury, for so few
Can suffer all the terror of that love:
The terror of that love has set us spinning in this groove

Greased with our blood.
                    These dry themselves and dress,
Resume their shirts, forget the fear and shame of nakedness.
Because to love is frightening we prefer
The freedom of our crimes. Yet as I drink the dusky air,
I feel a strange delight that fills me full,
A gratitude, as if evil itself were beautiful;
And kiss the wound in thought, while in the west
I watch a streak of red that might have issued from Christ's breast.

F. T. Prince

688   **Ultima Ratio Regum**

The guns spell money's ultimate reason
In letters of lead on the spring hillside.
But the boy lying dead under the olive trees
Was too young and too silly
To have been notable to their important eye.
He was a better target for a kiss.

When he lived, tall factory hooters never summoned him.
Nor did restaurant plate-glass doors revolve to wave him in.
His name never appeared in the papers.
The world maintained its traditional wall
Round the dead with their gold sunk deep as a well,
Whilst his life, intangible as a Stock Exchange rumour, drifted
        outside.

O too lightly he threw down his cap
One day when the breeze threw petals from the trees.
The unflowering wall sprouted with guns,
Machine-gun anger quickly scythed the grasses;
Flags and leaves fell from hands and branches;
The tweed cap rotted in the nettles.

Consider his life which was valueless
In terms of employment, hotel ledgers, news files.
Consider. One bullet in ten thousand kills a man.
Ask. Was so much expenditure justified
On the death of one so young and so silly
Lying under the olive trees, O world, O death?

Stephen Spender

689   **Meditation**

Now the ambassadors have gone, refusing
Our gifts, treaties, anger, compliance;
And in their place the winter has arrived,
Icing the culture-bearing water.
We brood in our respective empires on

The words we might have said which would have breached
The Chinese wall round our superfluous love
And manufactures. We do not brood too deeply.
There are our friends' perpetual, subtle demands
For understanding: visits to those who claim
To show us what is meant by death,
And therefore life, our short and puzzling lives,
And to explain our feelings when we look
Through the dark sky to other lighted worlds—
The well-shaved owners of sanatoria,
And raving, grubby oracles: the books
On diet, posture, prayer and aspirin art:
The claims of frightful weapons to be investigated:
Mad generals to be promoted: and
Our private gulfs to slither down in bed.

Perhaps in spring the ambassadors will return.
Before then we shall find perhaps that bombs,
Books, people, planets, worry, even our wives,
Are not at all important. Perhaps
The preposterous fishing-line tangle of undesired
Human existence will suddenly unravel
Before some staggering equation
Or mystic experience, and God be released
From the moral particle of blue-lit room.
Or, better still, perhaps we shall, before
Anything really happens, be safely dead.

Roy Fuller

690   **The End of the World**

Quite unexpectedly, as Vasserot
The armless ambidextrian was lighting
A match between his great and second toe,
And Ralph the lion was engaged in biting
The neck of Madame Sossman while the drum
Pointed, and Teeny was about to cough
In waltz-time swinging Jocko by the thumb—
Quite unexpectedly the top blew off:

And there, there overhead, there, there hung over
Those thousands of white faces, those dazed eyes,
There in the starless dark the poise, the hover,
There with vast wings across the cancelled skies,
There in the sudden blackness the black pall
Of nothing, nothing, nothing—nothing at all.

Archibald MacLeish

INDEX OF AUTHORS AND TITLES

(Numbers refer to Pages)

555

(Numbers refer to Pages)

(Numbers refer to Pages)

(Numbers refer to Pages)

(Numbers refer to Pages)

(Numbers refer to Pages)

(Numbers refer to Pages)

(Numbers refer to Pages)

(Numbers refer to Pages)

(Numbers refer to Pages)